Liberatheism

♫ I'm free, I'm free
And freedom tastes of reality.

I'm free, I'm free,
And I'm waiting for you to follow me. ♫

—The Who's *Tommy* ("I'm Free")

Liberatheism:
On Freedom from God(s)

David Eller

AN IMPRINT OF THE
GLOBAL CENTER FOR RELIGIOUS RESEARCH
1312 17TH STREET • SUITE 549
DENVER, COLORADO 80202

INFO@GCRR.ORG • GCRR.ORG

GCRR Press
An imprint of the Global Center for Religious Research
1312 17th Street Suite 549
Denver, CO 80202
www.gcrr.org

DOI: 10.33929/GCRRPress.2024.01

Copyeditors / Typesetter: Christian Farren
Cover Design:

www.shanealmgren.com

Library of Congress Cataloging-in-Publication Data

Liberatheism : on freedom from god(s) / David Eller
     p.   cm.
Includes bibliographic references and index.
ISBN (Print): 978-1-959281-10-8
ISBN (eBook): 978-1-959281-11-5
1. Atheism.   2. Religion—Agnomancy.   3. Islam and atheism.
I. Title.

BL2747.3.E454   2024

Ↄ

To
Darren Slade and John Loftus, two partners in my intellectual journey.

A Selection of Publications by David Eller

Beyond Liminality: Ontologies of Abundant Betweenness (Routledge, 2024)

Introducing Anthropology of Religion: Culture to the Ultimate, 3rd Ed. (Routledge, 2021)

Trump and Political Theology: Unmaking Truth and Democracy (GCRR Press, 2020)

Psychological Anthropology for the 21st Century (Routledge, 2018)

Cruel Creeds, Virtuous Violence: Religious Violence Across Culture and History (Prometheus, 2010)

Contents

Foreword

John W. Loftus

David Eller's luminous works contain important perspectives you won't find from anyone else in today's world. We are all in his debt. You aren't a fully informed person if you're not reading them, and this new book is no exception.[1]

Let me highlight just a few of his perspectives, those I found to be brilliant, important, and persuasive. First, as a professor of cultural anthropology, Eller has challenged me to think outside my cultural box. Rather than thinking exclusively in terms of westernized notions of faith, religion, and culture, he has forced me to adopt a global perspective. This global perspective has been a game changer for me. I used to think exclusively in terms of the westernized theistic gods of Judaism, Christianity, and Islam. And while I don't have a very deep knowledge of the other religious cultures and their gods, my consciousness has been raised to consider these other religious cultures more than ever. When that happens you will see the problem of religious diversity for what it really is.

From Eller, I was forced to acknowledge it is not the case that westernized notions of religion have any superiority to them. That was a shocker to me, but then at that time, I was still in my ignorance. Again, when we adopt a truly global perspective on religion, none of them have anything more going for them than the others. This means for me as an atheist that when I choose to argue exclusively against one deity over the others, by my very choice I'm acting as if one particular deity has more going for it than the others. That assumption is false. The reason it's false is because all religions are subjective, cultural, tribal, and relative. Our inherited religion is just a different expression of the same kinds of hopes and fears over the problems we face with life and death, morals, and society itself.

---

[1] I am thrilled he graciously wrote a Foreword for one of my books and several chapters for my anthologies.

Since the dawn of human history, religionists have been arguing over competing and even mutually exclusive religious faith claims. These claims on behalf of gods, goddesses, and other superhuman beings, along with their commandments, prophecies, and promises cannot all be true. If we try to strip religious claims down to an agreed-upon commonly shared bare minimum, what we might have left is the belief in a superhuman being, or beings, and/or superhuman force, or forces, the ground of all being, or the subjective feeling of transcendence. Even that bare minimum shared belief, variously described, is not such a bare, minimum, or shared belief though. Religionist beliefs differ over the existence of one paranormal being (i.e., one God) or in many paranormal beings (i.e., gods, goddesses, angels, spirits, ghosts, demons), or in one paranormal force (i.e., panentheism, deism) or many paranormal forces (i.e., karma, fate, reincarnation, prayers, incantations, spells, omens, voodoo dolls), or some sort of combination of them all. Religionists who agree with one another on these beliefs also disagree over who these beings and/or paranormal forces are, how they operate, and for whom they operate.

So if we were to use one word to describe what we know about religions, that word would be *diversity*. When dealing with such a diverse phenomenon where no religion has an advantage over others, we must treat all religious faith-based claims the same, privileging none. Eller points out that "The diversity of religions forces us to see religion as a culturally relative phenomenon; different groups have different religions that appear adapted to their unique social and even environmental conditions."[2]

Eller's works convinced me of the cultural and relativistic nature of religion. Given the historical track record to date, no religion based on faith will ever rise above the heap of them. For this would require something they cannot provide: sufficient objective evidence that can convince reasonable outsiders.[3]

Second, because of the above perspective, Eller helped change my view of the philosophy of religion. Although I was trained in that discipline and taught it at the college level, I now see clearly its irrelevance and inadequacy.[4] If atheist philosophers and students want to truly

---

[2] Eller, *Atheism Advanced: Further Thoughts of a Freethinker*, 233.
[3] It's from this perspective that religionists should approach their indoctrinated culturally adopted religion as outsiders. It's the best way to test whether any one of them is true, if there is one. On this see my book *The Outsider Test for Faith How to Know Which Religion is True*.
[4] See my 2016 book, *Unapologetic: Why Philosophy of Religion Must End*.

understand my call for the end of philosophy of religion, they must read his works.

Third, Eller has also challenged me to consider what it means to be consistently atheist in an atheist society. Of his book, *Atheism Advanced*, I called it "The Best Damn Atheist Book on the Market Today, Bar None, Hands Down, Without Question!"[5] Among other things, he effectively argued that Christians believe in a local Christianity or no Christianity at all. When I started writing my books, I wrote against a specific religious viewpoint, likened to a small limb growing out of the very large tree of religion. I wasn't arguing against animism, animatism, ancestor worship, ethical non-theism (like Buddhism), nor the many polytheistic gods and goddesses, nor did I argue against other monotheisms like the several branches of Judaism or Islam, nor against whatever original Christians believed, nor liberalism, nor deism. No. My focus had been against a small sect in time, evangelical Christianity. And among evangelicals themselves there is no consensus about true Christianity, relegating certain other branches as "cults." Christianity is best understood as a "local Christianity," one situated in a particular time and place held by particular localized people. What a particular Christian believes is a hybrid coming from schism after schism and the conclusions of hindsight through the process of syncretism.

While I have argued specifically about the dominant American fundamentalist or evangelical view in my book, Eller argues against religion itself. Along the way, Eller advances our understanding of just what atheism is. According to him, atheism is not just a view that stands in contrast with the dominant religious view of any particular society. Atheism in Hindu countries would be a-Hinduist, while atheism in Christian countries would be considered a-Christian. But this cannot be what atheism is about. We atheists have allowed the dominant religious view of our societies to set the definition for what atheism is, and even the language we use to debate the issues, Eller argues. Why is it that most debates in Western cultures are debates on such topics as "Christianity vs. Atheism"? Eller wants us to think in larger terms than that. According to Eller, the real debate should be set in terms of "Christianity vs. Itself," since there are so many branches of it, or "Christianity vs. All Other Religions," since that's the proper way to think about religion. Can you imagine a Christian wanting to debate that topic with an atheist?

Consequently, says Eller, "Nothing is more destructive to religion than other religions; it is like meeting one's own anti-matter twin. Other religions represent alternatives to one's own religion: other people believe

---

[5] "The Best Damn Atheist Book," http://tinyurl.com/49duxzj5.

in them just as fervently as we do, and they live their lives just as successfully as we do." He goes on to rhetorically ask the question: "But if their religion is relative, then why is ours not?[6]

Fourth, Eller convincingly argues that Western cultures are dominated by Christian language, rituals, symbols, arts, music, habits, and so forth. It's as if we are almost imprisoned in it. He writes:

> We find in practice that atheists in Christian-dominated societies speak and think in Christian terms just as surely as Christians do. We let Christianity set the agenda, identify the questions, and provide the language of the debate. We quite literally "speak Christian" just as fluently and just as un-self-consciously as they do.[7]

Eller continues:

> We need to stop speaking Christian so as to loosen the grip of Christian language on our thinking....We do well to begin our debunking of religion with a debunking of religious terminology.[8]

Eller calls upon atheists to eliminate our use of words and phrases like "heaven," "hell," "sin," "angel," "devil," "bless," "soul," "saint," "pray," "sacred," "divine," "baptism," "purgatory," "gospel," "the Mark of Cain," "Garden of Eden," "patience of Job," "a voice crying in the wilderness," "wolf in sheep's clothing," "wars and rumors of wars," "lost sheep," and others. They have no corresponding referent in other non-Christian parts of the globe. This Christian language only serves to continue the cultural domination that Christianity has in Western society; much like chauvinistic language does with respect to women.

Fifth, Eller argues that there is no specific "Science vs. Religion" problem, since some religions do not believe in any personal god, and because religious believers are not against most scientific disciplines. Believers are only opposed to those scientific disciplines that come into direct conflict with their own specific religious claims. Some religions don't even have a creation theory! Surely religious believers are not opposed to quantum theory, gravitational theory, meteorology, botany, or gemology (the study of gems), for starters. They are only opposed to specific claims within physics and biology when science crosses over into the arbitrary and sacred/profane boundary of specific religious claims.

---

[6] Eller, *Atheism Advanced*, 233.
[7] Eller, *Atheism Advanced*, 35.
[8] Eller, *Atheism Advanced*, 36.

Religious believers are not opposed to science as a whole, just some aspects of it. So the debate is not about science vs. religion but rather about specific local religions vs specific scientific claims.

These are all very important perspectives readers need to understand and articulate. Pushing the envelope of our understanding farther is the impact of this volume. In the front matter essay, Eller asks,

> What comes after atheism? My answer is liberatheism, not against god(s) but free of god(s). We can think of liberatheism as liber-atheism (free-without-gods) or liberate-theism (freedom from theism), but either way, the message is the same. The battle over god(s) is finished. We move on to a life and a world freed from god(s).

In his Introduction, Eller deals with the complexities, paradoxes, and contradictions of freedom, then focuses in on the responsibilities of freedom at the end. He wants us to consider the responsibility to liberate ourselves from masters, from god, history, or human beings:

> If no man or woman, no historical force or "law of nature," and no god dictates what we think, what we value, what we do, and what institutions we construct, then it is up to us to decide. We do not make such decisions in a vacuum; we are creatures of a particular culture, historical experience, and historical moment, overdetermined to choose some things and avoid others … But in order to extricate ourselves from old, tired, ill-fitting, and often pathological social realities, we must liberate ourselves from old, tired, ill-fitting, and often pathological authorities, including especially religions and their god(s).

Then he outlines the rest of the book by sharing the three steps in this process:

> The first step in this process, in theism-dominated societies, is atheism—saying no to god(s). The next step is liberatheism—getting free of god(s). The final step is not talking about god(s) at all.

This book finishes his trilogy, to which I say, bravo! We are in his debt. May his work gain a very wide audience. It can help lead us into an era where gods and goddesses can be ignored, along with their caretakers and spokespersons(!). Ignoring prescientific superstitions and paranormal pretend beings is our best hope for achieving human and animal flourishing on this pale blue dot of ours. Based on scientific literacy without gods, and our own capabilities for empathy, there is hope we can bring it about eventually. But if not, we might as well die trying. "Light a candle in the dark," Carl Sagan said. Adopt that as your purpose in life. It's one that can transcend all that we do, until such time as we can ignore religion altogether.

Preface

This book completes a trilogy begun almost twenty years ago. The 2004 *Natural Atheism* was an explanation, examination, and defense of atheism on the premise that humans are born without any religious ideas or beliefs and hence "natural" atheists. The 2007 *Atheism Advanced: Further Thoughts of a Freethinker*, as the name suggests, pushed atheism in new directions, especially beyond argument about the Christian god, for instance emphasizing that there are many other theisms and many other gods than Christianity and its god and noting how arguing about god(s) in a Christian context still has us "speaking Christian." The current book pushes further still, envisioning a future when we no longer fight about god(s) because we are free of god(s).

The central theme of the book, then, is freedom, and the book offers various ways on various subjects to free ourselves of idols. The introduction explores freedom, launching from the famous but foolish prejudice—best formulated by Dostoevsky in *The Brothers Karamazov*—that god-free people, liberated from the thrall of a supernatural authority, will commit every crime and atrocity. Instead, we explore the complexities of freedom, including what is called "ugly freedom" or the harm that free individuals do to themselves and others. We reason that freedom does not equal anomie or license and that discipline, maturity, and responsibility are not anathema to freedom. Rather, freedom is not really possible without discipline, maturity, and responsibility, so there is nothing to fear from god-free people—and plenty to fear from god-ful people.

The first chapter turns to another common and highly motivated bias against atheists; that is, that it must be impossibly difficult—and impossibly unpleasant—to be without god(s). I call this the "(melo)drama of atheism" because it portrays atheists as lonely, depressed, and anxious people, cast adrift in a meaningless and hostile universe. The current generation of atheists is often accused of trivializing the crushing existential burden that earlier atheists like Nietzsche or Sartre understood. Rather, I argue that atheism is not so hard and has either become easier to imagine existence without god(s) or that our predecessors exaggerated the angst of godlessness, perhaps because the idea was so new to them.

The second chapter aims to free us from many other misconceptions about atheism, too many of them promoted by our own main spokespeople. Primarily, atheism is commonly presented as a "belief" that there is no such thing as god(s), while it is not a "belief" at all. The chapter surveys major writings by contemporary atheists, identifying their misunderstandings, which necessarily leads us to sort out the concepts of belief, faith, and atheism.

The third chapter, like any "encyclopedia," is a summary of knowledge on the principal topics of atheism. It serves as a microcosm of the book and of the entire subject, a book-within-a-book if you will, and if readers read nothing else in the present volume, they will get a clear sense of how I view atheism and how I think it should be viewed.

The fourth chapter opens a series of chapters on the confusing and misguided state of theism, a state of which rank-and-file believers are probably blissfully unaware. In the fourth chapter, we meet a wide variety of theisms, not only the obvious non-Christian religions like Islam and Hinduism but a myriad of sophisticated Christian theisms building up to powerless-god theism, Christian existentialism, and death-of-god theology. A propos of the first chapter, Christian theists are not spared the burden and anxiety of freedom, and many sensitive Christian thinkers have already surrendered to the impossibility of a personal, powerful, and caring divine being. The fifth chapter introduces the related but distinct concept of anti-theism or the reasoned *preference* for the non-existence of god(s), for freedom from god(s), refuting once and for all the assumption that everything is better with god(s).

The next three chapters continue the critique of the beneficence of religion in general and theism in particular. The sixth chapter discusses the topic of "religious trauma" or the psychological, emotional, and often physical injury that ensues from religion. The seventh chapter dives more deeply into the question of non-knowledge or ignorance, investigating how and why religions (and other domains of society) often quite intentionally preserve and promote ignorance through the process of "agnomancy." The eighth chapter describes the profound damage that religion has done to philosophy, the oldest form of rational inquiry. It condemns the academic field of philosophy of religion as little more than an adjunct to Christian theology and apologetics. An ultimate betrayal of the commission to analyze and critique our pet ideas and concepts, as well as a colossal waste of brainpower and resources, philosophy of religion is encouraged to liberate itself from its role as a defender of Christianity to become a genuine philosophical approach to the question of religion.

The final two offer a bit more "practical" guidance for atheists. The ninth chapter illustrates how diverse atheism can be and is across cultures and religions, revealing just how completely encumbered mainstream American and Western atheism is with Christianity, how it is anything but free of the Christian god. The chapter begins with nonbelief in Islam, which is almost an oxymoron not only to biased pundits but to many well-known atheists. It is also looks at nonbelief in Hinduism and the alleged irreligiosity in Japan. Finally, the chapter argues that, far from the standard impression that atheists lack morality, in most if not all religious settings the complaints against religion are less propositional (less about "belief") than moral--that is, that religion fails the test of human beings with functional moral compasses. Last, the tenth chapter provides some practical advice on how to change people's minds from theism to atheism, taking advantage of the best knowledge and practices in psychology, education, marketing, and behavioral economics. The chapter invites us to think in terms of "attitude change" and away from conventional confrontational tactics like argument and debate.

This last chapter brings the project full circle, warning about the danger of confirming theists' worst impressions and stereotypes of us as bitter, angry, and condescending. Our standard practices of arguing and debating (not to mention ridiculing and insulting) tend to reaffirm the (melo)drama of atheism and the assumption that people who are free of god(s) are not the kind of people that our interlocutors want to be. In the end, the information and insights in the book call us to free ourselves of many of the things we say about ourselves and about and to others—and to accelerate toward the day when we no longer argue *about* god(s) but live *free from* god(s), when god(s) are simply not worth talking about anymore.

One note on usage in this book. Readers will have observed that I consistently say "god(s)" rather than "God" and also refer to god(s) in terms of "he/she/it/they" instead of merely "he." The word "God" is the proper name of the Christian god and should only be used as such; the preferred form "god(s)" is a constant reminder to theists that theirs (whichever god is theirs) is not the only god that people believe in out there. Likewise, "he/she/it/they" (and its other forms like "him/her/it/they," etc.), although a little clumsy, stresses the fact that some theisms posit a masculine god, some a feminine god, some multiple gods, and so forth. The effect of this usage is to decenter and "provincialize" the Christian mono-god and to force Christian theists to cope with rival theisms. I ardently urge others to adopt this usage.

Introduction:
The Problem of Freedom

> Free *from* what? As if that mattered to Zarathustra! But your eyes
> should tell me brightly: Free *for* what?
>
> —Friedrich Nietzsche,
> "On the Way of the Creator," *Thus Spoke Zarathustra*

So there is no such thing as god(s). Now what? We could continue to argue about god(s), but there are no new arguments, for or against. Not that apologetics—making excuses for god(s)—or philosophy or theology or the devotion of the rank-and-file believer has ceased. But the debate is over: there is no reason to think that there is any such thing as god(s).

Atheism, literally "no/without god(s)-*ism*," has been, throughout Western/Christian history, not *without* god(s) but *against* god(s). (-*Ism* as a suffix does not always mean "belief": patriotism is not "belief in patriots" any more than vegetarianism is "belief in vegetarians" or "belief in vegetables." Both, like atheism and many other *isms*, are positions or practices but not *beliefs*.) However, just as Nietzsche also warned that when you gaze too long into the abyss it gazes back into you, so arguing about god(s), especially when god(s) have been repudiated—when those god(s) are dead, to quote Nietzsche yet again—keeps those god(s) on our tongues and in our minds. Arguing about something is still talking about it, and like a ghost, the idea or memory of god(s) haunts us still.

What comes after atheism? My answer is *liberatheism*, not against god(s) but *free of god(s)*. We can think of liberatheism as liber-atheism (free-without-gods) or liberate-theism (freedom from theism), but either way, the message is the same. The battle over god(s) is finished. We move on to a life and a world freed from god(s).

What does this freedom entail? What does it offer us, and what does it demand of us? People, particularly American people, speak a lot about freedom, but not all of this speech is entirely sensible or consistent. The two silliest things I have heard recently about freedom, written 140 years apart, come from Dostoevsky's classic 1880 novel *The Brothers*

Karamazov and Christine Rosen's review of Elisabeth Anker's 2022 book *Ugly Freedoms*. Most readers may be familiar with Dostoevsky's infamous meme, "Without God, everything is allowed." The implication is that, freed from god(s), humans would run amok, perpetrating—and justifying—any and all crimes and perversions. In other words, as most theists, and even some nontheists, will tell you, a god is the source and the guarantor of morality (humans, presumably, being naturally immoral, like Lucifer in the Rolling Stones song, "in need of some restraint"). This is of course nonsense, but first it is worth noting that this is not what Dostoevsky said. Rather, in the key passage a fictional character recalls a conversation with the fictional atheist character Rakitin, in which he *asked Rakitin the question*, without God (i.e. the Christian god), "What will become of men then? Without God and immortal life? All things are lawful/allowed then, they can do what they like?" Rakitin never answered—other than to point out that "a clever man can do what he likes"—nor did anyone else in the story.

So we are left to grapple with the question ourselves. Or are we? Must we take every question, every frivolous accusation and baseless slander, seriously? There is no evidence to suggest that atheists are more "immoral" or generally worse people than theists, and if there were such evidence it would be easy to demonstrate (by crime rates and such). The allegation is part of what we will call, in the first chapter, "the (melo)drama of atheism" that theists are inclined to think the worst of atheists: it does not make theism *true*, but it promises to make it *preferable*. Further, the "divine command" theory of morality has been amply debunked. Actually, it has been more than debunked and most passionately so by a suffering theist, the anguished Søren Kierkegaard. Kierkegaard struggled with Yahweh's instruction to Abraham to sacrifice his son Isaac. How (hopefully Abraham wondered) is it moral to kill my son, but how is it moral to disobey my god? And why would this god issue such an immoral order? Kierkegaard realized that a deity *who is the source of morality and law is himself not bound by morality and law, is beyond good and evil*. In other words, Dostoevsky's characters—and everyone who thinks that the lesson is that without god(s) everything is permitted—have it exactly backwards. For a god, everything is permitted. Who can say no to him/her/it/them? Who can even, like Job, hold the god accountable without a browbeating? And in the final analysis, as history has shown with a vengeance, if the god(s) can establish any law, dictate any moral code, order any action, then for the human devotees anything and everything is permitted, and more than permitted but *compelled* if they believe their god has approved or required it, from polygamy and animal sacrifice to murder, holy war, and terrorism. After all, even the apostles recognized that "With God, all things are possible" (Matthew 19:26; also Mark 10:27)—including really bad things.

Which brings me to the second silly remark. In reaction to Anker's book on the uglier aspects of freedom, which we will discuss below, Christine Rosen of the right-wing magazine *Commentary* declared, "Freedom is freedom."[1] Whenever I hear such an unequivocal statement my anthropologist's ears prick up, since I know that almost never is anything so simple and straightforward. In this case, a more sophomoric attitude is barely imaginable. As much as Americans prattle on about freedom, there is hardly any concept less obvious, less simple, and less unequivocal. Two centuries ago, the great philosopher Hegel opined, "No idea is so generally recognized as indefinite, ambiguous, and open to the greatest misconceptions (to which it therefore actually falls a victim) as the idea of freedom: none in the common currency with so little appreciation of its meaning."[2] Almost sixty years ago philosopher Alan Ryan asserted that freedom "is not open to any simple definition," although he still clung to the vain hope that it is "not ambiguous."[3] Much more recently political scientist Wendy Brown contended that freedom "is neither a philosophical absolute nor a tangible reality but a relational and contextual practice that takes shape in opposition to whatever is locally and ideologically conceived as unfreedom."[4] Sixty years ago anthropologist David Bidney added the controversial but probably valid judgment that freedom, "in itself, is not an absolute good: one must define the conditions under which it is exercised."[5]

Carolina Humphrey provided an illustrative case of "alternative freedoms" in Russian variations of the concept. She found three non-synonymous words in Russian that could be translated as "freedom," none of them identical to the English word. *Svoboda*, she explained, appears in the context of political freedom or liberty but originally related to the group or "the security and well-being that result from living amongst one's own people."[6] Just as it did not apply to "me" but to "us," so it also clearly demarcated the "not-us" and entailed freedom from those unlike us and their foreign ways. *Svoboda*, she continued, "indicates the society of the people who are *not unfree*, but apart from that it suggests little about what

---

[1] Rosen, "The Foolishness of 'Ugly Freedoms.'"
[2] Quoted in Dudley, *Hegel, Nietzsche, and Philosophy: Thinking Freedom*, 1.
[3] Ryan, "Freedom," 105.
[4] Brown, *States of Injury: Power and Freedom in Late Modernity*, 6.
[5] Bidney, "The Varieties of Human Freedom," 22.
[6] Humphrey, "Alternative Freedoms," 2.

that society might be like."[7] A wider concept is *mir*, meaning all humankind, the world, or the universe, although it too had a more limited reference to the Russian peasants' local community, which was their whole world. *Mir* is not cognitive but more affective and emotional, providing "a feeling (*oschuchenie*) of freedom, which is given by self-realization" but still collectively rather than privately.[8] The third term is *volya*, "will" or individual freedom, particularly when a person is unfree or oppressed and yearns for release. It is freedom of action, which she warned carries a dark side, associating will or desire with demand and command. One can impose one's *volya* on others and bend them to one's own. Such freedom is not even necessarily healthy for the person exercising it: the sense of "everything-is-permitted-ness" (*vsedozvolennost'*)—powerfully reminiscent of Dostoevsky's quotation—can consume the person and result in great frustration if it is thwarted.[9] More poignantly, as we will consider again shortly, freedom (*svoboda* being the dominant term today) can be and regularly is abused, since it is available disproportionately "to anyone with the wealth or resources to exercise it":

> The present-day svoboda-freedom is thus associated with the arrogance of political-financial clout, with corrupt little islands of energy and agency, and it tends to be resented or frankly rejected, by everyone else....
>
> People are worried that this new "freedom" is not really freedom at all, but the downside of endless openness, namely "limitlessness" (*bespredel*), a new slang word that actually means unbridled-ness, lawlessness, mayhem, chaos.[10]

We do not have to travel around the world, though, to confront diversity and complexity in the idea of freedom. In this seminal essay "Two Concepts of Liberty" Isaiah Berlin distinguished "negative freedom" from "positive freedom."[11] The former comprises roughly *freedom from*, that is, the absence or removal of constraints on and obstacles to freedom of action, while the latter names *freedom to*, that is,

---

[7] Humphrey, "Alternative Freedoms," 3.

[8] Humphrey, "Alternative Freedoms," 3.

[9] Humphrey, "Alternative Freedoms," 6.

[10] Humphrey, "Alternative Freedoms," 7–8. Humphrey noted in closing that Western invocations of freedom are likely to be ineffective or counterproductive when filtered through Russian ears.

[11] Berlin, *Liberty: Incorporating* Four Essays on Liberty. (Essay originally published in 1958.)

what the person can do with her freedom or the potential or capacity to master one's life and determine one's destiny. Berlin did not suggest that there are no limits to freedom (i.e. there is no perfect "freedom from") nor that negative freedom grants absolute positive freedom (i.e. one cannot automatically do all that one is "free" to do).

Bidney, in his cross-cultural study of freedom, discovered four different types or categories—natural, cultural, normative/moral, and metaphysical. *Natural freedom* is the very ability to commence and complete independent action (with its negative and positive forms); it further consists of *biological freedom* or what we are physically and socially (e.g. in competition with others) able to do and *psychological freedom* which depends on our individual will, intelligence, and imagination. *Cultural freedom* is "the system of historically acquired rights and privileges prescribed on the authority of a given society" or more simply how society and culture construe and organize freedom, as in the Russian case above.[12] *Normative/moral freedom* in Bidney's analysis is freedom of action structured by reason and its ideals, laws, and principles. Finally, *metaphysical freedom* refers both to the "irreducible" (existentialists would say "inescapable") condition of choice—that human beings *must make choices and decisions*—and also to the practical/technical, historical (i.e. at any given time), and cultural conditions of "what is possible."

We could no doubt multiply categories and classifications of freedom, but the point is made that freedom is not a single or simple thing. More importantly, the discourses and uses of freedom will always be constructed from historical and social experience. In the case of Western notions of freedom, that experience, as Bidney and many others have understood, boils down to the struggle first against the church and then against the state. Martin Luther fatefully introduced the idea of freedom of conscience as a tactic for extricating Christians from the grip of the Catholic Church; individuals should be free to read scripture and decide for themselves what it means and requires. However, Luther fervently assumed that everyone, taking advantage of that freedom, would share *his* conclusions on the matter; instead, we soon had not two (Catholic and Lutheran) but three (add Calvinist) and eventually thousands of interpretations and their resultant sects and denominations. Either way, "freedom" was a weapon against religious authority (or at least religious authorities with whom you disagree); once committed to a particular sect, denomination, or biblical exegesis, talk of freedom tends to dissipate.

---

[12] Bidney, "The Varieties of Human Freedom," 12.

The other nemesis of freedom was (and is) "the state" but more specifically the king or emperor or monarch. As in the American Revolution, monarchy was inherently associated with tyranny (even a good king was bad), an encumbrance on our negative freedom to be thrown off. This was also John Stuart Mill's main argument in his celebrated 1859 essay *On Liberty*, where he characterized liberty as "protection against the tyranny of the political rulers," which was achieved through constitutional checks on government's power and through "certain immunities" from government interference that we call *rights*.[13] For him, freedom covered three different realms—freedom of thought or consciousness, freedom of tastes and pursuits (that is, to live our lives as suits our character), and freedom to assemble. Crucially, the only legitimate reason for curtailment of individual liberties in a modern "civilized" community in his view was "to prevent harm to others"; in other words, a free person should not be forced to do something or prevented from doing something against his will for his own betterment even if "to do so would be wise, or even right."[14]

Yet, while the Declaration of Independence from British autocracy reserves the right and the duty to alter and abolish any form of government that is destructive of citizens' life, liberty, and pursuit of happiness, once a new government is instituted it is much less congenial to rebellion and revolution (notice that the republic did not honor the Confederacy's wish to escape from the perceived tyranny of the federal government). Accordingly, Bidney sagely observed that, "Those who do not accept a given authority are inclined to contrast 'authority' and 'freedom' as if they were two opposing principles; on the other hand, those who do accept the authority of a given person or institution see no such conflict and find their freedom in conforming to the established authority."[15]

The effect of this history is a unique Western—and most intensely, American—conception of freedom, highly individualized to be sure but more precisely viewed as "self-reliance, as unconstrained agency, and as unbound subjectivity. It combines these interpretations together as normative expressions of a sovereign subject, one who obeys no other authority but one's own, who can determine the future and control the vagaries of contingency through their sheer strength of will."[16] This variety of freedom is unusually prickly and defensive, perceiving virtually

---

[13] Mill, *On Liberty*, 6–11.
[14] Mill, *On Liberty*, 14.
[15] Bidney, "The Varieties of Human Freedom," 26–27.
[16] Anker, *Orgies of Feeling: Melodrama and the Politics of Freedom*, 9.

any authority or rule or norm or even neighbor's need as an affront to the individual's liberty. As a result, freedom is brandished as absolute and as absolutely simple and self-evident. We have seen already that freedom is anything but absolute, simple, and self-evident, as there are inevitably at least two conflicts—the conflict between the individual's freedom and the social order, and the conflict between the individual's freedom and some other person's freedom (or well-being or very life).

It goes without saying that every law, regulation, norm, moral, or tradition is a restriction on someone's freedom, and such is the nature of living in a society. (One can retreat to the mountains or the woods to evade these limitations, but one also foregoes the benefits of modern civilization.) It bears saying, however, that, like all principles that sound good on the surface, freedom leads us into paradoxes and contradictions. Three of these paradoxes and contradictions bear closer inspection.

The first is what Elisabeth Anker called (much to Rosen's consternation, as we mentioned earlier) "ugly freedoms." In her book, Anker considers the noxious aspects of freedom, which is generally regarded as an unmitigated good in American culture. Tersely stated, freedom more than occasionally "entails a dynamic in which practices of freedom produce harm, brutality, and subjugation as *freedom*."[17] Slavery is a key example in American history: the freedom of some Americans to own property subsumed certain other people—African people—who were treated *as property* and whose freedom was explicitly and legally stripped from them. She mentions political thinker and slave-owner John C. Calhoun, who held that

> slavery was necessary for freedom. It entailed the freedom of local control and citizens' self-rule. Slavery comprised the freedom to improve the land in an orderly fashion as well as the freedom of private property, as it authorized white property owners to use the labor of their Black human property largely as they decided. Slavery was the basis for free white institutions, and it provided his fellow enslavers the freedom of mastery, prosperity, and leisure, including the leisure to write treatises of liberty.[18]

This is another instance of conflicting freedoms, in which the freedoms of enslaved black people—who were not viewed as fully human at all—were sacrificed for the freedoms of slaveholding white people. She also names the freedom to lease one's property to a renter as a relationship of ugly

---

[17] Anker, *Ugly Freedoms*, 9.
[18] Anker, *Ugly Freedoms*, 4.

freedom, which American law has sought to moderate with "renter's rights" legislation. In his critical analysis of free speech and the First Amendment, Stanley Fish retells a shocking example of the weaponization of freedom. A leading figure of the 1977 neo-Nazi march in Skokie, Illinois, Frank Collin,

> boasted that his strategy was to use the First Amendment "against the Jew." He counted on the amendment as a cover for his efforts to inflict damage, a damage vividly described by one of his followers: "I hope they're terrified … because we're coming to get them again. I don't care if someone's mother or father or brother died in the gas chambers. The unfortunate thing is not that there were six million Jews who died. The unfortunate thing is that there were so many Jewish survivors."[19]

To drive home their point, the marchers carried signs demanding "Free Speech for White People," as if White People were somehow deprived of freedom and Black people did not deserve it.

We could add the freedom of management to hire labor and thus control the terms of employment in regard to wages, hours, working conditions, and the very opportunity to work (ripped from workers when jobs are "offshored" or businesses are "downsized" or "right-sized"). In earlier days in some parts of the country, "company towns" compromised the freedoms of laborers by compelling them to rent their houses, buy their food, and obtain all of their other services from the same company that provided their jobs. One more example that observers have highlighted is the freedom of modern families to work outside the home and to enjoy their leisure, which is purchased on the backs of underpaid and precarious (and often foreign if not undocumented) housekeepers, nannies, cooks, gardeners, and other "help" who can barely afford to keep their own homes and families—and if undocumented, are afforded none of the protections of regular workers and can be deported at any time.

Anker also recognizes a second kind of ugly freedom, by which she means the sorts of freedoms exercised by disadvantaged or oppressed peoples that are discouraged and condemned by the dominant and "decent" segments of society. This "second valence" of ugly freedoms— what we might construe as freedoms that the society wishes they would not practice—includes resistance and protest, adaptation through "gamesmanship, sex, and theft," the creation of alternative and parallel social systems (perhaps like gangs), and diverse "self-destructive"

---

[19] Fish, *The First: How to Think about Hate Speech, Campus Speech, Religious Speech, Fake News, Post-Truth, and Donald Trump*, 31.

behaviors of the very sort that Mill insisted the government had no right to stop.[20] One could think of the urban African American culture described by Carol Stack in her classic *All Our Kin* as a window on second-valence ugly freedoms.[21] What mainstream society castigated as a "broken family" and a "culture of poverty"—single motherhood, temporary sexual partnerships, sharing of property, and swapping of childcare—were, in Stack's estimation, "strategies for survival" and reasonable expressions of freedom to cope with difficult living conditions, *many of those conditions generated by the ugly freedoms of mainstream society.*

A second paradox, and one of the uglier sides of freedom as stressed by Bidney, is the chronic "failure to differentiate clearly between self-destructive abuses of liberty and life-promoting uses of liberty."[22] In a word, *freedom can be self-destructive.* Of course, in Mill's highly libertarian view, the government or society has no authority to restrain citizens' self-destruction, even if it has an interest to do so. Nevertheless, Bidney's and Anker's points raise the deeper issue of the price we pay and the pain we suffer for freedom. At the most superficial level, my freedom may injure me (and the world) through overconsumption (and consequent obesity and weight-related medical conditions), personal debt, pollution, environmental degradation, etc. At a much more profound level, though, freedom itself can be burdensome, hurtful, indeed objectionable.

No one made the case more bluntly than Erich Fromm in his chilling 1941 *Escape from Freedom.* Fromm was one of many mid-century scholars who were stunned by the rise of fascism and authoritarianism, particularly in societies where democracy was presumably advancing if not secure. More troubling, a large percentage of citizens seemed to endorse or choose fascist/authoritarian leaders; after all, Mussolini and Hitler attained office legally through the ballot. Fromm reckoned that, although "European and American history is centered around the effort to gain freedom from the political, economic, and spiritual shackles that have bound men," the consequences were not as desirable as philosophers and revolutionaries expected.[23] Freedom from church and state, the aspiration of freedom fighters everywhere, shattered social bonds and dissolved age-old truths. Surely, the free person was "more independent, self-reliant, and critical" but simultaneously "more isolated, alone, and afraid."[24] For the citizen of modernity this social and intellectual isolation, Fromm

---

[20] Anker, *Ugly Freedoms*, 16.

[21] Stack, *All Our Kin: Strategies for Survival in a Black Community.*

[22] Bidney, "The Varieties of Human Freedom," 21.

[23] Fromm, *Escape from Freedom*, 17.

[24] Fromm, *Escape from Freedom*, 124.

concluded, "is unbearable and the alternatives he is confronted with are either to escape from the burden of his freedom into new dependencies and submission, or to advance to the full realization of positive freedom which is based upon the uniqueness and individuality of man."[25] Demonstrably, many twentieth-century (and early twenty-first-century) members chose the former, which is frankly easier and arguably more reassuring, and its most virulent form was (and is) surrendering and attaching to a demagogue and autocrat, a populist savior who promises meaning, order, and "greatness" while stroking the wounded pride of the declining or humiliated nation or its forgotten majority.

Interestingly but not surprisingly, another passage in *The Brothers Karamazov* has received less attention than the fretful question about the permission to do anything. In the fifth chapter, titled "The Grand Inquisitor," Dostoevsky through the Inquisitor asserted that

> nothing has ever been more insupportable for a man and a human society than freedom....In the end, they will lay their freedom at our feet, and say to us, "Make us your slaves, but feed us...." They will marvel at us and look upon us as gods, because we are ready to endure the freedom which they have found so dreadful and to rule over them—so awful it will seem to them to be free. But we shall tell them that we are Thy servants and rule over them in Thy name.

At least Dostoevsky and Fromm offered people an escape from the affliction of freedom. For existentialist thinkers like Jean-Paul Sartre and Albert Camus—who lived through World War II and its disorienting disillusions—there was, as Sartre put it in the title of one of his works, no exit. Sartre diagnosed humanity as *condemned to be free*, without any option other than to make a decision (literally, "cut-off/from") and to chart a course. One could, hypothetically, hand the decision-making over to another party, but paradoxically that was still a decision, and disappointingly it still did not solve the problem or absolve the responsibility: one had to choose *which* demagogue and autocrat to bow to, and even the most totalitarian regime could not make every choice for you. Prostrating to a god him/her/itself saddled abject believers with the burden of interpretation and application, desperately searching for a verse in scripture or a model in history to obey or emulate. Freedom then is understood as the congenital defect of humanity and all sentient beings, and religion is no relief.

---

[25] Fromm, *Escape from Freedom*, viii.

The third paradox, a source of the others, is the relation and tension between freedom and what we might variously call structure, rules, order, law, or society itself. A tradition stretching from Rousseau through Marx, and equating church and state with "society," posits society as the chains that bind (in positive and negative senses) otherwise and naturally free persons. In the ideology of absolute and uncompromising freedom rampant in the United States, any kind of obstruction of individual action is unfreedom at best and despotism at worst, even something as inoffensive and beneficial as wearing a mask during a pandemic; it is all "treading on me," intolerable to those who would "live free or die." This kind of freedom that Americans valorize is not only individuating but also atomizing and ultimately anti-social (which, for some people, is the point).

According to the *New World Encyclopedia* entry on freedom, scholars distinguish between freedom and *license*, that is, "anything goes": "In the modern world many people mistake license for freedom and become angry when they are censured for being selfish, rude, irresponsible and immoral."[26] This includes actions that are patently bad for the actor as well as for neighbors, compatriots, and the planet. Friedrich von Hayek, a dean of modern libertarianism, elevated freedom above all other virtues including happiness, arguing that freedom might make us (or those around us) miserable but was worth it nonetheless. Clive Hamilton indeed dubbed such an attitude *the freedom paradox*. However, he also counseled that "a certain level of social and psychological maturity is needed if we are to make proper use of the liberties that have been won."[27]

Maturity is one way to express it. Another is discipline. In their essay on freedom across cultures, Moises Lino e Silva and Huon Wardle declare that freedom (they use the word *autonomy*, literally self-rule) "is as much a mode of self-discipline as it is a rejection of external rule."[28] Aristotle himself taught that discipline facilitates freedom rather than negating it. It is a truism, but no less true, that structure or discipline makes free action possible: without the rules of grammar, there would be no free speech (or any intelligible speech), and without the rules and standards of, say, ballet, dancers would not be able to express themselves freely through dance.

If it is true that structure and order, even the oft-despised "society," enable freedom as much as they constrain it, it is equally so that freedom depends on other factors that are often neglected or denied. Two of these factors are money and power on the one hand and resources and

---

[26] *New World Encyclopedia*, "Freedom."
[27] Hamilton, *The Freedom Paradox: Towards a Post-Secular Ethics*, 18.
[28] Lino e Silva and Wardle, "Testing Freedom: Ontological Considerations," 18.

technologies on the other. As the case of Russian *volya* illustrated, people with the wherewithal have degrees of freedom that poorer citizens lack (and they can—and liberally do—indulge that wherewithal in ugly freedoms). Likewise, in a depressing study of young Americans, Fred Alford discovered that most "define freedom as the possession of money and power" and were comparatively uninterested in highfalutin principles like freedom of speech.[29] Consequently, in the land of the free, few of them felt very free: "I have a right to do anything I want, anything that's legal anyhow," one subject confessed, "But I can't *do* anything I want. That takes more than freedom. Freedom is concerned with my rights. What I get to do with them depends on how much money and power I can get."[30]

Anker tells another story of the unequal distribution of freedom. During a previous drought in California, rich inhabitants refused to reduce their water consumption since, they contended, their *ability to pay* for water guaranteed their *freedom to use* water. Anker calls this "consumptive sovereignty," the attitude that those who can afford it are free to take whatever they want from the world, public good be damned.[31] Such an ugly freedom denies—or just doesn't care—that others without the means cannot make the same choices and thus do not have the same freedom; in fact, it literally takes water out of their neighbors' mouths. It is freedom but selfish, privileged, and irresponsible freedom. It conveys the message, to paraphrase George Orwell's *Animal Farm*, that all of us are free but some are freer than others.

Along with the money and power to choose certain courses of action, the available resources and technologies open new avenues of freedom. As Maggie Nelson chides us, much of our modern freedom and the democracy that sustains it depend on abundant cheap oil.[32] Or to be more precise and thorough, such freedom depends on oil, the internal combustion engine, affordable automobiles, and the national highway system. Certain freedoms are simply not available until the technical means emerge to create them. Women became freer to control their reproduction once the birth control pill was invented (and that freedom will be severely reduced as abortion clinics disappear from the landscape). Cars and apartments gave young people more freedom to date and explore premarital sex. Medical knowledge and technology grant us the freedom to extend life (and force us to confront the decision to end life by "pulling

---

[29] Alford, *Rethinking Freedom: Why Freedom Lost Its Meaning and What Can Be Done to Save It*, 1.

[30] Alford, *Rethinking Freedom*, 12.

[31] Anker, *Ugly Freedoms*, 156.

[32] Nelson, *On Freedom: Four Songs of Care and Constraint*.

the plug"), to resist infectious diseases, to donate our organs or receive organ donations, and many more—also opening abundant new moral dilemmas. Tomorrow's advances and discoveries will undoubtedly provide new vistas of freedom, like the freedom to migrate to another planet or to clone ourselves or our loved ones (again, if we have the cash).

Recalling Anker's despicable example of irresponsible freedom, another way to think about not the *limits* but the *contours* of freedom is in terms of responsibility, even dare we say obligation and duty. Bidney believed that "the right to freedom in the modern state is based on considerations of justice and responsibility to the public good."[33] I am not so sure that is true, other than as an abstract ideal. All the same, whether or not freedom expects or demands any responsibility to the public, it does unavoidably expect and demand responsibility of us. Nietzsche asked and answered the central question: "For what is freedom? That one has the will to assume responsibility for oneself."[34] But responsibility for oneself is only half—or much less than half—of the issue. Philosopher Emmanuel Levinas insisted that *both freedom and responsibility* characterize the human condition, that responsibility is not just responsibility to self but *responsibility to others*, and that such responsibility is the very *source and form of freedom*. Interpersonal responsibility, social responsibility, "does not limit but promotes my freedom, by arousing my goodness. The order of responsibility ... is also the order where freedom is ineluctably invoked. It is thus the irremissible weight of being that gives rise to my freedom."[35] Indeed, in the strongest possible language, Levinas asserted that not only my freedom but my *self*, my *being*, is produced by being-with-others, that the person does not entirely *exist* independent of and prior to responsible social interaction.

Levinas can perhaps be forgiven for waxing a bit theistic about freedom and responsibility to others. For him, his god is the ultimate other, the Absolute Other, the personification of otherness. But we do not need to summon a god to understand otherness, and the god-lens may not be the best way to understand it anyhow. Gods, at least anything vaguely like the Christian or Abrahamic god, do not need us, and we have no immediate responsibilities to him/her/it/them, certainly none that affect his/her/its/their existence. In classical Christian theology, its god is entirely self-sufficient and without needs (except perhaps for adoration and occasional burnt meat). Besides, if ethics—using freedom responsibly and using responsibility freely—is the essence of the human condition for

---

[33] Bidney, "The Varieties of Human Freedom," 22.
[34] Kaufman, *The Portable Nietzsche*, 542.
[35] Levinas, *Totality and Infinity: An Essay on Exteriority*, 200.

Levinas, Kierkegaard's analysis above demonstrates that gods are not bound by ethics nor by responsibility to humans or other creatures (after all, Shakespeare and the ancient Greeks believed that the gods kill us for their sport). For humans, the only other we require to complete our humanity is another human—or even another creature, like a cat or dog—with whom we can and must enter a responsible relationship.

We have reached the supreme paradox, which brings us full circle to the end of this introduction and onward to the chapters of the book: if we are free, *how do we choose what we do with that freedom, and why?* Let us take Mill's two primary individual/personal freedoms (other than the freedom to meet and assemble), which he described as freedom of thought and freedom of taste/pursuit. The question is, why does one think this or that, why does one have a taste for and pursue this or that? Freedom is often read as autonomous (self-ruling) action, as choice and decision without external determination, but on what basis does one choose this action or decision over another? And what rule does one dictate to oneself? We accepted earlier that freedom does not equal license, or what we might more forcefully call anomie (no-rule), anarchy, or libertinism, doing whatever we feel like and whatever our base and animal impulses drive us to do. So freedom is always to some minimal extent self-limiting; to rule oneself is *to rule out some choices for and some facets of the self.* Further, though, the idea that freedom means and could ever mean complete liberation from external forces is a pipe dream, and not an especially pretty one. In fact, Lino e Silva and Wardle remind us that one possible etymological source of the word "liberty" is primitive Indo-European *leudh-*, people, belonging to a people, growing up in a community (reminiscent of Russian *svoboda*). "From this viewpoint," they reason, "liberties derive from growing with, and hence having rights in, a community."[36]

The fact is that personal freedom and interpersonal relationships and responsibilities are not in conflict but are mutually dependent and co-constitutive. We are not, as some romanticists sing, born free but become free as we grow in subjectivity (as a subject and not an object, as a being with its own will and perspective) and intersubjectivity (in reciprocal relations of knowledge, action, and care). Clifford Geertz made the point a half-century ago that humans are incomplete creatures, unfinished animals, who are completed and constructed out of external public resources (culture) through participation in a group (society).[37] In the process of *enculturation*, cultural beliefs and values are internalized by

---

[36] Lino e Silva and Wardle, "Testing Freedom: Ontological Considerations," 17.
[37] Geertz, *The Interpretation of Cultures*, 46.

individuals, furnishing their capacity to act *freely and responsibly*. Indeed, the word "education" (*ex-*, out + *ducere*, to lead) derives from roots that evoke guidance and preparation for participation in society, and the German word for education, *bildung*, still more overtly suggests the social construction or building of the free and responsible, the free-responsible, person. This is why Levinas insisted that the intersubjective and social dimension be incorporated in philosophical accounts of human knowledge and action, in contrast to the standard portrait of the solitary and self-made knower and actor.

So the free individual is the being who has learned to be free and has learned what to do with that freedom. Put another way, our autonomy or self-rule is decisively (and paradoxically?) informed by others, and this is as true for theists as for atheists; the only real difference is that atheists do not include a god or supernatural other. As philosopher Susan Wolf opined, reason or the ability to think well and logically and to arrive at true knowledge and good values (whichever those are!) is one basis for our autonomous choices, but reason is allegedly objective, universal, and thus *external* and in a way compulsory—even if the free person chooses to act *unreasonably*, that is, in disregard of the true and the good.[38] Closer to what we have been discussing is Wolf's second basis for freedom, namely one's own true self or values, but again, we have just established that a "self" and its values are social constructions and therefore products of the enculturation/education/*bildung* process, not only formal schooling but every experience in which we interact with others and the world. In other words, *by the time the free individual is ready to choose and decide, to act autonomously, she is already a product of external forces*, namely society and culture (including, for most, religion). Succinctly, most (if not all) of our individual tastes and pursuits, our values, wants, and ideas *are acquired*—we are not the author of them—and they are acquired during, through, and from social interaction. René Girard said roughly the same thing in his influential concept of "mimetic desire": humans imitate the desires of members of their society, which inevitably pits them against each other in competition for culturally-defined goods. Interestingly, he theorized that religion was not the cause of such mimesis but the effect of it, as a means to prevent society-destroying violence.[39]

Each "free" human being thus is the assemblage of ethically-oriented freedom-responsibility relationships with other people that

---

[38] Wolf, *Freedom within Reason*, 53–54.

[39] Girard, *Violence and the Sacred*. In Girard's theory, sacrifice is the original form of religion and is an outcome of mimetic desire, as the group's projection of hostility onto a scapegoat. Unfortunately, his hypothesis about sacrifice is totally wrong.

Levinas envisioned. Or as Oscar Wilde colorfully phrased it, "Most people are other people. Their thoughts are someone else's opinions, their lives a mimicry, their passions a quotation"[40]—except instead of "most people" he should have said "all people" or "humanity essentially." (Wolf's third basis for action was pure arbitrariness, undetermined by either reason or one's self and culture. This would be sheer chaos, rendering the individual's behavior utterly unpredictable and trampling the freedoms of neighbors.)

No matter how you look at it, freedom never is and can never be utterly unfettered. Or better, the view that education, training, character-building and person-building, reason, truth, and society are somehow insufferable—and optional and removable—domination of the individual is an immature, irresponsible, and frankly foolish position. It is a selfish and isolating kind of freedom, a pugnacious kind of freedom, and one that can quickly devolve into what Alford characterized as paranoid and conspiratorial freedom that fears that "the government" is keen to take away your rights, your property, your guns, and maybe your life.[41] It is also the kind of freedom that partisans usurp as theirs and theirs alone, that their "enemies" (domestic, like liberal elites, and foreign, like Muslims and immigrants) allegedly seek to destroy, and that "has become a cudgel with which to pummel political opponents."[42] We find ourselves back in the domain of ugly freedoms, what Brown considered the appropriation, including in democracies, of freedom "for the most cynical and unemancipatory political ends."[43] She was harshest in her assessment of the propensity of right-wing parties and leaders to advocate "an increasingly narrow and predominantly economic formulation of freedom" and then to promote themselves as freedom's only real ally, indifferent to any appeal to justice or equality.[44] For such freedom fundamentalists and fetishists, concerns about justice, equality, social or environmental responsibility—what Nelson calls "caring"—only cramp their rights to use (and to monopolize) property, wealth, and power for their personal advantage. At its zenith, which is not beyond our perception, this radical freedom-ism "rejects the view that promotion of human wellbeing is self-evidently good and should be the principal objective of any society"; to the contrary, if "society" exists at all, it is only a playing field or game board on which individuals make their moves and either win

---

[40] Wilde, *De Profundis*.
[41] Alford, Rethinking Freedom, 6–7.
[42] Alford, *Rethinking Freedom*, 2.
[43] Brown, *States of Injury*, 5.
[44] Brown, *States of Injury*, 10.

or lose.[45] The outcome of this intensely egocentric and juvenile approach to freedom is, in Anker's estimation, *unfreedom*, which we observe in contemporary society as

> mass political disenfranchisement, experiences of being overpowered by the agentless forces of globalization, increasing economic in equality and financial precarity across populations, tightening norms for acceptable individual behavior, and decreasing political agency for influencing collective governing decisions. Unfreedom refers to contemporary experiences in which citizens are continually demobilized and demoralized, excluded from politics, and made into consumers rather than active players.[46]

In this light, Hamilton was probably correct that the kind of freedoms we celebrate today "have actively worked against our freedom to choose to lead more fulfilling lives."[47] The freedom of the market—the freedom to buy what we want—is a trivial freedom, which is often bought at the price of surveillance, invasion of privacy, and production of shoddy and dangerous if not toxic goods. Many of our freedoms, and the ways we use them, are narcissistic, avaricious, pestilent, and downright deadly to ourselves and others. (As I write, the United States has just finished a weekend with thirteen mass shootings, thanks at least in part to our vaunted "freedom to bear arms." Is that merely the price of freedom?)

One more word that might be added to the qualifications for freedom, along with maturity, discipline, and responsibility, is humility. In his treatise on ignorance and liberty, Lorenzo Infantino postulated that the justification of liberty "rests on the recognition of human ignorance" or what he called *fallibilism*, the fact that no one has perfect knowledge and that we all get it wrong sometimes.[48] Americans and free-marketeers are happy enough to file this charge against the government: central planning or socialism should not be allowed because no government official is wise enough to make such complicated decisions. (But are we any wiser or better informed as individuals? Aren't "government officials" individuals too?) As Infantino summarized it, "Improvement in the conditions of our lives, therefore, does not come from the omniscience attributed to some enlightened legislator or planner," whether this "privileged point of view," this perfect planner and decider is a president,

---

[45] Hamilton, *The Freedom Paradox*, 7.
[46] Anker, *Orgies of Feeling*, 15.
[47] Hamilton, *The Freedom Paradox*, 8.
[48] Infantino, *Ignorance and Liberty*, n.p.

a Founding Father, a culture hero (such as Gilgamesh or Moses), or—although Infantino does not carry his argument this far—a god. Even a god cannot foresee every contingency or balance every interest; besides, whatever a god decides or ordains must be interpreted and applied through the eyes of the present. Infantino held that liberty itself "is bestowed by a normative network that marks the boundaries of our actions, indicates what we cannot do and leaves us free choice of how to act,"[49] in short, the rule of law and the equality of all citizens before that law. What he failed to grasp is that *humans put the law in place, that we* are *the lawgivers.* We also ultimately put truth in place; we are the truth-givers, and any notion of a monopoly of truth "destroys all systems of liberty."[50]

But what is a religion, at least the kind of religion we are most accustomed to like the Christian religion, other than a systematic monopoly of truth? We have reached the end finally, where we can engage with Dostoevsky's challenge to live without god(s), with these lessons in hand:

- freedom is complex, unstable, and malleable (didn't Daniel Dennett aver that "freedom evolves"?[51])
- freedom can be contradictory and paradoxical
- freedom in the form of decision and choice is unavoidable (we are, as the existentialists stated, condemned to be free)
- freedom can be ugly, self-serving, rapacious, even lethal—in other words, not every exercise or consequence of freedom is "good"
- freedom is not the absence or antithesis of order, structure, and rule and certainly not of society or culture—it is not anomie—but rather it is made possible and given shape by those forces
- freedom deployed positively requires much of us, including maturity, self-discipline, humility, and responsibility.

It is to responsibility that I want to return one last time. Wendy Brown condensed the paradox of freedom to the reality that "liberation from masters—god, history, or man—constrains us to an extraordinary responsibility for ourselves and for others."[52] That explains why she titled her book *States of Injury,* because freedom used irresponsibly can be and often is injurious to oneself and others. Freedom is a liberation but also a

---

[49] Infantino, *Ignorance and Liberty*, 31.
[50] Infantino, *Ignorance and Liberty*, 133.
[51] Dennett, *Freedom Evolves*.
[52] Brown, *States of Injury*, 24.

liability, since those who *can* choose *must* choose. If no man or woman, no historical force or "law of nature," and *no god* solves the riddle of humanity, then it is up to us to decide. We do not make such decisions in a vacuum; we are creatures and constructions of a particular culture, historical experience, and historical moment, overdetermined to choose some things and avoid others.

So the point is not, as Dostoevsky or his characters fretted, whether without god(s) all things are permitted. The point is that without god(s)—and, ultimately, even with god(s)—*humans do and must decide what is permitted.* We give ourselves the law and then conveniently forget that we are the authors of our own order. David Graeber and David Wengrow dissect freedom into three constituent parts. The first two are freedom to say no to authority and freedom to move, to get up and leave the system and society where we reside (to "get off the grid" if not to emigrate altogether). Both of these freedoms have eroded almost to the point of non-existence in the modern world, with the tightening of borders and the penetration of technologies of governmental knowledge and control. The third freedom is "the freedom to create new and different forms of social reality," to radically re-imagine how we live and what we value (Nietzsche's "revaluation of all values") and to put those alternatives into practice.[53] If we can actually do that—and in ways that are respectful of ourselves, our society, and our world—then the first two freedoms potentially come within our reach. But in order to extricate ourselves from old, tired, ill-fitting, and often pathological social realities, we must liberate ourselves from old, tired, ill-fitting, and often pathological authorities, including especially religions and their god(s).

The first step in this process, in theism-dominated societies, is atheism—saying no to god(s). The next step is liberatheism—getting free of god(s). The final step is not talking about god(s) at all.

---

[53] Graeber and Wengrow, *The Dawn of Everything*, 525.

1

The (Melo)Drama of Atheism, or It's Not Easy Being Free?

Many people think that atheists must be angry, bitter, and depressed, not necessarily (although often) because of some purported "atheist personality" but more immediately because the absence of god(s) is simply too much for a human to endure. "If one is really serious about" a universe without god(s), opined John Haught, atheism "should make all the difference in the world, and it would take a superhuman effort to embrace it."[1] Today's atheists, he insisted, especially the so-called New Atheists of the new century (chiefly Richard Dawkins, Christopher Hitchens, Daniel Dennett, and Sam Harris), are shallow thinkers, armchair atheists, "amateur atheists," "soft-core atheists" compared to their earlier compatriots, the "hard-core atheists" like Nietzsche, Camus, and Sartre. The superficial atheists of our day literally do not understand what they are asking for, since they fail to comprehend the "tragic heroism" and ultimately soul-crushing loneliness, alienation, and disorientation of a reality without god(s). Faced with the ultimate silence and solitude, they would suffer from excruciating freedom, which, as Erich Fromm warned (see Introduction), could only lead to such isolation, anxiety, powerlessness, and meaninglessness that most puny humans would likely beat a desperate retreat to the arms of a deity, any deity, including a non-supernatural one such as scientism or political authoritarianism.

That this description does not fit me at all, nor the vast majority of the atheists I have ever known, makes me suspicious of Haught's analysis (or should we say diatribe). Admittedly the New Atheists are not the intellectual or emotional equivalents of the giants of philosophy and psychology who preceded them, but are they—are *we*—mere idlers of idolatry, or is atheism today not as tragic and burdensome as he and his ilk assume? Maybe atheism was *never* as onerous and unpleasant as the great god-deniers of yesterday assumed. In this chapter, while acknowledging

---

[1] Haught, *God and the New Atheism*, 20.

that a godless world leaves humanity much work to do, I will argue that this work is not beyond human capacity and endurance—and further, *that there is no more human work for atheists than for theists, as a god who never shows itself leaves all the effort to humans anyhow*. In other words, by exaggerating the tragedy of godlessness, opponents have made a false melodrama out of atheism.

You Atheists Just Aren't Serious

Haught's case against the superficiality of contemporary atheism was largely a tirade against the New Atheists, published shortly after the initial wave of New Atheist books (Harris' 2004 *The End of Faith*, Dawkins' 2006 *The God Delusion*, Dennett's 2006 *Breaking the Spell*, Hitchens' 2007 *God is Not Great*, not to mention Victor Stenger's 2007 *God: The Failed Hypothesis*, David Mills' 2006 *Atheist Universe: The Thinking Person's Answer to Christian Fundamentalism*, 2006; Michel Onfray's 2005 *In Defense of Atheism: The Case Against Christianity, Judaism, and Islam*, John Loftus' 2008 *Why I Became an Atheist: A Former Preacher Rejects Christianity*, and my own 2004 *Natural Atheism* and 2008 *Atheism Advanced: Further Thoughts of a Freethinker*, among others). He first took modern atheists to task for their lack of theological sophistication: "The new atheism is so theologically unchallenging," he stated, "Its engagement with theology lies about at the same level of reflection of faith that one can find in contemporary creationist and fundamentalist literature."[2] This is more than a bit ironic since he was granting that much *theistic* writing is also simplistic in its theology. Nevertheless, it is a fair critique, one which I have previously made, and none of the horsemen of New Atheism is a religion scholar per se (Dawkins, biology; Dennett, philosophy; Harris, philosophy-cum-neuroscience; Hitchens, journalism). That their works are pitched at the level of "creationist and fundamentalist literature" is no great surprise, since that is their main target.

It is true that theological speculation can be and has become incredibly subtle and nuanced, but that is honestly no reason to take it particularly seriously. (See Chapters 4 and 8) Theology, literally "god-study," is, if not an impossible enterprise altogether, then little more than regurgitation of and exegesis of religious doctrine—and of *one or more particular religious doctrines*. That is, there is "Christian theology" and "Islamic theology" and "Hindu theology," etc.—and at a finer level of distinction, "Catholic theology" and "Baptist theology" and "Mormon theology," *ad infinitum*—each differing from and often contradicting the

---

[2] Haught, *God and the New Atheism*, xi.

others. Truly, there is no such thing as theology but only *theologies*, and it would be an interesting project to study and compare theologies, to perform a genuine comparative theology or a theology-ology. And when Haught confessed that his own theology posits "that the divine mystery can be approached only by way of faith, trust, and hope," it is difficult to see how atheism could and should take it seriously since we are not convinced that a "divine mystery"' exists in the first place (worse, Haught tried to add that "even though God cannot be known apart from faith and hope, most theology allows that faith and hope are entirely consistent with and fully supportive of human reason"—a vain statement that should replace "allows" with "pleads").[3]

His next objection was that New Atheism is not particularly new (in fact, the first chapter is titled "How New is the New Atheism?"). Again, this is fair enough: New Atheism did not excel in originality so much as in intensity. The books in the New Atheism canon "are not mild treatises like those that trickle tentatively, and often unreadably, from departments of philosophy. They are works of passion"—which amounts to a condemnation of philosophy of religion as much as of atheist writing.[4] Neither is it entirely true: much theology and philosophy of religion *is* a fairly passionate supplication to the author's favorite theism (usually Christianity). (See Chapter 8) This is also another potentially self-undermining point in Haught's argument, since it is very important to him that "faith" is not just intellectual assent but "the commitment of one's whole being," to a god in the case of theists but presumably to some or any other things. Passion, you would expect, would be integral to such commitment.

On this subject, Haught, like other theists, protested that New Atheism operates with a pinched notion of faith, construing it "in a narrow intellectual and propositional sense."[5] That is, faith in New Atheism equates to sheer belief in a truth-claim, which, if false, makes it a sign of "a weak intellect." Faith for theologians is different and greater, "a state of self-surrender in which one's whole being, and not just the intellect, is experienced as being carried away into a dimension of reality that is much deeper and more real than anything that could be grasped by science and reason."[6] (That sounds pretty passionate to me!) That is, indeed, how many theologians understand faith, which makes it sound like a thoroughly bad idea. However, Haught and others like him miss two essential points—

---

[3] Haught, *God and the New Atheism*, xii.
[4] Haught, *God and the New Atheism*, 25.
[5] Haught, *God and the New Atheism*, 5.
[6] Haught, *God and the New Atheism*, 13.

first, that such "faith" depends for any value at all on the *veracity of the thing committed to* (that is, "faith" in a non-existent entity is utterly misplaced), and second, that "faith" and "belief" are ultimately synonyms. Faith and belief cover exactly the same semantic ground and are in all instances interchangeable; both refer to multiple predicates and practices, including (1) acceptance of a claim as true, (2) confidence in a person or other entity, and (3) commitment to a person, entity, or cause. (See Chapter 2) The multiple meanings of "belief" and its verb form "believe" are obvious in the old saying, "You may not believe in (i.e., accept as true) God, but he believes in (i.e., is confident about and committed to) you."

Haught continued that New Atheism not only stresses that theism/religion/faith (admittedly, a confusion of quite different phenomena) is false but actually bad. A little too cleverly, he likened it to Buddhism's Four Noble Truths, the first New Atheist Noble Truth concurring that life is suffering. The second "Evident Truth" of New Atheism is that the cause of suffering is faith, and accordingly the third "Evident Truth" is that the cure for suffering is the elimination of faith. The fourth "Evident Truth," equivalent to the Buddhist Eightfold Path, is narrowed down to one, namely, science.

This is the spot from which Haught launched his main assault on New Atheism, in the second chapter titled "How Atheistic Is the New Atheism?" Twenty-first-century atheists, he declared, are intellectually, morally, and aesthetically pale relative to atheists of prior eras. They do not, in a word, appreciate the gravity of what they are advocating; they do not grasp "the terrifying consequences of the death of God."[7] They think that erasing god(s) from the universe is no big deal, while they should, Haught held, understand reality without god(s) as overwhelming, devastating, unbearable, and tragic beyond all human endurance.

Because New Atheism believes that it can have godlessness "at the least possible expense" to the human order, they think that life after god(s) will "remain pretty much the same, minus the inconvenience of terrorism and creationists" and that "our moral and social instinct, rooted in biology as they are, will remain unmodified except for slight cultural corrections that will need to be made after religion disappears."[8] I would do Haught one better and assert that New Atheism expects that life will be better after religion disappears. Either way, Haught was singularly irritated by the New Atheism focus on happiness and enjoyment (summed up by various appeals to "human flourishing" or "eudaimonia"): New Atheists like Harris assume that humans will go merrily on their way without

---

[7] Haught, *God and the New Atheism*, 20.
[8] Haught, *God and the New Atheism*, 19.

god(s), basically living the lives they lived before, honoring the same values and pursuing the same goals. Instead, Haught warned ominously,

> Go all the way and think the business of atheism through to the bitter end; before you get too comfortable with the godless world you long for, you will be required by the logic of any consistent skepticism to pass through the disorienting wilderness of nihilism. Do you have the courage to do that? You will have to adopt the tragic heroism of a Sisyphus, or realize that true freedom in the absence of God means that *you* are the creator of the values you live by, an intolerable burden from which most people would seek an escape.[9]

He asked menacingly, "Are you willing to risk madness?"

The great atheists of earlier decades and centuries knew better, Haught insisted. Compared to New Atheism, they—whether Nietzsche, Marx, Freud, or existentialist philosophers—"demanded a much more radical transformation of human culture and consciousness."[10] At the individual level, it would require a stronger, a higher, kind of human, an *übermensch*; at the collective level, it would entail a revolution of social institutions and relations, a revaluation of all values. Either way, the generations of *real* atheists, of serious atheists, of hard-core atheists, "understood that if we are truly sincere in our atheism the whole web of meanings and values that had clustered around the idea of God in Western culture has to go down the drain along with its organizing center."[11]

Haught was not the only observer to come to such conclusions about atheism, New or Old. In a series of blogs, philosopher Edward Feser surveyed what he called Old Atheism, showing the same disdain for New Atheism. His sense of the naïveté of today's prominent atheists and of the entire contemporary atheist movement is summed up in the "Atheist Bus Campaign" with "its preposterous slogan: 'There's probably no god. Now stop worrying and enjoy your life.'"[12] In place of smugness and simplemindedness, Feser asked atheists to ponder, "What would be the consequences if it were true?"

> As if atheism promised only sweetness and light. As if the vast majority of human beings would not find the implications of atheism—that human existence has no purpose, that there is no postmortem reward to counterbalance the sufferings of this life, nor

---

[9] Haught, *God and the New Atheism*, 22.
[10] Haught, *God and the New Atheism*, 19–20.
[11] Haught, *God and the New Atheism*, 22.
[12] Feser, "Adventures in the Old Atheism, Part I: Nietzsche."

any hope for seeing dead loved ones again, etc.—far more depressing than any purported deficiencies in traditional religious belief.[13]

With an insulting tone, not to mention offensive idiocy, that even Haught could not match, Feser declared that upon hearing the dire predictions of theists and Old Atheists alike, today's atheists mindlessly "shrug, thinking only of the heady prospect of guilt-free porn surfing, transvestite bathroom access, rectal coitus, and the other strange obsessions of the modern liberal mind."

The Unbearable Lightness
of Being Without God(s)

It is true that many sensitive and articulate atheists of yesteryear experienced the absence or unreality of god(s) as traumatic, perhaps more so than ordinary humans could withstand. The classic portrait of humanity's discovery that there is such thing as god(s), that we have left god(s) behind, that we ourselves have "killed" god(s), comes of course from Friedrich Nietzsche. In his 1882 *The Gay Science*, section 125, he pictured the universe flying apart without the gravitational pull, without the solid ground, of a god:

> What were we doing when we unchained this earth from its sun? Whither is it moving now? Whither are we moving? Away from all suns? Are we not plunging continually? Backward, sideward, forward, in all directions? Is there still any up or down? Are we not straying, as through an infinite nothing? Do we not feel the breath of empty space? Has it not become colder? Is not night continually closing in on us? Do we not need to light lanterns in the morning? Do we hear nothing as yet of the noise of the gravediggers who are burying God? Do we smell nothing as yet of the divine decomposition? Gods, too, decompose. God is dead. God remains dead. And we have killed him. How shall we comfort ourselves, the murderers of all murderers? What was holiest and mightiest of all that the world has yet owned has bled to death under our knives: who will wipe this blood off us? What water is there for us to clean ourselves? What festivals of atonement, what sacred games shall we have to invent? Is not the greatness of this deed too great for us? Must we ourselves not become gods simply to appear worthy of it? There has never been a greater deed; and whoever

---

[13] Feser, "Adventures in the Old Atheism, Part I: Nietzsche."

is born after us—for the sake of this deed he will belong to a higher history than all history hitherto.[14]

The pathos of this passage is almost overwhelming; the realization of the god's death is so awful that it must issue from the mouth of a madman, and most people cannot and will not hear it. Nietzsche concluded that the inescapable consequence of the death of god(s) and other idols was nihilism. Indeed, in the collection of notes and unfinished thoughts that was assembled under the title of *The Will to Power*, he foresaw "the history of the next two centuries," during which "what will happen, what must necessarily happen" is *"the triumph of Nihilism."*[15] We will say more about this shortly.

Similar to and prior to Nietzsche, Karl Marx presciently perceived not just god(s) but everything "melting into air" and not specifically through the agency of atheism. Rather, modern urban industrial life, and most potently of all capitalism with its dedication to "creative destruction" and the constant revolution of technologies and social institutions, was grinding down all received truths while immiserating the vast majority of humankind. Religion was at best a palliative, a painkiller, "the opium of the people," but also a symbol or metaphor of their real suffering (and to an extent, an additional contributor to that suffering). Religions and their gods and other beings were bound to fade but not from the arguments of atheists; rather, the masses would spontaneously abandon their religious illusions when the "condition that requires illusions"—namely, poverty, class inequality, and alienation of labor—was rectified. So, the liberation from god(s) is not a panacea in itself (atheism alone does not improve the practical circumstances of life for the oppressed classes) but would arise only after the hard work of dramatic, even radical social change. In other words, as Feser wrote in another essay, "You won't find in Marx the chirpy naïveté about the consequences of naturalism and of abandoning religion that you see in the New Atheists."[16]

If anything, as a physician of the human condition Sigmund Freud was still more pessimistic about the outlook of post-theism. Certainly, religion was for Freud a grand wish fulfillment, an infantile projection of magical thinking and family drama. But Freud did not expect that letting go of god(s) would automatically ensure human happiness. In fact, he did not believe that happiness was a realistic or possible goal for humans. In his 1930 *Civilization and Its Discontents* (the title of which in German,

---

[14] Nietzsche, *The Gay Science*, 181.
[15] Nietzsche, *The Will to Power*, Books 1 and 2, 1.
[16] Feser, "Adventures in the Old Atheism, Part IV: Marx."

Das Unbehagen in der Kultur, more closely translates to "Discomfort/Uneasiness in Culture"), written after World War I and in the shadow of rising fascism, he conceded that losing one's childish illusions, that is, growing up, would not afford less pain but probably more. Maturity means facing the "reality principle" and relinquishing the "pleasure principle"; more, living in a society (culture/civilization) means curbing our instincts and repressing our drives, leaving us frustrated and unhappy. As he added a few years later, in an essay titled "Analysis Terminable and Interminable," the recovery process undertaken in "psycho-analytic therapy—the liberation of a human being from his neurotic symptoms, inhibitions, and abnormalities of character—is a lengthy business" and indeed may never come to a full and satisfactory conclusion.[17]

At the same historical moment, two other monumental thinkers struggled with the implications of the non-existence of god(s). Albert Camus published his first book, *L'envers and l'endroit* (released in English as "Betwixt and Between," also translated as "The Wrong Side and the Right Side") in 1937, followed soon by *The Stranger* (1942), *The Myth of Sisyphus* (1942), *The Plague* (1947), and *The Fall* (1956). Jean-Paul Sartre, a contemporary of Camus, started his literary career in 1936 with *Imagination*, then *Nausea* (1938), *Being and Nothingness* (1943), *No Exit* (1944, originally *Huis clos* or "Behind Closed Doors"), and *Existentialism and Humanism* (1946). Both have been categorized as existentialists for their unflinching examination of human existence, defined by freedom and finitude: both described humanity as fundamentally if not absurdly free. Yet neither man found this to be a cause for celebration.

Already in his earliest work, Camus envisioned humankind confronting an indifferent universe where death was the only and final reality. In the fictional *The Plague*, children die for no good, certainly no just, reason. In the non-fiction *The Myth of Sisyphus* he declared that "in a universe suddenly divested of illusions and lights, man feels an alien, a stranger. His exile is without remedy since he is deprived of the memory of a lost home or the hope of a promised land."[18] (Recall from Greek mythology that Sisyphus was a trickster figure who twice escaped death and was sentenced by Zeus to eternally roll a boulder up a hill in hell.) Trapped in such a reality, Camus began his meditation on the myth with the infamous statement: "There is but one truly serious philosophical

---

[17] Freud, "Analysis Terminable and Interminable," 373.
[18] Camus, *The Myth of Sisyphus*, 13.

problem and that is suicide."[19] Is, he pondered, suicide a solution to the intrinsic problem of existence?

"I do not believe in God," he announced in his notebooks from the 1950s, and how could he, realizing the disenchantment, the alienness, the exile, the absurdity of life?[20] Yet in an almost Buddhist way, he was not interested in disproving god(s), and according to philosopher Craig DeLancey he was surprisingly openhearted to theists, as in his 1948 remarks to a gathering of Dominicans: "I shall never start from the supposition that Christian faith is illusory, but merely from the fact that I cannot accept it" and "I shall not try to change anything that I think or anything that you think (insofar as I can judge of it) in order to reach a reconciliation that would be agreeable to all."[21]

Sartre was somewhat more forthcoming with his atheism: in his *Les Mots* ("Words"), he recounted how at school in 1917 he "decided to think of the Almighty. Immediately He tumbled into the blue and disappeared without giving any explanation. He doesn't exist, I said to myself with polite surprise, and I thought the matter was settled. In a way, it was, since never have I had the slightest temptation to bring Him back to life."[22] Still, even though he apparently never regretted his conversion to atheism and bragged that he had "carried it through," he characterized atheism as "a cruel and long-range affair."[23]

Long-range perhaps (in that in an individual's life, and in a society's history, atheism may not be achieved), but why cruel? Sartre scholar Alexis Chabot holds that Sartre believed (just as Erich Fromm concluded) there was an urge to run back to the comforting arms of belief; atheism is never quite secure and constitutes a permanent "struggle against the temptation of faith, a struggle which is nothing else than the aspiration to Being."[24] But those familiar with Sartre's worldview know that Being is the one thing that we cannot have, that is absolutely unavailable. Humans, rather, are as condemned to Becoming as we are to freedom (recall his slogan that Existence precedes Essence, that Becoming precedes if not replaces Being). Surely most humans would prefer the repose of Being over the restlessness of Becoming—or worse, the finality of Nothingness. Chabot insists that Sartre deemed it "bad faith" when "any

---

[19] Camus, *The Myth of Sisyphus*, 11.

[20] Camus, *Notebooks 1951–1959*, 92.

[21] Quoted in DeLancey, "Camus's Atheism and the Virtues of Inconsistency."

[22] Sartre, *The Words*, 251.

[23] Sartre, *The Words*, 253.

[24] Chabot, "Cruel Atheism," 58.

human being refuses contingency and devotes him- or herself to the quest for Being."[25] If so, all theism, all theology, all religious faith is bad faith.

The "Sartrean human being," which for Sartre (and for us) is the honest and rational person, "thus knows, under his or her different masks, that God does not exist."[26] But most human beings are more like the audience of Nietzsche's madman, not ready and not able to hear the news and accept the truth. It is too much, this "awareness of contingency, inseparable from the revelation of an empty and silent sky," and so there is the ever-present lure of some absolute, of Being, of an absolute being, since "any ersatz of God is better than nothing."[27] And nothing, Nothingness (*néant* in French, the second term in Sartre's title *Being and Nothingness*), is exactly what reality seems to offer us. It is the condition and possibility of our freedom; religion and other such searches for the eternal and for a solid ground are the negation of freedom; and atheism is "the negation of the negation of freedom" (which is the same or different from freedom?)[28] In the end, Chabot feels, Sartre did not consider it feasible "to get to the bottom of atheism without experiencing the unbearability of contingency, the desolation of the empty heavens"; therefore, "because it is painful for him not to believe," the atheist is doomed to be an "unhappy figure oscillating between belief and its impossibility"[29]—a Sisyphus forever pushing the rock of god-belief up the hill, only to have it come rolling back down on him.

Cruel Theism

If atheism is a misery, a Nietzschean burden too great (in both senses of the term) for ordinary people to tolerate, an agony of silence and solitude, then surely theism (or religion of all sorts) is a relief, a peace, and a balm, a secure comfort in undying and unquestioned human and superhuman fellowship. Some Christians portray it this way, to a compulsive degree ("I've got joy, joy, joy, joy down in my heart"), the obsessive repetition of joy making us wonder if they protest too much.

But no, theism or religion more generally is not a guaranteed end to the intellectual and moral torment of the human condition, and delicate souls among the religious have reported suffering as great as any felt or foreseen by Nietzsche, Sartre, or Camus. In Christianity itself, whether or

---

[25] Chabot, "Cruel Atheism," 60.
[26] Chabot, "Cruel Atheism," 62.
[27] Chabot, "Cruel Atheism," 61.
[28] Chabot, "Cruel Atheism," 61.
[29] Chabot, "Cruel Atheism," 62–64.

not the doctrine can be traced back to Augustine (fourth and fifth century CE) or even to scripture, the concept of "original sin" has saddled believers with the weight of inescapable guilt. By the third Christian century, more perceptive if not neurotic followers were renouncing ordinary life in favor of an ascetic withdrawal into the desert—a self-imposed silence and solitude if not punishment—characterized by fasting, celibacy, sometimes self-inflicted pain, obsessive prayer, a sense of continuous affliction by and battle with demons, and an imminent vision of the end of the world. And this sentiment did not diminish with time: sixteenth-century Saint Teresa not only found herself assailed by the devil and his demons but averred that being purer of spirit than regular people made her *more* susceptible to demonic attack; according to Catholic scholar Father Antonio Moreno, John of the Cross reached the same conclusion, holding that "the devil accomplished more through a little harm caused to an advanced soul than great damage to many others." Moreno adds that once Satan identified Teresa as a worthy adversary and target, "she endured the terrible and subtle temptations of despair, false humility, false presumption, and false fears as well as the temptation to abandon mental prayer. These temptations put her soul's peace and love of God at risk."[30] Atheists by comparison are mercifully spared the fear of demonic aggression.

Martin Luther is another who found "doubt and struggle and despair" in his religious convictions, sometimes pitched for days into a dark depression that he called *Anfechtungen* (challenges). Like Augustine (and many others before and since) he was tortured by his own sinfulness and unworthiness:

> He could never escape his own failure. He had been taught to fear the righteous judgment of God and nothing seemed to bring him relief from that fear. He tried working harder but the defects in his walk with God only seemed even more conspicuous to him. He frequented the confessional and wore himself out with acts of penance, but he could never find a way out. "My conscience would never give me assurance," he later told his students, "but I was always doubting and said, 'You did not perform that correctly. You were not contrite enough. You left that out of your confession.'"[31]

It was out of this very moral suffering that Lutheranism and Protestantism more broadly were born. Luther's god's grace could never be earned or

---

[30] Moreno, "Demons According to St. Teresa and St. John of the Cross."
[31] Thompson, "Luther's Raging Torment."

deserved by such a flawed creature as himself or any human, but the deity gifted it anyhow.

Lutheranism unleashed a wave of religious interpretations of sinfulness and salvation, such as Calvinism and English Puritanism. Each placed a cumbersome burden on devotees, for instance, to fret if they were among the elect who had already won salvation (e.g. predestination, the antithesis of spiritual freedom) and to perpetually inspect and criticize themselves and each other for minute moral failures (which was in a serious way a perpetuation of the Catholic tradition of confession or constantly monitoring oneself for any slip from righteousness). Fascinatingly and extremely importantly, this path led to Christianity's own form of existentialism, a sort of Christian existentialism first and best personified by Søren Kierkegaard. Kierkegaard (a nineteenth-century theologian, philosopher, and poet) agonized as intensely for his faith as Sartre or Camus did for their unfaith, illustrating that theism does not and cannot remove the essential strains of human existence.

Kierkegaard's Christianity was no tonic for his anxiety and was the cause of much of it. Titles such as *Fear and Trembling*, *The Sickness Unto Death*, and *The Concept of Anxiety* indicate that he was as troubled by the human condition as any atheist of his time. Despair was his particular illness, indeed a "metaphysical sickness" and a "crisis" deeper and more deadly than any bodily malady. Further, Kierkegaard diagnosed the sources of despair roughly as the hard-core atheists did. The first is inherent and undeniable human finitude: each of us is a particular factual historical being limited in duration, endurance, and understanding. But finitude is also a kind of inauthenticity, of being less than one's full authentic self, of being—ironically—less than totally free from social norms and received ideas. Vincent McCarthy wrote that for Kierkegaard "the despair of finitude,"

> in contrast to that of infinitude, represents narrowness of feeling, knowledge and will. Rather than expanding himself in growth of these faculties, a person stays as he is and merges into the crowd and never develops as an individual. And no one is potentially as insensitive, ignorant, and weak-willed as the crowd.[32]

Thus, even with a god in the world, humans were still radically free, we might say condemned to be free, to be who they are. And since we are fated with Sartrian freedom, we also suffer the despair of possibility or contingency, of the lack of necessity, and of the associated pressure to

---

[32] McCarthy, *The Phenomenology of Moods in Kierkegaard*, 93.

"become" rather than merely to "be" (again, shades of Sartre). But the obligation to become is itself overwhelming: "Eventually everything seems possible, but this is exactly the point at which the abyss swallows up the self."[33] On the other hand, necessity too is a hardship, as it restricts freedom. "To lack possibility means either that everything has become necessary for a person or that everything has become trivial," Kierkegaard opined.[34] In the former case, humanity collapses into determinism; in the latter, it dissolves into the pettiness of the "philistine-bourgeois" lifestyle.

A person could dwell in ignorance of her condition and then maybe remain contentedly ignorant of her despair, but this was no solution. For Kierkegaard, the only treatment for the metaphysical sickness was faith in the Christian god, but even this provided no final cure. It was ineluctably blind: his classic notion of "a leap of faith" implied that we cannot know what we are leaping toward or whether it exists at all. No one, he admitted, can reason their way out of human despair or into religious faith. But more fatefully, the Christian faith is a comfortless home. As he was hardly the first to recognize, Yahweh promises neither happiness and prosperity nor even justice or morality. Any religion, Christianity included, that assured only good things and success for members could not be taken seriously and would be instantly and laughably refuted (the "prosperity gospel" notwithstanding). Yet, in the face of life's obvious pains and failures—if not evils—many Christians cling to the life raft of their god's omnibenevolence and justice. However, the Book of Job portrays graphically that Yahweh cannot be counted on for justice, nor does he owe feeble humans an explanation for his injustices. Kierkegaard himself grappled extensively with the injustice and immorality of the deity's order that Abraham sacrifice his son Isaac; this is the subject of *Fear and Trembling*. He could only conclude that his god is beyond moral laws and norms and, as the freest of beings, is free to violate morality and compel others to violate it at his whim. Faith, then, both the faith of Abraham and the faith of a modern Christian, calls for the "teleological suspension of the ethical" whenever confronted with a situation and command that breaks all everyday moral rules (and for which, as in the cases of Abraham and Job, no justification is given). But once again, this places an enormous burden on the individual, who must exercise his freedom to decide for himself whether to act morally or to obey his god when the two options contradict each other.

Out of such pained musings, and in the light of atheistic existentialism, a branch of theology identifiable as "Christian

---

[33] Kierkegaard, *The Sickness Unto Death*, 36.
[34] Kierkegaard, *The Sickness Unto Death*, 40.

existentialism" has coalesced. Associated with multiple Christian thinkers from Gabriel Marcel to Rudolf Bultmann and Dietrich Bonhoeffer, Christian existentialism naturally shares many of the features of secular/atheist existentialism, with a god (usually) added back in. One source summarizes Christian existentialism thusly:

- A person is autonomous and is fully free to make choices and fully responsible for them
- Rational grounds for theology and divine revelation do not exist
- True faith transcends rationalism and God's commandments
- The true God is not the God of philosophers or of rationalism
- The destruction of wars throughout human history proves there cannot be a rational understanding of God or humanity
- A Christian must personally resolve within herself the content of faith from being a myth or mystery to being reality or truth before they will allow an understanding and acceptance of salvation
- It is impossible to discover a personal Being and faith through rational reasoning.[35]

Probably the best-known and most representative figure in Christian existentialism is Paul Tillich, whose 1952 *The Courage to Be* seduced many an undergrad, including myself briefly (I composed a baccalaureate essay comparing his and Freud's conception of anxiety). Indeed, for Tillich, the fundamental challenge and threat to humanity is anxiety, which is "the state in which a being is aware of its possible nonbeing" or "the existential awareness of nonbeing"[36]—a formulation that could come straight out of Sartre and indeed echoes Sartre's *Being and Nothingness*. Equally echoing Kierkegaard, Tillich rephrased that anxiety "is finitude, experienced as one's own finitude."[37] Tillich specifically analyzed three types of anxiety, namely the anxiety of death, the anxiety of meaninglessness and emptiness, and the anxiety of guilt and condemnation (although I doubt that atheists do or must ache over the third of these). He asserted that the fear of death results from "contingency" or the fact that "our existence [has] no ultimate necessity," that each of us may not have existed, once did not exist, and eventually will not exist.[38] However, it is fair to say that such contingency is the root of all anxieties, including moral and legal ones (that is, any particular law or moral stricture may not have

---

[35] All About Philosophy, "Christian Existentialism."
[36] Tillich, *The Courage to Be*, 35.
[37] Tillich, *The Courage to Be*, 35.
[38] Tillich, *The Courage to Be*, 44.

existed and actually does not exist in other times and places), which we will shortly call Nietzschean nihilism.

Again, as in Kierkegaard, Sartre, and Camus, Tillich appreciated humankind's freedom, albeit a finite and not infinite freedom: "Within these limits he is asked to make of himself what he is supposed to become to fulfill his destiny."[39] Yet contingency and freedom cannot help but combine to produce despair, which is the reaction of "a being [who] is aware of itself as unable to affirm itself because of the power of nonbeing."[40] Referring to Luther's *Anfechtungen* and the "frightful threat of meaninglessness," which Luther interpreted as demonic assault, Tillich reckoned that the only answer to existential anxiety was courage or "the self-affirmation of being in spite of nonbeing."[41] As a Christian thinker, of course, "faith" was for Tillich the foundation and form of such courage, but he had to grant nonetheless that even a god could not eliminate humanity's existential emptiness and, much worse, that the conventional biblical god could not provide even the most basic succor—which was a task for a "God above God," that is, some kind of divine something-or-other "who appears when God has disappeared in the anxiety of doubt."[42]

The vacuity or incoherence of that stance speaks for itself. (See Chapter 3, especially ignosticism) But we have already dwelt too long in Christian materials exclusively. In other theisms, and in non-theistic religions, although they may not possess the philosophical self-reflection we have seen, the incapacity of religion to provide relief, or the reality of religion's own cruelty and burdensomeness, is apparent. In Western civilization, it is the void, nothingness, nonbeing (*néant* in Sartre's French) that preoccupies and panics deep thinkers.[43] Eastern religious traditions have often rather embraced the void. Hinduism understands the world that we take for reality as an illusion (*maya*) and strives for final release or liberation (*moksha*) from the cycle of death and rebirth (*samsara*). Buddhism too aims to extinguish the self (*nirvana* refers not to a life after death, and certainly not a heavenly paradise, but "blowing out" or "extinguishing") but goes a step further, teaching that there is no permanent stable self or soul in the first place (*anatta*, no-self). Emptiness (*sunyata*) is a key concept in Buddhism, but it is not to be feared; it is not

---

[39] Tillich, *The Courage to Be*, 52.
[40] Tillich, *The Courage to Be*, 55.
[41] Tillich, *The Courage to Be*, 172.
[42] Tillich, *The Courage to Be*, 182.
[43] See for instance Adams, *Nil: Episodes in the Literary Conquest of Void during the Nineteenth Century* for a survey of approaches to nothingness in Western literature, responses that range from disturbed to enthusiastic.

Sartre's *néant* but the very basis of being Buddhist and Buddhist being. Thich Nhat Hanh explains that emptiness

> means empty of a separate self. It is full of everything, full of life. The word "emptiness" should not scare us. It is a wonderful word. To be empty does not mean to be nonexistent. If the sheet of paper is not empty, how could the sunshine, the logger, and the forest come into it? How could it be a sheet of paper? The cup, in order to be empty, has to be there. Form, feelings, perceptions, mental formations, and consciousness, in order to be empty of a separate self, have to be there. Emptiness is the ground of everything. "Thanks to emptiness, everything is possible." That is a declaration made by Nagarjuna, a Buddhist philosopher of the second century. Emptiness is quite an optimistic concept.[44]

The idea that the void has some religious significance and therefore is not to be rejected or feared is actually present in the Abrahamic religions. David Biale, in a discussion of Jewish secular thought, contends that the Kabbalist tradition emanating from the teachings of Isaac Luria believed the void—specifically, the void left by the withdrawal of Yahweh—to be the very possibility of creation: "when God begins to create the world, he contracts himself away from a central point, leaving an empty space (*halal ha-panui*). Without this realm devoid of God, the world could not exist." [45] In short, the physical world that humans inhabit is precisely where the god is *not*.

Finally, in many ancient and indigenous religions with or without gods, the existence of gods and other supernatural beings is anything but a source of joy. Throughout history and around the globe, gods have utterly plagued and terrorized people, from the ugly mad god Kuemoi of the Piaroa (Venezuela) to the stupid vicious god of the Semai (Malaysia). Gods are frequently capricious, sometimes evil, and by no means always lovable and kind; even when they are benevolent, they are still dangerous and inscrutable. And this does not mention the plethora of other entities and forces, from demons and monsters to nature spirits and dead ancestors who make human life unpredictable and unpleasant. The members of many societies might or often do prefer that these beings did not exist. (See Chapters 4 and 5)

---

[44] Nhat Hanh, "The Heart Sutra: The Fullness of Emptiness."
[45] Biale, *Not in the Heavens*, 47.

In Praise of Popular Atheism

This excursion through the lands of hard-core atheism, existentialism, suffering, and angst in diverse religious traditions brings us back at last to Haught's critique of contemporary atheism. As we saw, he faulted twenty-first-century atheism for two failings—that it blissfully ignores the tragic personal consequences of a godless universe and that it minimizes the impact of godlessness on society and morality. We have good reason to dismiss both charges.

To start, do we latter-day atheists, soft-core atheists, and amateur atheists trivialize a godless universe, or did the classic fatalistic atheists like Nietzsche, Sartre, and Camus overdramatize it? Perhaps when the idea was still new it was more alarming and disorienting; few had genuinely considered it before. Professionally and legally, atheism was a perilous undertaking: one could lose one's job and friends—and at certain moments in time, one's life—for publicly disavowing deity. But more profoundly, because the idea was so fresh and so unprecedented, it probably did feel like an ominous prospect, one that could undermine sanity itself. People were taught that society could not function and that reality could not continue without a god to sustain it. I can imagine a similar sentiment among the Aztecs, who believed that the sun would weaken and die without a steady diet of hearts and blood and thus a trail of carnage from human sacrifice. The proposition of ending sacrifice must have seemed like a mortal threat to existence. And yet, when the practice of human sacrifice was abolished, they discovered—first with shock, then with relief—that the world survived and got along fine without the blood and death.

Likewise, Western Christians believed (and believe) that their god is not just one being among beings but the ground of being, the cornerstone or keystone—or more urgently, diffused throughout all the stones—of their civilization and their universe. Removing the god would cause the entire edifice of their world, like the walls of Jericho, to come tumbling down. Instead, á la the Aztecs, the world hardly shudders.

Further, as our brief tour of the world's religions has shown, many cultures and faiths do not possess a concept of god(s) at all, and their earth keeps spinning. Many, as we will discuss in other chapters, would in fact probably be happier and less traumatized with fewer or no supernatural beings to harass them. (See Chapters 5 and 6) And even the void, nonbeing, or nothingness is not equally terrifying to all societies. One wonders if Christianity has instilled more fear of the void in Westerners than is reasonable or healthy.

Whether or not our atheist predecessors exaggerated the difficulty of enduring a world without god(s)—and at least to an extent they clearly did—it has proven not to be so difficult after all. Similarly, I imagine that it was very hard to be a Christian in the early days of that religion, not only as a tiny minority first among the Israelites and then among the Romans and as a persecuted and often despised faction but as the devotees of a singularly demanding faith. Living in expectation of the imminent end of the world, dreading judgment and eternal damnation, called upon to dedicate one's entire life to the cause—*that* was an ordeal not for the faint-hearted. Being a Christian got considerably easier once the religion was in charge, and today one can be a Christian with hardly any effort or inconvenience and in fact with some notable privilege. To be sure, there are hard-core Christians (and other theists)—sometimes we dub them fundamentalists or extremists—but most Christians (and other theists) are soft-core, amateur, and part-time.

This goes equally for the public figures, the leaders, and the writers. There are still (far too many) professional and scholarly theists producing lofty theology, little of which is known, comprehensible, or useful to the vast majority of their flock (and, as we will see in Chapter 4, the professional theists and theologians have reached no consensus among themselves whatsoever). Instead, for every Dawkins, Hitchens, or Harris there is a Billy Graham, Lee Strobel, Joyce Meyer, James Dobson, and hundreds or thousands more clogging bookshelves with amateur theology and apologetics. Or rather than amateurs (since they get paid and often occupy institutional positions), I would call them *popularizers*. I think it best to conceive of the leading New Atheists (who are mostly respected intellectuals in their own fields—which do *not* include religious studies or theology) and many of the less famous atheist writers in their wake, as popular atheists, activist atheists, and in some cases celebrity atheists. There is nothing wrong with this: popularizers are the ones who bring it "to the people." Do they do atheism a disservice? I think no more so than popular Christian writers, activists, and celebrities. In fact, the more they bring it to the people, the more they make it of and for the people. And the more of and for the people atheism becomes, the less strange and ominous it becomes, for atheists and theists alike. Meanwhile, high-level scholars are writing on and from atheism, even if, as we will argue in the next chapter, often they get atheism profoundly wrong.

So, I posit that today's atheists are not ignoring the alleged tragic heroism incumbent on the godless. In fact, the only ones nowadays who seem to think that atheism must be tragic are theists, but they do not understand atheism or atheists; they only know, or believe, that the extinction of god(s) would make *them* awfully unhappy. In response, I would invite them again to put themselves in the shoes of the Aztecs. The New Atheists, and all of us living in the post-theist (and maybe post-atheist) world, either find that atheism is, frankly, no big deal, or by talking about it and living it they *make* it no big deal.

What of Haught's second complaint, that New Atheism trivializes the social and moral effects of reality without divinity? I would never defend the main horsemen of atheism as deep social or moral thinkers. None of them is a sociologist or anthropologist, nor are they moral philosophers, and some of them adopt the surprisingly theistic position of moral objectivism. This is surprising—and theistic—because Haught explicitly (and consistently with other theists) insisted that, "If absolute values exist, then God exists. But if God does not exist, then neither do absolute values," in which case atheists would have no ground to stand on from which to issue moral decrees.[46] He is wrong, of course, and conceded in the next sentence that theistic belief "is not necessary in order for people to be highly moral beings," but that concession is so full of incomplete thoughts and unexamined assumptions that it does not amount to much.

Haught's main criticism of New Atheist moral claims was that they are dismally conventional, that is, that they advocate pretty much the same morality we already have. He presumed that atheism must entail some extreme moral restructuring, no doubt of the liberal sort. Accordingly, other enemies and friends of atheism have expressed disappointment at the unlikely and increasingly conservative nature of much of the posturing of the prominent New Atheists. I share this concern. For instance, in a mid-2021 *Salon* essay, Phil Torres admonished Harris, Dawkins, and Hitchens for mouthing far-right rhetoric. In a scathing comment, he declared that these august figures "turned out to be nothing more than self-aggrandizing, dogmatic, irascible, censorious, morally compromised people who, at every opportunity, have propped up the powerful over the powerless, the privileged over the marginalized."[47] Harris specifically, but not uniquely, has been an ardent detractor of Islam; one-third of his debut book was an uninformed harangue against Islam, one of his online speeches was titled "The Problem with Islamic Fundamentalism is the Fundamentals of Islam" (as if the fundamentals of Islam or Christianity differ significantly!), and he displayed both ignorance and prejudice in opposing a Muslim cultural center in New York City, pontificating that it was too close to the "hallowed ground" (a religious concept) of the World Trade Center attack site and that violence

---

[46] Haught, *God and the New Atheism*, 26.

[47] Torres, "Godless Grifters: How the New Atheists Merged with the Far Right."

and hatred are "the true face of Islam" while simultaneously denying that there is any such thing as Islamophobia (thereby licensing his tirade—or multiple tirades—against it).[48] (See Chapter 9)

Anyhow, Torres recited several other grievances against Harris and major atheist and rationalist characters, including Michael Shermer, Lawrence Krauss, Peter Boghossian, and Richard Dawkins. These men (and they are all men) have variously castigated "wokeism" and "social justice warriors" (Shermer allegedly called them "a bunch of weak-kneed namby-pamby bedwetters" while many of them were in the streets risking their lives protesting police brutality), gay rights (Boghossian incredibly and foolishly tweeted in 2014 that he could not understand why anyone would be proud to be gay), and feminists (Dawkins unwisely entered the fray of a sexual misconduct case to advise atheist Rebecca Watson to "stop whining, will you?"). Sadly, more than one male atheist/humanist has been accused of sexual misbehavior himself, and Torres reports that Boghossian and a colleague, James Lindsay, attempted to embarrass gender studies by submitting a hoax article to a gender studies journal. Several of them have emerged as champions of "Western civilization" against the putative forces of "political correctness" and "cancel culture."

Now, no one is asserting that atheists are or must be morally perfect, and atheism necessitates no specific moral position; one atheist (former) colleague of mine was an outspoken Holocaust denier. So, it is easy to pillory individual atheists for their tactless and literally stupid moral and political (and, in the case of Holocaust denial, factual) stands. The more important question raised by Haught and others is what the death of god(s) means for morality and society. I would answer that here, unlike in some of their regrettable personal statements, the New Atheists are more correct than incorrect. The non-existence of god(s) does not oblige us to abandon every single current moral value and standard; indeed, to insist so is to mistakenly maintain *that religion was the source of those values and standards in the first place.* As I have argued previously and repeatedly, the elements of morality that are most meaningful and universal do not come from religion, and the elements of morality that come from religion (like wearing a beard, abstaining from coffee, or fretting about virginity) are not the most meaningful or universal. Further, some of the loftiest moral systems, like Buddhism, do not depend on gods at all.

---

[48] See my essay "The End of Harris" in the September/October 2010 issue of *American Atheist* magazine, for which, as you might predict, I caught a fair amount of flak for desecrating an atheist sacred cow.

Many details of current morality are not such bad ideas and are worth preserving. But that is not really the point. The point, as Nietzsche understood a century and a half ago, is that it is ultimately and unavoidably up to us to assess the value of our values *whether or not a god exists.* This is the message of Nietzsche's "nihilism" introduced earlier. Recall that Nietzsche prophesied that nihilism was the fated future of Western Christian society, that it "is the only possible outcome of our greatest values and ideals."[49] But nihilism for Nietzsche—accurately—does not mean that nothing exists or that nothing has value; rather, and here he is clear and emphatic, nihilism means "that the highest values are losing their value."[50] And the highest value, the foundation of all values in Western Christendom so far, was the Western Christian god him/itself. I would go so far—and think Nietzsche would approve—that "the death of God" is not so much about religion as about moral absolutes or absolutes of any kind; this god was only significant insofar as he/she/it secured and warranted our moral valuations. In the absence of a god, morals and values are set adrift, spinning and falling as in the vision of the madman.

Haught and Nietzsche, remarkably and properly, concur on one thing: without god(s) humans are free, and "true freedom in the absence of God means that *you* are the creator of the values you live by."[51] Ironically—and this is perhaps the insight of both atheistic and Christian existentialism—the existence of some god does not change the fact that *it is still up to humans to choose what values to value and to live by.* Do we, as Kierkegaard stressed, submit to kill our son or not? Do we stone to death adulterers, execute folks who work on the Sabbath, or murder disobedient children? Haught added to the sentence above the opinion that creating and revaluing values is "an intolerable burden from which most people would seek an escape." But do we not do that every day? Furthermore, the dissolution of absolute values is not the same thing as the disappearance or impossibility of value. While absolute or universal values and morals may not exist (and I hold that they do not), relative or local values and morals do, so Haught's jab that atheists "should not issue moral judgments as they do" is plain wrong.[52] As long as one can specify what one's values and moral principles are and acts consistently with them, that is enough— or has to be enough, since that is all there is.

Along these lines, I dare say that the maw of nonbeing and the horror of mortality are not how the average modern human being

[49] Nietzsche, *The Will to Power*, 2.
[50] Nietzsche, *The Will to Power*, 8.
[51] Haught, *God and the New Atheism*, 22.
[52] Haught, *God and the New Atheism*, 26.

experiences contingency in the first place. We all know, at least in the back of our minds, that we will die, but most of us do not confront the stark reality most of the time, and the void, nothingness, *néant* is too abstract for the typical non-philosopher. Instead, I would suggest that people encounter contingency in more mundane ways, starting with the dizzying pace of cultural and technological change: what was familiar and certain yesterday is questioned today and obsolete tomorrow. Another and more confusing and disorienting form of contingency is the impression that things are going wrong, the sense of decline or failure of what once seemed trustworthy and permanent; for contemporary Americans, this includes the erosion of American power and prestige around the world, as well as, in the natural realm, species extinction and imminent global overheating. A third form of contingency is diversity, that other people do not share your certainties—not your values nor your morals nor your truths—and that if you were one of "them" you would have *their* values, morals, and truths. A fourth form of contingency is the recognition of our vulnerability to forces beyond our control or even understanding; at the natural level this includes the outbreak of a new virus like COVID-19 that can disrupt our best-laid plans, and at the social level it includes what social scientists call "precarity" or exposure to unpredictable and insecure or inadequate employment, income, housing, and other conditions of life. In other words, one does not have to lose god(s) to be sorely aware of loss.

Conclusion:
Don't Worry, Be Happy?

"Are you willing to risk madness? If not, then you are not really an atheist," Haught haughtily proclaimed.[53] But we have seen that there is no justification for this proclamation. If a world without god(s) was an extraordinary and unsettling idea in the past, it is a rather ordinary idea today. The sky has not fallen; the earth has not spun out of its orbit. Further, religion does not immunize humans from the terrors of existence and instead introduces a whole set of terrors of its own.

Does atheism promise to solve all problems? Obviously not. So, when Edward Feser got offended by the atheist bus campaign and its slogan, "Now stop worrying and enjoy your life," he was worked up over nothing. (And how is that more flippant than the average message on a church marquee, which hardly qualifies as great theology?) Atheism neither increases nor decreases humankind's contingency, finitude, and mortality. What it does is clear away one fallacy—the idea of god(s)—and

---

[53] Haught, God and the New Atheism, 22.

leave humans to their own devices to go about the work of responding to those challenges. It liberates us from one illusion but not all illusions; we may succeed or fail, save ourselves or destroy ourselves, but the outcome is up to us, *as it always was*. Besides, it is silly to take a public outreach like the bus campaign as some kind of grand philosophy.

The fact that contemporary atheists are not committing suicide in droves or otherwise running amok refutes the predictions both of Haught and Feser and of Nietzsche, Sartre, and Camus. In fact, that the suicide rate in the United States, an especially religious Western country, is one of the highest in the world and that Americans lately commit more than one mass shooting per day leads us to doubt that religion is a preventative for self-annihilation.[54] On the other hand, nothingness may not be as awful as all that: Buddhist monks are able to peer into the void with benign tranquility. The menace of impending madness resulting from godlessness is located only in the fevered nightmares of theists, who know nothing of atheism and whose real nightmare is the potential for life to go on mostly unchanged without god(s). Rightly disturbed by the discovery that humans do not need god(s) to live happy, meaningful, and fulfilling lives, theists have tried to scare people into turning away from contemplating a godless universe and to warn people away from the grumpy, angry, depressed neighborhood atheist. Those of us who have not heeded the melodramatic alarm or never heard it at all have found not madness but freedom, which is not a panacea but a possibility.

---

[54] According to the World Population Review (https://tinyurl.com/4vkhrvcd), the United States currently has a suicide rate of 16.1 (which has increased dramatically in recent decades), equal to the rate in Botswana and much higher than countries like the Philippines (2.2), Indonesia (2.4), Turkey (2.4), or Egypt (3.0).

2

With Friends Like These:
Freeing Ourselves (and Others)
From Misunderstandings of Atheism

"I do not believe in God and I am not an atheist," Albert Camus wrote in his *Notebooks 1951–1959*.[1] What are we to make of that statement? Perhaps Camus was being wry and cryptic, as French philosophers are often wont to be. Maybe "atheist" meant something different to him or to 1950s-era France. Alternatively, it might have been too dangerous to avow atheism in that time and place. Or maybe he was just confused about the word.

If the latter is the case, then Camus would not be the first or the last to labor under misconceptions about atheism. Of course, theists are highly likely—and highly motivated—to get atheism wrong. Since they are not atheists and possibly have never spoken to one (at least not intentionally and civilly), they really do not know what we think; they can only see us through their own theistic eyes and assume that we are the reverse image, or, more perversely, some odd variation, of their own theism. Then, as sworn and mortal enemies of atheism, they are driven to portray us in the most unflattering light, to construct a ridiculous straw man that they can summarily caricature and assassinate. We need not take their (mis)characterizations of us seriously, except as a public relations problem.

What about atheists themselves? Surely they are accurately portraying their position. Surprisingly and distressingly, too many professional atheist writers and speakers commit a regular set of errors in describing the nature of atheism. This is a tremendously damaging tendency, for two reasons. First, we mislead current and future atheists, who are misinformed by the incautious pronouncements of prominent atheists. Second, we empower theists and other critics of atheism who use our words against us: "See, even atheists say that atheism is X, so we are justified in our criticism and condemnation of the idea."

---

[1] Camus, *Notebooks 1951–1959*.

In this chapter, we will expose and free ourselves from recurring and systematic mistakes in the atheist literature. We will not repeat or critique "arguments for atheism," which have been sufficiently covered, including by me[2] and are largely cogent and decisive; all but the most hard-headed theists and religious apologists (who still exist) concede that "the case for god(s)" is weak at best and lost at worst. Nor will we linger on the New Atheists, who have been thoroughly examined many times before, including in the previous chapter where we noted their unexpected and unfortunate turn toward reactionary social and political attitudes— ironically simultaneously debunking one of the pillars of Western civilization (i.e. Christianity) and defending Western civilizational traditions of sexism, racial thinking, and Islamophobia, among others. The New Atheists are broadly guilty of the common charge of scientism, not just of crediting science with the solution to all problems but of equating, as Richard Dawkins does, religion to science (albeit bad science). For instance, Dawkins wrote in his lauded *The God Delusion* that "'the God Hypothesis' is a scientific hypothesis about the universe," and Victor Stenger actually put this "god hypothesis" business in the title of one of his books.[3] Finally, all of the New Atheists, who are quality scholars on their own turf, operate with limited (by which I mean Christianity-centric) notions of religion and god, in which "god" means the Christian or Abrahamic god and "religion" means Abrahamic monotheism. Any college freshman student of religion knows better.

Atheism as Belief?

The basic issue in the study and advancement of atheism (or any other subject) is definition; if we get fundamental definitions incorrect, we have already started down the wrong path, where enemies wait to pounce. The most consistent fault in the atheist literature is the classification of atheism as a "belief" or some other related and sometimes stronger term. We would expect this blunder from theists, who perceive the world through the lens of belief. Accordingly, philosopher and theologian John Hick asserted in a philosophy of religion textbook, where suggestible students are likely to see it, that "atheism (not-God-ism) is the belief that there is no God of any

---

[2] See Chapter 1, "12 Steps to Atheism," in *Natural Atheism*.
[3] Dawkins, *The God Delusion*, 2. See also Stenger, *God: The Failed Hypothesis*, subtitled *How Science Shows that God Does Not Exist*.

kind."[4] Catholic historian Paul Johnson not only declared atheism "a positive set of beliefs" but a failed one at that.[5]

Francis Aveling, writing for *New Advent* Catholic Encyclopedia (in an entry more than a century old), called atheism "that system of thought which is formally opposed to theism" and reiterated his error by labeling it "a doctrine, or theory, or philosophy opposed to theism" and "the teaching of those schools ... which do not include God either as a principle or as a conclusion of their reasoning."[6] Notwithstanding that doctrine, theory, and philosophy are not synonymous, and that atheism is not a "system of thought" but a single thought (no god[s]), one wonders where these alleged schools are. Zofia Zdybicka, a philosopher and Catholic nun, nonsensically echoed this notion of a "doctrine"—or actually of three quite distinct if not incompatible doctrines, namely, (1) "negation of the existence of God understood as a fully perfect and transcendent being," (2) acknowledgement of "the Absolute but as lacking in one or more attributes of God" which explicitly includes pantheism, panentheism, and deism, and (3) "impossibility of proving God's existence" or agnosticism and skepticism.[7] On this argument, pantheism, panentheism, and deism—which are variations of theism—are atheism, as are agnosticism and skepticism, which makes it rather pointless to identify as an agnostic or skeptic rather than an atheist. She also conflated anti-theism (see Chapter 5) with atheism, whereas most if not all anti-theists are theists, while also lumping theists "who are not guided by any religious principles in moral life, who do not have any sense of sin," or "among whom prayer and religious practices disappear" with us atheists.[8] Finally, revealing her true colors and agenda, she opined that atheism can actually serve theists by "cleansing us of false gods and deified men, and to come to a deeper understanding of the truth about man as a person who finds his true dignity, freedom and dynamism in God."[9] I would condone this conclusion if we include among "false gods" all of the gods.

This view is maybe forgivable, or better yet ignorable, coming from a theist who is desperate to discredit atheism and establish her own theism. Tragically, it is far from restricted to theists; some of the leading atheists of the day say essentially the same thing. Julian Baggini is blunt: "Atheism is in fact extremely simple to define: it is the belief that there is no God or gods" (disappointingly adding that "Henceforth I shall talk

---

[4] Hick, *Philosophy of Religion*, 5.
[5] Johnson, *The Quest for God: A Personal Pilgrimage*, 2.
[6] Aveling, "Atheism."
[7] Zdybicka, "Atheism in *The Universal Encyclopedia of Philosophy*," 709.
[8] Zdybicka, "Atheism in *The Universal Encyclopedia of Philosophy*," 745.
[9] Zdybicka, "Atheism in *The Universal Encyclopedia of Philosophy*," 755.

simply of belief in God" by which he means the Christian/Abrahamic god).[10] Eric Chalfant, a media scholar and researcher into the history of atheism (but not identified clearly as an atheist or theist) (mis)states that "atheism must be understood as a positive belief, in the nonexistence of God rather than the absence of belief."[11] Daniel Harbour, in an otherwise intelligent person's guide to atheism, agrees that atheism is the "belief that God does not exist," although he at least regards it as "the plausible and probably correct belief."[12] Robin Le Poidevin, despite a sophisticated treatment of the arguments in favor of atheism, persists in describing it as "a definite doctrine," specifically of the person "who denies the existence of a personal, transcendent creator of the universe, rather than one who simply lives life without a reference to such a being."[13] To mention one more, Graham Oppy's introduction to atheism perpetuates the (mis)conception that atheism "is the claim that there are no gods, and atheists are those who believe that there are no gods"; yet more incomprehensibly, he says that "atheists also fail to believe that there are gods," implying that godlessness is some kind of failure.[14] For good measure, he repeats that "atheists are united in *believing* that there are no gods" (his emphasis) while entertaining any number of "other atheistic beliefs."[15]

Thankfully, not every atheist author labors under this (mis)apprehension. Stephen Bullivant, working to define atheism for *The Oxford Handbook of Atheism*, announces that in his chapter and throughout the volume atheism "is defined as *an absence of belief in the existence of a God or gods*" and not a belief in its own right; he continues that atheism "thus becomes an absence of something called 'theism.' Importantly, it does not *require* a specific denial or rejection of, nor any animus against, this 'theism.'"[16] Paul Cliteur, also in an essay attempting to define atheism, similarly posits that it "simply denies the claims of theism" instead of making a claim of its own.[17] Based on the construction of the word "atheism" as an "alpha privans" (the *a-* prefix attached to the noun *theism* negates or "denies what follows"), he offers that an atheist "is someone who does not subscribe to the central tenets of theism.... So an

---

[10] Baggini, *Atheism: A Very Short Introduction*, 3.
[11] Chalfant,"A Greimas Rectangle for a New New Atheism," 322.
[12] Harbour, *An Intelligent Person's Guide to Atheism*, 1.
[13] Le Poidevin, *Arguing for Atheism*, xvii.
[14] Oppy, *Atheism: The Basics*, 6.
[15] Oppy, *Atheism*, 9.
[16] Bullivant, "Defining 'Atheism,'" 13–14.
[17] Cliteur, "The Definition of Atheism," 8.

atheist denies what the theist tries to confirm."[18] This line of thought harkens back to George H. Smith, a pioneer in modern atheism, who explained decades ago that atheism

> *is the absence of theistic belief.* One who does not believe in the existence of a god or supernatural being is properly designated as an atheist.

> Atheism is sometimes defined as "the belief that there is no God of any kind," or the claim that a god cannot exist. While these are categories of atheism, they do not exhaust the meaning of atheism— and they are somewhat misleading with respect to the basic nature of atheism. Atheism, in its basic form, is not a belief: it is the absence of belief. An atheist is not primarily a person who believes that a god does not exist; rather, he does not believe in the existence of a god.[19]

This may sound like hair-splitting and deliberate evasiveness, but it is actually extremely significant. Indeed, the whole question of "atheism as a belief" hangs on a number of conceptual problems that boil down to a lack of clarity about what *atheism* and *belief* are. Bullivant is obviously correct when he maintains that atheism "is both a vexed and vexatious issue," sometimes from the malicious intent of anti-atheists but also from the fuzzy thinking of atheists themselves.[20] This partly stems from the mere fact that there is no such thing as the "true definition" of any word and always a contest to define words, but it also stems from the fact that atheism itself is a diverse notion. Bullivant helpfully suggests that a "zoological" approach would be useful, viewing "atheism as a 'family,' divisible" into two or more "genera" comprising various "species."[21]

Scholars, pro- and anti-atheist, have proposed various ways to parse the terrain of atheism. One of the most common, which Bullivant himself invokes, is the "positive" and "negative" atheism distinction. In his interpretation,

> Any person who does not, at present, have a belief in the existence of a God or gods is thus a negative atheist. By contrast, a "positive

---

[18] Cliteur, "The Definition of Atheism," 2.

[19] Smith, *Atheism: The Case Against God*, 7.

[20] Bullivant, "Defining 'Atheism,'" 11.

[21] Bullivant, "Defining 'Atheism,'" 15. This is consistent with philosopher Ludwig Wittgenstein's theory that most complex, and many familiar, words or concepts such as "religion" or "game" are really a constellation of terms sharing a "family resemblance."

atheist" is someone who is not only without such a belief, but holds a specific belief (which may, of course, be held with varying levels of certainty or interest) that there is no God or gods.[22]

There are two major objections to this interpretation, however. First, it deviates from Michael Martin's use of the same distinction: for Martin, negative atheism means identifying the inadequacies and errors in theist arguments, much as a defense attorney would poke holes in the prosecution's case (mounting a "negative defense"), while positive atheism, like a positive defense in court, musters its own evidence and arguments for the falseness of the charges against the defendant. In this regard—and Martin's usage is preferable—negative and positive atheism are *tactics* of atheism or of atheist argumentation specifically, not *types* of atheism. Both negative and positive atheism, in Martin's terminology, are without god-belief; they simply build the case against god(s) differently. The second objection is that, after all his good efforts, Bullivant re-imports the notion that atheism, albeit only "positive" atheism, consists of a belief.

The distinction that Bullivant has in mind is better captured by the terms "implicit" and "explicit" atheism, employed by Cliteur among others. Implicit atheism in most appearances of the term indicates non-awareness of godlessness, as in people who have never heard or thought about god(s); they obviously do not "believe" in god(s) because the whole concept of god(s) has never been presented to them. It is unconscious atheism or perhaps more precisely pre-theism. Many thinkers, including Cliteur himself, reject this condition as atheism proper, since, as he puts it, "Essential for the atheist position is weighing all the options, that is, all the traditional arguments for the existence of God."[23] Le Poidevin also excludes implicit or un-self-conscious atheism (without mentioning the term), again on his premise that atheism is a deliberate and definite doctrine: only one who actively *denies* god(s) counted as an atheist for him, "rather than one who simply lives life without reference to such a being."[24] I will have occasion to disagree below.

Atheists and anti-atheists have proffered any number of other typologies and categories. Bullivant lists among the "species" of (positive) atheism such creatures as "Promethean antitheism, existentialist atheism, Soviet scientific atheism, New Atheism, and so on."[25] Zdybicka surprisingly (for a theist apologist) vastly expanded the world of atheism

---

[22] Bullivant, "Defining 'Atheism,'" 15.
[23] Cliteur, "The Definition of Atheism," 10.
[24] Le Poidevin, *Arguing for Atheism*, xvii.
[25] Bullivant, "Defining 'Atheism,'" 15.

by first inventing three new species—anti-theism, pseudo-atheism (for the atheist who still "unconsciously believes in God, because the one whose existence is denied is not God but something else," whatever that means), and post-atheism or the complete vacuum left by the absence of the very concept and "problem" of God.[26] Then, to maximize the atheist zoo, she tacked on (1) "theoretical atheism" with its species "metaphysical" and "epistemological" and its subspecies pantheism, pancosmism, panentheism (all theisms, you will note), agnosticism, rationalistic/Kantian agnosticism, and skepticism, among others and (2) practical atheism for the person who may well believe in god(s) or at least pay lip service to the belief but behaves as if he does not, including the secular, the indifferent, the ignorant (which is the most dangerous sort, by the way), and just the insufficiently pious and observant. Although it hardly exhausts the subject, Cliteur inserts the idiosyncratic and not entirely meaningful categories of "private atheism" (supposedly rejecting "the theistic worldview" but keeping it to oneself), "public atheism" (a "creed" that one feels the compunction "to share with fellow citizens"), and "political atheism" (in which the state feels the compunction to expunge religion from society, as in communist Russia or China).[27] Once more, these are not *types* of atheism but styles of atheist activity or social engagement (of which, consequently, Cliteur approves only of the first, while I imagine that atheists would gladly discourage public and political theism; the only alternative is to live in the theist's world forever).

Atheism on Religion (and as Religion?)

If atheist scholars are not quite sure what atheism is, they are still more impoverished in their understanding of religion. Let us quickly dispatch one easy misunderstanding: atheism is not a religion, and no sane atheist would ever avow that it is, despite the oblivious pontifications of some theists, like Alister McGrath, who audaciously branded it "the religion of the autonomous and rational human being, who believes that reason is able to uncover and express the deeper truths of the universe from the mechanics of the rising sun to the nature and final destiny of humanity."[28] This is patent balderdash, to be sure, since atheism has none of the trappings of religion—no priests, no churches or other sacred spaces (indeed, no concept of the sacred), no scriptures, no rituals, and most

---

[26] Zdybicka, "Atheism in *The Universal Encyclopedia of Philosophy*," 710.
[27] Cliteur, "The Definition of Atheism," 15–16.
[28] McGrath, *The Twilight of Atheism: The Rise and Fall of Disbelief in the Modern* World, 220.

importantly no supernatural beings (and often no concept of the supernatural at all). Part of the problem, aside from McGrath's intention to impugn atheism, is his utter failure to define religion which, if he did, would quickly refute his contention. Cliteur, also critiquing McGrath, grasps that classifying atheism as a religion leads to myriad other mistakes: "Because McGrath thinks that atheism is the exact antithesis of Christian belief, he supposes that the atheist must also have certain opinions on these matters, but this is not the case."[29] That is, atheism seen through theist eyes is a mirror-opposite of theism, speaking the same language and sharing the same worldview, only in the negative.

There is a more amusing counter to opinions like McGrath's. If he holds atheism to be the religion of the autonomous and rational person, then what is theism? Is it the religion of the dependent, needy, and irrational person? I doubt he wants to go there. More basically, presumably a theist deems religion as a *good thing*, so it is difficult to understand how he means this accusation to be offensive. Does he, as I have mused previously, mean his barb as a compliment or an insult—that atheism is as good as other religions or as bad? And if we accept his declaration, is atheism entitled to federal protection and tax exemption?

We turn our back on such foolishness. But as we return to the atheist literature, we find equivalent confusion about religion and about the scope of atheism vis-à-vis religion. To be blunt, most high-profile atheists demonstrate a shocking lack of knowledge about the diversity of religions in the world. The result is that the scope of atheism is characteristically too wide and too narrow at the same time. We might say, aphoristically, that most atheism acts like anti-Christianity while fancying itself anti-religion, while theism is somewhere in between: theism is one kind of religion, and Christianity is one kind of theism.

Kerry Walters, another atheist companion, epitomizes the issue in writing, "Although 'atheism' is generically used to designate unbelief in any kind of deity, the word really denotes the rejection of a very specific variety of God-belief, the kind that's known as 'theism.' When *a-theists* deny the existence of a God, therefore, their skepticism is directed at the *theistic* God"; to guarantee that we understand the claim, Walters (mis)emphasizes, "The God whose existence atheists reject is the deity worshipped by modern adherents of the three 'Religions of the Book': Judaism, Christianity, and Islam."[30] If this were an isolated attitude, it would be odd, but others share it. Cliteur, for instance, says essentially the same thing in locating the target of atheism:

---

[29] Cliteur, "The Definition of Atheism," 9.
[30] Walters, *Atheism: A Guide for the Perplexed*, 16–17.

Theism is the same as—a more current term—monotheism. Theists are adherents to one of the three theistic religions: Judaism, Christianity, and Islam. Theists believe in one god.... [Hence] atheism in the sense outlined here is not opposed to religion as such. Atheism is concerned with *one specific concept* of god: the theistic god. The theistic god has a name and this is written with a capital: God.[31]

Cliteur's formulation is right in a small way and wrong in a big way. He is correct that, strictly speaking, atheism is not opposed to, is not even a comment on, "religion as such." There are many religions in the world, particularly among indigenous and ancient societies, that do not possess any sort of concept of god(s). These religions cannot be justifiably called theisms (a point that will figure prominently later in the chapter). Some of these religions teach about nature spirits or ancestor spirits or diverse demons and monsters or about non-personal supernatural forces like mana, chi, or karma; these various concepts can occur in any combination in any religion, sometimes alongside god(s). Properly defined, atheism has nothing to say on those matters, although most atheists-in-practice also dismiss those entities as non-real.

However, he is profoundly and stunningly wrong to limit atheism to the Abrahamic tri-omni god. And this error stands on the bizarre contention that other theisms like polytheism are not theism, *when theism is in the very name*. Atheists would reject Yahweh, Jehovah, and Allah but not Zeus, Odin, or Vishnu? I find the assertion incredible. I also find the term "theistic god" unintelligible, since it is so obviously redundant. I guess that by "theistic" Cliteur and others who would talk this way mean "personal," that is, a god who is a spiritual person, as opposed to some abstract idea of "uncaused cause," "wholly Other," or "ultimate ground of being." In fact, Cliteur expressly opines that atheism has nothing to do with abstract god-concepts such as those proposed by Paul Tillich, Rudolf Otto, and Ernst Schleiermacher.

I strenuously dissent, for two rather concrete reasons. First, a polytheistic god, or for that matter an abstract god, *is still a god*, and any belief system about them is still theism, and atheism has every right to judge them and reject them. Indeed, and second, atheism *must and does* judge and reject them: if a person accepts as valid and true the claim that some polytheistic, impersonal, or abstract god exists, *then that person is a theist* of some stripe or another. By definition, atheism excludes those conceptions too.

---

[31] Cliteur, "The Definition of Atheism," 3.

This illustrates what I mean by the simultaneously narrow and broad scope of much atheist literature. The New Atheists, for example, take religion as a whole—or, more broadly yet, faith as a whole *á la* Sam Harris (although one can have faith in many things other than supernatural beings or gods)—as their opponent, arguing gleefully that "religion" ruins everything and that "religion" is always immoderate and pestilent. Then they turn around and define "god" (almost always with the capital G) in the narrowest, that is, the most specifically Christian, way and attack this local god as if he/she/it is the sole member of the class of god(s) and the sole concern of atheists—in Dawkins' words, "the most unpleasant character in all fiction: jealous and proud of it, a petty, unjust, unforgiving control-freak; a vindictive, bloodthirsty ethnic cleanser; a misogynistic, homophobic, racist, infanticidal, filicidal, pestilential, megalomaniacal, sadomasochistic, capriciously malevolent bully."[32] And while I cannot help but concur that this scriptural character is pretty reprehensible, I cannot join Dawkins in assuming that all gods share these traits (since, as an anthropologist of religion I know much better), nor can I restrict myself to rejecting only this god with this sort of personality. Even the most benevolent god has no reality for me (in fact, it would be impossible to square a truly benevolent god with the nature of our universe). I mention in passing that Dawkins, in tune with the New Atheist trajectory, takes this god to be a "hypothesis," which is neither how devotees nor detractors understand him/her/it. A hypothesis is not something you "believe" (quite to the contrary, a hypothesis is something that you test and, if it is the starting point of scientific thinking, the null hypothesis, something that you hope and aspire to disprove) and certainly not something you pray and sing to.

Given all of these assumptions, it is perhaps unremarkable that few atheist scholars have bothered to define religion and that, when they have, their efforts have been less than satisfactory. Most writers apparently presume that religion means Abrahamic monotheism or, even more inexcusably, that all religions are like Abrahamic monotheism. Le Poidevin, on the other hand, takes a swing and a miss when he characterizes religion (partly anticipating Dawkins) as "a way of life based on a metaphysical conception of the world. Religious doctrine contains, therefore, what are essentially explanatory hypotheses."[33] That is interesting and problematic on a number of fronts. First, most theists will not recognize the notion of "a metaphysical conception of the world," and frankly I am not sure what he is driving at, since every conception of the

---

[32] Dawkins, *The God Delusion*, 31.
[33] Le Poidevin, *Arguing for Atheism*, xx.

world has some metaphysical underpinning. Second, he moves from "metaphysical conception" to "explanatory hypotheses," giving the impression that every metaphysics is explanatory and hypothetical; also, which particular metaphysical conceptions make a belief "religious" as opposed to something else? Third, elsewhere in his book, he differentiates between metaphysical and non-metaphysical religions, and if there are non-metaphysical religions then how can metaphysics be a defining feature of religion? Sadly, although his book includes a glossary— uncommon in atheism books—there is no entry for religion (nor for atheism or god), and his definition of theism describes Abrahamic theism. (See Chapter 3 for our glossary or encyclopedia)

Philosopher Bruce Milem (unclear whether an atheist or not) also at least realizes that atheism, theism, and god cry out for definition before we can say anything worthwhile about them, although incredibly the word "religion" never appears in his essay once. Theism by his estimation is "the proposition that reality is not solely an impersonal order, being either a personal order, that is, an order founded by at least one person, or an impersonal order plus at least one transcendent person"; atheism conversely is "the proposition that reality is solely an impersonal order."[34] This too does not quite get the job done, as there are other "personal orders" besides theism, for instance animism or ancestor spirit-belief; across the world's religions, and in (post)modern theology, we also find impersonal theisms like pantheism or Tillich's "ultimate ground of being" god. What is interesting and, I think, correct, is that Milem recognizes atheism not as a *belief* but as a *proposition*, or as I would prefer to say and will say, a conclusion on a particular question, namely the god(s)-question.

Once again, Stephen Bullivant injects some clarity into the discussion by noting that

> If atheism is defined exclusively in terms of (say) the prevailing Abrahamic monotheism, then all non-adherents in that society— including huge numbers of other types of theists, both poly and mono—are thereby made "atheists." But not even the proponents of such definitions, in practice, use the concept in so broad and unwieldy a way.[35]

In fact, the impact of constricting the definition of atheism to anti-Abrahamic-monotheism is that it condemns adherents of all other religions all over the world to the status of atheists, which is not what atheists intend

---

[34] Milem, "Defining Atheism, Theism, and God," 335.
[35] Bullivant, "Defining 'Atheism,'" 19.

but *has sometimes been what Abrahamic monotheists intend*, as we will see below.

Atheism versus Agnosticism

A third perennial problem in the atheist literature, and far beyond it, is a staggering confusion about the nature of agnosticism, a term that did not exist until the late nineteenth century. Baggini expresses the standard (mis)conception as clearly as anyone: agnosticism is "the suspension of belief or disbelief in God. The agnostic claims we cannot know whether God exists and so the only rational option is to reserve judgment."[36] Oppy uses almost identical words in his glossary definition of agnosticism: "Suspension of judgment about whether there are gods. An agnostic neither believes that there is at least one god nor believes that there are no gods."[37] Yet he includes agnostics among those "who fail to believe that there are gods" (*fail to believe* that there are gods?!), characterizing them as serious thinkers "who have considered the question of whether there are gods but have suspended judgment, neither believing that there are no gods nor believing that there is at least one god."[38]

Cliteur gets closer to the heart of the matter when he asserts that "the agnostic usually claims 'to leave open' the question of whether or not God exists. Agnosticism is the theory according to which things within a specified realm cannot be known."[39] This statement sheds valuable light on precisely why the agnostic supposedly "suspends judgment"—because required information is not just unknown but *there is nothing to be known*. Interestingly, Cliteur prevaricates that, "Probably the agnostic does not leave open the existence of *all* the gods that humans have venerated from the Stone Age to the twenty-first century, but only the existence of the god that is held in high esteem in the culture in which he or she lives, that is, the theistic god (or God),"[40] which begs the question of why someone would be hesitant to judge against the familiar local god but not against unfamiliar ancient or foreign gods. What does this agnostic know about strange old gods that she does not know about the local god? Dawkins expands on and perpetuates this myth in his popular book by reassuring us that agnosticism is the right path "in cases where we lack evidence one way or the other. It is the reasonable position"; elaborating on agnosticism

---

[36] Baggini, *Atheism*, 4.
[37] Oppy, *Atheism*, 158.
[38] Oppy, *Atheism*, 6.
[39] Cliteur, *The Secular Outlook*, 50.
[40] Cliteur, *The Secular Outlook*, 52.

further, he distinguishes "Temporary Agnosticism in Practice" from "Permanent Agnosticism in Principle" (his capitalization), the former a "legitimate fence-sitting" while we lack the evidence to reach a decision compared to "inescapable" indecision in the face of "questions that can never be answered, no matter how much evidence we gather."[41] Happily, I suppose, Dawkins places the god-question in the first column, which can be resolved as a "scientific question"; if he is correct, agnosticism either can be or has been overcome.

Yet many people, regular folk and scholars alike, persevere in using the term and even wearing it as an identity, that is, declaring, "I am an agnostic." What exactly are they affirming about themselves? According to Le Poidevin, who came back with a short introduction to agnosticism, the word tends to refer in common usage to "the 'I don't know' position on God's existence" or the "compromise between theism and atheism, a 'flapping around' in the middle."[42] Actually, in practice these two states are not entirely separate, because "I don't know" is an ambiguous thing to say. It can mean, "I don't have the information on the subject," as when asked to name the capital of Uzbekistan. However, it can also mean, "I haven't come to a conclusion on the subject" or "I don't have an opinion on the subject," as when asked which entrée you are going to order for dinner or which shirt you prefer to wear. Of course, you may not come to a conclusion because you lack the relevant information; this is the response a scientist might give to an unanswered factual question.

Either of these statements would qualify as "weak agnosticism" for Le Poidevin. "Strong agnosticism" by contrast makes the much more muscular claim that it is *impossible* to know the facts about some matter, such as the existence of god(s). A synonym, and better name, for this interpretation would be extreme skepticism or epistemological nihilism— that no knowledge exists or that there is no such thing as knowledge ("knowledge" often construed as demanding "certainty"). Both forms of agnosticism, though, are normally taken, and intended to be taken, as alternatives to theism or atheism, as a third position "between" god-belief and god-disbelief. But if we try to sustain this distinction, trouble follows. On the one hand, a number of the sources that we have examined in this chapter, including Zdybicka, situate agnosticism as a *kind* of atheism; Walters also calls it a variant of unbelief, which is the next best thing to atheism.[43] On the other hand, Shoaib Ahmed Malik (not clearly an atheist or theist) contends that some atheists (and no doubt theists as well) "have

---

[41] Dawkins, *The God Delusion*, 46–47.
[42] Le Poidevin, *Agnosticism: A Very Short Introduction*, 8.
[43] Walters, *Atheism*, 11.

problematically conflated *atheism* with *agnosticism*," mixing up "the *propositional denial* of God" and "*uncertainty* and *unknowability about God*."[44] So which is it: is agnosticism different from atheism or is it a type of atheism? To make things as muddled as possible, Chalfant associates agnosticism with uncertainty, making it possible for four options to co-exist—gnostic (certain) theism, gnostic (certain) atheism, agnostic (uncertain) theism, and agnostic (uncertain) atheism.[45] Dawkins drives this line of thinking to new heights by proposing seven degrees of certainty on the god-question, from absolute certainty (knowledge) that a god exists to absolute certainty (knowledge) that a god does not exist—with agnostics falling in levels three, four, and five depending on which direction they "lean."[46]

It would not be too wicked to conclude that thinkers are agnostic about the meaning of agnosticism; they do not seem to know what they mean by it or at least have reached no consensus on it. One way to cut through the murk is to note that all of the discussions of agnosticism reference *knowledge*, when the question we have been exploring is *belief*. Thus, Malik and Chalfant almost get it right when they discern some slippage in the discourse about atheism/theism and agnosticism. There *is* a conflation happening, between what one *believes* and what one *knows*, which are not, as I cannot stress emphatically enough, the same thing. The best course of action, as I have done elsewhere, is to return to the site of agnosticism's birth, in Thomas Huxley's late-1800s essay by that title. Huxley explained, quite clearly as I see it, that agnosticism

> in fact, is not a creed, but a method, the essence of which lies in the rigorous application of a single principle ... Positively the principle may be expressed: In matters of the intellect, follow your reason as far as it will take you, without regard to any other consideration. And negatively: In matters of the intellect, do not pretend that conclusions are certain which are not demonstrated or demonstrable. That I take to be the agnostic faith, which if a man keep whole and undefiled, he shall not be ashamed to look the universe in the face, whatever the future may have in store for him.[47]

Note—and mark it in bold—that Huxley did not conceive of agnosticism (*a-* + *gnosis*, without knowledge) as a "creed," that is, as a proposition to

---

[44] Malik, "Defining Atheism and the Burden of Proof," 279.

[45] Chalfant, "A Greimas Rectangle for a New New Atheism," 321.

[46] Dawkins, *The God Delusion*, 50–51.

[47] Huxley, "Agnosticism," 245.

believe or a position to adopt, nor yet as a theory, but *as a method*. While it is unfortunate that he went on to liken it to a "faith," I think he meant that in the sense of a principle to commit to. At any rate, as a method, what Huxley commended is not something *to be* but rather something *to do*, specifically, to stick to the facts and, when the facts run out, to admit that we have no (further) knowledge on the subject and accordingly to affirm only the conclusion or "belief" that the facts and evidence support. This categorically does not entail that knowledge is impossible; instead, it impresses upon us an intellectual modesty and caution not to claim or "believe" things for which there is no factual warrant and definitely not to "leap" from facts to unwarranted claims and "beliefs."

Huxley's agnosticism (now, a term I wish he had not entered into our vocabulary) is essentially equivalent to critical thinking or intellectual hygiene; it is asking ourselves, when we hear a claim or belief, "Is there a sound basis for that claim/belief?" and if not, rejecting it. An apt analogy is the courtroom, where ideally evidence of the defendant's guilt is introduced and tested. If there is no evidence, or if the evidence is "inconclusive," what does the jury do? Does it embark upon Dawkins' Permanent Agnosticism in Principle, or even his Temporary Agnosticism in Practice? (It is truly astounding that Dawkins actually quotes the key passage from Huxley and still misses its import.) Indeed, the time for practicing agnosticism is during the presentation of evidence; when the evidentiary portion of the procedure ends, the jury must make a decision. If there is no evidence to substantiate the charge (the positive claim of guilt) or if the evidence is refuted or is merely inconclusive—in fact, if the evidence does not support the charge beyond a reasonable doubt—then the jury does not continue to deliberate indefinitely, it does not sit on the fence, and it does not surrender with a shrug and an "I don't know." The jury is obligated, on the presumption of innocence (i.e. the presumption that the charge/claim is false until proven true), to accept and decide that the charge/claim is false.

So, a few things emerge as true. First, agnosticism is not a "position" at all but rather a process, a method; one is not "an agnostic" but thinks (or should think) "agnostically." Second, as a method, agnosticism is not exclusive to religion or god(s); one can and should think agnostically on all topics. Third, if one faithfully follows the agnostic method, then when one hears a claim or statement that is unsubstantiated by compelling evidence and logic, one should, like a responsible jurist, reject the claim/statement. One is not thereby *certain* that the claim/statement is false, but one has sufficient grounds to maintain that it is false—or maybe better, one has insufficient grounds to maintain that it is true. Do we, to answer Cliteur, "leave open" the question? We will gladly revisit it if and when new compelling evidence and logic are discovered (i.e., on appeal); until such time, we can rest confident in our initial determination. On the god-question specifically, with agnosticism as our guiding principle, the lack of any compelling evidence and logic in favor of god(s), the failure of theism to make its case beyond a reasonable doubt, is itself sufficient grounds to reject the god-claim. Even if the evidence for and against god(s) were 50/50, the prudent and obligatory path would be to dismiss the charge and acquit humanity of god(s).

Atheists Going Soft on Religion

Before moving from critique to constructive conclusions, I want to interrogate two other contemporary atheist writers who have made ill-advised concessions to religion. The first is Alain de Botton, whose *Religion for Atheists* purports to extract some useful lessons from religion for atheism. De Botton encourages us to consider "the possibilities of importing certain of their ideas and practices into the secular realm."[48] Among the virtues of religion, he touts community, kindness, education, tenderness, art, architecture, and institutions. However, he gives the impression that religion somehow invented and owns these virtues, which is patently and infuriatingly false. Community, kindness, etc. are in no way whatsoever the property of religion nor unique to religion; quite to the contrary, they are all normal human social ideas and practices that religion has incorporated and, to an aggravating extent, commandeered as its own. Some secular individuals and groups hesitate to emulate religion out of a wish to stand apart from it (while others emulate religion rather eagerly, like the Sunday Assembly, visit www.sundayassembly.org). Other local and national organizations aim to provide a community for the nonreligious to fulfill other human needs besides scientific inquiry and argumentation. So, while I heartily endorse the atheist and secularist world becoming a more fully functioning cultural alternative (and wrote about it myself in the final chapter of my *Natural Atheism* two decades ago), we do not have to give religion one ounce of credit for creating kindness, education, art, or anything else that makes us human. Further, when de Botton says "religion" he seems to mean not just Christianity but Catholicism particularly, which is his image and model of religion. And when he urges atheists to find religions "useful, interesting, and consoling,"[49] I can join him two-thirds of the way (as an anthropologist of religion I recognize religion as interesting and potentially useful) but not

---

[48] de Botton, *Religion for Atheists*, 11–12.
[49] de Botton, Religion *for Atheists*, 11.

the final third (I find nothing "consoling" about religion, whether Catholicism, Islam, Hinduism, or any ancient, tribal, or new religion). Plus, when he asserts that the *truth* of any religion is the "most boring and unproductive question one can ask,"[50] I must disagree. And when he invites us to visit the fictional Agape Restaurant "to speak to [fellow diners] for prescribed lengths of time on predefined topics" as assigned by some fictional *The Book of Agape*, I decline; why should I care what *The Book of Agape* or any other scripture has to say, and why should I let it interrupt my dinner?

If de Botton is mildly misguided, André Comte-Sponville is much more so. Comte-Sponville, an atheist philosopher, goes further than de Botton in aping religion, not only absorbing some of its practices (which it originally absorbed from secular human psychology and society) but speaking its language—specifically the Christian language—of "spirit," "sacred," and "soul." To start, he defines religion in a purely theistic way, as "any organized set of beliefs and rituals involving the sacred, the supernatural, or … specifically involving one or several gods."[51] More tediously, he gives god(s) far too much credit: "God, by definition, surpasses us. Religions do not," he writes, when we might respond that god(s) are obscure, contradictory, and likely meaningless talk.[52] But happily for him, the essence of religions is not god(s) but "communion" or "fidelity" which is attained "only by contemplating, repeating and rereading the same words, myths, and texts" through which "people end up communing in the same beliefs and ideals."[53] I find that notion kind of frightening, that we must reread and repeat the same words, myths (or any myths), and (scriptural) texts, but I also remember that any set of shared texts can constitute a community, from Shakespeare to the Declaration of Independence to Darwin or Harry Potter.

Comte-Sponville apparently worries that atheism will spiral into nihilism which "condemns us to seeing life as tragic": "What can people hope for who have never believed in God or who have ceased believing in him? Nothing, that is, nothing absolute or eternal, nothing beyond the 'darkest reaches of death.'"[54] Hopefully, we have already dispelled this nonsense. (See Chapter 1) His solution is to adopt a religious (read, Christian) worldview that includes "spirit" and "soul." Indeed, he clearly stipulates that, "Not believing in God does not prevent me from having a

---

[50] de Botton, *Religion for Atheists*, 11.
[51] Comte-Sponville, *The Little Book of Atheist Spirituality*, 4.
[52] Comte-Sponville, *The Little Book of Atheist Spirituality*, 1.
[53] Comte-Sponville, *The Little Book of Atheist Spirituality*, 20.
[54] Comte-Sponville, *The Little Book of Atheist Spirituality*, 50.

spirit, nor does it exempt me from having to use it."[55] He is correct after a fashion: again, strictly speaking, atheism does not entail the rejection of "spirit" (a religion could, and many religions do, lack god-concepts but include spirit-concepts, *of wildly differing sorts*), but if he means anything close to the Christian concept of soul—a unitary, immutable, immortal, immaterial part of a human that survives death and enters into eternal bliss or torment after death—then this concept must be proven and is just as anemic of proof as the god-concept. It is only late in his little book that he finally explains what he means by spirit, allowing readers up to this point to assume that he means something consistent with religious doctrine:

> The human spirit ... is our noblest part, or rather our highest function, the thing that makes us not only different from other animals ... but greater than and superior to them....

> Whatever it is, we can use it to think, to want, or to imagine.... It is the power to think, insofar as it gives us access to truth, universality, or laughter. It is likely that without the brain, this ability would be able to do nothing at all or would not even exist....

> The spirit is not a substance. Rather, it is a function, a capacity, an act (the act of thinking, willing, imagining, making wisecracks.[56]

Notwithstanding that he shows his species chauvinism in thinking that humans are "greater and superior" than/to other beings, he is not referring to some disembodied supernatural element at all but simply basic mind or imagination or will. He even asserts that *there would be no spirit without the brain* and in fact that it is not a "thing" at all, only the process or function of thinking, valuing, and so forth. In other words, he should have used other words than "spirit," since there is nothing spiritual, and nothing supernatural or superhuman, about his point. At the same time, his point is fairly insulting, that atheists somehow struggle to have "spirit" (mind/will/imagination/truth/humor) without god—which is condescending twaddle. "Being an atheist by no means implies that I should castrate my soul!" he cries melodramatically.[57] No, monsieur Comte-Sponville, but it does imply that we should select our words carefully, avoid speaking Christian when that is not what we mean, put

---

[55] Comte-Sponville, *The Little Book of Atheist Spirituality*, 134.

[56] Comte-Sponville, *The Little Book of Atheist Spirituality*, 134–35.

[57] Comte-Sponville, *The Little Book of Atheist Spirituality*, 134.

terms like "spirit" to the same test as "god(s)," and excise empty and ambiguous words from our vocabulary.

Conclusion 1:
The Three Kinds of Belief

We began this chapter by asserting that confusion about "belief" was at the root of many misunderstandings about atheism, even, as we have painfully exposed, among many atheists. In this first of two conclusions, we strive to impose some order on this most disorderly concept.

"Belief" is commonly used by scholars and non-scholars alike to denote a proposition that one takes to be true. In fact, in many analyses, *any* proposition that one takes to be true is a "belief" (which complicates the bankrupt old adage that knowledge is justified true belief; what then is unjustified and/or untrue belief—just belief?). On that line of thinking, if atheism is propositional (i.e. "there is no such thing as god[s]," then it is a "belief." But, as we discovered with the case of atheism itself, this approach to belief is both too narrow and too broad. It is too broad in considering all propositions as beliefs and too narrow in considering beliefs to be exclusively propositional.

To tackle these conjoined problems, let us stipulate that not all propositions (statements that make a factual claim or a truth claim) are beliefs. If I say, "A circle is a geometric figure on which all points are equidistant from a center point" or "A bachelor is an unmarried man," I am not expressing a belief; these are definitions. If I say, "Paris is the capital of France" or "The speed of light is 186,000 miles per second," I am not expressing a belief; these are empirical facts. One could insist that one also "believes" the definitions or facts, but such an insistence adds nothing (besides, one could say that one also believes that one believes the definitions/facts, *ad infinitum*). In everyday usage, "belief" tends to inject or imply some degree of doubt or insubstantiation; as I have done elsewhere, I define "belief" of this propositional sort (for there are other sorts, as we will shortly see) as *holding a position or making a claim without sufficient evidence and logic or in the face of disconfirming evidence and logic.*

At the same time, many if not most commentators maintain that belief relates solely to truth claims. Eminent scholar of religion Wilfred Cantwell Smith, for instance, equated belief with "holding certain ideas" and presumably holding them as true.[58] However, if we inspect the (in)famous trope, "You don't believe in God? Well, he believes in you,"

---

[58] Smith, *Faith and Belief*, 12.

we see the verb being used in two very different senses. The former, perhaps, is propositional: you do not think that God exists, or you reject the proposition "God exists" or "there is such a thing as God." It would be silly to interpret the latter in that manner, as "God thinks that you exist." This alerts us to the semantic range of the verb "believe" and the noun "belief." In English (other languages may divide up the semantic space differently or, as anthropologists have discovered, not contain a concept like "believe/belief" at all), the words cover three quite distinct territories. The first, admittedly, is propositional; we can call it the "correctness" function of the words. The second has nothing directly to do with propositions or correctness; an example would be, "I believe in my wife" or "I believe my friend will meet me at the restaurant." What this usage expresses is *confidence*; certainly, it presupposes that my wife and my friend (and the restaurant) exist, but that is not its main thrust. Rather, it conveys that I trust my wife and my friend. Often, when people say, "I believe in God," they mean that they *trust* their god (presuming, of course, that he/she/it exists). Third, belief may express *commitment*, as in "I believe in America" or "I believe in freedom"; in this formulation, "I believe in God" means "I am committed to my god" or "I am on my god's side." Naturally, the three meanings can overlap or coincide—one can believe that a god exists, be confident in that god's providence, and be committed to that god. On the other hand, the three meanings can detach: an ordinary Christian, for instance, may think it is correct that Satan exists, and even be confident in Satan's (evil) nature and intentions, but *not* be personally committed to Satan. In passing, it is worth mentioning that this is maybe what Camus was saying in his quotation to open this chapter: he did not have *confidence in* or *commitment to* the Christian god, although he might be willing to grant the being's reality.

Along with equating belief with propositional statements, theists and atheists alike often separate belief from "faith." Smith captured this approach clearly when he characterized faith as "deeper, richer, more personal" than propositional correctness; it constitutes involvement, even intense involvement. To "have faith" (since there is no verb form of faith) in something or someone is "to know it in personal committed fashion."[59] Theologian Richard Niebuhr similarly idolized faith but more perceptively realized that it too has multiple meanings: "Now it means belief in a doctrine; ... now confidence or trust; now piety in general or a historic religion."[60] But if faith sometimes means belief, then the sharp division between them collapses. Instead, "faith" like belief can refer to

---

[59] Smith, *Faith and Belief*, 6, 12.
[60] Niebuhr, *Faith on Earth: An Inquiry into the Structure of Human Faith*, 4.

propositional acceptance of a claim or doctrine, confidence or trust (as Niebuhr allowed), or commitment. In short, *the semantic range of belief is identical to the semantic range of faith*, and in any sentence in which "belief" can be sensibly used, "faith" could be sensibly substituted. (There are sentences like "I believe it is going to rain" in which "believe" is not really appropriate—the proper verb would be "predict"—so that "have faith" could not be sensibly substituted.) If there is any difference, it is that "faith" tends to be more emphatic than "belief," more indicative of strong confidence and commitment, but here too "belief" could accomplish the same job.

Crucially, this scrutiny of belief and faith sheds light on the functional equivalence of atheism and agnosticism. "Agnostics" may consider it wise or clever to "suspend judgment" on the question of the existence of god(s), but that attitude only addresses the first, "correctness" dimension of belief/faith. When a religion like Christianity instructs humanity to "believe in God," it demands more than propositional assent; it explicitly asks that humans put trust in this being, commit to this being, worship and praise this being, love this being with all one's heart and all one's soul. While an "agnostic" is postponing propositional belief, she is failing or refusing to offer belief as confidence or commitment—and a god like the Christian god makes no distinction between agnostic or atheistic failure/refusal.

Conclusion 2:
The Three Kinds of Atheism

So, we arrive at the definition of atheism, having trod a stony path across many errors and inconsistencies. Like belief, there is indeed more than one kind or proper usage of atheism; there is a veritable zoology or ecology of atheism, although the typologies that have been offered by other scholars are often not typologies at all but more like descriptions of diverse styles of representation and interaction (such as negative and positive atheism, as noted earlier). On other occasions, analysts have truly conflated atheism with things that are not atheism, including agnosticism, skepticism, and heterodox theisms (e.g. deism, pantheism, etc.). (See Chapter 4)

The rational course of action is, as with belief, to investigate how the term "atheism" is and has been used in practice. This means, firstly, going beyond etymological arguments (which attempt to settle the definition by appealing to the roots *a-* and *theism*, which at any rate could be interpreted as "no-god belief" or "no god-belief") as well as beyond dictionary definitions and popular (mis)understandings. I inquire instead, what *could* atheism mean? Or, to put it otherwise, on the god(s) question, what different things can possibly be meant? I have previously proposed and propose again that there are three distinct meanings for "atheism" which are valid and are different from other terms like agnosticism and such. I will call these *default* or *anthropological* atheism, *defamatory* or *accusatory* atheism, and *defensive* or *argumentative* atheism.

What, in other words, are the various ways to be "without god(s)"? The original, most basic, and across cultures and history the most common way is to have never been exposed to the concept to begin with. This is default/anthropological atheism, which we could also call natural atheism or, as previously encountered, implicit atheism. Many if not most of the societies and religions that have ever existed did not possess a concept of god(s) and certainly not one anything akin to the Christian tri-omni god. Granted, they may have believed in nature spirits, dead ancestors, supernatural forces, and various demonic or monstrous beings, but none of these entities approximated a god. Oppy recognizes this category too, preferring to call such people and societies "innocents" or "those who have never considered the question whether there are gods and who, for this reason, have no opinion on the matter. Typically, innocents are those who do not possess the concept of *god*."[61]

Oppy does not exactly accept them as atheists but welcomes them into the class of "people who fail to believe that there are gods." While I categorically reject the notion of "failure," such people are in either case without god(s). Likewise, many philosophers of religion withhold the label "atheist" for godless-by-default individuals and societies, preferring to name them "non-theists," but (1) this is pure semantics and (2) it offers no advantage analytically. These default-godless people and groups are still being construed in relation to god(s)—whether a-theist, non-theist, or, I might allow, pre-theist. Moreover, Oppy and the philosophers of religion make the same distinction that I do but merely label it differently. In the case of the latter, I feel that a primary motivation is to limit the population of atheists in the world. Baggini, I think, gets closer to the truth of the matter when he holds that atheism does not depend on (in his phraseology, is not "parasitic on") theism. Consider, he suggests, "what would happen if everyone ceased to believe in God. If atheism were parasitic on religion, then surely it could not exist without religion. But in this imagined scenario, what we would have would not be the end of atheism but its triumph."[62] I extend this example to embrace not just those who ceased to believe in god(s) but who *never started to believe*: those who have never learned or heard the concept of god(s)—for the concept must be heard and

---

[61] Oppy, *Atheism*, 6.
[62] Baggini, *Atheism*, 9.

learned before it is "believed"—would not call themselves atheists, but they would be as god-less as any latter-day atheist. An apt analogy is smoking: in a society that had never invented or observed smoking, no one would smoke; they would not call themselves "non-smokers," lacking the very word and idea of smoking, but they would be as smoke-less as a society that had collectively kicked the habit. Malik concurs that atheism "can potentially become an all-inclusive word for denial *and* absence of belief in God"; he does not "endorse this fusion," though, contending that "lack of belief in God and the denial of God's existence are two separate positions."[63] I accept, and will expound below, that they are different, but they are *different ways to be godless or a-theistic*.

The second type of atheism is atheism only from a particular perspective, yet it is probably the most frequent pre-modern application of the term. I call it defamatory or accusatory atheism because it is not a brand that a person ordinarily avows of herself but one that others ascribe to her. As Onfray rightly observes, in ancient Greece and Rome ἄθεος (*atheos*)

> was an expression of severe censure and moral condemnation. Sometimes, indeed often, "wrong belief" was equated with "unbelief." The accusation of atheist could be leveled not only at the man who did not believe in God, but at the man who did not worship the dominant deities of the moment, the local, socially prescribed forms of divinity. Even a person deeply committed to a god—if it was a foreign, unorthodox god—might find himself condemned as an atheist.[64]

Historians of atheism consistently stress that "atheist" was a term of moral and often legal opprobrium, leveled at figures from Socrates (accused of impiety) and poet Diagoras of Melos (sentenced to death for ridiculing the Eleusinian Mysteries) to Christians in the pagan Roman Empire before the ascension of Constantine. Early Christians were routinely denounced as atheists by their Roman countrymen because those Christians did not believe in—and more importantly from the Roman point of view, did not respect, prostrate before, and sacrifice to—the local gods. They were thus "atheists" in Roman eyes because they were without and/or opposed to the gods that Romans considered real and vital, both spiritually *and politically*. Indeed, Christian disregard of Roman gods was less objectionable as heresy than as *treason*, that is, disobedience to the state. As Onfray reminds us, throughout history religion has been intimately enmeshed with government and more fundamentally with social order, and

---

[63] Malik, "Defining Atheism and the Burden of Proof," 284.
[64] Onfray, *In Defense of Atheism*, 15.

the charge of atheism "has served politically to thrust aside, label, or castigate individuals who believe differently"—although they still believe.[65]

By the way, Islam envisions atheism or non-belief in a roughly similar manner. According to Kenan Sevinç, Thomas Coleman, and Ralph W. Hood, "Non-Muslims are considered 'non-believers' in that they do not have the Islamic faith," although they may practice some other religion or worship some other god(s).[66] The Arabic word *kafir* or *kufr* (infidel, non-believer) derives from the root for "conceal/hide," as the non-believer is understood to evade the truth of Islam, since no one is his right mind would *deny* its truth; the authors contend that "no existing term [in Arabic] corresponds directly to Western notions of atheism" because not believing in their god is inconceivable.[67]

This brings us to the third type of atheism, the type with which most readers (and atheist thinkers) are acquainted. In a society where god-beliefs are not only present but pervasive and dominant, one does not have the luxury of default, natural, implicit atheism. In such a setting, non-belief in god(s) can take just one form—defensive or argumentative atheism. That is, godlessness means, or is achieved by, freeing oneself from the culturally-available, -prevailing, and -privileged god. Unlike default/anthropological atheism, which is pre-theistic, defensive/ argumentative atheism is post-theistic, an atheism-after-god(s).

This does not, however, as we have argued throughout the chapter, entail that atheism is a "belief" on par with theism, and again, modern familiar atheism is more than a rejection of the propositional claim of the existence of god(s) but an absence or withholding of confidence in and commitment to any such being(s). Cliteur, for all his other flaws, appreciates this: "The atheist is not convinced by the proofs of theism. This being the case, he does what every sensible person would do. He says, 'I am not a theist.'"[68] This formulation may sound strange to some ears, so let us unpack it. The problem with many portrayals of atheists is that they depict atheists at the end of their thought process rather than during that process. We should recount the process itself something like the following. A person at some point in her life hears god-talk for the first time; it is manifestly true that no one is born with any knowledge of or beliefs about god(s) (or anything else). Either the first time the god-talk comes up or at some later date, after listening to multiple comments about god(s), the

---

[65] Onfray, *In Defense of Atheism*, 15.
[66] Sevinç, Coleman, and Hood, "Non-Belief," 2.
[67] Sevinç, Coleman, and Hood, "Non-Belief," 2.
[68] Cliteur, *The Secular Outlook*, 38.

person says, "I hear nothing to persuade me that this god that I keep hearing about is real." Perhaps the arguments for god(s) are found to be faulty and unconvincing (as they indeed are). Perhaps it is noticed that theistic predictions, like the efficacy of prayer or the end of the world, fail again and again. Perhaps knowledge of other religions and their god(s) reveals that the diverse gods are mutually contradictory and are merely cultural creations. By whatever road, the person concludes, "I see no merit in this god-talk. I am unconvinced by this god-talk. I dismiss this god-talk as undeserving of my attention." Maybe the person learns the counter-arguments against god(s), maybe not; it is irrelevant. The one sure thing is that the person does not "believe" that there is no such thing as god(s), and she does not need to be or claim to be "certain" that there is no such thing as god(s). Instead, she turns her back on and walks away from god-talk as vacuous and vain.

After discovering enough about the multitude of gods (and other alleged supernatural entities), after observing religious hypocrisy, after witnessing religious violence, after learning about scientific alternatives to theistic explanations, and so forth, the defensive/argumentative atheist may become firmer in her conviction that god-talk is pointless. She may say emphatic or exaggerated things like, "There are no gods" or "I know there are no gods." She may become a public atheist, to Cliteur's displeasure, or (horror!) an activist for official secularism and rationalism. All of this is beside the point and not the essence of contemporary post-theistic and anti-theistic atheism. The point, and the essence, is that despite or because of contemporary theism, she finds good reason to live godlessly and lives a good godless life.

The mistake among both atheists and theists is to assume, since defensive/argumentative atheism is the kind that they encounter often or exclusively, that it is the only or real kind of atheism. Hopefully, we have dispelled this misconception. It would be like knowing only one language such as English (or worse only one dialect of the English language) and assuming that it is the only or "true" language, that no other dialects/languages exist, or just as falsely, that any other must be just like the one you know. Even more dismally, one may assume—as theists often do—that non-theists and a-theists must also think and speak in the same terms and categories that theists do (one common and regrettable example: if the only two possibilities are to believe in God or in Satan, atheists must believe in Satan). Tragically, this misperception is not unique to theists. What I mean is that contemporary Western defensive/argumentative atheism, *precisely because it is defensive and argumentative and therefore locked in a struggle with its nemesis, Christian theism, is still far too theistic and Christian.*

In one of his most insightful moments, Onfray asks us to wake from what he calls "Christian atheism," an atheism that is still shaped if not haunted by Christianity and its god, and to work toward a genuinely *atheistic atheism*, one

> that encompasses more than negation of God and of a part of the values derived from him. It calls for a different *episteme*.... *Atheistic atheism* would place morality and politics on a new base, one that is not nihilist but post-Christian. Its aim is neither to reconstruct churches nor to destroy them, but to build elsewhere and in a different way, to build something else for those no longer willing to dwell intellectually in places that have already done long service.[69]

When we have reached this state, we will not only be without god(s) or against god(s) but *free of god(s)*.

---

[69] Onfray, *In Defense of Atheism*, 56–57.

3

An Encyclopedia of Liberatheism

Before thought can be free, language must be free. And one tool since ancient times for freeing both thought and language is the "encyclopedia," from the Greek *kyklos* (circle) and *paideia* (education, child instruction). Conceived as a "circle of learning," an encyclopedia is a single document or series of documents (like a "set of encyclopedias" such as *Encyclopedia Britannica*) that collects and organizes what is known on a subject—or more ambitiously in some instances, on all subjects. Although the practice of assembling and preserving knowledge in encyclopedic fashion dates back at least to early Greece in the fourth-century BCE work of Speusippus, and although other civilizations including China and the Islamic world have their own traditions of encyclopedia-making, it was only in recent centuries that the practice of arranging entries in alphabetical order developed.

It was in the Enlightenment era, and especially in the run-up to the French Revolution, that the encyclopedia not just took its modern form but became an important instrument of mental liberation. The *Encyclopédie* of Denis Diderot and Jean Le Rond d'Alembert, composed in the mid-1700s under the full title *Encyclopédie, ou dictionnaire raisonné des sciences, des arts et des métiers* (Encyclopedia, or a Systematic Dictionary of the Sciences, Arts, and Crafts), combined factual knowledge with "lengthy polemics on the controversial topics of the day."[1] The editors, who sought out contributions from the leading minds of the day, explicitly intended their project "to change the way people think," and it did. It attacked superstition, cast doubt on the veracity of Christian dogma and the Bible, and encouraged scientific inquiry and liberal politics, including the revolutionary notion of "natural rights." *Encyclopedia Britannica*, which appeared shortly thereafter as a more neutral and comprehensive source, eventually credited the French version for its role in the French Revolution and in the freeing of the early-modern mind; two centuries later, Clorinda Donato and Robert Maniquis' edited volume *The Encyclopédie and the Age of Revolution* claimed that the writers of the original *Encyclopédie*

---

[1] Encyclopedia Britannica, "History of Encyclopedias."

successfully argued and marketed their belief in the potential of reason and unified knowledge to empower human will and thus helped to shape the social issues that the French Revolution would address. Although it is doubtful whether the many artisans, technicians, or laborers whose work and presence are interspersed throughout the *Encyclopédie* actually read it, the recognition of their work as equal to that of intellectuals, clerics, and rulers prepared the terrain for demands for increased representation. Thus the *Encyclopédie* served to recognize and galvanize a new power base, ultimately contributing to the destruction of old values and the creation of new ones.[2]

The present chapter does not have such grandiose aims but continues the tradition of subject-specific encyclopedias, like an encyclopedia of philosophy, history, mathematics, or of medicinal plants or body-building. It consists of nearly three dozen key terms in the study of religion and atheism and even more so in the liberation from theism and religion in general. The entries discuss how the terms are used and, in many cases, how they *should be* used, to remove erroneous understandings. Our "encyclopedia" also serves as a concise summary of many ideas in this book, as well as a retrospective on some of the main ideas in my previous works. Not everyone, at first at least, will agree with all the treatments and (re)formulations of these words, but such is the nature of freethought and of the evolving freedom of knowledge. *Incipe disceptationem.*

Entries:

agatheism	belief	political
agnomancy	credition	theology
agnosticism	discredism	religion
agnotology	faith	religious
anatheism	god	trauma
animism	God	ritual
anti-theism	ignosticism	secular
apisteology	liberatheism	secularization
apologetics	misotheism	spirit
apophatic	myth	theism
theology	philosophy of	theology
atheism	religion	tri-omni god
atheology		unbelief

---

[2] Donato and Maniquis, *The Encyclopédie and the Age of Revolution*, 12.

agatheism

From *to agathon* (Greek for "the good"), agatheism "identifies God or the Ultimate Reality with the ultimate *good*.[3] Offered by philosopher of religion Janusz Salamon as a solution to the problem of religious diversity, and thus of the apparent irrationality of any specific religion in the light of all the other contradictory religions, agatheism wants to insert a universal, rational, and pre-religious reality underneath every (or nearly every—a significant qualification) actual historical religion. Emphasizing (exclusively) the goodness variable of the biblical tri-omni (omnipotent, omniscient, and omnibenevolent) god, Salamon maintains that agatheism "conceives the Absolute as *Agatheos* [good god] by attributing to it first and foremost the characteristic of perfect goodness (but *not necessarily* all the other attributes of God of the Western classical theism, since 'agatheism' is a 'thinner' concept than 'theism')"; accordingly, agatheism "ascribes to the Ultimate Reality the function of being the ultimate ground and ultimate end (*telos*) of all that is good."[4] Despite the fact that "perfect goodness" is an incoherent notion (something cannot be good for all purposes, for all persons and other-than-persons, and from all perspectives), and that Western classical theism has long struggled with the problem of evil, agatheism supposedly not only eliminates the problem of religious diversity—since all the various religions are construed as local and superficially- and trivially-different forms of the search for the good— but also establishes the rationality of this thin theism by grounding it in an allegedly natural human "agathological imagination" or "faculty of practical reason which is intentionally directed towards the ultimate good (of no choice of ours) and guides our mental activity."[5]

agnomancy

As criminology examines crime or practices of criminal or deviant behavior (along with other subjects such as police and prisons), so agnotology (the study of ignorance) has agnomancy as one of its primary areas of interest. From *a-*, no/without, *gnosis*, knowledge, and *–mancy*, magic/conjuring, agnomancy is a new term referring to the more-or-less (but often quite and overtly) intentional conjuring or construction of ignorance. Premised on the assumption that ignorance is not necessarily a natural or default state, agnomancy includes all practices and techniques

---

[3] Salamon, "Atheism and Agatheism," 197.
[4] Salamon, "Atheism and Agatheism," 201–2.
[5] Salamon, "Atheism and Agatheism," 202.

of ignorance-making, in various fields of society from corporations, governments, and religions to everyday life. Among these practices and techniques are obviously lying but also secrecy, censorship, propaganda, "spin," plausible deniability, discrediting sources (e.g. accusations of "fake news"), sowing doubt, and many more. (See Chapter 7)

agnosticism

Much confusion surrounds the notion of agnosticism or "being an agnostic." From *a-*, no/without and *gnosis*, knowledge, agnosticism is a term introduced by the famous rationalist and Darwinist, Thomas Huxley, in the late nineteenth century to reflect his own misgivings about belief and knowledge.

It is common to hear people say, "I am an agnostic" or "He is an agnostic." This (mis)use of the term suggests that "agnostic" is a *thing to be* rather than, as Huxley clearly stated when he coined the term, a *thing to do*. Huxley explicitly asserted that agnosticism is not a "creed" or a *position* but a *method*, a process, path, and action. In a very real sense, "agnostic" should not be understood as a noun at all but rather as a verb or perhaps an adverb ("to approach a question/claim agnostically"). In this same sense, agnosticism is identical to critical thinking or the scientific method and is merely a form of intellectual honesty: do not claim to know something unless you can demonstrate the evidence and logic to support the claim, and do not stray beyond what you can justifiably claim to know.

In its standard (mis)use, agnosticism typically implies indecision, "sitting on the fence," or worse, the impossibility of knowledge altogether, specifically in regard to god-claims. None of this is true. First, as already established, agnosticism is not a position and therefore not a position "in between" theism and atheism (there is no such position). Second, agnosticism is not specifically about god(s) or religious claims but is general mental hygiene for handling all questions of fact: one can and should think agnostically about all matters. Third, agnosticism in no way holds that knowledge is impossible, that is, that we "cannot know" whether there is a god or not. Instead, agnosticism stipulates that if we cannot demonstrate the evidence and logic to justify a god-claim, we should not make a god-claim, and that if god-claims (or any other claims) cannot be justified by "reason as far as it can carry you without other considerations" then we should forsake such claims.

Finally, since agnosticism, as the very name conveys, is about knowledge or the lack thereof, it is not a belief or about belief. One does not "believe in agnosticism," any more than one "believes in evidence" or "believes in logic." Agnosticism, however, has consequences for belief: insofar as belief is a truth-claim, and insofar as following the tenets of agnosticism ("thinking agnostically") demolishes any possibility of accepting any aspects of some belief as "knowledge" (that is, as something that we can say is true), then one should dismiss or abandon the belief. In short, when applied to the god-question, if agnosticism destroys all claims to "know" anything about any god(s), then the agnostic process or path leads inexorably to the atheist conclusion or destination. Therefore, agnosticism is not an alternative to atheism but the road to atheism; "agnostic atheist" is a redundancy, and "agnostic theist" is an oxymoron (there is no knowledge of god[s], so the theist almost necessarily must claim some special esoteric, secret "gnostic" knowledge) that violates the norms of agnosticism.

agnotology

Agnotology (*a-*, no/without, *gnosis*, knowledge) is a term and area of study created to complement or contrast epistemology or the study of knowledge. Popularized by Robert Proctor and Londa Schiebinger in their 2008 edited volume *Agnotology: The Making and Unmaking of Ignorance*, agnotology stresses that non-knowledge or ignorance (not stupidity, but the lack of knowledge or information) is not entirely natural or accidental. As Proctor phrased it in his introduction to the volume, ignorance or not-knowing is "more than a void"; it may of course be the initial or default state on any subject, but it also may be the product or effect of losing or forgetting what was previously known or "a deliberately engineered and *strategic ploy* (or active construct)" to render a person, group, or nation uninformed or misinformed.[6] Such ignorance, he concluded, overlaps with but is not identical or limited to "secrecy, stupidity, apathy, censorship, disinformation, faith, and forgetfulness."[7]

    Much of the work in agnotology has concentrated on industry and how corporations foment ignorance in order to manufacture, sell, and dispose of their products in irresponsible and destructive ways. However, agnotology also extends to other and essentially all domains of society, especially government and religion. Finally, as the study of ignorance, a key part of the topic is the previously-unidentified matter of agnomancy or the various techniques to "conjure" or create ignorance. (*See* agnomancy)

---

[6] Proctor, "Agnotology," 3.
[7] Proctor, "Agnotology," 2.

anatheism

Affixing *ana-* (return, repetition) to theism, anatheism is a paradoxical term for a modern "god after god." In Richard Kearney's book *Anatheism: Returning to God After God*, he describes it as "an invitation to revisit what might be termed a primary scene of religion: the encounter with a radical Stranger who we choose, or don't choose, to call God."[8] He considers it a wager, not a certainty and not even quite a belief, characterized by imagination, humor, commitment, discernment, and hospitality.

Anatheism is a response and supposed solution to a profound (even fatal) problem for conventional theism, namely, the utter failure of the Judeo-Christian god to show up and take sides against atrocities like the Holocaust. For many sensitive observers, it is impossible to believe in a good, powerful, knowing god in light of such suffering, and yet for many theists it is equally impossible to give up on god(s) altogether. The answer proposed by theologians and common believers alike was a congeries of post-theist theisms, like "death of God theology" which sought to rescue Christianity from the immanent absence (if not non-existence) of its god; Paul Tillich's liberal theology based on a god not as a metaphysical being but as "the ground of Being" and one's "ultimate concern"; Dietrich Bonhoeffer's post-Christian or "religionless" Christianity; and of course Kearney's anatheism. The god that Kearney and his peers pull out of the fire of Auschwitz, however, would be unrecognizable to most believers; its most cogent and disruptive quality is "the powerlessness of the divine."[9] That is, this god-after-god did not save his people from the concentration camps—and has not saved anyone from the misery of war, oppression, and genocide since—because he/she/it *cannot*, and so we should not expect relief and salvation. The best we can ask from this enfeebled god, the "only God worthy of belief"—or better, the only one in which non-contradictory and non-disappointed belief is still possible—"is a vulnerable and powerless one who suffers with us and is incapable of being relieved from this suffering unless we act against injustice."[10] (See Chapter 4)

animism

Animism, from the Latin *anima* (soul or more precisely "alive" or "moving," on the premise that living things are mobile) is the general

---

[8] Richard Kearney, *Anatheism: Returning to God After God*, 6–7.

[9] Kearney, *Anatheism*, 52.

[10] Kearney, *Anatheism*, 61.

notion that non-human beings (plants and animals), objects (like a mountain or river, the sun or moon, or a pot or tool), and/or forces (like the wind or rain, or even sickness or death) can and do have spiritual elements. Early anthropologist Edward Burnett (E. B.) Tylor is credited with coining the term in his classic 1871 book, *Primitive Culture*. Sometimes misconceived as "nature worship," animism does not necessarily or ordinarily entail the "worship" of natural entities or forces but instead a respectful "social" attitude, since those entities and forces are "person-like" or actually persons with will and intention. Depending on the society and religion, members may think that each individual being/object has its own "spirit" or "soul" or that there is a species- or type-spirit/soul for all like beings/objects (in other words, a shared animating kangaroo-spirit, etc.).

Animism, often dismissed as a "primitive" form of religion or spirituality, enjoyed a revival with Nurit Bird-David's 1999 essay "'Animism' Revisited: Personhood, Environment, and Relational Epistemology," in which she discussed the religion of the Nayaka of southern India. The Nayaka claimed to speak and interact with a class of beings known as *devaru*, recognized as "superpersons" or persons who did not occupy a single continuous body but who were emplaced in multiple physical sites simultaneously. Most importantly, as persons the Nayaka entered into relationships with the *devaru*, each with its own distinct personality: people recognize each spirit "by how it idiosyncratically interrelates with Nayaka (how it laughs with, talks with, gets angry at, responds to Nayaka, etc.)."[11] Consequently, interaction or conversation with *devaru* "is highly personal, informal, and friendly, including joking, teasing, bargaining, etc.... Nayaka and *devaru* nag and tease, praise and flatter, blame and cajole each other, expressing and demanding care and concern."[12]

Animism is often construed as a "type" of religion, but it can be found in most if not all religions. Indeed, animism—the tendency to identify minds or spirits in the physical world—may be the basic impulse of all religion.

anti-theism

Anti-theism (also antitheism) is a term introduced by philosopher of religion Guy Kahane in his 2011 essay "Should We Want God to Exist?" Although the word actually dates back at least to the 1830s, when the

---

[11] Bird-David, "'Animism' Revisited," S75.
[12] Bird-David, "'Animism' Revisited," S76.

Oxford English Dictionary defined it as not only disbelief in but *opposition to* the existence of a god, Kahane invoked it in response to Thomas Nagel's terse comment about his aversion to God. Anti-theism is thus not synonymous with atheism: atheism lacks or rejects a belief in god(s) or the very concept of god(s), while anti-theism expresses a preference for the non-existence of god(s), even if such entities do exist. Kahane based his argument for anti-theism on a better-or-worse analysis, that is, that things are worse if a god exists than if one does not. In other words, an anti-theist asserts that "it's a logical consequence of God's existence that things are worse in certain respects."[13] Kahane considered two ways in which life without a god could be preferable to live with one—impersonally or generally (for everyone or the overall good) and personally (for me or any particular individual)—and he found more support for the latter than the former. Predictably, he evaluated only a tri-omni (omnipotent, omniscient, omnibenevolent) god like the Judeo-Christian-Muslim god, but if a justification can be found for preferring that even an allegedly all-good god not exist, it is a devastating condemnation of gods. (See Chapter 5)

apisteology

In his 1989 *Faith on Earth: An Inquiry into the Structure of Human Faith*, theologian Richard Niebuhr made a single use of the term "pistological," as follows:

> We are, by necessity and by freedom, beings that are bound to a cause and bound to each other. However, we are warned against the effort of seeking to develop a "pistological" argument for the existence of God by the reflection that it is impossible for us to abstract from our faith as to pretend that in moving from the familiar ground of ordinary loyalties to faith in God we are moving from the known to the unknown. If the theologian undertakes to do what the philosopher does, he is not keeping faith with those to whom he is speaking for he counts himself a member of the community of faith in God.[14]

The editor of the book added this footnote: "*Pistological*—this word may have been coined by the author. I have not encountered it elsewhere. It is formed on the base of *pistis*, the word usually translated as *faith* in the New

---

[13] Kahane, "Should We Want God to Exist?" 674.
[14] Niebuhr, *Faith on Earth*, 63–64.

Testament but occasionally also as *faithfulness*.... In various handwritten notes the author also occasionally uses *pistology*."[15]

From the Greek *pistis* ("belief" or "faith," interchangeably: *see* belief *and* faith and Chapter 2), the term "pistology" has been adopted by theologians, defined as the branch of their field which deals with faith. However, no one seems to have considered that the word naturally suggests its opposite, a study of unbelief or unfaith which we could call "apisteology" (a Google search on the word in March 2022 yielded zero results). An alternative might be "apistology," but that term already exists as the name for the study of bees. Certainly there needs to be a field of study focusing on the lack of belief/faith, for which the term "unbelief" has been proposed. (*See* unbelief) However, despite its advocates' opinions, "unbelief" has a great deal of baggage, while also being clunky and too directly evocative of religion. Apisteology, being a completely new word, has no baggage and has no special associations with religion. As a field, apisteology would examine all instances and forms of nonbelief and nonfaith—that is, failure or refusal to accept particular propositions, positions, and theories—including denial of scientific facts and embrace of conspiracy theories. It would further comprise a consolidated study of nonbelief/nonfaith unifying cognitive/psychological, social/cultural, and biological/neurological perspectives.

apologetics

In everyday speech, an apology is an admission of guilt and contrition which usually asks for forgiveness for a wrong. This is, however, a rather dramatic divergence from the original meaning of the Greek term *apologia*, which referred to a verbal defense (literally, "to speak back"), as in the famous "apology" of Socrates in which he pleaded his case against the charges of impiety and corrupting youth. The word actually appears several times in the Christian scriptures, as in Acts 22:1 ("Brethren and fathers, hear my *defense* which I now offer to you") and Acts 25:16 ("I answered them that it is not the custom of the Romans to hand over any man before the accused meets his accusers face to face and has an opportunity to make his *defense* against the charges").

For various historical reasons, a verbal defense of their faith was a key practice in early Christianity, since followers were compelled to defend themselves against pagan religions, against unorthodox or heretical Christian doctrines, and often against legal charges of disloyalty to the Roman gods and emperors. Examples of written apologies from third-

---

[15] Niebuhr, *Faith on Earth*, 64.

century Christianity include Origen's *Contra Celsum* ("Against Celsus") and Tertullian's multiple tracts like *Apologeticus* (directed to Roman authorities), *Adversus Marcionem* ("Against Marcion," a heretic), and *Adversus Judaeos* ("Against the Jews"). The term persists today in the same general sense as a formal component of Christian thought. Contemporary arch-apologist William Lane Craig, in his *Reasonable Faith: Christian Truth and Apologetics*, wrote:

> Apologetics (from the Greek *apologia*: a defense) is that branch of Christian theology which seeks to provide a rational justification for the truth claims of the Christian faith. Apologetics is thus primarily a theoretical discipline, though it has a practical application. In addition to serving, like the rest of theology in general, as an expression of loving God with all our minds, apologetics specifically serves to show to unbelievers the truth of the Christian faith, to confirm that faith to believers, and to reveal and explore the connections between Christian doctrine and other truths.[16]

At the end of his 400-page book, Craig confidently declared, "I've argued that we can know that Christianity is true because of the self-authenticating witness of God's Holy Spirit [a breathtaking case of circular reasoning] and that we can show it to be true by means of rational argumentation and evidence [simply false]."[17] Another prominent instance of popular apologetics is Lee Stroebel's 1998 *The Case for Christ* (subtitled "A Journalist's Personal Investigation of the Evidence for Jesus").

Apologetics, a branch of theology and most decidedly *not* a department of philosophy of religion, often repeats traditional and familiar arguments for theism such as the cosmological (e.g. that the universe requires a supernatural cause or ground), the teleological (e.g. that the universe shows design or purpose and thus requires a designer), ontological (e.g. that a god by definition must exist), and the moral (e.g. that moral values demand a supernatural source) arguments. Unfortunately, all of these pleas have been exposed as faulty, and of course other arguments from scripture, tradition, authority, or miracles prove nothing.[18] Yet the abject failure of "reasons to believe" is only part of the trouble for apologetics. In fact, there is no such thing as "apologetics" if we mean a single unified body of claims and assertions. Rather, each religion and sect that possesses its own doctrines and dogmas does and

---

[16] Craig, *Reasonable Faith: Christian Truth and Apologetics*, 15.
[17] Craig, *Reasonable Faith*, 405.
[18] See Eller, *Natural Atheism*, Chapter 1.

must formulate its own apologetics. The clearest case is the *New Advent* Catholic encyclopedia, which explains that there are three "divisions" to the "science" (a laughable abuse of that word) of apologetics: "First, the study of religion in general and the grounds of theistic belief; second, the study of revealed religion and the grounds of Christian belief; third, the study of the true Church of Christ and the grounds of Catholic belief."[19] Protestants of all stripes would beg to differ, not to mention Muslims, Hindus, Buddhists, and all manner of religions that could mount and have mounted their particularistic apologies—all mutually exclusive.

One solution to the problem of the poverty of apologetics is to totally abdicate the responsibility to make the case for your faith and simply proclaim that it needs no proof or justification. This is the path taken by respected (for some unknown reason) theologian Alvin Plantinga, who has made a career on the assertion that belief in his god is "properly basic," self-evident like any other perception (illustrating thereby a gross ignorance of the philosophy of perception).[20] Fortunately for Plantinga, his god installed in humans a *sensus divinitatis*, a sense of the divine, by which our "knowledge" of him/her/it/them is fully warranted. Hence, any human with properly functioning mental faculties should immediately grasp the reality of this god, since this god equipped us with the mental faculties to immediately grasp him. That this argumentative anti-argument is breathtakingly circular, and that it could be made with equal conviction for each and every god or supernatural being, mysteriously evades Plantinga's grasp. (See Chapter 8)

All of the hoopla about apologetics ultimately overlooks the facts that (1) the rank-and-file believer has never heard the theistic arguments, could not recite or explain them, and does not lean on them for his/her belief and (2) that, when reason and evidence (inevitably) fail, he/she can always fall back on "faith."

apophatic theology

From *apo* (off, away from) and *phanai* (to reveal, uncover, or bring to light), the adjective "apophatic" has to do with those things that are not said or known. As such, apophatic theology, also known as negative theology, approaches or attempts to make sense of divinity in terms of what cannot be said or known of it. Apophatic or negative theology is an intellectual response to two intractable problems for theists. First, no matter which god(s) they are discussing and defending, he/she/it/they

---

[19] Aiken, "Apologetics."
[20] Plantinga, *Warranted Christian Belief.*

seem to be enigmatic, inscrutable, perhaps absent altogether; it is difficult (I prefer impossible) to say that one "knows" anything about him/her/it/them. Second (and perhaps as a result of the former), any god is conveniently beyond human understanding and language; all of our words and claims about him/her/it/them seem inadequate; the best we can do is to say what a god is *not*, for instance not mortal, not material, not mutable, etc. For some philosophers and theologians, then, unknowability itself was ascribed as an essential quality of the deity, Philo's "luminous darkness" of God. Augustine called the Christian god *aliud, aliud valde*—other, completely other—while John Scotus Erigena (ninth century) opined, "We do not know what God is. God Himself does not know what He is because He is not anything. Literally God is not, because He transcends being."[21] Or divinity may simply be beyond human language, all of our words failing to do it justice; the best we can do is to utter that God is not this or that (e.g., good, just, powerful, loving, etc.) because every utterance is insufficient. This view has been shared by other religions, and not only theisms, like Daoism. The opening lines of the *Daodejing* teach, "The Dao (Way) that can be spoken of is not the constant Dao. The name that can be named is not a constant name." Thus, the best knowledge we can have of divinity or ultimate reality is non-knowledge. How we can know anything about such an entity, including whether or not it exists at all, is not explained.

atheism

From *a-* (no/without) and *theos* (god), atheism is absence or lack of belief in any god(s). Atheism is commonly misunderstood as absence of or antipathy to religion as a whole, but since not all religions are theisms, this is an invalid stretch of the term. Oppositely, atheism is commonly misunderstood (primarily by theists) as a "belief" or even as a religion, whereas it is neither. Atheism is a position on or attitude toward a particular kind of religion (theism) which does not make it a religion itself (in fact, atheism has none of the trappings of a religion, such as rituals, myths, priests, scriptures, etc.). Atheism also is not a belief but rather the absence of a belief.

Atheism actually takes three distinct forms, although not all observers accept the term in all three usages. First, many cultures and religions do not have and never had a concept of "god" at all, and they can be properly called a-theistic; some philosophers of religion, as well as partisans of religion, prefer the term "non-theistic," but that is a matter of

---

[21] Quoted in Indick, *The Digital God*, 179.

semantics: whatever we call it, the very idea of "god" never occurred to these other cultures/religions. If one were to ask them if they "believe in god(s)," they would not answer yes or no; instead, they would answer, "I don't know what you mean." We can call this first subtype of atheism *default atheism, natural atheism,* or *anthropological atheism* (the latter because anthropological reports of such religions reveal no god-beliefs).

Interestingly, even many theists admit that theism is not the "natural" state of humans but rather that god-beliefs must be inculcated in individuals through persistent and strenuous effort. The founder of Methodism, John Wesley, acknowledged as much when he recognized humans as "natural atheists":

> After all that has been so plausibly written concerning "the innate idea of God"; after all that has been said of its being common to all men, in all ages and nations; it does not appear, that man has naturally any more idea of God than any beasts of the field; he has no knowledge of God at all; no fear of God at all; neither is God in all his thoughts. Whatever change may afterwards be wrought... he is, by nature, a mere Atheist.[22]

The second subtype or species of atheism is not avowed by anyone but, quite to the contrary, is applied to them by others. An example would be the ancient Roman accusation, often a legal charge, that early Christians were atheists. Obviously, Christians believed in a god, but Roman authorities sometimes censured them for believing in the "wrong" god or in a false or non-traditional god. We will call this practice *defamatory atheism* or *accusatory atheism*, because its thrust is to defame the accused. It is also similar to the Islamic concept of *shirk*, a kind of nonbelief or idolatry or polytheism that more closely means "association" or "making a partner," equating or associating something with the real god (Allah) that should not be equated or associated. Likewise, the Arabic word *kafir* or *kufr* which is sometimes translated as atheist or nonbeliever (infidel) derives from the root *k-f-r* which, according to the august religious scholar Wilfred Cantwell Smith, suggests spurning or disparaging a truth. Cantwell contended that Islam can hardly imagine someone thinking Allah does not exist, although they might reject or disobey Allah.[23]

The third subtype or species of atheism is the form most familiar to contemporary readers, especially those in theist-majority or Christian-majority societies. Where god-beliefs are present and dominant, atheism

---

[22] Wesley, "Sermon 95: On the Education of Children."
[23] Smith, *Faith and Belief*, 39.

is of necessity oppositional, disputing the existence of god(s). Such an atheism is tangled with theist talk, arguing about and against god(s), and does not have the luxury of default or natural atheism. We could call it *defensive atheism, debate atheism,* or *argumentative atheism,* and we would find it in the works of famous modern atheists like Richard Dawkins, Sam Harris, Christopher Hitchens, and others. However, despite the fact that it is the main kind of atheism we encounter, it is essential to understand that it is only one, and a relatively recent, kind of atheism.

Thinkers have offered other variations on atheism, such as "positive" and "negative." In one (mis)construal, positive atheism attempts to make atheism more attractive and friendly, while negative atheism engages in offense and ridicule. More properly, positive atheism refers to advancing the argument or presenting the evidence in support of atheism (akin to the positive defense in a court of law), while negative atheism simply highlights the faults and failures of the argument or case for god(s) (akin to the negative defense in court). These, however, are not *types* of atheism but rather *tactics* of atheism; the atheistic position remains the same. On the other hand, some non-god-believers have been labeled "apatheists" (apathy-theism) because they simply do not care about god-talk. Being thereby "without god(s)," they are functional atheists.

The same can be said for "agnostics." Agnosticism is not a position on god(s) at all but rather a process or method of knowledge. (*See* agnosticism) It is therefore obviously not a "middle position" or hesitation between theism and atheism. Insofar as some self-described "agnostic" is not actively believing in (and worshipping, loving, and obeying) a god, she is again an atheist (without god) in practice. The rather simple proof of this claim is that, if a god like the Christian deity exists, he/she/it/they will not differentiate at the end of days between the avowed atheist and the agnostic; neither believed, and neither will be saved.

Finally, Jeanine Diller recently offered the distinction between local atheism and global atheism. Local atheism, she held, is nonbelief in one particular god, that is, the rejection of one local theism like Christianity or Islam. Global atheism, on the other hand, is nonbelief in all god(s) or all local theisms. She went on to conclude erroneously that global atheism is almost impossible because it has an unbearable burden of proof—to know and debunk all god(s). She was wrong because an atheist need not disprove all gods, *or any gods*; atheism does *not mean the proof or the certainty that god(s) do(es) not exist.* As explained, atheism means the lack of god-belief, whether by default or dispute. And contrary to Diller's analysis, *every atheist is a global atheist,* lacking a belief in any and all god(s); if they believed in even one god, they would be a theist.

(Interestingly and importantly, she argued that a theist can be a "local theist" but cannot intelligibly be a "global theist," believing in all local gods—although, despite the fact that various god-beliefs contradict each other, some have tried.[24])

atheology

If theology is the putative (as well as impossible and nonsensical) "study of god"—almost always conceived as specifically the study of the Christian god by means of Christian literature and Christian experiences—then *atheology* is a reasonable complement or foil. Most simply and obviously, atheology could be understood as the study of not-god(s) or of atheism and atheists. Its main proponent, John Shook, taught us that the word has existed since the seventeenth century, when philosopher and Christian apologist Ralph Cudworth employed it to refer to "godless" ancient Greek philosophies. It did not get any traction until it was revived, ironically, by the unabashedly Christian philosopher of religion Alvin Plantinga, who defined "natural atheology" as "the attempt, roughly, to show that, given what we know, it is impossible or unlikely that god exists."[25] However, that sounds suspiciously like the definition of atheism, which makes us wonder if and how atheism differs from atheology (and if not, why we need it); further, "natural atheology" implies that there are other kinds, just as there are other kinds of theology besides natural theology.

A few other scholars have rolled out the term or had it retroactively attached to their work, including Martin Heidegger and Jean-Luc Nancy, but no one has done more to elaborate it than Shook. In a series of publications including his 2018 *Systematic Atheology*, he has defined and refined the fledgling discipline, calling it in one essay "the intellectual defense of atheism and the argumentative counterpart to theology."[26] In his major book he articulates that atheology "clarifies atheist unbelief about gods, analyzes and criticizes theological views defending convictions about gods, and assembles arguments defending atheism's judgment that it is unreasonable for anyone to think that a god is real"; systematic atheology specifically, as the antithesis of systematic theology, "organizes the philosophically sophisticated challenges to theism, and concludes that attending to gods has nothing to do with being a reasonable and well-informed person, a moral member of society, and a responsible

---

[24] Diller, "Global and Local Atheisms."
[25] Plantinga, *God and Other Minds*, vii.
[26] Shook, "Atheology," 263.

citizen."[27] He also grants that atheology deals with both "individual disbelief and public atheism," examining "varieties of disbelief in religions, explains how atheists justify and encourage nonreligious views, and defends their secular engagement with religion and religious aspects of society."[28]

Like theology with its multiple branches, atheology also comprises multiple projects. In contrast to revealed theology—atheism not admitting any such thing as divinely-revealed knowledge—Shook posits *rationalist atheology*, which deploys logic to discredit any claims about god(s) or religious experiences. In contrast to natural theology, *scientific atheology* musters empirical data to deprive god(s) of any place in nature. Where theologians practice moral theology, Shook advocates *moral atheology* or reflection on the "ethical opportunities and outcomes by abandoning commitments to god."[29] Finally, civil theology evokes a *civil atheology* which establishes the irrelevance of god(s) for a healthy functioning social order. In Shook's estimation, "complete atheologies" encompassing all four domains are rare since the nineteenth century, although social philosopher Jürgen Habermas and humanist Paul Kurtz have made attempts.

Although closely modeling atheology after theology is one possible and appealing approach, there is no particular reason why it must be a photonegative or antipode of its nemesis—and potentially good reasons why it should not, just as atheism is not merely the inversion or mirror-image of theism. Another way to commission a field of atheology is to imagine it, not as *a-theology* or the opposite or negation of theology but as *athe-ology* or the study of atheism(s) *in precisely the way that theology is* not *the study of theism(s)* but perhaps should be. Shook's version covers some of this ground, such as the "varieties of disbelief in religions," which we could and should extend to religions that do not contain god(s) in the first place. As an ambitious study of atheism(s) in all forms and effects, it could be a truly interdisciplinary undertaking, welcoming psychological studies of atheists, sociological studies of atheist groups and subcultures, anthropological studies of societies without theism, and philosophical studies of the atheism and its adjunct concepts. Finally, as a focus on unbelief, it would fall within the domain of the more comprehensive enterprise of apisteology. (*See* apisteology)

---

[27] Shook, *Systematic Atheology*, 9.
[28] Shook, "Atheology," 264.
[29] Shook, *Systematic Atheology*, 51.

belief

It is still common for philosophers and other scholars to define belief as not yet (or not ever) verified and justified knowledge ("knowledge," they say, "is justified, true belief"), and in everyday usage, as well as much academic discussion, belief tends to encompass anything that individuals think is true. Both of these approaches are inadequate if not utterly wrongheaded.

From old West Germanic *ga-laubon* (to hold dear, esteem, trust) and further back in time to *leubh-* (to care, like, love)—related to modern German *lieben* (to love)—the root of the English words "belief" and "to believe" is not oriented toward knowledge at all but toward affection and trust.[30] According to Malcolm Ruel, something similar is found in ancient Greek and Hebrew languages, where the equivalents of "to believe" — *pisteuo* and *'mn*, respectively— "express centrally the notion of trust or confidence....In classical Greek literature *pistis* [belief] means the trust that a man may place in other men, or gods; credibility, credit in business, guarantee, proof of something to be trusted."[31] The Hebrew term in particular "denotes even more directly a quality of relationship: it was used of the reliability or trustworthiness of a servant, a witness, a messenger, or a prophet, but it also served to characterize the relationship between God and his people, reciprocally trusted and trusting."[32] Likewise, in modern French, the verb *croire* (to believe) has different meanings depending on the preposition it takes: *croire à* means "to believe that something is true," while *croire en* means "to have confidence" or "to trust in" and *croire que* means something akin to "to hold an idea or opinion."[33] Meanwhile, anthropologists have discovered that many languages lack a term for "belief" altogether or that, if they have one, they do not evoke it in religious contexts.

Thus, a few things become clear. First, "belief" is not exclusively about religion; one can have "beliefs" on any subject. Second, "belief" is not a synonym for "knowledge," nor is it a class of which "knowledge" is one (true and justified) member (and what would the other members be, those false and/or unjustified beliefs?). If one inspects the everyday use of the English word "belief" and its verb form, we find a semantic range (the various meanings and applications of a word) that covers three quite different areas. One, to be sure, is propositional or epistemic: for instance,

---

[30] Online Etymology Dictionary, "Belief."
[31] Ruel, "Christians as Believers," 38.
[32] Ruel, "Christians as Believers," 38.
[33] Pouillon, "Remarks on the Verb 'To Believe,'" 2.

when a speaker says, "I believe in angels" or "I believe in climate change," she is communicating that she claims angels or climate change are real. (Coincidentally, every such "belief in" consists of one or more "beliefs that," i.e., claims about the existence and traits of the subject at hand.) We could call this the *correctness* dimension of belief. Another usage is closer to the original German, Greek, and Hebrew senses, conveying not factual accuracy but *confidence* or trust. Such confidence/trust may be well or poorly placed, based on previous behavior, but it is not (at least not only) a fact-claim. Yet a third instance of belief expresses *commitment* or devotion. The differences between these three dimensions are clear in the religious context in the distinction between "believing in the devil" in the sense of (1) asserting that the devil exists (correctness), (2) being sure that the devil will do harm (confidence), and (3) devoting oneself to the devil (commitment)—the first two of which a good Christian would agree with but not the third.

While "belief" covers all of these domains (and is also often used when other terms like "opinion," "preference," "value," "prediction," etc. would be more appropriate), in contemporary debates about religion it is ordinarily the first (correctness, propositional, truth-related) use that is most often and emphatically meant. Belief and knowledge do both deal with this issue, but in diametrically opposed ways. Knowledge is a truth-claim that is sufficiently supported by facts and logic. Belief, insofar as it is a truth-claim and not a position of confidence or commitment, is one that is not sufficiently supported by facts and logic or that, much worse, is held despite being contradicted by facts and logic.

credition

Credition is a term coined by scholars at the Credition Research Project housed at the University of Graz in Austria. According to Hans-Ferdinand Angel in his contribution to the *Encyclopedia of Sciences and Religions*, credition (from the Latin *credere*, believe, which also yields such words as "creed" and "credible") is a more technical and neutral substitute for the unscientific and baggage-laden term "belief." The new term also puts belief on par with other psychological phenomena like cognition, emotion, perception, and so forth. Credition emphasizes belief as a mental process—"that is, on what happens 'while someone is believing'"—rather than the standard and tired relation between belief and knowledge and associates it with other mental processes like "empathy, perception, action control, memory, and the self-concept."[34] So far, credition researchers have identified four functions that drive credition:

1. An enclosure function, which originates and modifies "those subsets of mind-sets, which are activated when a process of believing starts," i.e. "emotionally shaped propositions, such as vague ideas, confirmed knowledge, values, moral claims, and intuitions," some of which are "mightier" than others
2. A converter function, which translates belief into action by, among other things, "reducing the number of choices and abbreviating the time of decision-making"
3. A stabilizer function, which tends to "maintain" and "reduce the volatility" of creditions by putting them in contact and consonance with other "attitudes and mind-sets"
4. A modulator function, which "highlights in a specific way the differences of individuals and the differences of situations," understanding that beliefs are not static entities but rather that credition is affected by body states, circumstances, and (although not discussed) cultural context.[35]

In the flagship publication of the project, *Processes of Believing: The Acquisition, Maintenance, and Change in Creditions*, Angel and his colleagues examine credition/belief across a range of disciplines from philosophy and theology to economics and anthropology, but predominantly neuroscience, suggesting the highly neurological and cognitivist nature of the project.[36] Whether the initiative will bear fruit and inspire followers is yet to be determined, but for now it reveals the complex, dynamic nature of belief, which is simultaneously epistemic, emotional, and visceral (embodied) and by no means limited to religion.

discredism

Discredism is a term coined in my *Atheism Advanced: Further Thoughts of a Freethinker*. The neologism is derived from the Latin *credere* for "to believe," which also yields such English words as "credible," "credence," "credentials," "credit," "*dis*credit," and of course "creed." In its conjugated form (*credo*, "I believe") it is specifically the first word in the famous and formative Christian dogmas known as the Nicene Creed and

---

[34] Angel, "Credition, the Process of Belief," 536.
[35] Angel, "Credition, the Process of Belief," 537–38.
[36] Angel et al., *Processes of Believing*.

the Apostles' Creed. The prefix *dis-* also comes from the Latin for "apart" or even more actively "to part," "to separate from," "to deprive of," "to exclude/expel." (Ironically, Dis is also the name of the Roman god of the underworld, perhaps giving the prefix its negative connotations.) Together, the prefix *dis-* and the root *cred* produce "discredism" which means "no belief" or "without belief" but much more. Discredism implies not just the passive or indifferent absence of belief but an active, intentional, and principled *dis*missal of and *dis*regard for belief. It is a deliberate rejection of and *dis*tancing from the entire notion of belief, *dis*sociation from the practice of believing, and ideally and hopefully a *dis*abling of the power of belief. It is the position or lifeway of permanent *dis*posing of belief(s).

A further point of the new term is to differentiate between atheism, as the lack or rejection of belief in god(s) specifically, and discredism, as the lack or rejection of beliefs of all sorts, based on the discussion of belief above. Discredism is, therefore, a comprehensive attitude to claims of any kind at all: if the evidence warrants a positive conclusion, accept the claim as true; if the evidence warrants a negative conclusion, reject the claim as false; if the evidence warrants no conclusion, tentatively *dis*card the claim until more information comes to light. But at no point is "belief" warranted, wise, or helpful as such. "Belief" can never be anything better than premature arrival at a position (literally "jumping to a conclusion") and can often be much worse, like accepting an unjustified and more-than-likely false claim.

faith

From Old French *foi* (faith, belief, trust, confidence) and, earlier in time, Latin *fides* (trust, faith, confidence, reliance, credence, belief), the English word "faith" is often used interchangeably with religion (as in "the Christian faith" or "the Jewish faith"). This is clearly unacceptable, as (1) the word originally had nothing to do with religion specifically and (2) it is not entirely applicable to certain instances of religion (for instance, "the Buddhist faith," "the Norse faith," "the ancient Egyptian faith," and many others, including most or all indigenous and traditional religions). Furthermore, the word has applications, and is commonly applied, well beyond the context of religion.

On the other hand, scholars—especially religious ones—like to make a distinction between belief and faith. One of the champions of a distinct and expansive sense of "faith" was Wilfred Cantwell Smith. In his 1979 *Faith and Belief,* he restricted "belief" to the realm of "holding certain ideas" or what we might call the propositional or truth-claim aspect of thought and speech.[37] Faith, in contrast, "is deeper, richer, more personal"[38]; it is also a quality or characteristic of persons, indeed in his estimation the most important and essential quality/characteristic, specifically the ability and tendency to "get involved," to engage intimately with an idea, tradition, and relationship, "to know it in personal committed fashion in one or another of its varied forms."[39] As such, Smith esteemed it as "the fundamental religious category, even the fundamental human category."[40] At the same time, he granted that there are multiple kinds of faith across the world's religions and even that faith is not unique to religion; one can be intensely engaged with many a tradition, concept, person, or relation.

Since faith is not synonymous with belief for Smith, he saw the absence of faith not as disbelief but as "nihilism: a bleak inability to find either the world around one, or one's own life, significant; an absence of mutuality, in that one cannot respond to the universe or to one's neighbors knowing that one will be responded to.... The current terms for this are alienation, loss of identity, uncommittedness."[41] Interestingly, though, Smith did not regard all faith as equally praiseworthy; there was also the "mean, cramping faith of blind and fanatical particularism," religious, national, racial, and so forth.[42] Apparently forgetting his own warning, he concluded, "Faith is a virtue. Believing is not. To believe is not in itself virtuous."[43] But then neither is faith.

Theologian Richard Niebuhr also attempted to institute a study of faith or "the structure of human faith," but he noticed something that Smith did not:

Is not the word faith so highly equivocal or even indeterminate in meaning that it cannot be significantly used in such various connections in the course of one conversation? Now it means belief in a doctrine; now the acceptance of intuited or self-evident truths; now confidence or trust; now piety in general or a historic religion. In some cases the word applies to man's relation to the supernatural but again it refers to human interpersonal relations.[44]

---

[37] Smith, *Faith and Belief*, 12.
[38] Smith, *Faith and Belief*, 12.
[39] Smith, *Faith and Belief*, 6.
[40] Smith, *Faith and Belief*, 7.
[41] Smith, *Faith and Belief*, 13.
[42] Smith, *Faith and Belief*, 13.
[43] Smith, *Faith and Belief*, 142.
[44] Niebuhr, *Faith on Earth*, 4.

With this observation, he put his finger on a fact that is often ignored or obscured by students of religion. To begin, "faith" is often used in the propositional sense, as in faith in a claim or doctrine; on those occasions, it is interchangeable with "belief"—the only difference being that English lacks a verb form of faith equivalent to the verb "to believe." But one can surely "believe" that a god exists or "have faith" that a god exists without a shift in meaning. Niebuhr next mentioned that faith can imply or denote confidence or trust; however, in our discussion of belief we emphasized that belief has the exact same semantic potential: one can say, "I believe in my friend" or "I have faith in my friend." In fact, Niebuhr ended this quotation by acknowledging that faith applies equally to human and superhuman actors and relationships. Finally, we can extend Niebuhr's comment, and add it to Smith's, by stressing that faith conveys a sense of commitment, but so does belief in its third usage discussed above. In other words, *faith and belief have exactly the same semantic ranges and can be and are used interchangeably in everyday speech.* "Faith" may carry a certain connotation of intensity compared to "belief," but that is inconsequential. In every meaningful way, *faith and belief are synonyms*.

god

A god (*theos* in Greek, *deus* in Latin, *Gott* in German) is a type of spirit, but it is profoundly unclear across religions exactly what type. There is no settled, cross-culturally satisfactory definition of "god," but folks living in Christianity-dominated societies tend to imagine him/her/it as an infinitely powerful, perfectly moral or beneficent, usually creative (i.e. creator of the universe), and wholly "other" spiritual being. By "wholly other" we mean that he/she/it is totally unlike humans or anything else in nature. Richard Swinburne, a prominent Christian philosopher, defined god as "a person without a body (i.e., a spirit) present everywhere, the creator and sustainer of the universe, able to do everything (i.e., omnipotent), knowing all things, perfectly good, a source of moral obligation, immutable, eternal, a necessary being, holy and worthy of worship."[45] However, this is not a definition of god at all but rather a description of a particular god, namely the Christian god. It does not fit all cases. Among the ancient Greek gods, for instance, some were good, some bad or both or neither. Some were eternal, but many were born from other gods (or humans), and many died. Some played no part in creation, as creation was obviously complete before they were born. Often, each had a discrete assignment in a

---

[45] Swinburne, *The Coherence of Theism*, 2.

supernatural "division of labor"—i.e. a god of sea, a god of war, a god of love, a god of wine, etc. And concepts like "holy" and "worship" are not universal across religions.

Anthropologists Robert Levy, Jeannette Mageo, and Alan Howard proposed to distinguish gods from other spirits as inhabiting opposite ends of "a continuum of culturally defined spiritual entities ranging from well-defined, socially encompassing beings at one pole, to socially marginal, fleeting presences at the other."[46] Gods would fall on the former end, spirits the latter. The writers offered four variables that differentiate gods and spirits—structure, personhood, experience, and morality. By structure they meant that gods are the focus of more detailed social institutions, including priesthoods, shrines, and festivals, as well as specific territories; spirits are not the subject of such elaboration, being more "fluid," "emergent, contingent, and unexpected."[47] By personhood they held that gods are more physically and socially human, while spirits are "vague ... only minimally persons."[48] By experience they maintained that gods are actually less directly experienced whereas spirits are more commonly encountered and often more immediately the objects of human concern. Finally, gods are more likely agents and paragons of moral order than are spirits, who tend to be "extramoral" or evil. Gods, they argued, are paradigms and preservers of social order who establish and sanction human morality, but spirits "are threats to order and frequently must be purged so that order may be re-established."[49]

Unfortunately, this dichotomy is not supported by the empirical evidence. First, as already noted, gods are not always particularly good or moral, nor do they always take an interest in human affairs. At the same time, spirits may be the objects of extremely elaborate ritual behavior, while gods (especially distant "high gods") may be so abstract and remote as to inspire little human interest and action. Also, spirits, since they are more immediate, are often *better known and more like* persons than gods, with distinct names and personalities. Worse still, the line between gods and spirits on the one hand and humans on the other is not hard and fast: in many societies and religions, humans can and do become spirits and even gods, and—if Christianity shows us anything—gods can and do become human.

---

[46] Levy, Mageo, and Howard, "Gods, Spirits, and History," 11.
[47] Levy, Mageo, and Howard, "Gods, Spirits, and History," 14.
[48] Levy, Mageo, and Howard, "Gods, Spirits, and History," 15.
[49] Levy, Mageo, and Howard, "Gods, Spirits, and History," 16.

God

As a proper noun, God is the name of the biblical deity of the Judeo-Christian tradition, also known as Yahweh or Jehovah (both renderings of the unspoken and unspeakable tetragrammaton or four-letter word YHWH). For this reason, the capitalized form "God" should only be used when naming this particular god; alternatively, to caution listeners and readers that "God" is only one of the many gods in the world's religions, "the Christian god," "the Judeo-Christian god," or "the biblical god" are advisable options. When referring to other gods, their proper names (Zeus, Thor, Vishnu, etc.) should be used, and when intended as a common noun the form "god" is preferable. Using the capitalized form of god when discussing other gods or godhood in general is Christian-centric, factually incorrect, and, from a certain Judeo-Christian or biblical perspective, sacrilegious.

ignosticism

In Michael Martin's magisterial 1990 *Atheism: A Philosophical Justification*, his first argument in favor of atheism was the problem of religious language or the words that theists (and, too often, atheists) use to talk about religious entities and the beliefs about them. Since people must use words to speak about god(s) and other religious concepts, he raised the objection that such religious language may be, and ultimately proves to be, contradictory, incoherent, or totally meaningless—literally referring to nothing and carrying no content.[50] If words are contradictory, incoherent, or meaningless, then any statement formulated in those words is questionable if not completely unintelligible—as they say, "not even false" since it literally bears no sense. (The difference between "false" and "not even false" or simply meaningless is the difference between the sentences "Two plus two equals five" and "Two plus two equals red [or truth, or booga-booga].")

Although he did not speak the term, Martin's position is recognizable as ignosticism (a play on agnosticism, more explicitly bringing "ignorance" to the front). Attributed to humanistic rabbi Sherwin Wine, it is equated to "theological noncognitivism" as defined by Steven Conifer in 2002 as the view that "the sentence 'God exists' is cognitively meaningless" and thus does not deserve any serious consideration.[51] Subsequently, the great humanist and skeptic Paul Kurtz proposed

---

[50] Martin, *Atheism: A Philosophical Justification*.
[51] Conifer, "Theological Noncognitivism Examined."

"igtheism" in his 1992 *The New Skepticism: Inquiry and Reliable Knowledge*.

Despite the fact that all three of these terms are relatively obscure and uncommon, they do underscore a basic problem also recognized by apophatic theology, that is, that our ordinary words are often if not entirely inadequate for talking about god(s) as most modern Christians understand (or think they understand) the word. (*See* apophatic theology) What does it mean to say, "God is love" or "God loves us"? Is this, for instance, the same kind of love that humans feel for their mates, their children, their pets, or their favorite sports team? What does it mean to say, "God is three persons—the Father, the Son, and the Holy Spirit"? What is "a living god"? What does it mean to say, "God exists" if he/she/it/they do(es) not exist in the same fashion as other beings? What, in the end, does it mean to say, "God"?

The problem is intensified, perhaps beyond tolerability, when we learn that other languages possess entirely different vocabularies. There is, for example, no place in Christianity for such words as, and Christian terminology cannot be translated easily if at all into or as, *nirvana, pratītyasamutpadā, samsara, kufr, jukurrpa, pirlirrpa*, or any of an indefinite variety of words native to other religions (let alone words exogenous to religion such as "atom" or "quantum" or "entropy"). What we are virtually forced to conclude is that each religion is really just a religious language and, further, that each religious language is a "language game" that believers learn how to play in such a way that the words and statements in that language (seem to) make sense to the speaker/believer *but not to anyone who is not already fluent in the language game*. The very word "god" has quite different meanings—or no meaning at all—depending on the religion. (*See* god) To put it simply, Christians do not only or mainly "have Christian beliefs" so much as "speak Christian." And when atheists—in a majority-Christian-speaking society—engage with and argue about Christian concepts like god, they are inadvertently speaking Christian too.

A different and superior approach to the debate about the existence of god(s) would be to answer the theist as follows: "I do not know what you mean, and neither do you."

liberatheism

The neologism "liberatheism" can be interpreted in two ways. From the Latin *liber* (free) and atheism, liberatheism can mean the freedom that comes with atheism; additionally, but equally valuably, from "liberate" and "theism," it can mean being liberated from theism or more strongly *liberated from the very idea of god(s)*. God(s) and other putative supernatural beings constrict and oppress humans in multiple ways, not least by the apprehensions that such invisible entities inflict on people by their very (putative) existence, as well as the distortion and damage that such ideas do to individual thought-processes and social institutions. Relieved from the idea of such imaginary presences, humans are free to live their lives, meet their challenges, and choose their destiny.

Despite the fact that atheists do not share theists' belief in god(s), contemporary argumentative atheism is hardly free of god(s). (*See* atheism) Atheists who actively engage in debates about god(s), as opposed to apatheists who just don't care, still think and talk about god(s), and of course individual nonbelief in god(s) does not negate the effects of religious leaders and institutions on politics and society. We might go so far as to say that current atheism, even (if not especially) in its most aggressive forms, is not yet atheism at all—it is hardly "without god(s)"—but is closer to *agontheism* (*agon-*, struggle, contest), a conscious struggling or wrestling with god(s). And so long as one is wrestling with an entity or idea, one is not free of it.

Liberatheism is not another "ism"-identity to adopt: no one is asked or encouraged to "be a liberatheist." Liberatheism is a vision, a project, and an aspiration. We can ponder, and we may have reached the moment when we must ponder, what life will or can be like *after we stop talking about god(s) altogether*. One is reminded of the "three metamorphoses" described early in Friedrich Nietzsche's *Thus Spoke Zarathustra*. In the first metamorphosis, the individual becomes a camel, bearing the burden of timeworn ideas and beliefs. In the second metamorphosis, the camel becomes a lion that says, "No" to the burden and combats the old ideas and beliefs, still entangled with them. This is the stage of present-day atheism. But eventually, hopefully, the lion becomes a child, who says, "Yes" to something new, something fresh, something previously unknown and maybe unthought, maybe previously unthinkable. What that something will be, we cannot predict. And someday our progeny may have to break free of our ideas and beliefs, our truths and morals, and create something new again.

Liberatheism, like atheism, will not solve all of humanity's problems. It was never meant to. It will solve one problem—the problem of the tyranny of god-belief—but that only releases human energy and ingenuity to begin to grapple with the world's practical and social issues, from global warming to racism and injustice. Is humankind up to the challenge? We cannot know. But we can know that religion has never solved any practical or social problem, not once, and that the freedom to think and implement new solutions is our best and only hope.

misotheism

Adding *miso* (hate) to *theos*, misotheism is hatred or condemnation of god(s). Misotheism is not synonymous with atheism; despite the misguided fact that many theists believe that atheists hate god, scholars like Bernard Schweizer insist that only theists can be misotheists, since a god must exist in their minds in order to hate him/her/it.[52] The idea of misotheism appears in the Book of Job, which illustrates the essence of the position: in the first and second chapters Satan challenges Yahweh to visit such suffering on Job that the latter "will curse thee to thy face," and once the torture begins Job's wife also counsels him to "curse God, and die." Had Job chosen this course of action, he would have been a misotheist. Since then, many other people have measured god(s) by the pain and anguish of the world, great and small—from personal misfortunes and losses to world-historical tragedies like the Holocaust—and arrived at a disdain if not hatred for god(s). Misotheism, naturally, only poses a problem for religions in which humans are expected to love god(s); in many of the world's faiths, gods are not loveable, and people are welcomed if not encouraged to entertain all sorts of mixed or negative attitudes toward deity. Atheists, on the other hand, may despise the *idea* of god(s) and/or what people do in the name of religion, but they cannot strictly speaking hate any god(s) since they recognize no such thing as god(s).

myth

From the Greek *mythos* for speech, story, or virtually anything delivered by word of mouth, "myth" in everyday discourse refers to false tales and statements, from fantastic accounts of imaginary gods to simple claims about the existence of Atlantis or the efficacy of some snake oil remedy. Myth tends to relate to religion in particular, where the assumption is that the events told are untrue and fanciful, as in "Greek mythology." Note that no one ever refers to their own religious beliefs as myths (i.e. no Christian calls the Genesis story the "Christian creation myth").

When scholars apply the term myth in religion, they are not, however, necessarily presuming falsehood. Instead, a myth is generally a narrative with supernatural or at least superhuman characters; often it

---

[52] Bernard Schweizer, *Hating God: The Untold Story of Misotheism*.

recounts a creation event. As formulated by the classic comparative religionist Mircea Eliade, a myth "narrates a sacred history, it relates an event that took place in primordial Time, the fabled time of the 'beginnings.' In other words, myth tells how, through the deeds of Supernatural Beings, a reality came into existence...."[53] Emphasizing this creative content *and creative power* of myth, anthropologist Bronislaw Malinowski went further, disputing not only its "false" but its "symbolic" quality: myth for him was not a just-so story but a "charter" or model or blueprint for life; it "expresses, enhances, and codifies belief; it safeguards and enforces practical rules for the guidance of man."[54] Thus, while the events portrayed in myth occurred in the past, even the distant or primordial past when the world was first taking shape, its force and effect are in the present and the future.

Accordingly, theorists of myth have moved beyond "interpreting" (let alone debunking) myth to assessing its impact on the individual and society. For instance, anthropologist Claude Lévi-Strauss described how myth could be therapeutic by providing sick people with a lens through which to understand and overcome their suffering; he went so far as to compare a ritual cure with Freudian psychoanalysis by noting that "both succeed by recreating a myth which the patient has to live or relive"—the difference being that the therapeutic myth is a personal/biographical story while the religious myth is a collective/cosmological one.[55]

Insofar as myths depict "beginnings," they may tell of the origin of the universe itself, of humanity or specific aspects of humanity (our bodily form, the pain of childbirth, the inevitability of death), of various aspects of nature, or of social relations and institutions. One of the most important but neglected expressions of myth then is "political myth." A political myth, which may or may not feature supernatural characters *but always features "superior" characters*, imputes an old, sometimes ancient, and occasionally even sacred origin to political offices and institutions or to the political group (nation or country) itself. A clear example of non-supernatural but still more-than-ordinary (or at least "more-than-us") characters at the origin of the nation is the "Founding Fathers" of the United States, who authorized much of the country's politics by literally authoring its fundamental document, the Constitution. Other lesser myths report on George Washington never telling a lie or Abraham Lincoln going to great lengths to keep a promise; many of the country's specific traditions, from the Fourth of July or Thanksgiving

[53] Eliade, *Myth and Reality*, 5–6.
[54] Malinowski, *Magic, Science, and Religion and Other Essays*, 83.
[55] Lévi-Strauss, *Structural Anthropology*, 199.

celebrations to the putative design of the American flag, refer back to (but not always accurately reflect) early formative historical moments.

In other modern countries, political myth does much heavier lifting. The Russian myth of Arctida or Hyperborea (to which not all Russians subscribe), a typical "golden age" myth, recalls an ancient society in the far north populated by grand citizens, much better than people today—"robust, noble, reliable, truthful, courageous, generous, skillful, knowledgeable and wise"—who once ruled most or all of the northern hemisphere. They were also the ancestors of the white race, making them superior to all other peoples and races and certainly entitling them to a national (and racially exclusive?) state, if not to domination of the whole world.[56]

As evinced by the case of Hyperborea, political myth can often have pestilent features and consequences. Raoul Girardet reckoned that contemporary political myths tend to have four elements, namely a golden age (before things went wrong or were stolen from the group), a notion of "unity" (an allegedly homogeneous people or nation—which excludes "others" and even insiders who do not share the beliefs and values of "us"), a conspiracy against "us," and a savior who will restore "our" pride and glory (making us "great again").[57]

philosophy of religion

Philosophy, the ancient Greek "love of wisdom," has been applied to every topic from morality to science and certainly to religion as well. Ideally, philosophy would explore and clarify knowledge at the most fundamental level, critiquing concepts and showing us what we do and do not know. However, the subdiscipline of philosophy of religion has for most of its history completely abandoned this responsibility. Instead, for the greater part of the past two thousand years, as even philosopher of religion John Hick confessed, it was "generally understood to mean religious philosophizing in the sense of the philosophical defense of religious convictions. It was seen as continuing the work of 'natural,' distinguished from 'revealed,' theology. Its program was to demonstrate rationally the existence of God, thus preparing the way for the claims of revelation."[58] In short, philosophy of religion has been, and to a disturbing extent continues to be, an adjunct or almost a duplication of theology and apologetics. (*See* apologetics *and* theology)

---

[56] Shnirelman, "Hyperborea," 121.
[57] Girardet, *Mythes et Mythologies Politiques.*
[58] Hick, *Philosophy of Religion,* 1.

Hick would have us believe that philosophy of religion has since shaken off its unabashedly theological and apologetic clothing, but this is far from true. While he maintained that the discipline "studies the concepts and belief systems of the religions as well as the prior phenomena of religious experiences and the activities of worship and meditation on which these belief systems rest and out of which they have arisen," the rest of his treatment belies its enduring Christian bias.[59] For example and most baldly, the first chapter of his book is "The Judaic-Christian Concept of God," followed by such chapter titles as "Arguments for the Existence of God," "Revelation and Faith," and "Human Destiny: Immortality and Resurrection," with a nod to "The Conflicting Truth Claims of Different Religions" and "Human Destiny: Karma and Reincarnation." The situation is not much different, or much better, in other standard summaries of and introductions to the field.

In addition to its skewed topical treatment, closer inspection proves that philosophy of religion is overtly biased in favor of religion rather than upholding its duty to be objective and critical. The majority of philosophers of religion are devotees who apparently perceive their job as not so much to analyze and critique religion as to protect and advance it. Further, the work that passes for scholarship in the field displays a conspicuous pro-religion and anti-nonreligion prejudice. For all of the reasons discussed here, a number of scholars outside and inside the field have called for a radical reformation of philosophy of religion, if not for its total abolition. It could be replaced, then, with an academic and scientific activity that seeks to explain the origin or root of religion, its diversity, and its functions, drawing on methods and insights from a range of disciplines including philosophy, cognitive science, anthropology, and sociology. (See Chapter 8)

political theology

Political theology stands at the intersection of religion and politics or of god(s) and government. For all of recorded history, and probably long before, political rulers and social superiors have strived to justify their authority and the laws, roles, and institutions through which they dominate. Saul Newman asserted that "the problem of political theology is a way of thinking about the foundations and legitimacy of power," whether in a traditional chiefdom, an ancient kingdom, or a modern state.[60]

---

[59] Hick, *Philosophy of Religion*, 1.
[60] Newman, *Political Theology: A Critical Introduction*, xx.

Religion naturally provided and continues to provide a ready and effective legitimation tool.

In traditional and indigenous societies, it was often believed that the chief or other elites possessed some special spiritual quality. One familiar example is the concept of *mana* in the Pacific Islands: *mana*, a supernatural force of vitality and efficacy, gave leaders, warriors, and hunters their unique capacities. In the Madagascar kingdom of Merino, a force called *hasina* granted leaders their power over society and nature itself. In the ancient city-states of Mesopotamia, it was understood that the city's god owned and controlled the land and people and that the law was given to the king, not invented by the king (sometimes, as depicted in the carvings on Hammurabi's law code, literally handed to him by the god); in ancient Egypt, the king or pharaoh was a living god whose will was divine. In classical China, emperors promoted the notion of "the mandate of heaven," the choice of the gods to bestow power and authority on a particular person or dynasty; of course, when the emperor was defeated or nature turned against the empire (in the form of natural disasters like floods, droughts, or earthquakes), it was obvious to all that the mandate had been withdrawn and transferred to whoever rose to power.

For the nearly two millennia of Christian hegemony in Europe, the Christian god predictably made rulers legitimate. Dating back to Constantine in the early fourth century, emperors and popes enjoyed both worldly and otherworldly authority. So emerged the doctrine of the "divine right of kings"—that, as with Chinese emperors, the local god favored some individual or family and conferred on him/her/them the right to rule. Also as with Chinese emperors, the god could rescind the right and assign it to another, who subsequently held the divine right until it was again taken away. In the meantime, whoever ostensibly had the right commanded unquestioning obedience, disobedience amounting to sacrilege.

In modern democracies, while there are many who still believe that power (or even a political instrument like the Constitution or the flag) is god-given, religion is not a stable or even possible foundation for political power. In the early twentieth century, during the interwar period in Germany, political scientist Carl Schmitt reoriented political theology in a series of essays published together under that title. For him, the key to political theology was *sovereignty*, which he defined or diagnosed in his famous opening line, "Sovereign is he who decides on the exception."[61] In other words, it was explicitly *not* in the law that we find the basis of power but the other way around: power comes from, or is located in, the capacity

---

[61] Schmitt, *Political Theology: Four Chapters on the Concept of Sovereignty*, 5.

to *make the law and break the law*. The classic case of the exception is the suspension of a constitution and/or the declaration of martial law. Such events demonstrate the fragility of the law, of "ordinary politics," and the fact of individual will as the ultimate source of law and social order. At such moments, the sovereign (king, autocrat, dictator) rises god-like on the political horizon, a figure who rules but is not restrained by the rules. Decision-making during the exception displays a miraculous quality, breaking through mundane politics and inaugurating new political and social realities, even "truths." Indeed, Schmitt went so far as to posit, "All significant concepts of the modern theory of the state are secularized theological concepts."[62] However, it may be equally or more accurate to insist that all religious/theological concepts are spiritualized political/social concepts, since human groups, institutions, and powers are real and are then elevated or sublimated into superhuman ones.

religion

Given the amount of energy expended by theists and atheists alike sparring over religion, it is remarkable how little consensus there is among scholars as to what precisely religion is. Even the etymology of the word is disputed: some sources trace it to the Latin *ligare* (to bind), emphasizing its unifying potential, while others associate it with *relegere* (*re-* re/again, *legere* read), stressing its repetitive and obligatory nature. In either case, the word "religion" was not used by the ancient Greeks or early Christians; indeed, many societies and languages have no word that is equivalent to "religion."

Worse, many contemporary Christians and other theists equate theism with religion, but in actuality theism is only one kind or component of religion. (*See* animism *and* god) Some religions contain god(s) and others, perhaps the majority, do not; instead of or in addition to god(s), the world's myriad religions contain nature spirits, dead human ancestors, supernatural forces or powers, and an innumerable variety of other beings and entities. Equally innumerable are the attempts to define religion, each highlighting one or more aspects of it. Founding sociologist Émile Durkheim, for instance, characterized religion as "a unified system of beliefs and practices relative to sacred things, that is to say, things set aside and forbidden—beliefs and practices which unite into one single moral community called a Church, all those who adhere to them."[63] Anthony Wallace insisted that a religion is essentially "a set of rituals rationalized

---

[62] Schmitt, *Political Theology*, 36.
[63] Durkheim, *The Elementary Forms of Religious Life*, 62.

by myth, which mobilizes supernatural powers for the purpose of achieving or preventing transformations of state in man and nature."[64] Clifford Geertz put symbols at the center of his especially celebrated definition: "(1) a system of symbols which act to (2) establish powerful, pervasive, and long-lasting moods and motivations in men by (3) formulating conceptions of a general order of existence and (4) clothing these conceptions with such an aura of factuality that (5) the moods and motivations seem uniquely realistic."[65] Other influential thinkers on the subject include Rudolf Otto, who attributed it to the mysterious experience of "the holy" and "the other," as well as dismissive scholars like Karl Marx and Sigmund Freud who considered it to be false consciousness to justify exploitation or projection of infantile psychological processes, respectively—both expecting and hoping that it would soon wither away. (*See* secularization)

Some experts on religion conclude that the concept of religion has become, in the words of Kevin Schilbrack, so "sprawling, overly inclusive, and unwieldy"[66] that they endorse the idea of jettisoning the category altogether. Simply, they advocate that there is no such thing as "religion." However, while there is no settled definition of religion, and its boundaries are vague and porous, there is a place for such a term (perhaps some systems and institutions are "more or less religious" than others, or perhaps we could speak of individuals and groups acting "religiously"). One variable that appears to unify most (but not all) phenomena that we call "religion" is a notion of supra-human agency, that is, beings that are unlike humans in some ways (particularly, more powerful and more eternal or immortal, although not always totally immortal) but like humans in others (particularly, possessing a mind or personality). Then, humans find themselves in diverse kinds of social relationships with these beings, from loving protection to frightening victimhood. Either way, the message of religion might be construed that humans are not the only "persons" in the universe and that these non-human and supra-human (but not necessarily supernatural) persons interact with us for good or ill.

Finally, since theism is not synonymous with religion, atheism is not synonymous with nonreligion or anti-religion. Strictly speaking, the scope of atheism is only theism, namely, the absence of or opposition to the concept of god(s). There are many religions that do not include god(s)—that are a-theistic or non-theistic—which atheism does not

---

[64] Wallace, *Religion: An Anthropological View*, 107.
[65] Geertz, *The Interpretation of Cultures*, 90.
[66] Schilbrack, "What *Isn't* Religion?" 291.

directly address. It is sloppy speaking and thinking to imagine a binary with "religion" on one side and "atheism" on the other.

religious trauma

Religion, whether or not it is true, is widely held to be "good for you." In fact, the "argument from benefit" is one standard argument in favor of religion: like Pascal's infamous and foolish wager, one is recommended to believe, even if the evidence does not support belief, because of the supposed good that derives from it.

However, scholars, religious leaders, psychotherapists, and laypeople have become increasingly aware of the damage that religions do to their members. Terms like "toxic faith" or "spiritual abuse" are now common ways of speaking about the harm caused by religion, but perhaps the central term and concept is religious trauma. Medically, trauma is an injury to the body; the notion was expanded to include psychological or emotional trauma, both the specific event that causes pain or damage and the lingering effects like post-traumatic stress disorder. One of the first experts to identify religious trauma, or a "religious trauma syndrome," was Marlene Winell, who was most interested in "the condition experienced by people who are struggling with leaving an authoritarian, dogmatic religion and coping with the damage of indoctrination."[67]

Though interesting and worthwhile, this focus is far too narrow. It concentrates on certain kinds of religions (the authoritarian, dogmatic kinds) and certain relationships to those religions (leaving or escaping them) but does not recognize or sufficiently emphasize the mental or social injury suffered by those who remain in those religions or who belong to non-authoritarian, non-dogmatic ones. In any religion, as in any group or organization, there are opportunities for "manipulation and exploitation, enforced accountability, censorship of decision making, requirements for secrecy and silence, pressure to conform," and other abuses, to which religion singularly adds "misuse of scripture or the pulpit to control behavior, requirement of obedience to the abuser, the suggestion that the abuser has a 'divine' position and isolation from others, especially those external to the abusive context."[68]

Predictably but tiresomely, most of the research on (and healing from) religious trauma has been done in the Christian context. However, the diverse religious traditions of the world have their unique practices and patterns of traumatization. Two of the most common are sacrifice and self-

---

[67] Winell, "Religious Trauma Syndrome."

[68] Oakley and Kinmond, *Breaking the Silence on Spiritual Abuse*, 21–22.

injury. Throughout history and across cultures, humans have killed living beings—including other humans—and destroyed nonliving things for some alleged religious purpose or gain. Even more universal, and probably responsible for more agony, is self-directed harm. In virtually all of the world's religious traditions, members are expected, often recurrently, to hurt themselves through cutting, bleeding, scarring, piercing, fasting, sleep deprivation, and a myriad of renunciations and self-deprivations. In some traditions, individuals may become athletes and aficionados of pain, adopting lives of asceticism. In the extreme case, believers may offer themselves as martyrs to their god(s) and beliefs.

Across the world's cultures, members or leaders of one religion have persecuted and punished members of other religions or sects, or those without religion (admittedly, in some regimes like Soviet Russia and Communist China, atheists have also persecuted religionists). In still other situations, religion has blended with cultural and "ethnic" differences to produce ethno-religious conflict, as in Northern Ireland (Catholic versus Protestant), Sri Lanka (Sinhalese Buddhist versus Tamil Hindu), and Bosnia (Serbian Orthodox Christian versus Croatian Catholic versus Bosnian Muslim). Again at the extreme, one group or country may make war on another for religious reasons, whether we call it a crusade, a holy war, or a *jihad*.

Finally, of course, there are instances when individuals in positions of religious authority, or ordinary members in the name or practice of religion, commit crimes and abuses against others. The most prominent and egregious example is the sexual abuse of children by Catholic priests, but Catholic officials are hardly the only specialists who have mistreated their flocks. Devotees have killed their children, spouses, and other kin for religious reasons, while many parents have let their children suffer and die unnecessarily by depriving those youngsters of reasonable medical care in favor of prayer and faith healing.

So, the emerging and burgeoning field of religious trauma has much to offer victims of religion, but it also has a long way yet to go to recognize and excise all of the forms in which religion traumatizes its followers. (See Chapter 6)

ritual

From the Latin *ritus* for custom, usage, or especially a religious ceremony or observance (ceremony is essentially a synonym for ritual, as is rite), ritual is a central element of religion in virtually all of its manifestations, even if an often-disparaged element. The negative attitude toward ritual in many Western/Christian societies stems from Protestant influence, which disdained many of the ritualistic trappings of Catholicism. Yet Protestant denominations are hardly without their ritual activities, and we cannot allow one religion's or sect's perspective to color our objective understanding of something as common and powerful as ritual.

Ritual is frequently denigrated because it is thought to be rote and meaningless, even irrational. More to the point, William Sax opined that the objection to ritual is less about its rationality than about its *effectiveness*; that is, ritual is usually taken to be utterly pointless and vain action which cannot possibly achieve its stated aims (like making rain or curing disease).[69] For those who would rescue ritual from absolute contempt, the solution is often to reinterpret the behavior in ritual as "symbolic" (a polite way of saying "vain and useless"), that is, to focus on its "meaning" rather than its intent and assumed efficacy.

This attitude, as generous as it seems, misrepresents the attitudes of ritual participants and mischaracterizes ritual as understood by local societies and religions. In fact, few religions and their languages speak of "ritual" at all; rather, from India to Pacific islands, what we call ritual they call something like "the work of the gods" or, in Australian Aboriginal English, "business." As Sax put it, "What *we* see as ritual, *they* see as technique," and successful technique at that.[70] To be clear, when people engage in actions to elicit rain or heal illness, they are not seeking "meaning," they are seeking rain and health.

Of course, ritual is not unique to religion; human social life is replete with ritualistic behavior. Indeed, any activity that is regularized, conventional, formalized, and repetitive is ritualistic to an extent. We even find ritualized behavior in non-human species, often associated with issues where the stakes are high, such as mating, competing for status, and territoriality. So "communication" is important in ritual, including communicating the fact that a ritual is taking place, what philosopher John Skorupski labeled "interaction-code behavior," the point of which "is to establish or maintain (or destroy) an equilibrium, or mutual agreement, among the people involved in an interaction as to their relative standing or roles, and their reciprocal commitments and obligations."[71] One productive way of conceiving religious ritual in contrast to secular/everyday ritual or animal ritual is that religious interaction and agreement transpires *between humans and non-human/supra-human actors*. Two special problems present themselves in such circumstances.

---

[69] Sax, "Ritual and the Problem of Efficacy," 6.
[70] Sax, "Ritual and the Problem of Efficacy," 4.
[71] Skorupski, *Symbol and Theory*, 77.

First, since the supra-human actors are usually if not always much more powerful than us, we must be especially careful and respectful in how we approach them. Second, since these supra-human actors are usually invisible, we cannot be certain if the interaction worked—or if the beings were present at all.

There are many types of ritual, and students of religious ritual have suggested various typologies, none of them perfectly adequate. Anthony Wallace, for instance, organized rituals into technical (intended to achieve a natural or supernatural goal), therapeutic and anti-therapeutic (to heal and harm), salvation (to effect changes in the individual's personality), ideological (to control groups and society as a whole), and revitalization (to repair society in times of crisis) categories. Catherine Bell constructed a different classification, distinguishing between rites of passage (to transform individuals from one state to another, like child to adult or single to married), calendrical or commemorative rituals (often celebrating actual historical events, like the Fourth of July), rites of exchange and communion (with gifts or sacrifices to spirits), rites of affliction (to cure illness or misfortune), rites of feasting, and political rituals (to "construct, display, and promote the power of political institutions [such as king, state, village elders] or the political interests of distinct constituencies and subgroups").[72]

In one of the most influential analyses in the history of ritual studies, Victor Turner theorized a ritual process that is most evident in so-called rites of passage. In his model, an individual occupies a particular status (juvenile, single, polluted, ill, etc.) prior to the ritual. The first stage of ritual action accomplishes a separation from that status and perhaps from the group, which may be enacted and symbolized as a death. Once separated, the individual enters the second and crucial stage, the "liminal" phase, in which statuses and social distinctions are erased; often symbolized by nakedness, silence, and physical ordeals (such as fasting, sleep deprivation, or bodily operations like scarring or circumcision), it is during this phase that transformation occurs, not unlike a caterpillar in its chrysalis. At some point in time, the individual emerges from liminality and returns to society a changed person (adult, married, purified, healthy) in the third and final stage of aggregation.[73]

We may well discover elements of liminality in secular/everyday rituals as well as religious ones and even outside of ritual contexts. The crucial point, though, is that rituals, wherever and whenever they occur (including in relatively trivial moments like high school graduations or

---

[72] Bell, *Ritual Perspectives and Dimensions*, 128.
[73] Turner, *The Ritual Process: Structure and Anti-Structure*.

getting one's first driver's license), are generally and strongly felt to be transformative—that individuals, relationships, and the world itself are different after the ritual compared to before. In this quite non-trivial sense, rituals are anything but ineffective but are techniques not only to communicate to others that changes have happened but *to achieve those changes*. They are part, and a profound part, of the human process of world-making.

secular

"Secular" as a noun or adjective is popularly taken to mean "without religion" or "opposed to religion." However, from the Latin *saeculum* (generation, age), secular actually refers not to nonreligion or antireligion and not even to the physical or material world (in contrast to a putative spiritual or heavenly realm) but to time, that is, the current age or era. Modern statisticians for instance use the phrase "secular trend" to describe long-term processes, with no religious connotations. The Catholic Church itself uses the phrase "secular clergy" for parish priests and other office-holders who do not enter the ascetic life of the monastery but minister to the everyday needs of their congregation. Eastern Orthodoxy likewise calls their married priests and deacons "secular clergy," in distinction to their celibate monks. Obviously, "secular" does not necessarily require absence of or hostility to religion.

Secular in its contemporary sense was coined only in the mid-nineteenth century by George Jacob Holyoake, a British non-believer, who characterized secularism as

> a series of principles intended for the guidance of those who find Theology indefinite, or inadequate, or deem it unreliable. It replaces theology, which mainly regards life as a sinful necessity, as a scene of tribulation through which we pass to a better world. Secularism rejoices in this life, and regards it as the sphere of those duties which educate men to fitness for any future and better life, should such transpire.[74]

secularization

Secularization is the theorized process in which religion over time becomes an ever more peripheral and trivial aspect of life, until that inevitable day when it disappears or is cast off once and for all. The French

---

[74] Holyoake, *The Principles of Secularism*, 11.

philosophes of the eighteenth century were intensely critical of religion and expected and desired, even plotted, its decline and demise. The nineteenth-century sociologist Auguste Comte divided human history into three epochs, the "theological" stage being the first and most primitive, followed by the "metaphysical" stage of philosophy and rational inquiry and, in his own time, the third "positive" stage, distinguished by science and the pursuit of facts, which would dispense with any lingering theological or metaphysical speculation.

If there is an arch-theorist of secularization, it is Karl Marx, who diagnosed religion as an illusion and false consciousness—the opium of the people and the sigh of the oppressed—and prophesied that it would spontaneously vanish when humanity's practical needs were met. In 1882 the philosopher Friedrich Nietzsche announced that "God is dead," although he had to put the words in the mouth of a madman, and Sigmund Freud foresaw the end of religion in his 1927 *The Future of an Illusion*. Founding sociologist Max Weber also felt that the modern world with its bureaucracy, urbanization, industrialization, and increasingly managed way of life was unconducive to religion and that society had become "disenchanted," bereft of its religious or spiritual element.

Out of these observations and predictions grew secularization theory, summed up by sociologist Steve Bruce in the understatement that "modernization creates problems for religion."[75] Another sociologist, José Casanova, boiled secularization theory down to three primary propositions. The first is structural differentiation: religion separates from other domains of society isolated in a "religious institution" (like "the church") from other institutions (like "the state"). The second is privatization: religion becomes something that individuals do inside their homes, heads, and hearts without wider public impact. The third is absolute decline: people spend less time and energy on church attendance, prayer, and such religious behavior, contributing to the diminution and disappearance of religion in society.[76]

However, as events have demonstrated, the anticipated death of god and religion has not come to pass, and religion has returned with a vengeance (often quite literally), if it ever actually receded. In 2006 Casanova revisited his theory and restated that the "functional differentiation and emancipation of the secular sphere—primarily the modern state, the capitalist market economy, and modern science—from the religious sphere" was and remains "the defensible core of the theory

---

[75] Bruce, *God is Dead: Secularization in the West*, 2.
[76] Casanova, *Public Religions in the Modern World*.

of secularization."[77] Accordingly, multiple scholars have suggested that we live today in a "post-secular" reality in which secularization did not quite happen but neither did religion escape unscathed. Instead, both the secular and the religious have evolved, partly in interaction with each other.

spirit

Derived from Latin *spiritus* (breath) and *spirare* (to breathe/blow), "spirit" is commonly understood to refer to some non-material component of human (and, in various religions, at least some other) beings. Webster's Dictionary accordingly defines spirit as "an animating or vital principle held to give life to physical organisms," as crucial but intangible as breath. In fact, other English words draw this same connection between breath and life, such as expire (to "breathe out," to lose or end one's energy or vitality, sometimes even to die), conspire (to "breathe together," to combine one's energy or vitality with another, as in a conspiracy), perspire (to "breathe through," to give off one's energy or vitality through the skin), inspire (to "breathe in," to absorb energy or vitality from some external source), aspire (to "breathe at/toward," to focus or direct one's energy or vitality on some goal), and respire (to "breathe again," to repeatedly gain and lose energy or vitality, in other words, to stay alive), among others.

 Humanity's religions—indigenous, ancient, modern/"world," and new/emerging—posit all sorts of spirits, not all of them perfectly immaterial. In some religions, spirits may have bodies, permanently or temporarily, as well as the power to invade and "possess" human bodies. The vast majority of these beings/entities also have other human-like qualities, specifically mind or will or what scholars call "agency"—the capacity to act rather than merely to be acted upon. They are both animate and intelligent, whether they are benign, malign, or simply indifferent to humans. No matter their local details, spirits share the sort of "life force" or "vitality" that enlivens humans and other material beings and are identified with breath and motion. In fact, ancient Greek *pneuma* means air or breath, from *pnein* for to breathe (giving us words like pneumatic and pneumonia) and stood as a symbol for spirit. In ancient Hebrew, *ruah* also means both breath and spirit, and it is commonly used in the Hebrew scriptures to designate the power of their god that injects life into matter and order into chaos. Recall that Judeo-Christian mythology teaches how the universe was created by the speech of God (the out-rush of air in verbal form) and how Adam was created by God's breath into dust. In these and

---

[77] Casanova, "Secularization Revisited: A Reply to Talal Asad," 12–13.

many other traditions, it becomes clear that "spirit" is a metaphor taken literally, air or breath or life itself ascribed an independent existence from the creature who lives and breathes.

theism

Theism (*theos*, god) is commonly understood as a kind—and for many partisans, a superior kind—of religion, one that posits one or more gods, however defined. (*See* god) There are many types of theism, most basically *mono*theism (one god) and *poly*theism (multiple gods). But this hardly exhausts the forest of theisms. Henotheism grants that there is more than one god but prescribes belief in and worship of only one. Apeirotheism (*apeiro*, infinite) teaches that there is an infinite number of gods. Pantheism (from *pan*, all) would have it that the universe and everything in it is identical or equivalent to god; alternatively, pantheism might refer to recognition or even worship of all the gods (as in "pantheon"). On the other hand, panentheism contends that its god is more than the universe but somehow includes or subsumes the universe as one of his/her/its/their parts or properties. Deism, meanwhile, tends to acknowledge a creator-god, often envisioned as a cosmic engineer or divine watchmaker, who gave the universe its start but then retired from active involvement in his/her/its/their creation (thus an absent, inert, or hidden deity). Many other permutations of theism can be, have been, and will be presented. The upshot is that theism is a highly complicated and contested concept and that theists are nowhere near agreeing on the quality or quantity of god(s). And theism is not even a "type" of religion so much as a component or module of religion: *every* actual religion that contains a god, including Christianity, also includes other kinds of putative supernatural beings. There is no such thing as "pure" theism. (See Chapter 4)

theology

Theology (*theos*, god + *logos*, study/word) is the highly sophisticated yet essentially impossible if not nonsensical (if there is no such thing) "study of god(s)." Exactly how one would study a phenomenon that is mysterious and potentially or actually unknowable (*see* apophatic theology), and what exactly would serve as the source of information for such a study, is difficult to comprehend.

Despite these difficulties, some scholars have classified theology as not only a branch but the culmination of metaphysics, including Aristotle who called theology the highest of the "theoretical philosophies/sciences" since "it deals with the highest of existing things," namely god(s).[78] Other theologians from Aquinas to Paul Tillich have similarly conceived of the activity as elucidating the first principle, the uncaused cause, or the primary (or for Baruch Spinoza, the only) substance, that which is eternal, unmovable, and independent, upon which all contingent things depend. Of course, if there is no uncaused cause or eternal immutable substance, then the whole project of theology is futile.

This concern has not stopped theologians from claiming scientific status for their field. In his 1887 Abstract of Systematic Theology, James Petrigru Boyce, the first president of the Southern Baptist Theological Seminary, asserted that theology "means literally a discourse concerning God but in analogy with other words, as geology, chronology, and biology, it means the science which treats of God."[79] Even today, *The Catholic Encyclopedia* clings to this entitlement, stating that adding –*ology* to *theos* make theology

> the science treating of God, subjectively, the scientific knowledge of God and Divine things. If defined as the science concerning God (*doctrina de Deo*), the name of theology applies as well to the philosophical knowledge of God, which is cast into scientific form in natural theology or theodicy.[80]

Such pleading notwithstanding, the assertion that theology is a science is dubious if not absurd. It produces no quantitative (or any other kind of) facts, derives no laws, advances no hypotheses, formulates no theories, posits no mechanisms, makes no predictions, and affords no solutions or technologies. It assumes its "knowledge" ahead of any investigations into that knowledge, as plainly stated by Louis Berkof in his *Systematic Theology*: "We start the study of theology with two presuppositions, namely (1) that God exists, and (2) that He has revealed Himself in His Divine Word."[81]

The flat-out if not audacious speciousness of such talk—presupposing that which must be proven and is so far unproven, and using religious scriptures written by human hands as the source-material for your "science"—exposes theology as nothing more than apologetics and exegesis. It is apologetics because it beseeches for belief (*see* apologetics), and it is exegesis because it amounts, and could only amount, to reading,

---

[78] Aristotle, *Metaphysics*, 186.
[79] Boyce, *Abstract of Systematic Theology*.
[80] Pohle, "Theology," 580.
[81] Berkhof, *Systematic Theology: New Combined Edition*, 19.

repeating, and expanding the claims previously made in religious writings—that is, saying more about what people have already said about god(s). Paul Badham granted as much when he admitted that, in practice, theology "usually means studying the sources of Christian belief like the Bible and the Creeds, and exploring the meaning of Christianity for today."[82] Truly, what else could it mean? But our critique is yet more fatal to theology, since there is not and cannot be any such thing as "theology" but only diverse and competing *theologies*—Christian, Jewish, Muslim, Hindu, etc. and beyond that sectarian and denominational theologies such as Catholic, Baptist, Methodist, Mormon, *ad nauseum*.

Inadvertently pinpointing the vacuum at the heart of theology, Charles Hodge in his 1872 *Systematic Theology* counted as the "methods" of theology the following: induction from the Bible (as a "store-house of facts"), speculation (deistic, dogmatic, and transcendental), and mysticism.[83] It hardly merits more of our time and energy to consider such an enterprise, but this has not prevented theology from becoming remarkably subtle and impressive-sounding (and well-funded). It is commonly divided into several subfields, including systematic, natural, historical, practical, dogmatic, and biblical (which is wildly redundant or tautological, since all Christian theology ultimately circles back to the Bible). Different scholars and institutions foment different categorizations, and other religions would design their theology differently (for instance, not appealing to the Bible but the Qur'an or the Vedas, etc.). No matter how you look at it, though, if theology is understood as the study of god(s), it is until proven otherwise a study without a subject.

tri-omni god

A shorthand for the three putative qualities of the biblical or Abrahamic god, "tri-omni god" refers to a god that is omnipotent (all-powerful), omniscient (all-knowing, literally all-seeing), and omnibenevolent (all-good). It is often then fallaciously assumed that all gods, or at least all gods worth worship, possess these three qualities. (*See* god)

unbelief

Unbelief is a term that has been advanced by a number of writers as a substitute and umbrella term for nonreligion. It is one proposal in the

---

[82] Badham, "What is Theology?" 101.
[83] Hodge, *Systematic Theology*, 9–15.

ongoing project to name, organize, and analyze what a recent champion of the term, Nickolas Conrad, calls "the rupture with traditional forms of religion or spiritual practices."[84] Admittedly, "atheism" will not do, not only or mostly because it is too "rigid" in Conrad's estimation but because its scope is more narrow, limited to the absence or rejection of god-beliefs (notwithstanding that people—atheists and theists alike—frequently take "atheism" to mean the absence or rejection of religion in total.) (*See* atheism *and* religion)

In contrast to atheism, Conrad argues that unbelief "is a more responsible category because its ambiguity allows a much greater degree of inclusion."[85] Whether or not ambiguity is a virtue in scientific technology is questionable, but certainly religious unbelief includes more than atheism, although perhaps not as much as Conrad, and Gordon Stein in his earlier *The Encyclopedia of Unbelief*, would have it. Conrad endorses Stein's definition of unbelief, as "the position of 'not holding orthodox beliefs or traditional opinions—on religious matters," which gives it the expansive subject-area of "blasphemy, heresy, the rejection of belief, atheism, agnosticism, humanism, and rationalism."[86] In a word, unbelief is synonymous with "heterodoxy."

Despite the enthusiasm for the neologism in some camps, there are two significant objections to it as currently conceived. First, unbelief is not directed only at religion; there are also many other beliefs and belief-systems to not believe in. (*See* apisteology) So, religious unbelief is one species of the much wider genus of unbelief, which itself requires a more informed understanding of belief and believing. (*See* belief *and* credition) Second, unbelief cannot and must not be equated with "heterodoxy" or "heresy" for the simple and obvious reason that *a heterodox or heretical belief is still a belief.* There does need to be a study of blasphemy, heresy, and heterodoxy, but it is more than a disservice to list those among unbelief. And of course, evaluating unbelief by the standard of "orthodox beliefs" or "traditional opinions" presupposes that there is such a thing as orthodoxy or tradition. Instead, some beliefs are orthodox to certain individuals or groups at certain times and places, and others are not. That is to say, unbelief as Stein and Conrad see it is relative to *someone's* orthodoxy, and what is blasphemous, heretical, or heterodox today may be orthodox and traditional tomorrow (take, for example, Christianity in the first decades of the ancient Jerusalem "Jesus movement").

---

[84] Conrad, "An Argument for Unbelief," 1.
[85] Conrad, "An Argument for Unbelief," 7.
[86] Stein, *The Encyclopedia of Unbelief*, xv.

4

So Many Theisms: Freeing Atheism From Monotheistic Assumptions

How are we atheists expected to engage theists when those theists cannot even agree among themselves on precisely what they believe? And yet both sides plunge ahead as if they know what they are talking about, rather than stopping, pausing, and taking the time to define just what they mean by "god(s)." Or more correctly, both sides hardly acknowledge that there is a need to consider "god(s)" and merrily proceed to argue about "God" by which both sides mean something like a generic version of the Christian god. It makes sense that in a Christian-dominated society with a Christian-dominated discourse most of the energy would be expended on the neighborhood god or what Jeanine Diller calls the "local theism." (See Chapter 5) However, unless we want to be cast in the role as merely the "local atheism"—which entirely misunderstands atheism as the absence and dismissal of *all* gods, not just Yahweh or Jehovah (and, on a good day, Allah)—we need to be aware of the staggering diversity of thoughts and opinions about god(s). More urgently, *theists* need to be aware of the staggering diversity of thoughts and opinions about god(s) and about their own god, many images of which would be unrecognizable and unpalatable to them.

This chapter is a service to atheists and theists alike, who have little appreciation of the wide and expanding range of ideas about god(s). Theologians and philosophers of religion are cranking out, and have long been cranking out, clever and cutting-edge descriptions and theories about the Christian god itself, in addition to building their apologetics repertoire to invent new arguments for that god, largely to cope with the sore fact that the traditional, conventional figure of god—to be frank—is no longer believable even to them. But short of the collapse of the standard personal interventionist god, humans have simply entertained all kinds of conceptions of what god(s) and theism might be like, limited only by their imagination, *since god(s) and theisms are purely a product of the imagination.* All of this spectacle, this desperate god-definition and god-creation, is as good an argument for atheism as anything that atheists could come up with.

Other Religions, Other Gods

We noted in Chapter 2 that for many educated professional atheists, atheism is (wrongly) portrayed as anti-monotheism, on the incredibly misguided premise that, as Cliteur puts it, theism means monotheism. To compound the confusion, he avers that atheism only contends with the "theistic god" (and presumably therefore with theistic theism!) as opposed to other kinds of gods. This is also false (although it may be an accurate enough description of mainstream Christian-oriented atheism), but it does raise consciousness that there *are* diverse kinds of gods in the world's religions.

The easiest and most obvious distinction to make is between monotheisms and polytheisms. Polytheisms posit a number of gods, usually with specific powers and portfolios, perhaps overseen or ruled by a supreme god. Almost all ancient theisms were polytheisms, as in Egypt, Greece, Rome, India, etc. Greek religion was chock full of gods (not always very nice beings), giving us the term "pantheon" for "all the gods," as were Egyptian, Roman, Norse, and other lesser-known pre-modern religions (like that of the Caroline Island of Ulithi with its high god Ialulep, god of sailors Ialulwe, god of canoe-builders Solang, trickster god Iolofath, and so on). None of this cornucopia of gods fits the description of the tri-omni god known and beloved by Christians and fellow theistic theists.

Hinduism is probably the most familiar living polytheism, commonly characterized as featuring three gods—Brahma the creator, Vishnu the protector, and Shiva the destroyer—but in actuality populated by an indefinite number of deities such as Saraswati (Brahma's wife), Ganesha, Agni, Indra, Durga, Kali, Lakshmi, Ganga (the Ganges River personified), Hanuman, Varuna the god of water, Bhaga the god of fortune, Surya the sun god, untold local gods, and the multiple incarnations or avatars of gods like Krishna. Plumbing below the surface of this multi-god theology, Hindus do not always worship all the gods—it would take too many hours and resources—but dedicate themselves to a specific god, a form of religion referred to as *henotheism*. Thus, individual "Hindus" may be practical devotees of Vishnu (Vishnavites), Shiva (Shivaites), or some lesser god like the excessively hungry and desirous goddess Gangamma.[1] Not satisfied with labeling Hinduism a polytheism because

---

[1] See Flueckiger, *When the World Becomes Female*.

of the complex relation between the gods and between gods and devotees, the eminent nineteenth-century linguist and religion scholar Max Müller coined the term *kathenotheism* (*kath' hena*, one at a time) for such a system that comprises many gods but ultimately understands and worships them as one. This reminds me of a joke or wisdom tale (it is often difficult to tell them apart) about a Hindu holy man who spent his life crisscrossing the continent counting gods; on his death bed he tallied up the results and concluded that the answer was "one."

Polytheisms are typically anathema to monotheisms: Islam castigates polytheism as *shirk*, sometimes translated as idolatry but more indicative of "association" or "equivalence," that is, associating or equating what is not god (i.e. other putative deities) with what is god (namely, the one true god, Allah). Yet, polytheisms pre-date monotheisms (it is sometimes asserted that the Egyptian pharaoh Akhenaton's fourteenth-century BCE worship of the sun god Aton was the first monotheism in history, but it was quickly erased by Egypt's polytheistic priests after his death), and they are also more cognitively digestible than monotheism. A god of circumscribed power for each plant, animal, or natural feature or force makes a kind of primitive sense, and it also sidesteps the "problem of evil," as no single god has the power or authority to control or prevent all the adverse events of the world. In a recent short but sophisticated essay Eric Steinhart defended polytheism for its "many metaphysically attractive features and merits."[2] Supposedly superior to the atheist (zero gods) or monotheist (one god) position, Steinhart's idiosyncratic *ordinal polytheism* contains an undetermined number of gods, ranked in order of increasing perfection; further, this brand of polytheism suggests multiple universes: "The result is a series of ranks of actual universes. Of course, one of those is our universe. Our universe is created by our local god."[3] He even believed that the gods of ordinal polytheism "can be modeled with mathematical precision: they can be modeled as necessarily existing computers that generate universes." Of course, none of this resembles any polytheism in practice, which entails multiple gods in *this* universe, but it does demonstrate the possibilities of theisms once we let our fancies take flight.

Whatever the religion, gods often if not always share the scene with all manner of supernatural beings, making it imprecise to call such religions "theisms" and rendering the gods themselves from relatively to mostly peripheral to the religion. Few if any of these gods have the traits of the Christian god. For instance, the Azande (central Africa) god Mboli

---

[2] Steinhart, "On the Number of Gods," 75.
[3] Steinhart, "On the Number of Gods," 81.

or Mbori is a remote deity with little moral interest in humans, and Azande society was much more concerned about witches than their god. The !Kung or Ju/hoansi bushmen of the Kalahari had a high god Gao Na and a lesser god Kauha, but the spirits of the ancestors were a more immediate problem. The gods (*kamuy*) of the Ainu people of northern Japan were associated with various natural sites (shore, sea, and sky) and species (bear, wolf, and fox). The Nuer (east Africa) "god" *kwoth* was simultaneously a being (the creator *cak ghaua*), numerous other beings (*kwoth nhial*, god of the sky and *kwoth piny*, god of the earth), and natural phenomena like rain and lightning. Theist debaters and apologists, theologians, and philosophers of religion seldom if ever comment on these gods.

Religions like those of the Ju/hoansi, the Ainu, the Nuer, and many more, including polytheisms, suggest that "god" might not be the best term for the local conception of powerful spirits. "God" is a Western Christian imposition on indigenous thought that implies a creator, a law-giver, and an immutable moral guarantor, which is not what many of these societies believe in. Another and preferable way to think about significant supernatural beings is found in Amazonian societies, who consider their major spirits to be not "gods" but *masters* or *owners* of various species, places, and forces. Thus we might envision the *kamuy* of bears, the *kwoth* of sky, Poseidon the "god" of sea, or Mars the "god" of war as the masters/owners of bears, sky, sea, or war, etc. with whom humans must interact and to whom we must defer.

Then there are religions like those of Australian Aboriginal societies that do not have gods at all, for whom "god" was not an indigenous or intelligible concept until Christianity arrived.

The Wild World of Christian Theisms

We might forgive ordinary theists for ignoring this thicket of theisms and their gaggle of gods. On the other hand, we should not forgive scholars of religion their ignorance of their own subject-matter—or perhaps we should expose them as the partisan defenders of *one particular* favored theism and not serious scholars of religion at all. Worse, not only have Christian thinkers practiced a studied myopia about religion and god(s), but within that confined space they have devised more species of theism than most theists and atheists would ever imagine.

To put it bluntly, not all Western Christian-inspired scholars have accepted that there is a single personalistic "theistic" god. Baruch Spinoza is the most famous example. A seventeenth-century Talmudic-trained

Jewish thinker influenced by the classical Greek philosophical concept of "substance," Spinoza came to contend that there was one god but that it was not a person separate from the universe. Aristotle used the term substance (literally, stand-under) to designate the matter or form of which a thing is made, which makes it unique. Classical Christian theology (e.g. Thomas Aquinas) held that the Christian god was the (necessary) ground on which the (contingent) material universe stands, and Spinoza resolved these two viewpoints by declaring that there is only one substance in reality, which is both God and the material universe. As philosopher Michael Levine explains the position, for Spinoza,

> there exists one and only one particular substance which he refers to as "God or nature"; the individual thing referred to as "God" is one and the same object as the complex unit referred to as "nature" or "the cosmos." On such a scheme the finite things of the world are thought of as something like parts of the one great substance, although the terminology of parts is somewhat problematic. Parts are relatively autonomous from the whole and from each other, and Spinoza's preferred terminology of modes, which are to be understood as more like properties, is chosen to rectify this.[4]

This philosophy or theology, which to summarize it very simplistically maintains that all is God and God is all, is called *pantheism* (*pan-*, all + *theos*). Like polytheism for Steinhart it eliminated the problem of evil but it also, in Spinoza's thinking, eliminated a personal god who loves and cares for us. Not terribly surprisingly, Spinoza was detested as an atheist by contemporary Christian scholars, a case of defamatory or accusatory atheism as discussed in Chapter 2.

Of course, not every instantiation of pantheism follows Spinoza's logic, but at the far opposite end of the spectrum from his oneness of god and nature is an infinity of gods or *apeirotheism* (*apeiros*, infinite). Thomas Davidson advocated for apeirotheism in the late nineteenth century on the basis of the notion of an infinite number of substances, something like Leibniz's or Alfred North Whitehead's theory of monads or conscious sentient points in space-time. For Davidson, this thing called god was not diffused through the universe as in Spinoza but was present and concentrated in each monad/point, making reality a "society of gods."

Prior to his adoption of apeirotheism, Davidson had dabbled with *panentheism* (*pan-*, all + *en-*, in), the idea that "all is in god" but not, unlike Spinoza's pantheism, that all is identical to god. Coined by Karl Christian

---

[4] Levine, "Pantheism."

Friedrich Krause also in the nineteenth century (a very fertile period indeed for birthing new theisms), panentheism means that

> the non-divine individuals are included in God, are fully within the divine life. God knows all that exists without externality, mediation, or loss (though God's knowledge and valuation are more than the creaturely experiences that are wholly included in the divine experience). God empowers all that exists without externality, mediation, or loss (though there is genuine indeterminacy and freedom of choice and action which God empowers in the creaturely realm). This is in contrast to traditional theism, which has tended to regard God as utterly distinct from the creation and the creatures.[5]

For a truly abstruse theological concept, panentheism has received considerable attention, particularly in the last decade or so. In their edited volume, Loriliai Biernacki and Philip Clayton and their contributors find it spread across religious traditions from Judaism and Islam to Hinduism, Buddhism, Confucianism, and Jainism; Biernacki goes so far as to promote panentheism as a tool "to help us imagine God for the twenty-first century" and to ponder "how God might be interwoven into our messy reality down here, how we might find a materialist God in our world of matter and morality."[6]

Elizabeth Burns finesses panentheism by offering a "conjoined panentheism" that construes the deity as two forms or modes (whatever that means), namely "God the World" and "God the Good." In her system,

> "God the World" captures the notion that the totality of everything which exists is "in" God, while acknowledging that, given evil and suffering, not everything is "of" God. "God the Good" encompasses the idea that God is also the universal concept of Goodness, akin to Plato's Form of the Good.[7]

Burns insists that her conjoined panentheism (is it a bi-theism?) not only restores personhood to its god, avoids the problem of evil (since the bad stuff in the world is conveniently not divine), and allows deity to grow and

---

[5] Nikkel, *Panentheism in Hartshorne and Tillich: A Creative Synthesis*, 4.

[6] Biernacki, "Introduction: Panentheism Outside the Box," 1.

[7] Burns, "How to Prove the Existence of God: An Argument for Conjoined Pantheism," 5. *The International Journal for Philosophy of Religion* dedicated an entire special issue (85, no. 1) to the topic of panentheism.

change with humans but somehow proves the existence of a god—although a god that few theists would recognize or worship.

Speaking of The Good (an idea that has plagued us since Plato), Janusz Salamon aims to solve the problem of religious diversity, the incompatible beliefs and conceptions of god(s) as well as other beings and forces across religions, by means of *agatheism*. Agatheism (*to agathon*, the good) simply stipulates that its god, also known as "the Ultimate Reality," is identical to the ultimate good. To make his point as (un)clear as possible, he explains that his brand of theism

> identifies the Ultimate Reality religiously conceived with the ultimate good which is postulated as a transcendental condition of our axiological consciousness through which we perceive and evaluate the goods at which our actions are aimed and towards which our hopes are directed. Agatheism conceives the Absolute as *Agatheos* by attributing to it first and foremost the characteristic of perfect goodness (but *not necessarily* all the other attributes of God of the Western classical theism, since "agatheism" it is [sic] a "thinner" concept than "theism," capturing the agathological core of a broad range of religious concepts of the Absolute).[8]

In this tour-de-force of theological sophistry, Salamon first invokes the view of "Ultimate Reality religiously conceived," a mysterious formulation since it does not define what "religiously conceived" means or what other kinds of conceptions might be available. Then he equates his god with goodness but "not necessarily" with the other traits ordinarily granted to the Christian god (such as power or knowledge or, for that matter, paternity), a "thin" or stripped-down god, for sure. Finally, he assumes that goodness is a widely shared trait of gods, which we know to be false; some gods are not good at all, some are indifferent or capricious, and some like those of the Piaroa or the Semai are nasty pieces of work. (See Chapters 1 and 5)

Since, as has been commented and complained since ancient times, divine goodness is problematically related to its other common traits (and contradicted by human experience), theists and theologians have had to concoct ingenious theisms to rescue their god(s) from contradiction. One proposal is *open theism*, which gives us a god who does not have total knowledge and control over humankind or the universe. James Rissler summarizes it as follows:

---

[8] Salamon, "Atheism and Agatheism," 201–2.

Because God loves us and desires that we freely choose to reciprocate His love, He has made His knowledge of, and plans for, the future conditional upon our actions. Though omniscient, God does not know what we will freely do in the future. Though omnipotent, He has chosen to invite us to freely collaborate with Him in governing and developing His creation, thereby also allowing us the freedom to thwart His hopes for us. God desires that each of us freely enter into a loving and dynamic personal relationship with Him, and He has therefore left it open to us to choose for or against His will.[9]

This view of a god is similar to the *created co-creator* theory of Philip Hefner, who would have us understand that the deity created humans who, as free creatures, in turn become co-creators of the god's creation, perhaps furthering the god's plan for existence and perhaps not.[10] Such a theology conveniently lets divinity off the hook for anything that goes badly, while elevating humans to a semi-divine status, as some critics have warned. Meanwhile, even advocates of open theism like Clark Pinnock, Richard Rice, John Sanders, William Hasker, and David Basinger in their 1994 book *The Openness of God* concede that, as Rissler puts it, "their view is at odds with the great majority of the Christian tradition" (the subtitle of their book, after all, is *A Biblical Challenge to the Traditional Understanding of God*).[11]

At the end of this road of divine impotence is *deism*, supposedly a popular opinion among America's founders. Deism answers one philosophical or metaphysical question—how did the universe come to be?—but eschews all other questions. The god of deism is often portrayed as the grand watchmaker, a craftsman who designed reality and then retired, even withdrew; having set the universe in motion, he/she/it does not participate or intervene in it. Such a god is obviously uninvolved in our day-to-day lives (for instance, does not answer prayers or perform miracles) and is amoral if not immoral (since remaining neutral to great injustices and evils is immoral in itself). Not to be outdone by the theists, some deists are *pandeists*, who hold that the creator-god *became* the universe after creation and is suspended in it like a statue (and thus incapable of subsequent action), or *polydeists*, who think that multiple gods collaborated in creation (although their distribution of labor is not always specified).

---

[9] Rissler, "Open Theism."
[10] Hefner, *The Human Factor: Evolution, Culture, and Religion*.
[11] Rissler, "Open Theism."

Given all this cacophony of theisms, why not cut out the middleman and anoint yourself a god? That is the claim behind *suitheism* (*sui-*, self) or *autotheism*. Self-deification is not a new idea—many ancient kings and emperors, as well as mystics throughout history, declared themselves divine—but the term "suitheism" is attributed to American spiritualist authors David Michael Cunningham and Traeonna Amanda R. Wagener in 2001. Their later book *Creating Magickal Entities* (which by the way does not use the term) teaches readers how to make spiritual entities or beings; they truly enough allow that "many gods and goddesses came into being as thought-forms personified," these human thoughts "slowly transformed into the gods and goddesses that we know today."[12] In the process of empowering inanimate objects by blowing, speaking, or singing on/to them, the authors elucidate that "you play a role of a god by 'breathing life' into the object."[13]

I Believe in God, but I Don't Know What God Is: Apophatic or Negative Theology

One point where all religions converge is in finding their purported beings and forces, and not only their gods, mysterious. Frankly, they have no choice in the matter, as the actions and wills of these supernatural phenomena are unpredictable, inscrutable, capricious, and utterly inconsistent with any alleged goodness or benevolence attributed to them (and as we have established, goodness and benevolence are *not* always attributed to them). It seems that anything we humans say about the supernatural realm is doomed to inadequacy if not futility; as the *Daodejing* (formerly *Tao Te Ching*) opens:

> The *dao* [the way] that can be described is not the eternal *Dao*.
> The name that can be spoken is not the eternal Name.
> The nameless is the boundary of Heaven and Earth.
> The named is the mother of creation.[14]

Understandably, the more grandiose the alleged nature of the beings or gods, the greater the problem of comprehending and discussing them. Words fail, and the finite human mind cannot grasp them. Some theologians of Christianity and similar theisms have resorted to the shrewd but craven step of surrendering any attempt to say what their god *is* and

---

[12] Cunningham with Ellwood and Wagener, *Creating Magickal Entities*, 10.
[13] Cunningham with Ellwood and Wagener, *Creating Magickal Entities*, 72.
[14] Lao Tzu, *Tao Te Ching*, 1.

instead turned to saying what he/she/it *is not*. This branch of theological (non)thought is known as *apophatic theology* or, reasonably, *negative theology*. Apophasis in general (from the Greek *apophemi*, to say no) is a rhetorical trick of broaching a subject by denying the subject or denying that it should be broached, for instance talking about it by asserting that you are not going to talk about it (e.g. a politician stating, "I am not going to speak about my opponent's drinking problem"). In his insightful study on apophatic discourse or "what cannot be said"—not only in religion but in philosophy, literature, and art—William Franke expounded that apophatic or negative theology amounts to "the denial of all descriptions and attributes as predicated of God," either because our words are too small for the task of describing the ultimate reality or because we have no words for it at all.[15]

Franke found apophatic thought in ancient Neoplatonic philosophy, where the concept of the *via negative* or negative path "emerges as a way to render possible a discourse about transcendent realities, especially 'the One,' for which all positive expressions are found to be inadequate. It is possible to say only what the One is not, hence to talk about it only by negatives."[16] Plotinus, a Roman Neoplatonist, judged that the idea of the One or the Absolute "can be achieved only by negating all finite determinations and stripping away (*aphaeresis*) everything that is articulable and sayable."[17] Christianity lends itself easily to apophasis, since, despite all of the ink (and blood) spilled over arguments about its god's qualities (particularly the tri-omni qualities of perfect goodness, knowledge, and power), this god remains unknowable. Early Church father Tertullian (*Apologeticus*, section 17), for instance, opined:

That which is infinite is known only to itself. This is which gives some notion of God, while yet beyond all our conceptions—our very incapacity of fully grasping Him affords us the idea of what He really is. He is presented to our minds in His transcendent greatness, as at once known and unknown.

A century later, Cyril of Jerusalem reiterated, "We explain not what God is; but we honestly confess that we have no exact knowledge of Him; for on the subject of God, it is great knowledge to confess our want of knowledge."[18] (In other words, his is an "agnostic" or knowledgeless

---

[15] Franke, *On What Cannot Be Said*, 1.
[16] Franke, *On What Cannot Be Said*, 9.
[17] Franke, *On What Cannot Be Said*, 10.
[18] Cyril, *The Catechetical Lectures of S. Cyril, Archbishop of Jerusalem*, 60–61.

theism.) In the same catechetical lecture, Cyril stressed that this god "is unspeakable as to His beginning, and form, and nature" and that the many attempts at "delineation" of divinity "all have failed."[19] Six more centuries passed without any progress in comprehending their lord, John Scotus Erigena in the ninth century doubling down, "We do not know what God is. God Himself does not know what He is because He is not anything. Literally God *is not*, because He transcends being."[20] (Even God is agnostic about godness!) Apophatic theology received the endorsement of the Catholic Church in the Fourth Lateran Council of 1215, which announced that "between the Creator and the creature there cannot be a likeness so great that the unlikeness is not greater," rendering any comparison impossible and any language unusable (and complicating the scriptural claim that humankind is made in the god's image).[21] As for the august systematizer of Christian knowledge, Thomas Aquinas, Franke reckoned that he accepted "indescribability and even radical anonymity as necessary to God":

> Thomas's analogical language for talking about God is not one that in the end yields knowledge in any scientific sense. What words like "good," "wise," and "true" mean as applied to the perfections of God is completely beyond our comprehension.... Even Being, *esse*, as it exists in creatures, must be denied of God, with the result that "the Being of God is unknown" ("*Esse dei est ignotum*").[22]

Although Christian negative theology is the most interesting to atheists in Western Christian-dominated societies, most if not all religions have their apophatic traditions. Ancient Vedic Hinduism possessed a concept of *neti neti* ("not this, not that") which conveyed the inexpressibility of ultimate reality. Much of Buddhist philosophy and metaphysics is constructed on a foundation of negation and negation of negation: the *Madhyamaka* (middle way) thought of second-third century Buddhist scholar Nagarjuna negated every conceivable combination of traits, like real and unreal, leading to "the four negations," in this case "not real," "not unreal," "not both real and unreal," and "not neither real nor unreal."[23] Another strict monotheism, Islam, also has an apophatic stream; for the Mu'tazilite sect, according to tenth-century scholar Abu al-Hasan al-Ash'ari, Allah

---

[19] Cyril, *The Catechetical Lectures of S. Cyril*, 64.
[20] Quoted in Indick, *The Digital God*, 179.
[21] Medieval Sourcebook, "Twelfth Ecumenical Council: Lateran IV 1215."
[22] Franke, *On What Cannot Be Said*, 27.
[23] Lion's Roar Staff, "What Are the Four Negations?"

is neither body, ghost, corpse, form, flesh, blood, substance, nor accident and He is devoid of color, taste, smell, tactual traits, heat, cold, moistness, dryness, height, width, or depth ... He is indivisible ... and is not circumscribed by place or subject to time ... none of the attributes of the creature which involve contingency can be applied to Him ... He cannot be perceived by the senses or assimilated to mankind at all.[24]

The nature of apophatic speech is immanent in everyday Christian (non)understandings of their god. This being is commonly considered immortal (*not* mortal), immaterial (*not* material), invisible (*not visible*), immutable (*not* mutable or changing), infinite (*not* finite), and so forth—all merely negations of normal and necessary characteristics of real beings and objects. On the other hand, a second set of divine qualities is composed of ordinary adjectives that are exaggerated to infinity, like all-knowing (omniscient), all-good (omnibenevolent), and all-powerful (omnipotent). And other traits, such as "love," "a father," or "a being" in the first place, are attributed to the god without any clear sense of what they might mean in a supernatural context. In other words, when people use these words and ascribe these features to their god, they literally do not know what they are saying. In the face of such nonsense, Franke insisted, and David Kelsey concurs for his own reasons as we will see below, that silence is the proper response. If only theists would take their own advice.

I Believe in God, but I Hate God:
Misotheism

"Curse God and die," Job's wife counseled in reaction to the torments Yahweh allowed to be inflicted on her spouse (Job 2:9). Although he declined to do so, instead remaining faithful to his tormentor and abuser (see Chapter 6) as this cruel deity desired, if Job had followed his wife's recommendation he would have been the world's first recorded misotheist. *Misotheism* (from *miso-*, hatred), like misanthropy or misogyny, denotes hatred or contempt, in this case for a being whom one is expected and commanded to love and who, supposedly, loves and provides for you. Of course, misotheism assumes two questionable propositions—first, that a god exists and second, that this god is or should be lovable. A related term, *dystheism* (*dys-*, bad) presupposes that the god is not entirely good, or is entirely bad, in the first place. Like Descartes' (in his own mind, refuted) "evil genius," or more like the vile god of the Piaroa or the Semai, or

---

[24] Quoted in Aijaz, "Islamic Conceptions of Divinity," 120.

merely the imperfect and often troublesome gods of polytheistic religions—or the playful and sacrilegious trickster gods of many religions—there is often no expectation that a god will be good or should be revered and worshipped. Such gods also circumvent the problem of evil, since they never promised goodness.

Although the word "misotheism" has been in the English lexicon for a century or more (and occurs in ancient Greek writings as well), it was only in 2011 that Bernard Schweizer composed a wide-ranging but not faultless study (e.g. he got both antitheism and agnosticism wrong) of the subject, which he located more frequently in poetry and fiction than in religion. Noting that alternative terms include *theostuges* ("hateful to God," appearing in Paul's Epistle to the Romans), "passionate atheism" (a phrase of which I disapprove), or "metaphysical rebel" (in Camus), Schweizer characterized misotheism variously as hatred, contempt, hostility, condemnation, or anger toward the deity, which are not exactly the same things: one can be hostile, angry, or critical without necessarily being a hater. Notwithstanding the question of whether one has the *right* to be mad at or to demand a justification from a god (Yahweh certainly communicated his position that Job enjoyed no such right), what would make a believer irritated at his lord? Schweizer affirmed that generally misotheism "is a response to suffering, injustice, and disorder in a troubled world. Misotheists feel that humanity is the subject of divine carelessness or sadism, and they question God's love for humanity."[25] This attitude is summed up well by a passage from Zora Neale Hurston's *Their Eyes Were Watching God* (and not really liking what they saw), quoted by Schweizer:

> All gods who receive homage are cruel. All gods dispense suffering without reason. Otherwise, they would not be worshipped. Through indiscriminate suffering men know fear and fear is the most divine emotion. It is the stones for altars and the beginning of wisdom. Half gods are worshipped in wine and flowers. Real gods require blood.[26]

Similarly, poet Percy Shelley castigated a Greek god (and indirectly the Christian god) in his *Prometheus Unbound* (Act I, lines 83–87), accusing the divinity of culpability for "this world of woe/to whom all things of Earth and Heaven do bow/In fear and worship: all-prevailing foe!/I curse thee! Let a sufferer's curse/clasp thee...." More than a century later, after

---

[25] Schweizer, *Hating God: The Untold Story of Misotheism*, 8.
[26] Quoted in Schweizer, *Hating God*, 145.

the horrors of the concentration camps and gas chambers but addressing a pogrom in 1649, Elie Wiesel put the Judeo-Christian god on trial.[27]

It is quite clear from these excerpts and examples that, as Schweizer saw it, "a sense of divine injustice is a major factor contributing to the development of a misotheistic outlook."[28] For this situation to arise, three things must be true. First, a god must be believed in, and this god must be expected to be an agent of justice; accordingly, a misotheist cannot properly be an atheist (atheists are not, contrary to many biased opinions, "angry at god," since they do not accept the existence of any such being to direct anger at, although they may be pretty fed up with the god's followers), but a misotheist may eventually free herself from this belief and become an atheist.[29] Second, the potential misotheist is most likely, as Schweizer phrased it, "beholden to ideas of liberation and justice" ("beholden" sounding like the wrong word here), that is, motivated by different and higher moral principles than simply god-belief.[30] As Schweizer must grant, misotheists are essentially decent, moral people. Third, the future misotheist must be disappointed by the lack of anticipated justice and care from his putative god.

Delving deeper into the world of misotheism, Schweizer suggested three diverse types—agonistic, absolute, and political. Agonistic misotheism (*agon*, struggle/contest as in "protagonist" or "antagonist") is the condition of clinging to a god but struggling with that god's insufficiency, inactivity, or absence. Agonistic misotheists like Hurston and Wiesel grapple "with the understanding that God is not entirely competent and good, while resenting the need to praise and worship him":

These misotheists wish that they were wrong in their negative assessment of deity and would prefer God to be benevolent and caring after all. At the same time, they are racked with grave doubts, and they keep up a constant quarrel with God. I call this "agonistic misotheism" because this stance is characterized by an ongoing internal struggle and by the agony over one's negative relationship with God....

---

[27] Wiesel, *The Trial of God*.

[28] Schweizer, *Hating God*, 9.

[29] For the ethics of misotheism that conditionally accepts belief in god(s) only for the sake of argument, see Slade, "Failed to Death," 118–66.

[30] Schweizer, *Hating God*, 14.

Agonistic misotheists are torn between hope and despair; they suffer from their inability to believe in a good god, and they often seek refuge in the figure of Christ....[31]

On closer inspection, they do not "hate" their god but are bitterly disappointed in him/her/it and call upon their god to do better.

Absolute misotheism is associated with Shelley, English poet Algernon Charles Swinburne, *His Dark Materials* novelist Philip Pullman, and most explicitly with Nietzsche. Figures like these are not at all sad that the local god is such an abysmal failure; rather, they "exult in the demise of the deity." Although Nietzsche is renowned for his depiction of the terror and nihilism of a godless universe (see Chapter 1), he joins his fellow absolute misotheists in being, according to Schweizer,

rather triumphant and cheerful, especially when the demise of God is seen as the dawn of a new day (Nietzsche and Pullman) or when God's fall is an occasion for creative experiments with alternative gods (Swinburne)....[A]bsolute enemies of God differ from agonistic misotheists because they are not doubting, they are not trying to enter into a dialogue with God, and they are not secretly hoping to be proven wrong in the condemnation of God.[32]

While there may be a temporary experience of loss and disorientation, the disappearance of god(s) finally means freedom for humanity.

Political misotheism, lastly, links religion and god-belief with social hierarchies, systematic oppression, and "exploitative institutions." Political misotheists like Mikhail Bakunin, Pierre-Joseph Proudhon, and most famously Karl Marx treat the reigning god and religion as an enemy not only of reason or individual happiness and meaning but of public and political good, that is, of any attempt at "establishment of a just social order."[33] They do not delude themselves, though, that excising god(s) alone will automatically deliver equality and justice; indeed, in Marx's estimation, the withering of god(s) will be more an effect than a cause of the amelioration of human economic and political suffering.

As indicated, Schweizer opined that misotheism, or at least what he called "true misotheism," is "only imaginable in the context of a monotheistic religion."[34] Perhaps by *true*, he meant *thorough*, since in

---

[31] Schweizer, *Hating God*, 17.
[32] Schweizer, *Hating God*, 18.
[33] Schweizer, *Hating God*, 42.
[34] Schweizer, *Hating God*, 29.

polytheisms adherents may disdain one or more gods, worship one or more others, and ignore the rest. But there is no good reason to privilege a monopolistic god for love or hatred over pluralistic gods. The only factor that exposes a mono-god to greater and more pointed condemnation is that, as the sole ruler of the universe, he/she/it has no one to blame for his/her/its shortcomings but him/her/itself.

I Believe in God, but God is Useless: Anatheism

Schweizer was correct that many people, especially those who are well informed on human history, recent and ancient, have become deeply disillusioned with their god, a god who not only allows (as in the case of poor Job) or maybe perpetrates evil and injustice but who stood by and did nothing during the Holocaust and other great catastrophes and tragedies before and since. Some have dropped the illusion and entered the ranks—merrily, warily, or wearily—of the atheists. Others cling to the illusion, blithely forgiving their god for his/her/its ineptitude and callous indifference or searching for some "greater good" that can come from such suffering, or blind to the problem in the first place; they remain conventional theists. A curious bunch, however, has substituted the old illusion with a new one—the old illusion of a god who could help but did not with the new illusion of a god who couldn't help at all. Philosopher Richard Kearney named this fresh alternative *anatheism*.

Anatheism (*ana-*, back, backwards, again, anew) was proposed by Kearney as "a third way beyond the extremes of dogmatic theism and militant atheism."[35] (In response, first, I thought we already had a third way in the form of agnosticism, and second, is dogmatic theism the only kind of theism, and militant atheism the only kind of atheism? Are we not presented here with a false dilemma?) As his subtitle, *Returning to God After God*, expressed, anatheism is imagined as "another way of seeking and sounding the things we consider sacred but can never fully fathom or prove." But why do we need another seeking and sounding? It is because "we've given up" the old god.[36] And why did we give up the old god? It is because he let us down so miserably.

Although Kearney does not say it, one reason why so many people, including philosophers and theologians, have given up on god(s) is the same reason why others have turned into misotheists—frustration and disappointment with god(s). In fact, it might be preferable to call it

---

[35] Kearney, *Anatheism*, 3.
[36] Kearney, *Anatheism*, 3.

apogoiteusitheism (*apogoiteusi,* disappointment) or *eknevrismotheism* (*eknevrismos,* frustration) instead of misotheism, if those were not such unwieldy words. Kearney knew we could not go back to the pre-disenchantment, pre-failure god, but he also felt that we could not or should not go on without a god.

Kearney's anatheism, his "god after God," his "faith beyond faith" (all vacuous phrases to my ear) features two primary characteristics. First, it is not "faith" in the familiar, tired sense of confidence or certainty in the truth of one's theistic propositions. It is more of a "wager" with five components—imagination, humor, commitment, discernment, and hospitality. It is hard to argue against hospitality, although it has nothing fundamentally to do with god(s) or religion. Humor is in short supply in standard theism, although imagination is rampant (and not in a good way). Commitment is a quality of conventional faith, which leaves us with discernment, defined as "where we distinguish between a blind leap of faith and wise one. The wager of response is not irrational."[37] Isn't it?

While Kearney's wager leaves me cold, his second proposal makes me sad. To be brutally blunt, he pronounced that a key element of anatheism, of god after the traditional god, is "the *powerlessness* of the divine."[38] To drink this sour wine to the very bottom, he conceded that after the shocking and revolting events of the twentieth century, and the shocking and revolting silence of any god(s), the last remaining kind of theistic belief available to us is "the basic recognition that the only God worthy of belief is a vulnerable and powerless one who suffers with us and is incapable of being relieved from this suffering unless we act against injustice"; "Post-Holocaust faith does not believe that God could have stopped the torture—and didn't."[39] With an apparently straight face, Kearney asked us to endorse (1) that the formerly all-mighty, all-moral king of the universe is actually feeble and helpless, (2) that the best this being can do is "suffer with us," and (3) that such an entity is "worthy of belief." We can unite with him on one point, though: while anatheism is not atheism, "it does agree with enlightened atheism that the God of theodicy [i.e., the god who is susceptible to the problem of evil, since he allegedly has the ability and will to banish it] is dead."[40]

He does not use the term, but Yale theologian David Kelsey offers us another version of anatheism. His more recent effort to rescue an enfeebled god from the judgment of history is inspired by a specific

---

[37] Kearney, *Anatheism,* 44–45.
[38] Kearney, *Anatheism,* 52.
[39] Kearney, *Anatheism,* 61.
[40] Kearney, *Anatheism,* 167.

challenge faced by priests and pastors, that is, what to say to parishioners who have suffered a personal tragedy, such as the death of a loved one. The shepherds want to console their sheep, but he insists—and he is probably correct—that the customary nostrums doled out on these occasions are no help, may actually be hurtful, and are scripturally unsound. These religious platitudes include "It is all god's plan," "S/he is in a better place," or truly traumatizing things like "It is god's justice" or "S/he must have deserved it." Through four hundred pages of gobbledygook that only another theologian could love (or care about), Kelsey sermonizes on the true nature of the Christian god. First, he establishes the apophatic if not ignostic point that we cannot employ normal language to describe this god. (See Chapter 3) Common theological words like powerful or sovereign or providential "must be used analogically when attributed to God's intrinsic dynamic self-relating ... [W]e have no way to know just how such language means in relation to God's intrinsic reality."[41] So we don't know what (or "how") we mean when we call this god powerful or good or whatever, which makes saying such things futile. What we can say with certainty, he avows, is that his god's key quality—or as he puts it, what makes God *God*—is not power or goodness or sovereignty but *glory*, and to such glory, humans must (and must want to) prostrate; the best response of puny humans would be awed silence, but the next best response is praise.

Of this unspeakable and unknowable god, Kelsey also knows three more things. First, the god aspires to create, *ex nihilo*, "realities genuinely other than God" which are "in their finite ways" good, true, and beautiful. Deity's second goal is to "reconcile creatures to God when they are estranged," and his/her/its third and highest goal is "to glorify creatures eschatologically"[42] (all of this in a theology-speak that is utterly opaque to the uninitiated). To dim the light on concepts like "good," he claims that good is relative and that each "kind of being is inherently disposed to its own 'good,'" whatever that means (what, I wonder, is the good of a mosquito or a coronavirus?).[43] But why doesn't this god do what we understand as good for us or what we ask it to do? That, he responds, is a complete miscomprehension of what this god is. To ask "why" the god does something, or hesitates or refuses to do something, is to impose our expectations and demands on him/her/it. It is, he states directly, to assume that "God is 'useful' to creatures whose lived worlds are profoundly

---

[41] Kelsey, *Human Anguish and God's Power*, 97.
[42] Kelsey, *Human Anguish and God's Power*, 181.
[43] Kelsey, *Human Anguish and God's Power*, 191.

distorted by evils and the deep suffering they occasion."[44] Instead, we should grow up and accept "the Triune God as intrinsically 'useless'"—that is, he/she/it is not here for our benefit and use.[45] To return to Kelsey's original question, then, what should religious leaders tell their lambs in times of trouble? The answer is basically this: your anguish is "something that makes a difference to God because God resists it by freely being closer to us *as we are experiencing such suffering* than we can be to ourselves in the experience of suffering."[46] Who here finds that comforting or reassuring? God's right there with you, buddy, but he/she/it cannot and will not lift a holy finger to help. Such a god is verily useless, and for that, Kelsey concludes, we should praise his/her/its intrinsic glory.

How, I wonder, is a powerless god, a useless god, better than no god at all? From there, it seems like a small step, and a more cognitively and emotionally satisfying step, to just relinquish the whole god-concept.

I Believe in God, but God Is Dead: "Christian Atheism" or Death of God Theology

Nietzsche announced it in the 1880s: God is dead. Not many theologians, or regular theists, took much notice of the announcement (which is as Nietzsche predicted: it was not yet time to hear the news). But as Kearney echoed more than a century later, God—or at least some god or somebody's idea of god—"died in Auschwitz," a god who could not and would not end genocide, and good riddance to him.[47] Half a century before Kearney, without the benefit of the word "anatheism," liberal/existentialist theologian Paul Tillich also reported the death of "the God of theological theism," that is, the kind of god that regular theists believe in, the being who knows all and rules all, the "invincible tyrant" who sits on the throne of heaven and makes the decisions that determine our lives. This is the god who had died, or who had been killed, and whom "Nietzsche said had to be killed because nobody can tolerate being made into a mere object of absolute knowledge and absolute control," especially when that knowledge and control behooves us not.[48]

Soon after Tillich realized that "God has disappeared in the anxiety of doubt,"[49] and seventy years after Nietzsche's madman

---

[44] Kelsey, *Human Anguish and God's Power*, 369.
[45] Kelsey, *Human Anguish and God's Power*, 367.
[46] Kelsey, *Human Anguish and God's Power*, 359.
[47] Kearney, *Anatheism*, 61.
[48] Tillich, *The Courage to Be*, 185.
[49] Tillich, *The Courage to Be*, 190.

proclaimed God's demise, a movement emerged within Christianity that revealed that the impact of Nietzsche's message had sunk in. Known as "death of God theology," one of its earliest voices was Gabriel Vahanian, whose 1957 *The Death of God: The Culture of Our Post-Christian Era* argued that the modern world has a "cultural incapacity for God." (This idea is reminiscent of founding sociologist Max Weber's theory of secularization, namely, that modern society with its urbanization, industrialization, bureaucracy, and rationalization had become infertile soil for religion, leading to "disenchantment" or the evaporation of spiritual interest and practice from modern life.) According to Vahanian, it was the very "cultural tradition of Christianity" which had ironically "bequeathed us the idea of the death of God."[50] God had disintegrated under a barrage of materialism and "immanentism," that is, focus on the worldly here-and-now, but also under the strain of "religiosity," which is some benighted version of religion. He affirmed, "God's death is not accidental. It belongs wholly to, and is grounded in, man's natural inclination to religiosity," which I suppose refers to the impulse to congregate in churches, pray and worship, and anthropomorphize our god(s), in other words, to dream that he/she/it/they listen and care.

Accordingly, Vahanian blamed much of the fault of religiosity and its toxicity to his god on "organized religion." When Christianity is organized it is "less apt than when it is not organized to inform and transform genuinely and creatively" the individuals and societies where it resides; "Where Christianity became organized, it almost immediately arrogated to itself what rightly belonged to culture and to the sphere of the secular," not least power and truth."[51] Church-based Christianity, he thundered, "does not transform the world, but enslaves it."[52] We could hardly disagree.

Prior to the modern age, those who railed against Christianity were, in Vahanian's estimation, *anti-Christian*. Now, we are "not even anti-Christian"; we are already *post-Christian*, inhabiting a world that is "impervious to the conception of Christianity," that is blind and deaf to the religion's entreaties, that finds its claims and its language "unnatural."[53] This is what he meant by today's "radical immanentism" resulting in "a cultural and religious incapacity for God."[54]

---

[50] Vahanian, *The Death of God*, 230.
[51] Vahanian, *The Death of God*, 8.
[52] Vahanian, *The Death of God*, 9.
[53] Vahanian, *The Death of God*, 140, 146.
[54] Vahanian, *The Death of God*, 190.

Before we get too excited about this shift in theology, we should remember that gods are obstinate and labile things, with a way of coming back to life after they have been slain. Indeed, while prideful Christian theologians like Thomas Altizer like to think that their religion is unique and superior because its god died and resurrected, in fact, the world's mythology is replete with dying gods such as Dionysus, Tammuz, Zalmoxis, Baal, Osiris, and Inanna, many of whom rose from the dead—the Sumerian goddess Inanna (awkwardly for Christianity) after three days.

So, the death of the Christian god is not as fatal a blow to the religion as we might expect and wish. This is what Altizer, one of the most influential death-of-God theologians, told us less than a decade after Vahanian. Altizer's key book, *The Gospel of Christian Atheism*, boldly stated that Christianity could endure just fine with a dead god. Indeed, the whole edifice of Christianity stands on a foundation of the death of its god—well, the death of a material mortal copy of its god. But it is somewhat more problematic and paradoxical to insist that an "honest Christian must admit that the God he worships exists only in the past." More extravagantly, this honest Christian should not mourn the vanquished deity but celebrate "the gospel, the good news of the glad tidings, of the death of God," and should actually will this death.[55] At the extreme, "the proclamation of the death of God is a Christian confession of faith."[56]

How, then, does Christianity carry on without its god? The answer for Altizer and some other death-of-God theologians is that this god died once already and was just fine. The incarnation of Yahweh as Jesus was a negation of the god's self, as was the crucifixion of Jesus (the god's literal if temporary death) and in a sense the original act of creation in Genesis, when the god negated himself by creating that which was not-god. In other words, "The death of God in Christ is an inevitable consequence of the movement of God into the World, of Spirit into flesh."[57]

But there is more at stake here. First, the pre-incarnation god, the Old Testament god, died or ceased to exist when Jesus was born. That god of (admittedly imperfect) justice and law was replaced by a god of love. (Is it the same god? The question has no answer because it is gibberish.) Second, the incarnated god, the Jesus-god, the Father-in-the-Son, died too or rather repeatedly dies, born again into and for each new era. The so-called "God of faith," meaning the god believed in and worshipped by any

---

[55] Altizer, *The Gospel of Christian Atheism*, 15.
[56] Altizer, *The Gospel of Christian Atheism*, 102.
[57] Altizer, *The Gospel of Christian Atheism*, 110.

particular age, church, or culture, "so far from being unchanging and unmoving is a perpetual and forward-moving process of self-negation, pure negativity, or kenotic metamorphosis."[58] (Kenosis is a theological term referring to the "self-emptying" of Jesus to make way for the spirit and will of his father-god.) Hence, the death of god is really not, for Altizer, an atheist's boast; rather, "Only the Christian can truly speak of the death of god, because the Christian alone knows the God who negates himself in his own revelatory and redemptive acts."[59]

This is all very interesting theoretically, but it has some remarkably practical ramifications. First, death-of-God theology or Christian atheism depicts a very different kind of god from the one that the masses venerate. Whatever remains after the god's death (the remains or corpse of the dead divinity), it is not the "celestial and transcendent Lord," the benevolent white-haired grandfather in the sky that most acolytes and preachers envision. It is a very alien and unconsoling god, often a highly impersonal god, deprived of most or all its personal qualities—stripped down to a "ground of being" or "ultimate concern" without feelings or action-potentials. Second, both Vahanian and Altizer concluded that, like the conventional god, the conventional church has run its course. Vahanian was explicit that churchly, ecclesiastical, or organized Christianity is dead on arrival, since it tries in vain to freeze in institutional form an ever-adapting—dare we say, evolving—god. Altizer too reckoned that the faithful should part with "the established form of faith" and "confess the death of God and give himself to a quest for a whole new form of faith," which is why he recognized his project as a radical theology, a revolution in Christianity.[60] Nor could it be a one-time revolution but rather a continuous one, permanently erecting and tearing down religious structures as relentlessly and adamantly as any Marxist or Nietzschean. This included, incredibly, moral structures and supposed moral truths that most Christians, and some New Atheists, still cling to. The radical death-of-God Christian, the Christian atheist,

> will sacrifice an established Christian meaning and morality, abandoning all those moral laws which the Christian Church has sanctioned, and perhaps even negating the possibility of an explicitly Christian moral judgment. Certainly he will be forced to renounce every moral imperative with a transcendent ground, and this means that he must foreswear the possibility of an absolute moral law, and at

---

[58] Altizer, *The Gospel of Christian Atheism*, 84.
[59] Altizer, *The Gospel of Christian Atheism*, 102.
[60] Altizer, *The Gospel of Christian Atheism*, 147.

best look upon all forms of moral judgment as penultimate ways which must inevitably act as barriers to the full realization of energy and life.[61]

It is hard to see how the death-of-God Christian is fundamentally different from the existentialist atheist when, after "the death of the Christian God, every transcendent ground is removed from all consciousness and experience, and humanity is hurled into a new and absolute immanence," where nothing survives of this god except a fading echo of his/her/its name.[62]

Conclusion:
Farewell to a God We Never Knew

What is a twenty-first-century atheist—or theist, for that matter—to make of the stunning contortions in theism and theology? A few salient and inescapable points emerge. First, there has never been any consensus across religions on the number or nature of god(s). There is, in a word, no such thing as *theism* but only many incongruous and clashing *theisms*, along with other religions that are *not* theisms. The Christian god him/her/itself has been imagined in myriad ways, not only as a big person who loves and judges us but as an entity or phenomenon that is one with the material universe, or somehow "in" the material universe or bearing the universe "in" him/her/it, or an inert amoral creator, or the human self-deified. Numerous scholars and mystics have renounced the attempt to understand their god at all, resorting to negative statements about what he/she/it is not—and usually arriving at the position that their god is not like anything and is finally unknowable (i.e., theological agnosticism). In theology for the twentieth century and beyond, imbibing existentialism and death-of-God philosophy and living through the categorically ungodly history of two world wars and many more disasters, injustices, and genocides, some sensitive souls have shaken their fists at their god, denouncing him/her/it for culpability in the suffering and death of millions of allegedly beloved creatures. Some have reasoned that the only kind of god that could probably exist is a drastically emasculated one, a powerless and useless deity who can be forgiven, and should for some unfathomable reason still be praised, for his/he/its inability to help us or save us in any way. A few have crept up to the precipice of atheism, admitting that their

---

[61] Altizer, *The Gospel of Christian Atheism*, 147.
[62] Altizer, *The Gospel of Christian Atheism*, 150.

god, or the god they thought they knew and that ordinary folks believe in, is gone.

Second, it is obvious that theology and theism, philosophy and piety, have wandered very far apart, meaning that the god of the academic theologians and philosophers of religion has long left behind the god of the commoners in the Divine Kingdom, of the lowly serfs of the Heavenly Demesne. The plebeians largely persist in believing in a holy being, a person, one who dispenses justice, hears and answers prayers, performs miracles, and generally gives a damn about humanity and our world. And there are still plebeian theologians and preachers out there, who peddle the bankrupt god. For more discerning types, though, that kind of god is no longer possible, no longer believable. To preserve the idea, or merely the word, "god," they have so truncated and evacuated the god-concept as to make it foreign if not offensive to ordinary church-goers. But then the most radical theologians advised Christians to exit their churches anyhow.

In a word, the most significant movements in theology have told the vast majority of Christians that god is not what they believe. If lay Christians read their erudite volumes, what they would hear is, "You are wrong about your religion. The god you believe in does not exist, and maybe never did."

Third and lastly, it strikes us that anatheism or death-of-God theism—which is arguably the only kind of theism that has any purchase in the contemporary world—not only offers no advantages over atheism (except prolonging the agonizing passing of god) and is hardly different from atheism. An unknowable god and no god are indistinguishable, and a powerless, useless, or dead god is good for nothing. Followers may still call themselves Christian, but they are alone in the cosmos, as condemned by freedom to create their own morality and their own institutions—even their own god—as any existentialist or "strong atheist" like Sartre or Camus. (See Chapter 1) To them I say, go ahead and take the final step, shed the empty carcass of god. You literally have nothing left to lose.

To the old-fashioned theists who refuse to let go of their medieval or ancient image of their god or have not yet heard the news that this god is dead and no longer believable, I say this: we atheists will not debate with you until you all—across Christian sects and denominations, across monotheisms, and across theisms—can settle on some version of god. Until then, we do not know what you are talking about when you say "god," and neither do you. Come to some resolution with each other first, then we can talk.

This should buy us an extended (if not eternal!) respite from god-debates.

5

Anti-Theism:
On Preferring To Be Rid Of God(s)

If god(s) did exist, would it be reasonable to prefer that he/she/it/they did not? If we had the choice, would we want a life under the thumb of god(s) or one free of god(s)?

In 2011 Guy Kahane published an influential essay posing the provocative question, "Should we want God to exist?" His launching point was an offhand comment by Thomas Nagel in his 1997 book *The Last Word*, to the effect that, "I hope there is no God! I don't want there to be a God; I don't want the universe to be like that."[1] Kahane reckoned that Nagel did not so much reject the possibility of a god like Yahweh as actually dread it; it was not that he disbelieved in such a god but fervently hoped it was not real.

Kahane insisted that Nagel's position is not equivalent to atheism, at least not the ordinary kind of atheism. In fact, Nagel's emotional objection to god(s) makes the most sense if a god does exist; if there is no such thing, then there is nothing to object to. Kahane labeled this view "anti-theism" because it is not a claim about the existence of god(s) or the truth of any particular religion; rather it is a statement of choice or preference—the choice or preference that god(s) not exist. He contended that "a theist *could* be an anti-theist"; indeed, we might argue that *only* a theist could be an anti-theist (or a misotheist, as in the previous chapter), since anti-theism presupposes some god(s) to wish not to exist. (Presumably, most if not almost all atheists are also satisfied with the non-existence of god[s], although a tiny minority might grieve the lack of divinity while simply being unable to accept the notion.)

Kahane's task was to ask how anyone, given that the conventional image of a god is all-good, all-knowing, and all-powerful (the famous "tri-omni" god of omnibenevolence, omniscience, and omnipotence), could rationally not want such a being in the world. The claim as he saw it was that "if God exists—or, if God had existed—things would be worse" than

---

[1] Nagel, *The Last Word*, 130.

they would be without a deity.[2] Expanding on the point, Kahane offered that anti-theists do not posit that a god is or must be evil (although that would be sufficient reason to not want it) but that

> it would be bad (or at least worse) if God *exists*. They claim that *despite* His supreme goodness it would be worse if He exists. God's existence must therefore be worse in a way *compatible* with His omnibenevolence and perfect goodness, indeed with His omniscience and omnipotence. It must be an *unavoidable logical consequence* of His very existence. It cannot be something God could be blamed for, if He does exist.[3]

Kahane thus searched for a justifiable basis to choose a world without god(s), which hinged on the notion of a better or worse world with god(s) in it. However, better and worse, or good and bad, are always and necessarily relative, that is, things are better or worse *for someone*, and things can be a little better/worse or much better/worse without being perfectly wonderful or perfectly terrible. He perceived two ways to weigh the evidence. First, the existence of god(s) might be better or worse for me or some other individual "personally"; alternatively, god(s) in the world might be better or worse "impersonally," that is, "overall" (in his words) or collectively for most or all human beings (and possibly non-human beings as well). Without much effort, he established that, "If you believe God does exist, you should also feel a touch of regret; if you believe He doesn't, you should feel at least some relief."[4]

Even so, Kahane concluded that it was probably better impersonally or collectively if the familiar god exists than not. I find this conclusion dubious, if only because I do not know how to assign the comparative merits of god(s) for different kinds of humans and other beings. For instance, if there is anything like the Christian god in the universe, then the vast majority of humans who ever lived will suffer eternally in hell for not believing in him/her/it, not to mention the sentient beings on other planets who may have never heard the good news or have rejected it (if, say, human missionaries reached them or an extraterrestrial savior visited them). On the other hand, no such god, no eternal torment. How do we total up the good and the bad "overall"? And since, if such a god exists, we do not know what the world would be like without him/her/it, it is difficult to determine the desirability of such a world—

---

[2] Kahane, "Should We Want God to Exist?" 680.
[3] Kahane, "Should We Want God to Exist?" 680.
[4] Kahane, "Should We Want God to Exist?" 687.

although it is hard to fathom that it could be much worse than the one we know.

Ultimately, since no one inhabits an impersonal standpoint anyhow, this problem does not detain us for long. Kahane agreed, asserting that "anti-theism's prospects are better if it is understood as a claim made from the *personal* standpoint" such that "It would be far worse *for me* if God exists than if He does not."[5] This transcends the trivial observation that evil-doers would much prefer not to be punished for their evil deeds or that atheists would much prefer not to be punished for their disbelief (although that is true too!). More soberly, Kahane considered that a god like the Abrahamic god "places an unreasonable burden on human good—that it is *too demanding*":

> Suppose, for example, that only in a world where God doesn't exist can we be fully independent, or enjoy complete privacy. The anti-theist could try to argue that the loss of such good is too demanding—so demanding that we could reasonably prefer God not to exist, even if this would also make the world significantly worse.[6]

Independence and privacy are two real considerations: in a god-filled world, we could never be the genuine authors of our own lives and values, and we could never feel genuinely alone, some god (like a supernatural Santa Claus) always knowing if we're sleeping or awake, bad or good. Worse, such a god imposes a virtually impossible standard of good and bad, one that we can never meet, leading us to feel like perpetual failures and inherent wretches.

Kahane also proposed that "the very existence of God might compromise our dignity as rational beings." One conceivable affront to our rationality is the requirement to believe things that are patently absurd or at best unproven and unprovable. Another might be the demand to accept that the injustices in this world will be rectified in some future afterworld. And we might wonder why such a god gave us free will in the first place (if such exists) only to penalize us for using it. Such a god deprives us of crucial amounts of freedom, the freedom to think and the freedom to act. And of course, it insults our dignity to think that we are as little children for the entire span of our time on earth. Most damning, Kahane countered a common theist objection: "Theists sometimes claim that if God does not exist, life has no meaning. I am now suggesting that

---

[5] Kahane, "Should We Want God to Exist?" 688.
[6] Kahane, "Should We Want God to Exist?" 688.

if God does exist, the life of at least some would lose its meaning."[7] Some lives "would be made absurd by His existence," leaving his creatures no better off than in the existentialist nightmare of Sartre or Camus.[8] (See Chapter 1) In the end, Kahane stated that anti-theism from a personal standpoint is rational and defensible:

> We could defend it either by showing that God's existence would make such demands on our good that it would not be reasonable to expect us to prefer it, or, more promisingly, by showing that it would undermine the life projects that give meaning to the lives of at least some of us....Nagel's hope is intelligible, and could well be correct. I do not pretend to have given conclusive grounds for hoping that God does not exist. I do think, however, that I have given enough reason to doubt that we should want God to exist.[9]

The Prehistory of Anti-Theism

Kahane did not invent the idea of anti-theism but re-introduced the term, because it existed prior to his essay, although often with a quite different meaning. For instance, in a 1993 article Christopher New used it (in the form of "antitheism" without the hyphen) to denote belief in a negative or opposite deity, in the sense of "anti-Christ" versus Christ—which, amusingly but consequentially, he insisted was defensible with the same arguments marshalled for theism if not more effectively so. The only reason, he opined, why philosophers, theologians, apologists, and lay theists defend theism instead of antitheism is that they prefer a "comforting" good god over a threatening evil one (unless, presumably, one is a Satanist).[10] Three years before Kahane, Stefan Baumrin resurrected the term with yet another definition, asserting that an antitheist "is one who actually espouses atheism and would try to convince theists of the error of their ways."[11] In other words, for Baumrin antitheism was aggressive or proselytizing atheism, mobilized to resist and undo theism because of theism's "evident evils."[12] This is actually a very serviceable alternative definition and certainly a valid description of many atheists.

---

[7] Kahane, "Should We Want God to Exist?" 691–92.
[8] Kahane, "Should We Want God to Exist?" 692.
[9] Kahane, "Should We Want God to Exist?" 693–94.
[10] New, "Antitheism: A Reflection."
[11] Baumrin, "Antitheism and Morality," 73.
[12] Baumrin, "Antitheism and Morality," 74.

Apparently, the word predates even these usages, reaching back to the 1830s when the *Oxford English Dictionary* defined an anti-theist as "one opposed to belief in the existence of a god." In an 1877 lecture, University of Edinburgh professor of divinity Robert Flint gave anti-theism its most capacious meaning, applying it to anything that diverges from Christian monotheism:

> Polytheism is not atheism, for it does not deny that there is a deity; but it is anti-theistic since it denies that there is only one. Pantheism is not atheism, for it asserts that there is a god; but it is anti-theism, for it denies that God is a being distinct from creation and possessed of such attributes as wisdom, and holiness, and love. Every theory which refuses to ascribe to a god an attribute which is essential to a worthy conception of its character is anti-theistic.[13]

It is typically incoherent and constipated Christian thinking to denigrate a rival theism like polytheism (which has theism in the name) as anti-theism because it does not conform to Christianity's specific variety of theism.

I raise these previous citations and definitions because they are important to the case. Kahane may have inaugurated the contemporary analysis and debate on anti-theism, but we are not beholden to his particular construction of it. I will make two fundamental contentions in this chapter. The first is that the literature on anti-theism, like philosophy of religion as a whole, is far too enmeshed with Christianity. (See Chapter 8) This is conspicuous, for instance, in Kahane's use of "God" with a capital G and capitalized "He" and "Him," as well as the apt observation of Kraay and Dragos that Kahane does not define theism, probably because he presumed no need to: aren't we all talking about the Judeo-Christian god? No doubt Kahane would have accepted a definition like the one that Kraay and Drago put forward: "There necessarily exists a being, God, who is essentially omnipotent, omniscient, and perfectly good, and who is the creator and sustainer of all that (contingently) is," the standard tri-omni god.[14] This echoes Richard Swinburne's classic and more complete definition of God as "a person without a body (i.e., a spirit) present everywhere, the creator and sustainer of the universe, able to do everything (i.e., omnipotent), knowing all things, perfectly good, a source of moral obligation, immutable, eternal, a necessary being, holy and worthy of worship."[15] What Swinburne and his proponents fail to grasp is

---

[13] Flint, *Anti-Theistic Theories: Being the Baird Lecture for 1877*, 23.
[14] Kraay and Dragos, "On Preferring God's Non-Existence," 159.
[15] Swinburne, *The Coherence of Theism*, 2.

that this is not a definition at all but rather *a description of a particular god, namely the Christian—or to be charitable, the Abrahamic—god*. (See Chapter 3 on god and God)

Even the slightest amount of cross-cultural knowledge of religions, the sort that theologians and philosophers of religion should possess, establishes firmly that the attributes ascribed to the Abrahamic god are not universally ascribed to the gods of the world. Not all gods, for instance, are creators of the universe; some, like Zeus or Thor, are second or third-generation gods, born long after the universe began. Gods also die, demonstrating that they are not necessarily eternal. Nor are all gods perfectly good or morally obligatory; Zeus again was something of a scalawag, the Azande (central Africa) god Mbori or Mboli was morally indifferent to humans, and Loki was a trickster god. Many gods, as we will learn below, were not considered holy (indeed, the very concept of "holy" is absent in many societies) or worthy of worship, including Loki. Finally, it is not altogether clear what distinguishes a god from other spirits, such as nature spirits or ancestor spirits; in many religions, dead humans may become gods. And of course, not all religions included gods in the first place.

Accordingly, we cannot approach the question of anti-theism with the false binary of the Christian/Abrahamic god versus not-god, a specious dichotomy that infects not only theology and philosophy of religion (which is essentially Christian theology and philosophy of Christianity) but also much of Western atheism, which jousts almost exclusively with the Christian god. It is fine for those who would narrow anti-theism to anti-Christian-god (and theism, like Flint, to pro-Christian-god), but as scholars and social scientists our ambitions must be more informed and inclusive. A diminishingly small number of interlocutors seem to understand this issue, like Michael Tooley who separates theism from monotheism, the latter "defined in terms of the deity of some particular religion"—a "trivial" distinction to Tooley, but not to us, which even he appreciates compromises "the best discussions of the pro-theism versus anti-theism issue."[16] Tooley also mentions Buddhism in passing, granting significantly that Buddhism affords us a view of a "godless world" but yet a morally rigorous and intellectually sufficient—in other words, a very habitable—world.

My second contention follows from Nagel's visceral reaction to god(s) and religion and more so from Toby Betenson's "recasting" of anti-theism. Betenson asserts, properly I think, that anti-theism "should be understood in terms of reasonable preferences that are not necessarily

---

[16] Tooley, "Axiology: Theism Versus Widely Accepted Monotheisms," 46.

connected to rational judgments about the comparative value of possible worlds."[17] In other words—and this is why the present chapter begins as it does—evaluations of better or worse worlds are just one way to approach the anti-/pro-theism question. But I take this cue a step further. Evaluations—or as some scholars including Kraay and Dragos have expressed it, *preferences*—need not be and frequently and perhaps inherently are not "rational"; at the very least, they are not *objective*, as all evaluations are relative to some standard of value, and different individuals, groups, and societies operate with different standards of value. *My* reason for preferring not-god(s) might differ from someone else's preference for not-god(s) and not at all conform to the value-standard of a pro-theist. That is to say, what I think is a worse world might not be a worse world to another person. But, unless my values and reasoning are utterly flippant and contradictory, they cannot be legitimately criticized by someone else who happens not to share them.

Ultimately, I hold that the basic Kahanian test of better/worse worlds is incomplete; all that it offers is disputes about what world one values (for instance, one with total human privacy and autonomy or one without). What I want to illustrate in the rest of this chapter, then, is that there are many reasons why someone might and does prefer not this god or the other or any god whatsoever. Phrased differently, a person may take an anti-theist stance for diverse reasons and does not have to pass a litmus test administered by Christian (pro-)theists to justify that stance. And since preferences are not matters of truth but matters of value at best or of taste and tradition at worst, they are not necessarily subject to verification or falsification.

On Preferring Not the Local God

As already noted, conventional debates about anti-theism assume almost universally that the god in dispute is the Christian (again, we could say Abrahamic, but honestly, few philosophers are thinking of Judaism or Islam, let alone Baha'i or Sikhism) god. Further, they tend to postulate that this god manifests certain virtuous qualities like goodness and knowledge; analysts are often thus flabbergasted that anyone could not want this being. But we understand now that their god is not the only target of anti-theist inclinations and that not all local gods own such sterling traits. People in other societies where other gods reign struggle with those gods and sometimes wish they would go away.

---

[17] Betenson, "Recasting Anti-Theism," 164.

Two ethnographic cases illustrate the point, both in famously nonviolent societies. The Semai of Malaysia are renowned as perhaps the most peaceful people in the world, which would seem to be an unambiguously good thing. However, Robert Knox Dentan reckoned that their nonviolence was better viewed as passivity and "surrender" to their relations with violent neighboring and dominant societies marked by cruelty and brutality, including killing and enslaving Semai. Semai nonviolence, in a word, was learned and strategic helplessness. In the best tradition of cultural holism, in which religion reflects social realities, Dentan explained that Semai theology (if we can use that term) "displays and reinforces a sense of terrorized helplessness learned from the experience of slaving, slavery, and general cruelty."[18] The Semai deity was accordingly represented by or present in the thunder squall, which like an invisible enemy erupts unexpectedly and aggressively. More explicitly, they described their god as "a stupid, incontinent, violent dupe," a "vicious ludicrous monster" simultaneously feared and ridiculed. Both interpersonal violence and their god earned their "frightened distaste."[19] Fortunately, the inanity of their god permitted the Semai to engage in one of the key tactics of the weak—duplicity—which gave them a certain kind of leverage: For instance, "Semai say they tricked God into giving them access to His *hnalaa'* power."[20] Further, in Semai demonology humans and evil spirits stalked and hunted each other in a "whirling totality of eater and eaten, the wheel of predation."[21] Luckily, the Semai could "domesticate" the dangerous spirits, even entering into loving relationships with them, for which purpose the séance was the chief device.

Speaking of eating and being eaten, the generally nonviolent Piaroa of Venezuela occupied a universe in which eating was fraught with danger. The existential threat of consumption related, predictably, to their theology. In the Piaroa genesis story, there were two creator gods, named Kuemoi and Wahari. Kuemoi was the Master of Water, an ugly and insanely ferocious cannibal; Wahari was the Master of Land and the maker of the Piaroa people. The two gods were competitive sorcerers who vied for control over each other's domain. Invading Wahari's terrestrial realm, Kuemoi formed plants, animals, and fire—fire symbolizing "culture" (as in the Prometheus myth) or the human knowledge and skills for controlling and exploiting "nature." Wahari, in addition to fashioning humans in his

---

[18] Dentan, *Overwhelming Terror*, 66.
[19] Dentan, *Overwhelming Terror*, 84.
[20] Dentan, *Overwhelming Terror*, 88.
[21] Dentan, *Overwhelming Terror*, 93.

land-based kingdom, created fish and fishing in his adversary's watery kingdom. Most importantly, he transformed the non-human species into their present edible forms, for prior to his supernatural intervention, plants and animals enjoyed both spiritual and anthropomorphic characteristics. Stripped of their human-like traits, they became proper food for humans.

The extreme and almost excruciating (dare we say existentially anxious and unbearable) result of the gods' actions was that the entire world was made poisonous and hazardous. Culture was poisonous because it was created by a mad god who was literally on drugs (another kind of poison) at the time. Food itself was poisonous; animals and large fish were particularly risky to eat, because they were the most human-like, but even small fish, birds, and plants posed a threat. Consuming any of these things was perilous, not because they were physically unsafe but because they were spiritually vengeful: animals and fish were originally "people" who had been converted into non-human beings by the gods. Consequently, fish, terrestrial animals, and plants were jealous and angry over losing their humanity and their capacity to have culture. Therefore, while humans ate them, they avenged themselves by "eating" humans (and causing illness) reciprocally.[22]

Both the Semai and the Piaroa could sensibly prefer that their god(s) did not exist (especially in the Semai case) or had never existed (especially in the Piaroa case). Without the Semai god, the people would not be prone to random and irrational torments. If the Piaroa gods had never existed or had existed with different personalities, it would be a simpler, safer, and saner world (for humans, anyhow). Nor is this a mere local version of the much-vaunted "problem of evil." Evil was not the same conceptual problem in either society as it is in Christianity, because the local gods were never expected to be omnibenevolent. Human suffering or misfortune demanded no intellectual gyrations for these groups; it was built into their reality *because of their gods*. In short, if posed the option, both the Semai and the Piaroa might well be anti-theists, preferring their god(s) not to exist or not to have existed, and they would have good reason for holding that opinion.

On Preferring Not the Christian God

As we have seen, people could conceivably choose a world in which their local god(s) did not exist. This crucial fact also reminds us that local peoples had or have their own god(s) and that therefore the Christian god

---

[22] Overing, "Images of Cannibalism, Death, and Domination in a 'Non-Violent' Society."

was and is often a foreign intrusion. They might, then, for understandable reasons, *prefer that the Christian god does or did not exist*, although they might not mind if their indigenous non-Christian gods or spirits remain.

The most obvious reason why a person, group, or society might want the Christian god not to exist is that they already have a god or gods—or other spiritual entities besides gods—with which they are comfortable and satisfied, or at least know how to handle. Muslims, for instance, could reasonably prefer the Christian god not to exist, partly to avoid the supernatural competition and partly because the Christian god, at least in some interpretations, has features that confuse and outrage them, such as incarnation and trinity (both serious violations of the Islamic doctrine of *tawhid* or the absolute oneness of Allah). Hindus may be content with Brahma, Shiva, Vishnu, or one of their multiple avatars. In fact, the Christian god is a divisive issue in more political versions of Hinduism like Hindutva ("Hinduness") which holds that the Indian and Hindu identity are one and the same. Such Hindu nationalists often demand that local Christians return to Hinduism, and in highly Christianized areas such as the northern state of Nagaland Hindu nationalist groups operate Hinduization campaigns like the Vivekananda Kendra mission with the goal of "transforming our people's inherent God-wardness into the right spiritual urge rising out of the teaching of the Upanishads" in order to reconstruct the Hindu nation and effectively realize the anti-theist (i.e., anti-Christian-theist) project.[23]

It is also important to understand that, once local peoples fully perceived the nature and intentions of the Christian god, they realized that it serves, if not seeks, to falsify, replace, and even demonize their prior beliefs. For example, Australian Aboriginal peoples including the Warlpiri at first welcomed Christian missionaries, because all religious knowledge was valued, and the local attitude was that other individuals might have knowledge that could be added to one's repertoire. However, they soon recognized that Christians did not want to share the field with traditional religious ideas but to displace and vilify those ideas. Like indigenous peoples all around the world, they found themselves trapped on mission stations (consider, for example, early New England "praying towns," which were virtual religious prisons for Native Americans), their ceremonies banned, their sacred objects confiscated or destroyed, and their religious beliefs scorned. Families were fragmented over religious differences, and children were often removed from their pagan homes.

Arguably more disorienting, if the Christian god was real, and if the teachings about him were true, then everything that non-Christian and

---

[23] Longkumer, "The Power of Persuasion," 213.

pre-Christian peoples had previously believed would be false or literally satanic (which is commonly what Christian missionaries tell them). This presented a grave affront to the ancestors or the nature spirits or whatever else people had believed and practiced before the Christian god was introduced to them. It also meant most likely that the ancestors, missing the opportunity to know Christ, were consigned eternally to hell. For this and all of the ancillary effects, the locals could easily prefer that the Christian god (and colonizing Christian missionaries with them) not exist.

The situation in nineteenth-century Polynesia sheds an interesting and revealing light on the distaste for the Christian god. During the 1810s and 1820s throughout the Pacific region, natives destroyed their traditional religious objects and buildings, smashing, burning, or burying statues, altars, and temples. This "Polynesian iconoclasm" was contemporaneous with the arrival of Christianity and would seem to be an instance of the radical break from the past that Christian conversion allegedly entails. Yet in many ways, it was completely continuous with Polynesian pre-contact culture with its seasonality of power and social structure. Each year around November, when the constellation Pleiades was rising, social rules were loosened and social distinctions minimized or ignored: on Tahiti, "people drank large quantities of kava and sang blasphemous cursing songs. Commoners and nobles, men and women, then bathed together in the ocean....Over the next four days, sexual orgies and feasting took place....During this period of revelry the high priest was secluded and blindfolded so that he would not see the violations of sacred restriction."[24] Power struggles during this period might eventuate in the destruction of temples and the desecration of sacred objects. However, months later as Pleiades sank below the horizon, order was restored: sacred statues were displayed in "a dramatic performance through which gods were called to sanctify their images and then sent away, leaving only priests and high chiefs as their representatives."[25] There was always a tension that traditional rules and power might be overthrown and not reconstituted as before. Such occurred in June 1815 as the stars descended: the Christian chief Pomare seized control, ordering local chiefs and priests to dispose of heathen temples and objects, clearing the way for a new sacred order dedicated to the new god, Jehovah, with new "temples"—Christian churches—and new rules and powers founded for his regime.

It was not long before the peoples of the region "realized their mistake" and began to turn against the new god. What the unsuspecting converts did not know, and could not know until they experienced it for

---

[24] Sissons, *The Polynesian Iconoclasm*, 14.
[25] Sissons, *The Polynesian Iconoclasm*, 17.

themselves, was that Christianity brought not only a new god but a new seasonality of power—or no seasonality at all. Unlike the old religion, Christianity granted no periodic respite from structure and hierarchy. And unlike the old gods, the Christian god was "[r]elentless and active day and night throughout the entire year," merciless as throughout the Christianized world in "the repression of youthful exuberance and bodily display."[26] There was truly no relief from belief: the natives had not merely substituted one god for another but had submitted themselves to a god more absolute and smothering than they had ever met or imagined. Most contemporary Christians are accustomed to, perhaps even glad for, a god who never takes or gives a break, but the Polynesian case reminds us of just how strange—and how stifling—that sensation is when encountered for the first time.

To further illustrate the point of the unusual and locally undesirable qualities of the Christian god and its religious ethos, Julia Cassaniti discovered a natural laboratory in the villages of Thailand. It has often been questioned whether "high" religious concepts like *nirvana* and *anatta* (no-self) penetrate to the ordinary folks of a society, but Cassaniti reports that lay Thai Buddhists understand and practice more of Buddhist virtue than they are usually credited for. Central to their ideal of the Buddhist person is *tham jai* or "making the heart," which relates to the scriptural notion of *anicca*, impermanence, instability, or change—the very opposite of Christian metaphysics. Not at all ignorant of or indifferent to formal doctrine, laypeople "invoked *anicca* for what seemed to be the purpose of self-work, advising themselves to temper their emotional reaction to a catastrophic event, or even to temper the emotions against the mere possibility that such a catastrophe might occur."[27] Accordingly, they strove for and generally achieved *jai yen*, "cool heart" or calm: "People didn't seem to get angry, or sad, or full of joy, or excited, as far as I could tell."[28] The Buddhist noble truth of detachment leads to an attitude of *ploy*, "to let go" or *plong*, "to dispose of, to lay down a burden, … letting go" (and again, not the angst and despair that critics insist must accompany peering into the void of nothingness; see Chapter 1). This "local model of personal agency" shaped by Buddhism teaches that letting go "brings about positive results, and this detaching is practiced through the cultivation of calm, cool, affective orientations (as captured by making the

---

[26] Sissons, *The Polynesian Iconoclasm*, 133.
[27] Cassaniti, *Living Buddhism*, 27.
[28] Cassaniti, *Living Buddhism*, 41.

heart in *tham jai*). Merit making and the work of karma serve to mobilize the effects of these practices."[29]

Significantly, a neighboring Christianized village displayed a very different and not better way of being in the world. For instance, when a female missionary from America spoke at the village church, as we would expect—and many Western Christians would applaud—she

> became more and more riled as she spoke, her face turning red from the heat and her animated speech. She waved her hands in the air and told us about fire and brimstone and an angry God and the importance of following his word....
> "We have to convert those people down there to Christianity!" the missionary said, "or else they'll burn in Hell!"[30]

This performance was a demonstration of the polar opposite of *jai yen*, the affective state valued by Thai Buddhists but not by Thai Christians. Predictably, each disapproved of the other: Buddhists felt that the Christians were too loud and verbose, selfish and "hot," while the Christians disparaged the Buddhists as too lazy, passive, cold, "all *jai yen*." Cassaniti justifiably concludes that being calm and detached is not an innate Thai way of being but is "a religious and cultural one." Which is better—being cool and detached, or being hot and intensely attached? There is no meaningful answer to that question outside of one value system or the other.

On Preferring Not Any God(s)

In a recent essay, Jeanine Diller drew a line between "local" and "global" theism and atheism. Local theism refers to any one of the myriad of culture- and religion-specific god-beliefs, from Christianity, Islam, and Hinduism to the Azande, Semai, Piaroa, and Tahitian ones described above. Each of these reputed gods has a particular set of properties and, just as important, a particular set of personal/psychological and social/institutional effects. Local atheism is the disavowal of one or more specific god(s). Global theism, which would necessitate the belief in all of the gods currently or ever worshipped (or feared or despised) in the world, is a logical impossibility; Diller admits that "there is no coherent global theism: all coherent theisms are local theisms ... or conjunctions of compossible local theisms" because the disparate god-beliefs are simply

---

[29] Cassaniti, *Living Buddhism*, 179.
[30] Cassaniti, *Living Buddhism*, 71.

too contradictory to be entertained simultaneously.[31] On the other hand, she correctly assesses that there is no logical problem with global atheism: "It is consistent to deny that there is a God on one, some or all notions of God," although she erroneously places an unbearable burden of proof on the would-be global atheist.[32] As I have argued elsewhere, every atheist is a global atheist: if an atheist disbelieved in some gods but not others, she would be a theist (and indeed that is the status of all local theists).[33] To be clear, being an atheist does not mean that you can *prove* that every iteration of god(s) does not exist; rather, it means being unconvinced by any god-concept and any argument for god[s] that one has heard or, obviously, has not heard.

The relevance of Diller's perspective, not at all explored by her or anyone else that I have seen, is that there is a parallel difference between local and global anti-theism. All of the potential anti-theisms that we have examined so far are local anti-theisms: Semai and Piaroa presumably would prefer their particular local gods not to exist, while Tahitians and Thai Buddhists might prefer the Christian god not to exist because they were happy with their own gods—or with no gods potentially for Buddhists. But there are people who, for various reasons prefer for no god(s) to exist. They may indeed desire the very idea of god, the god-concept, and all of the concomitant god-talk, not to exist.

Again, I take a cue from Stefan Baumrin, who sagely stated that there are "various ways in which ideas can be pernicious":

> One way is to get in the way of other clearer thinking, or more efficient … effective thinking. Another way is by encouraging one to think along lines that lead nowhere—that dead end in the mind like exitless mazes, or that lead to mounds of incommunicable fantasy. Yet a third way is to lead one to do evil.[34]

Some people may feel, reasonably—by which I mean for reasons that they can articulate and that follow from a set of consistent principles—that the god-concept is just such a pernicious idea. They are global anti-theists.

To start with a minor but still worthy example, a person might prefer that god(s) not exist in favor of other sorts of supernatural beings and/or forces. On whatever basis—that a god is too powerful, too exclusive, too abstract, etc.—such a person might throw their support to

---

[31] Diller, "Global and Local Atheisms," 9.

[32] Diller, "Global and Local Atheisms," 9.

[33] Eller, "Atheism is Global Atheism."

[34] Baumrin, "Antitheism and Morality," 79.

less omnipotent, more inclusive, and more immanent beings like nature spirits or dead ancestors, entities with limited portfolios and restricted powers. Or they might find appealing the notion of impersonal supernatural (or semi-supernatural) forces like *qi* (formerly chi) or karma, which provide order and even justice in the world without resorting to god(s). Unlike most gods, *qi* and karma can be predicted and managed (apparently acupuncture works more dependably than faith healing). And both alternatives might be favored because they do not impose the stultifying absoluteness of at least some god(s), including the monotheistic tyrant that the Polynesians struggled against. It merits stressing that there is nothing logically inconsistent in an anti-theist (or even an atheist) accepting other non-god beings and forces. Strictly speaking, anti-theism (or atheism) only directly excludes god-concepts, although many practicing anti-theists (and atheists) extend their reasoning beyond god-talk since there is no compelling evidence for these other claims either.

Moving along to more malignant impacts of god-ideas, Baumrin first emphasized the hurdle or obstacle that an idea can present to clear and effective thinking. Perusing the historical record and the current culture, there is little room for doubt that god-concepts, especially in the Western world, have been impediments to thought and knowledge. One can cite admonitions like, "The wisdom of this world is foolishness in God's sight" (1 Corinthians 3:19). Accordingly, the arch irrationalist Tertullian wrote, "After Jesus Christ we have no need of speculation, after the Gospel no need of research. When we come to believe, we have no desire to believe anything else; for we begin by believing that there is nothing else which we have to believe."[35] He went on to pronounce:

My first principle is this. Christ laid down one definite system of truth which the world must believe without qualification, and which we must seek precisely in order to believe it when we find it.... You must seek until you find, and when you find, you must believe. Then you have simply to keep what you have come to believe, since you also believe that there is nothing else to believe, and therefore nothing else to seek, once you have found and believed what he taught who bids you seek nothing beyond what he taught....I warn people not to seek for anything beyond what they believe, for that was all they needed to seek for.

Finally, Tertullian affirmed his unequivocal Rule of Faith which "allows of no questions among us," such that "it is better for you to remain ignorant

---

[35] Quoted in Miller, *Classical Statements on Faith and Reason*, 5.

for fear that you come to know what you should not know. For you do know what you should know."[36]

Christian god-belief persisted in subordinating reason to faith, or knowledge to belief, in the work of Augustine and beyond. Augustine's Sermon 43.7 asserted that belief precedes knowledge when he instructed "*Crede, ut intelligas*" (believe in order that you may understand), arguing vacuously that faith is a kind of knowledge. Anselm nearly quoted Augustine when he confessed "*Credo, ut intelligam*" (I believe in order that I might understand). But Augustine's stance on knowledge and reason was much harsher. In his classic *Confessions* (Chapter XXXV) he denounced the "temptation of curiosity":

> For besides that concupiscence of the flesh which lieth in the gratification of all senses and pleasures, wherein its slaves who "are far from Thee perish," there pertaineth to the soul, through the same senses of the body, a certain vain and curious longing, cloaked under the name of knowledge and learning.... This longing ... originates in an appetite for knowledge....

Later Protestant thinkers shared his dim view of knowledge. Martin Luther condemned reason as "God's worst enemy"—"the devil's bride" which "faith must trample under foot." "There is," he declared, "on earth among all dangers no more dangerous thing than a richly endowed and adroit reason," which "must be deluded, blinded, and destroyed."[37] Ditto for Luther's contemporary, John Calvin, who taught that human reason had been "partly weakened and partly corrupted" by sin and that knowledge (of God at least, which was the only kind of knowledge that interested him) was "open only to him whose mind has been made new by the illumination of the Holy Spirit."[38] "Thus we can see," he judged, "that the reason of our mind, wherever it may turn, is miserably subject to vanity."[39]

The unhealthy effects of god-belief endure into the present, giving Christian god-believers a license to reject sound scientific facts and theories such as evolution, Big Bang cosmology, the age (and even the shape) of the earth, and climate change, to name but a few. Some modern Pacific Islanders, for example, seduced by Christian god-talk, dismiss global warming as a breach of their god's promise not to flood the earth again, even as they witness their island homes submerging. But I would

---

[36] Quoted in Miller, *Classical Statements on Faith and Reason*, 9–10.
[37] Quoted in Kaufmann, *The Faith of a Heretic*, 75.
[38] Quoted in Miller, *Classical Statements on Faith and Reason*, 72–74.
[39] Quoted in Miller, *Classical Statements on Faith and Reason*, 81.

push the deleterious influence of god-ideas further. If, as is the case of the vast majority of theisms, the god(s) can intervene in the natural and human world—from performing miracles by the Christian god to treating humans as virtual pawns in their machinations by the Olympian gods—then human knowledge is virtually impossible. Knowledge depends on the regularity of the world, but if the god(s) can alter, interrupt, or entirely reconfigure worldly events—at the quantum or the cosmic level—then we mortals are stranded in a reality not of knowable lawful order but of mysterious and unfathomable divine whim.

Baumrin's second type of pernicious idea drives the thinker into blind allies, dead ends, and ceaseless rounds of pointless and profitless speculation. God-concepts are certainly responsible for this sort of intellectual waste and not only in the form of oracles, mediums, and diviners who have attempted for millennia to infer the intentions and wishes of deities in everything from stars to animal entrails. Christianity is only the most exquisite example of angels-on-the-head-of-a-pin conjecture, as manifested by early (and not so early) controversies about the virtue of faith versus works or the nature of Jesus (was he fully divine, was he fully human, was he divine and human, was he adopted by the Hebrew god, ad infinitum?) not to mention the Marcionite "heresy" that the biblical god was a lesser and malicious god, distinct from the higher benevolent god of the New Testament (officially, it would seem, embracing polytheism or minimally duotheism).

(Christian) theology and (Christian) philosophy of religion have continued to expend vast resources without demonstrable accomplishments; no theistic question has ever been settled on divine attributes, liturgical practice, morality, political theology, or any other subject. More pathetically, theologians and philosophers of religion pollute academia with pages and pages of blather and nonsense. (See Chapter 8) And the same holds for other religions, with, for instance, Buddhism spawning a sprawling interpretive literature and Islam splitting into several major schools of Qur'anic interpretation. Both of those traditions, like Christianity and every other major religion, have also splintered into many, often hostile sects and new religious movements, such as Mormonism, Seventh-day Adventism, Christian Science, and too many more to count, while also refracting through the politics and culture of the day. This does not include the myriad false announcements of the end of the world or the interminable squabbles over religious authority and policies regarding priest marriage, the ordination of women, virginity, divorce, birth control (interestingly all gender/sex issues), etc.

Finally, theistic thinking often leads—and cannot help but lead—to irresolvable paradoxes or, worse, meaningless utterances. A case in point is the claim (not made for all gods) that a divinity is all-knowing: if he/she/it knows all, does that include the future, and if it includes the future, then is the future already cast and therefore human choice moot? Do humans have free will (a culture-/religion-specific concept not part of all religions), or is everything determined? Is it already settled who will get to heaven and who is consigned to hell (i.e. predestination)? And what does it mean anyhow to say that a god is three persons in one?

Baumrin's third sign of a pernicious idea is its capacity to inspire the believer to harmful behavior. Here we are not invoking the familiar and tired "problem of evil," which is often touted, by theists and atheists alike, as the strongest objection to the existence of a god. Actually, the problem of evil is relatively uninteresting. First, as we have established, not all gods have been claimed to be "perfect" or "omnibenevolent" (which, conceivably, might be two different things—being "right" might not always equal being "good"). Tooley even gives us pardon to "jettison" putative properties of "God" that are derived from "various properties that characterize the gods of familiar monotheistic religions,"[40] but it is not clear which and how many of those properties are negotiable and safe to discard or what kind of god remains after this editing.

At any rate, as mentioned, many of the world's gods do not raise a problem of evil; they overtly either allow it or commit it. But when a god like the Christian god faces a complaint about evil, as Job's god did, there are a number of salvage arguments. Like Job's god, we can respond that the human mind is too small to appreciate the perfect goodness of the god's actions, no matter how awful they seem. Alternatively, we can reply that evil is part of a grand divine plan or is the price for still higher goods—an argument that accepts evil but contextualizes or balances it, rendering such a god at best "net good" (more good than bad) *but not all-good*. (I think of the Texas attorney general's disgusting comment after the Uvalde school shooting that "God has a plan," evidently a plan that requires nineteen dead elementary school children.) That is, to return to Kahane's words, there might be impersonal or overall good to offset the personal bad, which would support personalist anti-theism even if we accept impersonalist/overall pro-theism. In passing, the "god's plan" retort might not be a boon to pro-theists, as it implies that there actually might be less, or at least different, evil in the world *without* the god and his/her/its plan.

So we will not linger on the so-called problem of evil, but we can still ponder here not the evil that the god does or permits but rather the

---

[40] Tooley, "Axiology: Theism Versus Widely Accepted Monotheisms," 68.

harm and suffering that followers of the god perpetrate. We might begin with blood sacrifice, which many gods, from tribal gods to Greek and Roman gods to the biblical god until his one last great self-sacrificial act, have been keen to demand; untold animals and humans have bled, screamed, and died to fulfill a hungry, angry, or otherwise motivated deity. Additionally, humans have been inspired to hurt themselves in various and creative ways for their god(s), from minor discomforts and renunciations to life-threatening self-mutilations, asceticism, and martyrdom.

Meanwhile, red-hot theisms with their insistence on orthodoxy and the resultant incessant controversies over the minutia of god-talk have been uniquely responsible for the persecution of "heretics" who disagree about this or that detail of doctrine or practice. No god-idea, no painful interrogation and execution for a heretical god-idea. It is fair to say that religions have been responsible for an extreme amount of trauma. (See Chapter 6)

More disastrously for the reputation of gods and god-believers, the god-concept has made some spokesmen for divinity extraordinarily unkind, if not sadistic. Tertullian delighted in the promise that he, a guaranteed future citizen of heaven, would be able to watch the anguish of the hell-bound:

> At that greatest of all spectacles, that last and eternal judgment how shall I admire, how laugh, how rejoice, how exult, when I behold so many proud monarchs groaning in the lowest abyss of darkness; so many magistrates liquefying in fiercer flames than they ever kindled against the Christians; so many sages philosophers blushing in red-hot fires with their deluded pupils; so many tragedians more tuneful in the expression of their own sufferings; so many dancers tripping more nimbly from anguish than ever before from applause. (*De Spectaculis*, XXX)

Aquinas echoed this pleasure in the righteous fate of the eternally punished, writing in his deeply respected *Summa Theologia* (Question 94, Article 1), "In order that the happiness of the saints may be more delightful to them and that they may render more copious thanks to God for it, they are allowed to see perfectly the sufferings of the damned." Both Aquinas and Augustus before him, and many since, have reasoned that persecution for wrong theistic opinions was justice, indeed mercy, since it saved the sinner's soul while protecting others from his or her treacherous falsehoods.

Beyond these postponed if not imaginary pleasures, theism is well documented to be particularly susceptible to fanaticism and violence (a fanatical animist or ancestor worshipper is somewhat harder to picture). Sociologist Rodney Stark, no anti-theist, conceded as much in his study of monotheism:

> The image of God that is most potent in terms of social effects is, for that very reason, the most dangerous. It is precisely God as a conscious, responsive, good supreme being of infinite scope—the One True God as conceived by the great monotheisms—who prompts awareness of idolatry, false Gods, and heretical religions. *Particularism*, the belief that a given religion is the *only true religion*, is *inherent in monotheism.*[41]

Although arguing, somewhat opportunistically, that much of (mono)theistic violence is "collateral," he nevertheless assented that, because of unavoidable differences of opinion—and more importantly, because of the infinitely high stakes—"*internal* and *external conflict* is *inherent* in particularistic religions."[42] Lloyd Steffen among many others concurred, comprehending that theism is dangerous because of its tendency toward "ultimacy" and "absolutism." Ultimacy alone "is an incendiary concept" because the believer thinks that she is acting in the interest, if not on the command, of the highest conceivable being; absolutism, as "a totalizing or all-encompassing, all-enclosing philosophical idea that points toward a specific idea of ultimacy … invites people into self-deceptive interpretations of moral meaning, insisting that acts it commands be deemed good even when they are destructive of goodness."[43] Other causes, to be sure, can stimulate means-justifies-ends violence, including nation, class, race, and more, but none raises the stakes to a cosmic level, in which Good battles Evil. And in a cosmic struggle, there is no neutral ground, and there is no compromise or surrender.

These considerations explain Tooley's assessment that a number of classic pro-theism arguments are in fact bad arguments, specifically god as the source of objective values, moral obligations, and objective meaning. The history of religions, society, and philosophy makes very dubious the notion that there is any such thing as objective values or meaning, and if there is, theism has not helped us identify them. Further, gods are not the only source of moral obligations; many of the obligations

---

[41] Stark, *One True God: Historical Consequences of Monotheism*, 116.
[42] Stark, *One True God*, 117.
[43] Steffen, *The Demonic Turns*, 23–30.

they impose on us are hardly praiseworthy (like holy war) or are trifling (like growing a beard or abstaining from coffee); and there is no agreement across religions on the finer points of morality. At the same time, most societies agree on the broad outlines of morality (like not killing), which do not take a god to figure out, and indeed Buddhism decrees a demanding morality without any necessary appeal to god(s). And then there is the oft-commented point that, if we can submit a god to moral scrutiny, then there must be a moral standard outside of and higher than the god—which even pro-theists illustrate when they apply the better/worse world standard.

For the moment, I would add one more plank to the platform of anti-theism, which expands on a suggestion by Erik Wielenburg, who muses that a world with god(s) may be *more absurd* than a godless world. Wielenburg defines absurdity rather narrowly, as a situation in which it is "difficult or impossible" for people who make a claim—in this case, a god-claim—"to be happy"; then he reasons that the onerous commandment to love others as we love ourselves "makes life absurd in the sense that a universe in which such a God exists includes truths that most human beings would find it difficult to accept and live happily."[44] But I think we can and should construe absurdity much more broadly, as that state in which reality does not conform to our ideas and expectations such that predictability, meaningful action, and sense itself break down. One thing does not follow from another, and we end in contradiction, paradox, paralysis, and non-sense. This can take the form of empty terms or propositions such as "all-good" or "god is three persons," which sound plausible but evade any real meaning. Some, like Tertullian, positively reveled in the absurdity, famously saying of the doctrine of the resurrection, *prorsus credibile est, quia ineptum est ... certum est, quia impossibile* (it is entirely credible, because it is unfitting [often translated as "absurd"] ... it is certain, because it is impossible). For the rest of us, unfittingness, absurdity, and impossibility are not a mark of credibility and certainty.

There are many ways that a god potentially makes the world more nonsensical, depending as always on the specifics of the god. The ancient philosopher Theognis felt the sting of absurdity when he cried in distress:

Dear Zeus, you baffle me. You are king of all; the highest honor and greatest power are yours, you discern what goes on in each man's secret heart, and your lordship is supreme. Yet you make no distinction between the sinner and the good man, between the man who devotes himself to temperate and responsible acts and the man

---

[44] Wielenburg, "The Absurdity of Life in a Christian Universe," 147–148.

who commits deeds of hubris. Tell me, son of Cronus, how can you deal such unfairness?[45]

The same complaint could be lodged against the Judeo-Christian god, who promises justice but never delivers. This is the very god who created Satan, set him loose, bargained with him over Job's life, and allowed him to run amok until the last days. This is the very god who asked Abraham to kill his son Isaac without explanation, a request that troubled Kierkegaard deeply. (See Chapter 1) This is the very god who expects that his creatures believe in him and yet hides from us.

An anti-theist might defensibly conclude that a secular and scientific worldview, while not inherently sympathetic to humans, is less absurd. Surely modern physics includes mysteries and paradoxes, especially at the quantum scale, but these do not make life unthinkable and intolerable, and they impose no specific social or moral obligations on us. In fact, they affect the average citizen not at all while rousing scientists to greater investigation. And the scientific, godless worldview seems to describe reality more accurately, or at least testably, without adding circles-within-circles of theological rationalization. We would not be the first to note that the universe has exactly the qualities we would expect in a godless universe—and precious few of the qualities of a godful one. Like Laplace, the scientific worldview has no need of the god hypothesis and works better without it.

Conclusion:
Many Ways to Not Want God(s)

At the end of their critique of Kahane, Kraay and Dragos thank him for his effort and acknowledge that "there may be other ways to defend this view [of anti-theism], and these should be explored and evaluated."[46] In this chapter, we have done precisely that. We have explored a number of ways to represent and defend anti-theism apart from Kahane's Christian-centric better/worse world approach. Readers may deem some of these ways more convincing or appealing than others, but the point is to consider how anti-theists can and do justify their position to themselves. To that end, we have investigated not hypothetical thought-experiments but, as much as possible, real empirical cases of potentially or actually wishing god(s) not to exist.

---

[45] Quoted in Wheelwright, *The Presocratics*, 29–30.
[46] Kraay and Dragos, "On Preferring God's Non-Existence," 173.

Equally if not more important, the chapter has argued that we cannot use the Christian/Abrahamic god as the paradigm of god(s), nor can we use Christian reasoning for the evaluation of other people's attitudes toward their own gods or of non-Christians' attitudes toward the Christian god. Betenson declared that anti-theism "could look like this: 'I accept that God's existence would make the world better, but I don't want the world to be like that!'"[47] Perhaps the cost of this better godly world is too high: it offends our dignity, obstructs our maturity (permanently infantilizing us in relation to a supernatural father), fosters false hopes, vilifies and crushes our prior beliefs and values, traps us in absurdities, inspires too many of us to violence, and finally subjects us to the tyranny of theism by a being who surveilles our every thought and action and never gives us a moment's rest from his rules or excuses our slightest imperfections (unless we come groveling).

But anti-theism, the anti-theism I envision and endorse, could also look entirely different, more positive and liberating, more akin to a reformulation of Wielenburg's position, to wit: I do not accept that a god's existence would make the world better, and I am sufficiently happy in a world without god(s). If we want a better world, the work is up to us.

---

[47] Betenson, "Recasting Anti-Theism," 171.

6

"The Truth" Hurts:
Religious Trauma, Spiritual Abuse, and the Myth of Benevolent Belief

One of the standard and bankrupt arguments for god(s) is that belief is inherently beneficial, which can take several forms. Among them is the truly exhausted and easily countered "wager" of Pascal, who insisted that we are better off believing in (his particular) god because we lose nothing if we are wrong and potentially gain everything if we are right. Of course, as we established in Chapter 2, the Christian god is not looking for followers who hedge their bets by adopting a self-seeking propositional belief in him; this lord expects and demands deeper belief/faith in the shape of confidence and commitment. Another form of the argument from benefit is that religious belief makes us better people, individually and collectively. Religion is the alleged source (through some god[s]' law) and guarantor (through some god[s]' punishments) of morality, and personal morality ensures that individuals and institutions will treat fellow humans with dignity and respect and shield them from harm.

The first objection to such an argument is that it contributes nothing to the case for the existence of god(s): whether god(s) *would be beneficial* does not prove that such things as god(s) are real. The second objection is that there is no consistent evidence that god-believers are better people or build better societies than non-god-believers. On the contrary, multiple lines of evidence suggest that they are not and do not. For instance, sociologist Phil Zuckerman's study of two especially secular and nonreligious countries, Denmark and Sweden, depicted them as especially peaceful, orderly, just, and content nations.[1] Both also appear high on the Human Development Index's list of most livable countries (along with other secular Western states like Norway, Switzerland, Iceland, and the Netherlands), and another famously non-religious country, Japan, is also renowned for its low incidence of crime and

---

[1] Zuckerman, *Society without God.*

violence. An additional line of research provides the flip side of the coin: as Gregory Paul's cross-cultural study of religion and societal health demonstrated, "in almost all regards the highly secular democracies consistently enjoy low rates of societal dysfunction" than their more devout counterparts.[2] Some extremely religious countries, such as Afghanistan, are wracked with violence and injustice, and the United States is both strongly religious and extraordinarily violent and crime-ridden among wealthy Western democracies.

A third and comparatively ignored line of evidence against the benevolence of religion is the palpable harm that religion frequently does to individuals and families. This situation has recently attracted more attention, under the heading of *religious trauma* or *spiritual abuse*. Since the discovery or recognition of religious trauma, a considerable literature and practice has grown up around it, highlighting at best the burdens and at worst the damages that come with the religious life. On the more whimsical side, Patricia Klein, Evelyn Bence, Jane Campbell, Laura Pearson, and David Wimbish reflected on the experiences of growing up "born-again," which as we all know include various strictures on thought and behavior, from an obsession with the Bible to proscriptions on movies, card games, and musical instruments such as drums, tuba, and saxophone, all of which lead born-agains to perceive themselves—and those outside the born-again community to perceive them—as "peculiar people."[3] In a more somber vein, around the same time psychologist Donald Sloat documented the true hazards of being raised in a Christian environment.[4] Books such as these were rapidly followed by others like *Toxic Faith* and, remarkably, a number authored and/or published by pro-religion sources including *The Subtle Power of Spiritual Abuse* (emerging from publisher Bethany House), *Recovering from Churches that Abuse* (released by Zondervan Publishing House), and *When God Becomes a Drug* (written by an Episcopalian priest).[5] This obviously illustrates that acknowledging abusive religion does not automatically result in a rejection of religion; instead, it can call for reform and improvement and the creation of "better" religion. On the other hand, some of our more adamant atheist friends like Dawkins condemn the religious education of youths as child abuse, deeming it sufficient reason to dispose of all religion. For critics like these,

[2] Paul, "Cross-National Correlations," 1.
[3] Klein, Bence, Campbell, Pearson, and Wimbish, *Growing Up Born Again*.
[4] Sloat, *The Dangers of Growing Up in a Christian Home*.
[5] Arterburn and Felton, *Toxic Faith*; Johnson and VanVonderen, *The Subtle Power of Spiritual Abuse*; Enroth, *Recovering from Churches that Abuse*; Booth, *When God Becomes a Drug*.

urging people back to reformed religion is akin to advising an abused wife to return to her abusive husband.

At any rate, since the late 1980s, an entire industry of study and intervention into religious trauma has emerged, with many psychologists and counselors offering treatment for the condition and its symptoms and selling self-help manuals and workbooks. Entire organizations and networks have appeared, such as the Religious Trauma Institute (religioustraumainstitute.com) and, from a strictly nonreligious perspective, Recovering from Religion and the Secular Therapy Project, both instigated by Darrel Ray in 2009 and 2012, respectively. There are Facebook groups dedicated to exposing and healing from religious trauma, and the Global Center for Religious Research has initiated the North American Committee on Religious Trauma Research (gcrr.org/religioustrauma), which found that about one-third of U.S. adults have likely experienced religious trauma, with up to 20% of Americans exhibiting multiple major symptoms.[6]

What and Where is
Religious Trauma and Spiritual Abuse?

One thing that most if not all professionals working in the field would agree on is that, as Lisa Oakley and Kathryn Kinmond stipulate in their fairly recent book, spiritual abuse is abuse and religious trauma is trauma.[7] This realization impels us to examine the concepts of trauma and abuse. The National Institute of General Medical Sciences (NIGMS) understands trauma originally as physical injury to the body which is, further, sudden and episodic, with a distinct beginning and ending. That conception of trauma has been much expanded, in two particular ways. The first is the inclusion of psychological trauma or, according to NIGMS, emotional and mental injury. The American Psychological Association adds that psychological trauma may be episodic like physical trauma or may be— and often is—an emotional *response* to such an event, manifested as "shock and denial" and other long-term effects such as "unpredictable emotions, flashbacks, strained relationships and even physical symptoms like headaches or nausea."[8] The second, as the preceding words suggest, is the identification of "post-traumatic stress disorder," that is, lingering and traumatizing symptoms that arise after the particular traumatic event

---

[6] Slade, et al. "Percentage of U.S. Adults Suffering From Religious Trauma," 1–28.

[7] Oakley and Kinmond, *Breaking the Silence on Spiritual Abuse*.

[8] American Psychological Association, "Trauma."

has occurred and, in most instances, concluded. As psychologists have learned, PTSD can be as debilitating as or more debilitating than the initial trauma.

There can be, without doubt, literal physical traumas—including life-threatening and fatal ones, as we will discuss later—associated with religion, but most of the focus of religious trauma research has been on the emotional and social consequences. Hence, one of the leading figures in the field, Marlene Winell, defines religious trauma, or more ambitiously the "religious trauma syndrome," as "the condition experienced by people who are struggling with leaving an authoritarian, dogmatic religion and coping with the damage of indoctrination."[9] This is a far too narrow definition, as we will see, so the North American Committee on Religious Trauma Research widens the term to encompass any injury that "results from an event, series of events, relationships, or circumstances within or connected to religious beliefs, practices, or structures that is experienced by an individual as overwhelming or disruptive and has lasting adverse effects on a person's physical, mental, social, emotional, or spiritual well-being."[10]

Others have recommended variations on the notion of religious trauma. From a psychotherapeutic perspective and writing in the *Journal of Aggression, Maltreatment, & Trauma*, Rachel Novšak, Tina Rahne Mandelj, and Barbara Simonič speak of "religious-related abuse" or "occasions when religion or certain religious beliefs correlate with various types of abuse":

> At such moments, by applying certain perspectives of religion and faith, one justifies or allows for various insults, accusations, and sometimes physical punishment.... Abusers can use religion to legitimize their behavior, as a sort of permission, and to deny responsibility and mitigate feelings of guilt for their abusive behavior, thereby maintaining a positive self-image. In such cases, their religious beliefs play a key role in facilitating violence instead of preventing such behavior.[11]

As inclusive as that definition is, it is interesting if not revealing that they specify only a "correlation" between religion and abuse, not a causal connection. Then they infinitely inflate the concept by suggesting that "all

---

[9] Winell, "Religious Trauma Syndrome."

[10] Global Center for Religious Research, "Religious Trauma Research."

[11] Novšak, Mandelj, and Simonič, "Therapeutic Implications of Religious-Related Emotional Abuse," 32.

abuse can be considered religious-related abuse simply because abuse by definition damages an individual's spiritual self."[12] But most scholars and therapists would not go so far as to call all abuse religious-related abuse, since it stretches the term beyond meaningfulness, and surely pro-religion types would not appreciate attaching religion to all abuse. And atheists like myself deny that there is any such thing as a "spiritual self."

Three times in their article, Novšak, Mandelj, and Simonič also use the term "spiritual abuse," which has appeared in other places and overlaps with, whether or not it is equivalent to, religious trauma. More than three decades ago, David Johnson and Jeff VanVonderen characterized spiritual abuse as "the mistreatment of a person who is in need of help, support or greater spiritual empowerment, with the result of weakening, undermining, or decreasing that person's spiritual empowerment."[13] The problem here, beyond the fact that atheists and rationalists mostly reject the notions of "spirit" and "spiritual empowerment," is that the statement emphasized the effects of such abuse but not the cause, which as presented might or might not be religion itself. Ronald Enroth three years later tightened the definition to situations "when leaders to whom people look for guidance and spiritual nurture use their positions of authority to manipulate, control, and dominate,"[14] but surely it is not religious leaders alone who commit such offences.

One of the most thorough explorations of spiritual abuse is provided by Oakley and Kinmond, who list a number of definitions from the literature:

- "Spiritual abuse happens when a leader with spiritual authority uses that authority to coerce, control or exploit a follower, thus causing spiritual wounds."
- Spiritual abuse results from "someone using their power within a framework of spiritual belief to practice and satisfy their needs at the expense of others."
- "Spiritual abuse is misuse of power in a spiritual context."
- Spiritual abuse is "a misuse of power in a spiritual context whereby spiritual authority is distorted to the detriment of those under its leadership."[15]

---

[12] Novšak, Mandelj, and Simonič, "Therapeutic Implications of Religious-Related Emotional Abuse," 32.

[13] Johnson and VanVonderen, *The Subtle Power of Spiritual Abuse*, 20.

[14] Enroth, *Recovering from Churches that Abuse*, 9.

[15] Oakley and Kinmond, *Breaking the Silence on Spiritual Abuse*, 20–21.

Then they delineate their own sense of the term as "coercion and control of one individual by another in a spiritual context. The target experiences SA as a deeply emotional personal attack," adding:

> This abuse may include: manipulation and exploitation, enforced accountability, censorship of decision making, requirements for secrecy and silence, pressure to conform, misuse of scripture or the pulpit to control behavior, requirement of obedience to the abuser, the suggestion that the abuser has a "divine" position and isolation from others, especially those external to the abusive context.[16]

Finally, publishing in the same fateful year (1991) as Johnson and VanVonderen, Stephen Arterburn and Jack Felton described what they called "toxic faith" or "a destructive and dangerous relationship with a religion that allows the religion, not the relationship with God, to control a person's life."[17] This formulation presupposes a couple of specious things, first that there is such a thing as God (the only one of the gods that concerns them), and second that allowing the relationship with their god to control a person's life would be healthy faith. Whether it is synonymous with toxic faith or simply one manifestation, they also invoked the idea of "religious addiction," the symptoms of which are an excessive devotion to religious belief and practice, like "compulsive churchaholism" (attending church too much, reading the Bible too much, praying too much, although it is never explained how much church, Bible, and prayer are just right). Did they contradict themselves when they also said that good faith, "real and pure faith, is not practiced in moderation"?

> One cannot trust God too much or seek God too much. Persons whose faith has grown to encompass every aspect of life are spiritual faith giants to be modeled. A little faith, a faith that knows only a bit about God, is a form of toxic faith.[18]

No wonder god-believers are confused.

At any rate, Arterburn and Felton's third chapter is an exposition of twenty-one beliefs of toxic faith, which include:

---

[16] Oakley and Kinmond, *Breaking the Silence on Spiritual Abuse*, 21–22.
[17] Arterburn and Felton. *Toxic Faith*, 31.
[18] Arterburn and Felton. *Toxic Faith*, 45.

- That God's love is conditional and depends on what the devotee does
- That God/religion will give the sufferer instant and absolute peace and relief
- That God will heal you or your loved ones if you pray hard enough
- That religious leaders are above reproach or criticism
- That material wealth is a sign of spiritual purity
- That giving money to the church will earn you spiritual credit
- That a believer can be saved by good works
- That God is spiteful or vengeful
- That the follower must slavishly commit time and energy to religious causes
- That the follower must submit utterly to authority
- That some believers are spiritually superior to others
- That a true believer waits passively for God to intervene
- That every answer and insight is in the Bible
- That God will find you the perfect spouse
- That every bad thing that happens to you is really good (the authors countered that God really does allow bad things to happen, he just doesn't cause them)
- That faith shields you against all problems and pains
- That God is vindictive and punitive against sinners
- That Jesus was nothing more than a mortal teacher
- That God is impersonal and distant
- That God's intention for us is to be happy (no, the authors explained, God's goal is not for us to be happy)
- That the believer can become perfect like God.

The problem here, as the reader can surely detect, is that all of these toxic beliefs appear in one or more versions of mainstream Christianity (and other theisms) and indeed are actively and positively preached in those churches, synagogues, mosques, ashrams, etc.

When You Can't Live With It
and You Can't Live Without It

"Religion is supposed to be good for you. Yet people get hurt in religious systems, sometimes seriously," cautioned Winell in the opening words of her seminal commentary on religious trauma.[19] As we have hopefully settled firmly by now—as defenders of the faith have settled for us—a god, even an omnibenevolent god, and his/her/its/their institutions are no assurance of benign experience for disciples of such god(s). People in religious contexts or religious relationships can perpetrate, or have perpetrated against them, all sorts of traumas, abuses, and violence, much of it quite quotidian, the same kinds of trauma, abuse, and violence that people encounter anywhere. However, while acknowledging that spiritual abuse is abuse like any other, Oakley and Kinmond also stress that there are unique factors that distinguish it from secular or everyday abuse. Among these features they mention "the notion of divine position" (that is, that the abusive religious leader—priest, minister, mullah, guru, or what have you—enjoys an extraordinary, even supernatural privilege over normal members), "the use of scripture and the pulpit to enforce and challenge behavior," "the spiritual context within which spiritual abuse occurs which allows many of the behaviors seen in spiritual abuse to occur and births discourses which I have argued are foundational for the experience to occur," "the threat of spiritual consequences for individuals who do not conform" (i.e. excommunication, eternal damnation, etc., which secular leaders and institutions cannot muster as threats), and "the impact upon core faith beliefs following the experience of spiritual abuse."[20]

This last item reminds us that "faith beliefs" figure in religious trauma both as causes and effects. As a cause, Winell pinpointed the primary culprit of religious trauma/spiritual abuse as *dogma*, and members of dogmatic religions suffer under two circumstances—living the religion and leaving the religion. And tediously, as I have repeated in this book and throughout my work, the primary culprit of dogmatic religion in her account and in most accounts of traumatic religion is fundamentalist or evangelical (especially, according to Oakley and Kinmond, Pentecostal and charismatic) Christianity. In a word, Winell informed us that it is hard for adherents of strict conservative Christianity to live with their religion and to live without it.[21]

The diverse yet conventional analyses of religious trauma tend, as in Oakley and Kinmond's study, to center on power and control. They analyze this abusive power dynamic into a number of variables:

---

[19] Winell, *Leaving the Fold*, 1.

[20] Oakley and Kinmond, *Breaking the Silence on Spiritual Abuse*, 73.

[21] See also, Harvey, "The Power and Control Dynamics of Growing Up in an Abrahamic Faith Environment," 279–94.

- Accountability, that is, the obligation of followers to report and explain their actions, and often their thoughts, to the leader or the group and thereby to surrender much of their freedom, privacy, and agency (i.e. decision-making capacity)
- Censorship, particularly silencing questions or criticisms and breaking or banning relationships with non-members; also, protecting the secrets, including the indiscretions, of the group
- Conformity, in its various subforms: demands of excessive or exclusive commitment to the group, obedience to the very figures who are abusing them, sexist and misogynist roles for women, isolation from the outside world, rejection or ejection of non-conformists, and disapproval of apostasy (leaving the group)
- Financial demands
- A complex and contradictory self-image as simultaneously superior and special (a "spiritual elite," "chosen/called people," and "remnant") and powerless in the face of authorities and their authoritative truths.[22]

All of this further depends on intensive manipulation, particularly in terms of (1) offering positive-sounding rationales for controlling members' behavior, (2) undermining and discrediting the individual members' ability to think and act for themselves, and (3) most basically but sinisterly, controlling and altering the members' very perceptions of reality.

Winell contributed more insights into the machinations of dogmatic religions.[23] First, she cited fear, the ever-present and oppressive anxiety that believers experience when they understand that their every thought and action is scrutinized and judged by an unforgiving deity. But there are other sources of fear. There is the fear of not being fervent enough, or not being "on fire for God." There is terror of the devil and his minions; such believers often see demons as constantly at work in their lives. Then of course there is the great personal fear of damnation and the great collective fear of Armageddon and not being spiritually right when the moment comes. This attitude piles shame (for not being good enough or zealous enough) on top of guilt (for worrying about your own interests

---

[22] Oakley and Kinmond, *Breaking the Silence on Spiritual Abuse*, 24.

[23] Most recently, Winell has expanded her vision to the phenomenon of "collective religious trauma" or the shared and even structural and institutional harms that result from what she calls "institutionalized religionism" to equate it to institutionalized racism. She hopes that institutionalized religionism will be recognized and combatted like racism, but in a society like the United States where religion is so embedded, that seems unlikely. See Winell, "It's Not Just Personal: The Collective Trauma of Religion."

and not appreciating the sacrifice Jesus made for you). All of this leads the believer to denigrate, or worse despise, the self.

Among the other forces operating on the member of a dogmatic congregation are, as mentioned and well known, isolation and the vulnerability it brings. Sequestered from the social mainstream, individuals are susceptible to the domination of authorities and of group pressure and conformity (groupthink). Winell also referred to the distortion of language, including distortion of the meaning of freedom itself:

> *Freedom* in the Bible also means something very different from our usual notion of being able to make choices. It compares more closely to being free of lice. In the following verse, it is clear that the believer is no closer to having free will. *Freedom* simply means "available for subjection to God" instead of to sin.

> But thanks be to God, that you who were once slaves of sin have become obedient from the heart to the standard of teaching to which you were committed, and having been set free from sin, have become slaves of righteousness. (Romans 6:17–18).[24]

One hears echoes of George Orwell's *1984*, where the Ministry of Truth existed to disseminate lies and propaganda, corrupting and disabling language through Newspeak. In Orwell's totalitarian world, and in Winell's dogmatic religion, members find themselves trapped in a closed system of thought with no resources to challenge it. In the end, their "truths" are a web of "fantasy and denial."

Winell and others understand, moreover, that the church or worship setting is certainly one site of religious abuse and resultant trauma but not the only one. As we noted in the previous discussion of religious upbringing, the family is another context of abusive experiences, in a circular relationship with the church. Referencing Sloat's aforementioned critique of the Christian home, Winell described the dread of their god that is put into children, the guilt that is activated to control and manipulate them, the neglect and disparagement of individual thoughts and feelings, the shutting down of any questions or doubts, and a rigid catalogue of dos and don'ts ironically paired with the parents' and family's frequent failure to "practice what it preaches," exposing the child to impossible contradictions and hypocrisies.

---

[24] Winell, *Leaving the Fold*, 81.

Another popular and more recent writer on the subject, Teresa Pasquale, in her aptly titled *Sacred Wounds* also returns to the religious home and family system, where she discovers

- Codependency
- Enmeshment, such that "it is hard to identify personal feelings, thoughts, and aspirations—this person so wound around someone else or another community that it is impossible to know the 'I' outside of the 'we'"
- Addiction, especially to simple black/white, good/evil patterns of thought that instill "fear of ambiguity and ... promise a sense of peace and ease with their brand of certitude"
- Unhealthy attachment.[25]

Pasquale is more thorough than most in classifying the kinds of traumatic experiences that people face in religious settings, such as

- Physical or sexual assault by a leader or layperson
- Physical, sexual, or emotional abuse outside the church but within the faith community (e.g. domestic violence by a devout spouse), in response to which the victim is "shamed or guilted into believing that it was his or her fault due to church doctrine or distorted faith text references—and had those references or the abuse reinforced as 'OK' by anyone else in the family/faith system"
- Marginalization and condemnation of the individual for their inferior, sinful, and wrong racial, ethnic, linguistic, and particularly gender or sexual identity according to doctrine
- Submission of a woman to a man in ways that adversely impact her physical, emotional, or psychological well-being
- Castigation for asking questions, which is seen as sinfulness or weak faith
- Excommunication, ostracism, shunning, or otherwise excluding people for their thoughts, feelings, and actions
- Making anyone "feel he or she doesn't belong, or is less than or sinful, or unworthy, based on nothing more than being who he or she is or communicating feelings."[26]

---

[25] Pasquale, *Sacred Wounds: A Path to Healing from Spiritual Trauma*, 79–80.
[26] Pasquale, *Sacred Wounds*, 65.

So far we have only spoken of the pain of being *in* the religion. But Winell was insistent that getting *out* of the religion can be traumatic in itself; in fact, her book's title, *Leaving the Fold*, directs the emphasis there. She overtly likened departing one's religion—or more often, departing one's particular church or religious community, since many if not most escapees remain committed to religion—to divorce or the death of a loved one, with similar qualities of loss and grief, such as "anger, guilt, depression, lowered self-esteem, and social isolation."[27] Naturally a religious group, like any group or organization, *wants* it to be difficult to leave, partly because attrition is bad for the group and partly to avoid setting the example of a successful life without the religion, its leaders, and its dogma. Enroth collected nineteen factors that impede the departure from religion, including the learned dependence on the community and authorities, lack of skill at thinking for oneself, in fact lack of social skills for survival in the world outside the community, "culture shock" at the ways of the outside world, feelings of rejection and isolation (especially if one's family and friends remain in the fold), and negative emotions like shame, guilt, anger, and bitterness.[28]

"Every aspect of my life had to be reexamined, healed, and redesigned," Winell testified of her personal experience of turning her back on her conservative Christian past.[29] This connects to another literature and to a problem that is bigger than religious apostasy, one that relates to all major loss and trauma. Also during the early 1990s, as religious trauma was initially identified and described, Ronnie Janoff-Bulman alerted us to the profound challenge of "shattered assumptions." She drew on still earlier work by C. M. Parkes concerning the bereavement process, who introduced the concept of "assumptive world," that is, a person's sense of reality, "which contains everything that we assume to be true on the basis of our previous experience. It is this internal model of the world that we are constantly matching against incoming sensory data in order to orient ourselves, recognize what is happening, and plan our behavior accordingly."[30] Eminent child psychologist Jean Piaget would call such assumptions "schemas," while historian of science Thomas Kuhn would use the term "paradigms," but whatever the name they provide a picture of reality as well as cognitive and emotional skills for navigating that reality.

---

[27] Winell, *Leaving the Fold*, 15.
[28] Enroth, *Recovering from Churches that Abuse*, 103–4.
[29] Winell, *Leaving the Fold*, 4.
[30] Parkes, "Bereavement as a Psychosocial Transition," 56.

Every individual inhabits an assumptive world, which is constructed from many sources, including religion for a large proportion of people but never religion exclusively; whatever public or cultural resources it is built out of, it is necessarily filtered through each person's unique biographical history and the interpretations they make of their life experiences. Once in place, although somewhat malleable, this assumptive world is stubbornly resistant to change, and people have many tricks for preserving it against anomalous and contradictory information. (See Chapter 10) However, as a bereavement scholar, Parkes stressed that life-changing events (like a serious illness or a loved one's death) sometimes or often "require people to undertake a major revision of their assumptions about the world."[31] In other words, it shatters their assumptions. Janoff-Bulman discussed three bedrock assumptions that underlie and facilitate all others, namely, that the world is benevolent, that the world is meaningful, and that the self is worthy.[32] Note that Janoff-Bulman did not claim, nor do I, that these three core assumptions are true, merely that they are common and for the most part healthy and enabling; we are better able to function if we believe (although "believe" is not quite the right word here; "take for granted" might be better) that the universe is kind and meaningful and that the self is good.

There is no indication that Janoff-Bulman or Parkes had religious trauma in mind, but their perspectives apply equally to it as to other sorts of trauma. To start, a religion may teach that the world is *not* benevolent or that the self is *not* worthy (in fact, conservative Christianity and most strains of Christianity teach that the world is corrupt and the self is inherently sinful or wicked), constructing a different bedrock of assumptions; granted, conservative Christianity does hold that the world is meaningful—if only as some unfathomable divine plan—but this meaning does not necessarily make the world more affirmative or affirming (life can be seen as a test or trap or temporary prison). So religious experience and training may instill a different and less healthy assumptive world than Janoff-Bulman imagined. Then, unpleasant, harmful, and abusive doctrines and encounters in the religion may shake those assumptions; members may be *told* that the world and the self are good but *feel* quite the opposite. The fear and anxiety that the religious doctrine instills are exacerbated by the fear and anxiety caused by malignant experiences inside the religion. These experiences are shattering enough; when the victim finally exits her religion (but, again, not always or usually religion entirely), she is traumatized again by the

---

[31] Parkes, "Bereavement as a Psychosocial Transition," 55.
[32] Janoff-Bulman, *Shattered Assumptions*, 6.

forfeiture not only of the religious community but of the assumptive world held together by its beliefs and relationships. For many, at least initially, their newfound freedom from religion does not feel liberating. Instead, by departing their religious reality they enter "a state of conceptual disintegration" where much of what they believed to be true is now false. "The victim is stuck between two untenable cognitive-emotional choices: preexisting assumptions that are no longer viable in describing the world and oneself and new assumptions that not only involve a total reworking of prior views but are themselves extremely negative and threatening."[33]

What follows for many former religious adherents, if their community, their beliefs, and their god were key elements of their assumptive world, is a period of recovery, which means world-rebuilding and assumption-adjustment and reconstruction. This can be a slow and arduous process, dependent on trust that has already been weakened. To be sure, not all defectors from religion go through an equally harrowing process—some accept and enjoy their freedom immediately—but for those who do, we who are already free of religion should not minimize their anguish. And we should take one more lesson from this investigation, as I have recommended elsewhere: arguing with people who have an essentially religious assumptive world is unlikely to dislodge them from their dogmas and communities, because they absorb those arguments through the screen of their religious assumptions. If and when "deconversion" occurs from arguments and facts, it will probably be a slow, fitful, and somewhat disorienting path for the believer.

The Varieties of
Religious Traumatic Experience

As important and useful as this information about religious trauma, spiritual abuse, and toxic faith is, it hardly scratches the surface of the matter. Typically, for both theist and atheist observers, the content of the primary literature deals almost solely with Christianity, in fact with conservative/fundamentalist/evangelical Christianity, which may be the main local problem for Western Christian societies but is far from the only religion in the world. The books surveyed above also tend to construe religious trauma as an individual phenomenon—one that pits a single victim usually against a single abuser—rather than as a structural or institutional affair. As noted, Winell's classic text focused as much on the ordeal of leaving a religion as the ordeal of staying in it. And, depressingly for non-religious types, much of the writing comes from a pro-theist angle

---

[33] Janoff-Bulman, *Shattered Assumptions*, 93.

which, while admitting that abuses happen in religion, is deeply committed to exonerating religion from responsibility and, therefore, to keeping the sheep in the fold. To paraphrase the National Rifle Association, they maintain that the only thing that can stop a bad guy with religion is a good guy with religion. Finally, religious trauma/spiritual abuse/toxic faith is thorny—but not inherently thornier than ordinary secular varieties—because it remains subjective, or, in the words of Pasquale, such trauma "is in the eye of the beholder."[34] On the one hand, an experience or relationship can be difficult or painful but not viewed as "traumatic," and if it is traumatic, it may not be viewed as *bad* trauma (i.e. there may be some notion of "no pain, no gain") or as damage. On the other hand, outsiders and professional therapists may see trauma and abuse where members, including victims, do not; this is conveyed by Novšak, Mandelj, and Simonič when they declare, "Despite the fact that people do not experience their religious context as abusive, this does not mean that the abuse is not occurring."[35]

To remind readers of some of the other consequential expressions of religious trauma, we might begin with the irrational "panic" over "satanic ritual abuse" that gripped much of the United States in the 1980s and 1990s. Arising from the general moral hysteria of the era and from the "recovered memory" movement in psychology (as in the 1980 book *Michelle Remembers*, which purported to document the memories of Michelle Smith, patient and future wife of the co-author, psychiatrist Lawrence Pazder, subsequently debunked), accounts of satanic abuse—especially sexual and child abuse but also allegedly murders—became commonplace. Less than a decade later, S. J. Kelley, in the *Cultic Studies Journal*, described ritualistic abuse of children which supposedly took place mostly at "day care centers or family child care providers" (who for some reason were Satanists). In those locations, children

> are abused psychologically as well as physically through group cult ceremonies, animal sacrifices, supernatural threats, ingestion of drugs and other substances, and distortion of traditional belief systems. Investigators and therapists often fail to recognize the signs of ritualistic sexual abuse, while others remain skeptical that this type of abuse actually occurs. Increased incidences of functional disturbances,

---

[34] Pasquale, *Sacred Wounds*, 22.
[35] Novšak, Mandelj, and Simonič, "Therapeutic Implications of Religious-Related Emotional Abuse," 40.

inappropriate sexual behavior, psychological distress, and other mental health disorders are associated with sexually abused children.[36]

A feverish 1996 essay based on a study of 802 psychotherapists reported 6,821 client cases, suggesting a true epidemic of lurid conduct including forced sex, child pornography, drugs, beatings, torture, animal and human sacrifice, and "baby breeding" (presumably to use in said sacrifices), often perpetrated by parents, although even the authors expressed some skepticism about the details.[37] Few if any such allegations have ever been substantiated.

Back in the real world, other much more verifiable forms of religious abuse and traumatic experiences have been documented. For instance, there really have been numerous homicidal and suicidal religious groups and "cults." In the former category, the Japanese doomsday religion Aum Shinrikyo, anticipating the end of the world in a violent conflagration of evil against good, attacked the Tokyo subway in June 1994 with sarin gas, causing seven deaths and six hundred injuries. In the category, we also find Heaven's Gate/TELAH, the Branch Davidians, and the Peoples Temple headed by Jim Jones. Heaven's Gate, formally known as TELAH or "The Evolutionary Level Above Human," was an ersatz California religious group mixing Christian theology with modern technology and science fiction; so convinced were they that their computer-chip-based "souls" would be uploaded for delivery to a more advanced planet that they killed themselves *en masse* in March 1997, after some of the male members had castrated themselves to liberate themselves from their more animalistic parts. Jim Jones transplanted his Peoples Temple from the United States to Guyana, where more than nine hundred devotees drank poison in November 1978 after an investigative team including Congressman Leo Ryan arrived to look into charges that members were held against their will (for which Ryan was shot and killed by some more committed members). Straddling suicide and homicide, the Branch Davidians, an offshoot of Seventh-day Adventists based in Waco, Texas and preparing for the apocalypse, attracted the attention of the Bureau of Alcohol, Tobacco, and Firearms (ATF), which attempted to seize the group's weapons. The ATF raid resulted in four dead agents and sixteen more wounded, along with six Branch Davidians; the subsequent siege of the compound by the FBI in April 1993 ended with fires that

---

[36] Kelley, "Ritualistic Abuse of Children: Dynamic Impact," 228.

[37] Bottoms, Shaver, and Goodman, "An Analysis of Ritualistic and Religion-Related Child Abuse Allegations."

destroyed the building and killed seventy-six members, each side blaming the other for the disaster.

Not all new and bizarre religions are as murderous as these four, but they do have a long and checkered history of preying on and exploiting their members. Among the more recent and notorious are NXVM (pronounced "nex-i-um"), the Kansas-based Angel's Landing, and The Movement for the Restoration of the Ten Commandments, whose leaders burned down their church and killed more than five hundred supporters in 2000. Older organizations that abused and traumatized their members include Children of God (a California group in the 1970s through 1990s that practiced "flirty fishing" or sexual advances to attract male recruits and was also accused of child physical and sexual abuse; it survives as Family International), the polygamous Church of the Lamb of God in the 1970s, the Rajneesh movement of the 1970s and 1980s (which poisoned the residents of a town in Washington state), and the Order of the Solar Temple (yet another cult that doomed many of its followers to murder or suicide in the 1990s), to name but a few. Across such organizations, financial and sexual violations have been rife.

By definition (of those who use the term "cult," which is really not part of the social-scientific vocabulary), these cultish groups are outside the mainstream of "good" religion. However, there is no assurance that good, mainstream, institutional religion will protect its flock from abuse; rather, the shepherds are often the prime and systematic wolves. The most egregious case is the sexual abuse of children in the Catholic Church. An investigation of church records conducted by the John Jay College of Criminal Justice in 2004 revealed eleven thousand allegations of child sexual abuse by Catholic clergy between 1950 and 2002, implicating 4,450 priests. The sexual crimes themselves were enhanced by an institutional cover-up to protect priests at the expense of young victims. A report on clergy sex abuse in Boston by Thomas Reilly concluded:

> Top Archdiocese officials ... decided that they should conceal—from the parishes, the laity, law enforcement and the public—their knowledge of individual complaints of abuse and the long history of such complaints within the Archdiocese....In the very few cases where allegations of sexual abuse of children were communicated to law enforcement, senior Archdiocese managers remained committed to their primary objective—safeguarding the well-being of priests and the institution over the welfare of children and preventing scandal.[38]

---

[38] Reilly, "The Sexual Abuse of Children."

But while the Catholic Church, due to its size and centralization (not to mention its hypocritical rule of celibacy), has garnered special attention, other sects and denominations have their own epidemic of abuses and violations. In 2022 the Southern Baptist Convention issued the report of its internal Sexual Abuse Task Force, documenting large-scale abuses in that Protestant organization. To name one egregious case outside the United States, Apollo Quiboloy, pastor of the Filipino megachurch "Kingdom of Jesus Christ, The Name Above Every Name," was charged in 2021 with sex trafficking for transporting girls and young women to feed his sexual appetites. The seventy-one-year-old Quiboloy, self-designated "Appointed Son of God," is also a friend and adviser of former Philippines president Rodrigo Duterte.[39] Then there are the untold physical, sexual, and emotional abuses that transpire behind the closed doors of religious homes.

Speaking of traumatic religious home life, another source of needless suffering and sometimes death is religion-inspired medical neglect and denial of medical treatment. Many devout parents believe that faith alone will cure their sick little ones; some actually believe that seeking medical care is disrespectful to their god, a sign of their lack of faith. Withholding reasonable and effective care would be criminal in most circumstances, but as many as thirty states in the United States allow religious exemptions and defenses for such behavior, The criminal code of West Virginia, for instance, stipulates that the classification of murder of a child does "not apply to any parent ... who fails or refuses ... to supply a child ... with necessary medical care on religious grounds," and Idaho grants an exception for religion-based manslaughter, criminal injury, neglect, and non-support from prosecution.[40] From Christian Science to Jehovah's Witness and the Amish, multiple religious groups discourage or forbid particular medical treatments (like blood transfusions) or any medical treatment at all. The COVID-19 pandemic witnessed many parents and religious leaders refusing vaccinations or simple interventions like masks or postponement of public religious services and even denying the plague altogether; meanwhile, by one account more than a thousand American clergy died from the disease, no doubt some unnecessarily and foolishly.[41] The full toll of faith-based medical neglect cannot be determined, but a study by Seth Asser and Rita Swan in 1998 counted 172 child deaths resulting from withheld medical care in the previous two decades, more than eighty percent occurring in five sects—the Church of

---

[39] Gotinga, "Pastor Claiming to Be 'Son of God' Charged with Sex Trafficking."
[40] Quoted in Swan, "Faith-Based Medical Neglect," 343–44.
[41] Dixon, "A Survey of COVID-19 Deaths among American Clergy."

the First Born, End Time Ministries, Faith Assembly, Faith Tabernacle, and First Church of Christ Scientist.[42] Plenty of other children (and adults) surely had their illnesses and injuries pointlessly prolonged and intensified for religious reasons.

Then there are the bogus and destructive "therapies" inflicted on individuals who are legitimately sick or who are only deemed sick according to religious doctrine. "Faith-healing," which inevitably fails (except as a placebo in the short term) deters the ill from seeking valid medical treatment. Meanwhile, in religious traditions where homosexuality or non-binary gender identity is regarded as sickness (if not sin), coercive interventions dubbed "reparative therapy" or "gay conversion therapy" are practiced, often on young people. Not only are such "treatments" ineffective, but they are actually harmful and traumatizing:

> There is ample evidence that societal prejudice causes significant medical, psychological and other harms to LGBTQ people. For example, research on the issue of family acceptance of LGBTQ youth conducted at San Francisco State University found that compared with LGBTQ young people who were not rejected or were only a little rejected by their parents and caregivers because of their gay or transgender identity, highly rejected LGBTQ young people were:
>
> - More than 8 times as likely to have attempted suicide
> - Nearly 6 times as likely to report high levels of depression
> - More than 3 times as likely to use illegal drugs
> - More than 3 times as likely to be at high risk for HIV and STDs.[43]

Elsewhere (in the fifth chapter of *Atheism Advanced* and in a book dedicated to religious violence, *Cruel Creeds, Virtuous Violence: Religious Violence Across Culture and History*), I have charted in detail the myriad forms that traumatizing, debilitating, and fatal religion-inspired violence can perpetrate on victims, human and non-human. There is not room to rehearse all of that material here, but it is worthwhile to mention and summarize it.

Probably no religious practice has claimed more victims and caused more agony than sacrifice, although it is neither the oldest nor the most universal expression of religious violence. It was widespread among

---

[42] Asser and Swan, "Child Fatalities from Religion-Motivated Medical Neglect."
[43] Human Rights Campaign, "The Lies and Dangers of Efforts to Change Sexual Orientation or Gender Identity."

the farming and herding peoples in pre-modern indigenous cultures, including the ancient Hebrews, whose scriptures ordain a plethora of sacrificial customs mostly of mammals but also of birds and even non-animal and non-living objects. The Vedas of ancient India were also sacrifice-driven writings, and most Christians continue to understand their religion as founded by a sacrifice (although some theologians dispute the sacrificial nature of Christ's death, which would be a surprise to rank-and-file Christians if they knew). In many a traditional society, blood sacrifices were a regular part of an array of ceremonial events, from male initiation rituals to the planting of a field or the raising of a building. And contrary to the predictions of scholars like René Girard,[44] sacrifice did not disappear in more centralized and state-level societies; instead, it escalated, as in the sacrificial cults of Greece, Rome, Egypt, Dahomey (Africa), and Hawaii, as well as, most magnificently, the Aztec. In the last few of these cases, humans were routinely sacrificed for various purposes, from feeding the gods to accompanying and serving the kings in the imaginary afterlife (so-called retainer sacrifice). Girard was wrong that sacrificial violence is the origin of religion and of culture itself (a just-so story disproven by the fact that the oldest societies, hunters and gatherers, did not perform sacrifice), but it is true that sacrifice reveals something about the essence of religion: countless beings bled and died so that their (imaginary) life-force could be tapped and used by humans, suggesting that religion is about the management and manipulation of the world's fecund power.

If there is a universal act of religious violence and trauma, it is self-injury, and humans have been fiendishly creative in inventing ways to hurt their bodies for spiritual purposes. From the smallest hunter-gatherer society to the most complex religious institution (like the Catholic Church), people have cut, scarred, pierced, sliced, beaten, flagellated, and bled themselves, knocked out teeth, and hacked off parts of their genitals, as well as deprived themselves of food, sleep, and basic comforts. Again, male (and sometimes female) initiation rituals tended to involve surgical changes to the body, which were also often tests of toughness for young men. Religious specialists such as shamans were frequently a primary target of ritual self-mutilations, up to and including symbolic death; once fully fledged, the performance of shamanic curing rituals for the benefit of others often caused further pain to the healers. Sometimes, as in the case of shamans, the idea was that physical suffering released or instilled spiritual power; in other cases, like Christian enthusiasts, beating and depriving the self was punishment, self-discipline, and emulation of their mythical founder (i.e., suffering like/for Christ).

---

[44] Girard, *Violence and the Sacred.*

The next step up from garden-variety self-deprivation and self-mutilation was the ascetic, the virtuoso of religious pain, who adopted a lifestyle of hardship and misery. "Professional" religious practitioners from Christian and Buddhist monks to Jain *digambar* ("sky-clad" or naked and homeless) saints accepted a permanent status of self-denial; ideally, older Hindu men would choose the way of a *sannyasin* or wandering self-renouncer without property or family, the better to concentrate on their spiritual purification (and no doubt leaving many an elderly wife and children in dire straits). At the end of the road to self-destruction is the martyr, who is willing and eager to die for religion, whose death is a testimony to the fortitude of their faith and, hopefully, a model to attract converts. Christianity naturally has a robust history of martyrdom, as does Islam, particularly Shi'ite Islam, in which believers scourge themselves in memory of past martyrs like Muhammad's compatriots and kinsmen Ali and Husayn and welcome death as a witness (the root meaning of both "martyr" in English and *shahid* in Arabic) to their religious truth. The message in all this behavior is that religion is largely about transformation and that "spiritual" transformation often requires physical adversity and pain.

Not satisfied to traumatize the self in some misguided spiritual quest, many religions have been keen to traumatize others in the form of persecution. Persecution (a legalistic concept, from the Latin *sequor*, "I follow/go after" and related to prosecution) is not always religious but is uniquely virulent when linked to religion. The central notion in persecution is wrongness and intolerability: the victim of persecution is bad, offensive, evil, and dangerous to himself and to others. Pagan Romans persecuted Christians (mostly for the crime of refusing to revere and sacrifice to the emperor), and once in power Christians returned the favor, persecuting pagans and, soon afterward, fellow Christians with the wrong beliefs, that is, heretics. Christians also persecuted (and persecute) Jews and, when they were available, Muslims and followers of other faiths. Meanwhile, Muslims persecuted (and persecute) Jews, Christians, Hindus, and members of minority and heretical Islamic sects such as Ahmadis, Barelvis, and Sufis. Contemporary Myanmar persecutes its Muslim Rohingya minority, and China appears bent on liquidating its Uyghur Muslim minority as suspected terrorists and obstacles to Chinese hegemony and economic development. Far from feeling shame for these assaults against religious diversity, perpetrators often feel quite proud of it: both Augustine and Aquinas in Christian history believed that heresy or religious deviance was a crime, indeed worse than any secular crime, and that punishing it was just and good, even a kindness to the victim, whose body might suffer and die but whose soul was saved. The lesson in persecution is that, while not all religions are prone to such violence, the closer they get to (mono)theism, the more intolerant of difference they become.

Religions also evince a remarkable capacity for blending with other social variables like race, class, and nationality into religiopolitical identities when they contribute to ethno-religious conflict. Not every ethnic conflict has a religious component, nor is religion ever the sole component in ethnic conflict, but religion commonly provides an extra level of intensity and authenticity to such struggles. On the island of Sri Lanka, minority Tamil Hindus clashed with majority Buddhist Sinhalese (proving that Buddhism is not always a religion of peace and tolerance) over land and political control; for Sinhalese Buddhists, the mythical grant of the island to them by the original Buddha himself sanctioned their claim. In India, Hindus have fought Muslims as well as Sikhs, and in Palestine Jews and Muslims are locked in a contest that periodically erupts into war. As Yugoslavia disintegrated in the 1990s, the conflict in Bosnia was sometimes seen, and actively promoted by Orthodox Christian Serbs, as a battle against global Islam in the form of Bosnian Muslims. And religions can be fratricidal, as in Northern Ireland, where The Troubles that broke out in 1969 (but have a much longer history) pitted Protestant "loyalists" who desired to remain in the United Kingdom against Catholic "nationalists" who sought to integrate Northern Ireland into the independent Republic of Ireland. In all of these cases, more was at stake than religious disagreement; religious differences were associated with inequalities in wealth, education, housing, rights, and political power, yielding an incendiary mix of religious beliefs and worldly interests.

At the extreme, religion can contribute to, and legitimate, open warfare. Most readers will be familiar with the Islamic concept of *jihad*, which is often translated as "holy war" but actually means "struggle" in Arabic and does not always denote violent conflict. Nevertheless, Islam does authorize war in defense of religion, the Qur'an (sura 2:190–1) teaching that fighting and killing "in the way of Allah" is perfectly justified. The notion of "holy war" of course originates in Christianity, although it has roots in Greco-Roman ideas of "just war" and in the ancient Hebrew idea of *milhemet mitzvah* or commanded war—commanded by Yahweh, that is—as in Deuteronomy 20:18: "But thou shalt utterly destroy them; namely, the Hittites, and the Amorites, the Canaanites, and the Perizzites, the Hivites, and the Jebusites; as the Lord thy God hath commanded thee." The Crusades (wars of the cross), a series of Christian campaigns to wrest the "Holy Land" from Muslim clutches in the eleventh and twelfth centuries, are the paradigm of religious war, although European Christian authorities also warred against heretics and new sects such as Waldensians, Hussites, and Cathars or Albigensians, and the Thirty Years' War (1618–1648) between Catholic and Protestant kingdoms devastated Europe. Other religions have martial elements to them, from the warrior monks of medieval Japanese Buddhism to the elite Khalsa branch of Sikhism. Together, ethno-religious conflict and religious war permanently debunk the myth that religion is intrinsically a force for peace.

Conclusion:
The Tangled Web of Religion and Trauma

It is understandable that American and European commentators in their Christian-saturated context, especially coming from a therapeutic perspective, would focus on the kinds of religious traumas that they encounter most frequently in their practices. We, as observers and students of religion in all its forms, cannot be content with such a limited horizon. Indeed, even Western therapists, scholars, and lawmakers are likely to meet victims of other types of religious trauma, from refugees of ethno-religious conflicts and religious wars (including acts of terrorism) to women victimized by religion-authorized genital mutilations or attempted "honor killings." There is a world of religious trauma beyond the tribulations of dwelling in or deserting conservative Christian homes and churches.

   Further, while I am not one to go easy on religion, we should also recognize that there are more connections between religion and trauma than the causal relationship. Undoubtedly, religion is a cause, direct or indirect, of much abuse, violence, toxicity, and trauma. Yet, for many people, religion also *explains* suffering and misfortune, whether this (inherently false) explanation consists of a divine test, a spiritual punishment, a demonic possession, a consequence of a broken rule or taboo or a neglected ritual obligation, or the nefarious scheming of a witch or sorcerer. The Azande of Africa famously attributed every negative event as the work of witches, and it is depressingly common for believers around the world today to blame witches, often child witches, for all the problems and failures in their lives (and to persecute those alleged witches, often to death). In other instances, sophisticated belief-systems like Hinduism and Buddhism explain the burdens and sorrows of life as the outcome of misdeeds in a past incarnation and, ultimately, as the inescapable effect of *samsara* and *dukkha*, the imperfection or brokenness of existence.

Second, religion can serve as an *expression* or *reflection* of real-world suffering and trauma. Joop de Jong and Ria Reis, in their account of an African religious movement of women who could not bear children or whose children had died, called religion of this sort an "idiom of distress," defined as "an embodied symbolic language for psychosocial suffering that derives its legitimacy from its shared metaphors, meaning and understanding in a group."[45] Such distress may come from tragic life events like losing a child, but it may also be part of the everyday structural situation of disadvantaged people, primarily the poor, racial and ethnic minorities, and women. Around the world, women are more likely to report spiritual attack and spirit possession, and to join spirit-possession religions like Brazilian Candomblé, as consequences of their real-world anguish. But men are not immune, as Francisco Ferrándiz found among the young males in the Venezuelan possession religion of María Lionza. These men indulged in unprecedented self-injury featuring "cuts with knives or razors, piercings with needles, ingestion of limited amounts of glass or toxic liquids such as kerosene," and other self-mutilations.[46] Possessed by and channeling the "rage, fury, frustration, courage, daring, valor, [and] fierceness" of spirits of Vikings or African slaves, they symbolically expressed the traumas "of their own current lives with the poverty, crime, social disorder, and violence of shantytown existence."[47]

Third, religion may function and may be sought as a *remedy* or *therapy* for trauma, whether that trauma is believed to have natural or supernatural origins. Earlier we discussed shamans and faith healers. The *curandera* in Latin American societies provides healing treatments for sick and troubled patients, who are often diagnosed as coping with "soul loss." Janice Boddy noticed that women in Hofriyat village (Sudan), who were thought to be possessed by *zâr* spirits, performed rituals and entered sects not to exorcise the spirit but to learn to live with it. Boddy hypothesized that the "purpose of the healing rite is to tame the *zâr* and establish a social relationship between it and its human host."[48] The woman will probably co-exist with the *zâr* for the rest of her life; possession, Boddy concluded, is thus "therapeutic" for the woman who is labeled a "bride of the *zâr*" and who, while possessed, "is not human, not

---

[45] De Jong and Reis, "Kiyang-yang," 302.
[46] Ferrándiz, "Open Veins: Spirits of Violence and Grief in Venezuela," 49.
[47] Ferrándiz, "Open Veins," 47.
[48] Boddy, "The Work of Zâr," 118.

Hofriyati, not even, in most cases, female"[49]—which did not relieve her from possession but did relieve her from many of the normal burdens of a woman in this rigidly patriarchal society. Often, since no real "cure" is possible, the goal of religious intervention is to help the individual accept and find dignity in duress, as in the Algerian Muslim music-and-dance tradition of *dīwān*. Tamara Dee Turner reasons that *dīwān* provides "a space for suffering with the intent to emotionally and physically engage with it through musicked trance dancing and manage it in ways that exercise the relational nature of suffering."[50] She insists that *dīwān* "functions quite practically as mental-emotional healthcare," giving comfort from forces ranging from "injustice and offense to racism and genocide."[51] However, like the Hofriyat cult, Algerian trance and music do not cure, since the human condition is incurable: "Life was deemed to be full of inevitable suffering," but religion grants the power and courage for "'going deeper' into suffering. Again, it resonates with the ethos to fully feel it, realize it, and complete it," making the pain of living bearable and honorable.[52]

This last point speaks to the ultimate moral of the story of religious trauma and its challenge to us but primarily to the theists, theologians, and therapists who deal with it and often try to spare religion from its own nastiest tendencies and to return victims comfortably to the fold. As we have said and as is painfully obvious, no religion can promise members a life of uninterrupted peace, bliss, and prosperity. Religion cannot take away all the hurt, but must religion itself hurt? Various writers on religious trauma, and trauma in general, concede that trauma is subjective and that suffering is not entirely negative or meaningless; Christianity indeed accepts and more than occasionally invites pain as a path to virtue. So, many a religious practitioner—from the shaman-in-training and the ascetic to the ordinary believer—embraces distress and even torment as the price of believing if not of being alive.

But let's take the next step: what if the "dogmatic religion," the "toxic faith," is true? What if their god really does hate homosexuality, considers humans innately sinful and wicked, or wants men to have dominion over women? What if, in more extreme cases, the weary sun really does need human hearts and blood, or a human god-king really does need servants in the afterlife, or the self or its unruly body really does deserve a good whipping? What if witches are inveterate evil-doers,

---

[49] Boddy, "The Work of Zâr," 122.
[50] Turner, "Music and Trance as Methods for Engaging with Suffering," 76.
[51] Turner, "Music and Trance as Methods for Engaging with Suffering," 77–78.
[52] Turner, "Music and Trance as Methods for Engaging with Suffering," 87–88.

shamans are dead shells of supernatural power, and heretics endanger their own and everyone else's immortal souls? The more kind-hearted theists and religionists, and many theologians and philosophers of religion, want to distance themselves from the uglier aspects of religion, but if they intend to stake their careers and their spirits on the truth of religion (well, their own religion, not other religions), then they cannot retreat into platitudes about the goodness of god(s) and the beneficence of belief—although they may, as Kearney and Kelsey do, abandon hope in an all-powerful and all-good god in favor of a powerless and useless one (their own words) who can do no more for us that suffer along with us. (See Chapter 4)

If it is the case that a god has any rules and preferences at all—and if they don't, what are they for?—then (1) fulfilling these rules and preferences may be difficult and unpleasant and (2) some individuals may fail to fulfill them. For such struggling believers, religion may be traumatic, even abusive, but that's just the way it is. Outside of Buddy Christ for whom everything is OK, god(s) and other putative supernatural beings and forces sometimes make life *more* arduous, grim, and tortuous for both adherents and non-adherents, not less. It is not easy to be a Christian, to be godly, many Christians admit. In this reality, in this regime of truth, humans may feel abused, they may *be* abused, but that is the divinely-decreed universe they occupy, and nothing can be done about it. And trying to deny or alleviate the trauma is somewhere between delusion and blasphemy. Being a good devotee may be laborious, even excruciating, even traumatizing, but it is *good* trauma from religion's perspective, trauma for a happy cause and with a happy ending; being a bad devotee—or not a devotee at all—leads irrevocably to a dreadful (but deserved) destination.

The elimination of religion does not promise a panacea of unceasing pleasure and joy; such is not the lot of human existence. But it does free humanity from the gratuitous abuses and traumas that illusory god(s) and other make-believe beings so exquisitely if not delightedly inflict on us creatures—and their devotees inflict on the rest of us.

7

Agnomancy:
Conjuring Ignorance in Religion
(and Throughout Society)

Given everything we know, why do people continue to believe in god(s)? More than sixty years ago, as we discussed in a previous chapter, theologian Gabriel Vahanian insisted that Christianity suffered from "dishabilitation" in the modern world, that is, it was both *disabled* and *homeless* in a secularist and "immanentist" (focused on the present and here-and-now) society. The result, he reasoned, was a contemporary "cultural incapacity for god" and, along with Thomas Altizer and similar thinkers, the "death of god." Why does this dead god still seem so very much alive—and not only alive but tenaciously traditional, confoundingly conventional—the same old grandfather in the sky?

The incomplete refutation if not erasure of god(s) is not from lack of trying on the part of atheists, secularists, humanists, rationalists, and scientists of all sorts. The information is there; the arguments are there; the debates are there. Of course, it is always possible, although not entirely likely, that devotees of the dead or otherwise shrunken god have not heard the news, have not heard the *facts*. Many if not most atheists think that if we can only deliver the facts to believers, if we bombard them with more facts and better arguments, they will see the light and come to know that there is no such thing as god(s). This is why the bulk of atheist writing takes the form of repeating (dare we say rehashing) the "arguments against god(s)" and the scientific evidence that debunks or at least renders obsolete and superfluous any god-talk.

There has certainly been progress in the erosion of god-belief, but the stubborn persistence of god(s) suggests that something is wrong. Too many theists do not know the anti-god facts and logic, and too many who do know the facts and logic do not *know* it, that is, have not accepted it, embraced it, and capitulated to it. They ignore the evidence of a godless reality; they are in a state of not-knowing that god is dead and that god-belief is no longer viable.

Ignorance is a powerfully pejorative word in English. It implies stupidity or an inability to think. In some circumstances, stupidity may be a cause or an effect of ignorance, but it is wrong to conflate the two: a person can be intelligent enough but *not know*. Ignorance (the negation of the Latin *gnoscere*, to know but also to be acquainted, recognize, or perceive) strictly speaking means that one is not aware of or does not possess knowledge. No one, of course, is ignorant on all subjects, so ignorance is specific to some domain(s) of knowledge, in the present instance perhaps science and critical thinking but also modern-day theology which often dispenses with the traditional personal god. (See Chapter 4) Like "faith," "ignorance" lacks a verb form; we can only say "to have faith" or "to be ignorant," and the verb "to ignore" is related but substantially different (ignoring may be one cause, or effect, of ignorance but is not synonymous with it).

More significantly, the typical attitude toward ignorance is that it is a simple absence of knowledge or information; it is also the default or starting point in a process that leads to knowledge and then to correct conclusions. In other words, one begins without knowledge, then one acquires knowledge, and finally, one understands and accepts the truth of the matter. In this interpretation, ignorance is a void to be filled, and once filled, knowledge not only dispels ignorance but also dispels any false thoughts or beliefs that were held during and due to the condition of ignorance. That is, knowledge should be transformative.

In this chapter, we will examine recent research on ignorance, which sees it as anything but a simple and innocent default state of knowledgelessness. Ignorance is far too often an achievement, a result of forces and activities that are frequently both intentional and sinister. Accordingly, we will investigate just what these forces and activities are, not only but especially in religion. A wide array of individuals, parties, and institutions *want us ignorant* and employ shrewd tactics to accomplish their goal. We will explore these ignorance-conjuring tricks in religion and consider their damaging consequences in and beyond the realm of religion, coming face to face with why more arguments and better facts—more knowledge—alone do not automatically eradicate ignorance and false or falsified belief.

Agnotology:
The Study of Ignorance or Not-Knowing

The problem of knowledge—what it means to know and how we know what we think we know—has been an enduring subject of philosophy, perhaps the first subject if we consider Socrates challenging the citizens of Athens to elaborate on what they know and forcing them to confront the imperfections of their supposed knowledge. Socrates famously asserted that he himself knew that he knew nothing and merely asked questions. Further, not knowing was a virtue of sorts: The only true wisdom is in knowing you know nothing, he reportedly taught, making self-awareness of ignorance the drive to inspect one's own and society's claims of truth and certainty. The Hellenistic philosophical school of Skepticism made ignorance or the lack (or impossibility) of knowledge its key tenet. Almost two millennia later French philosopher René Descartes used human proneness to error as a tool and motivator to clear away all alleged knowledge via radical doubt and to search for anything that we can know with absolute confidence, arriving at his most lauded discovery that the only thing I can know beyond dispute is that I exist (*cogito ergo sum*, I think therefore I am—which in the era of virtual reality and digital bots, androids, and simulated persons is no longer as sure as he surmised). Of course, on that foundation of total ignorance Descartes quickly and easily reconstructed all of Christian doctrine (on the unjustified premise that a god would not lie to us, that is, would guarantee us trustworthy knowledge). At the end of the 1700s Immanuel Kant claimed to find the very boundary of our possible knowledge, which could only come from and be of "phenomena" or sense perceptions; we could never know "things in themselves" beyond and behind our perceptions, but this did not prevent him from re-positing the Christian god, the ultimate thing beyond perception and knowledge.

Although the question of knowledge has always existed in philosophy, the term "epistemology" (Greek *episteme*, knowledge) did not appear in English until the mid-nineteenth century. It was immediately noticed by thinkers like James Ferrier that there was no equivalent study of not-knowing, presumably because, as we indicated at the outset, not-knowing was construed as the unproblematic condition of not-yet-having-knowledge. In 1854 Ferrier introduced a project to analyze ignorance, which he regarded as a "defect, imperfection, privation, or shortcoming," specifically "the deprivation of knowledge."[1] For this new field, he proposed the awkward neologism *agnoiology*.

No one really took up Ferrier's suggestion for over a century, until ignorance became a pervasive and conspicuous issue in society. The first scholar to seriously engage with the topic of ignorance was Michael Smithson in his 1989 *Ignorance and Uncertainty*. Smithson understood both that ignorance had been overlooked (ignored?) for too long as a

---

[1] Ferrier, *Institutes of Metaphysics*, 397.

philosophical and practical matter and that when it was included it was generally and wrongly "treated as either the absence or the distortion of 'true' knowledge."[2] Instead, he counseled that ignorance is or can be "a social creation, like knowledge.... Ignorance, like knowledge, is socially constructed and negotiated,"[3] although not always equally between partners or between perpetrators and victims.

Smithson's definition of ignorance—"A is *ignorant* from B's viewpoint if A fails to agree with or show awareness of ideas which B defines as actually or potentially valid"—highlighted the fact that ignorance is inevitably judged from somebody's perspective, relative to somebody's knowledge-claims or truth assertions; "Indeed, we cannot even talk about particular instances of ignorance without referring to the standpoint of some group or individual."[4] There is thus inherently an authority or power dimension to knowledge: *who* has knowledge, and *who* gets to determine what knowledge is? Further, knowledge is not simple and unitary; rather, it "is multiple, and has distinct levels," including the distinctions between being in error (in which case you do not know that you are ignorant) and being aware of a gap in your knowledge on the one hand or between *informational* ignorance (lacking certain data) and *epistemological* ignorance (the failure not so much to access as to *process* data—although there are many contradictory "processes" through which we can put information, from integrating it into our mind and jettisoning old false knowledge and beliefs to ignoring it, resisting it, or actually attacking it as biased or coercive).[5] At any rate, Smithson composed a typology of ignorance, dividing it first into *irrelevance* and *error*. Under irrelevance (knowledge that does not matter to us), he placed untopicality (facts that are off-topic), undecidability (issues that are too unsettled to be called knowledge), and taboo. Under error, he situated distortion (with two subtypes—confusion and inaccuracy) and incompleteness (consisting of absence and uncertainty, the latter subdivided into ambiguity, probability, and vagueness).

The next major advance in the development of a discipline of not-knowing was a 2008 edited volume by Robert Proctor and Londa Schiebinger, in which they coined the term *agnotology* (*a-* + *gnosis*, closely related etymologically to agnosticism) or the study of non-knowledge. In his introduction to the volume, Proctor first lamented over "how little we know about ignorance," particularly given "(a) how much

[2] Smithson, *Ignorance and Uncertainty*, 5.
[3] Smithson, *Ignorance and Uncertainty*, 6.
[4] Smithson, *Ignorance and Uncertainty*, 6.
[5] Smithson, *Ignorance and Uncertainty*, 6–7.

ignorance there is, (b) how many kinds there are, and (c) how consequential ignorance is in our lives."[6] He then expounded on the nuances of ignorance, noting for instance that it "is more than a void—and not even always a bad thing": privacy (keeping others, particularly the government, ignorant of many of your personal thoughts and actions) is a virtue; legal "blindness" of juries and judges makes the justice system function; not-knowing motivates science; and there is plainly too much information in the world for anyone to know all of it, which is why we rely on area-experts. Most fundamentally, he rightly advised, researchers and citizens alike "need to think about the conscious, unconscious, and structural production of ignorance, its diverse causes and conformations, whether brought about by neglect, forgetfulness, myopia, extinction, secrecy, or suppression. The point is to question the *naturalness* of ignorance."[7] At its most pernicious, ignorance is "a deliberately engineered and *strategic ploy* (or active construct)," something that is *done to us*.[8]

The chapters in their volume cover a range of topics, from censorship and journalism to race, indigenous knowledge, archaeology, and science and industry. Unsurprisingly, much if not most of the work in agnotology (whether or not the term appears) centers on corporations and the ways in which and the reasons for which they strive to keep customers, regulators, the general public, and the government ignorant of their conduct. Among the first such studies were Gerald Markowitz and David Rosner's 2002 *Deceit and Denial: The Deadly Politics of Industrial Pollution*, followed by the singularly influential and insightful 2008 book by David Michaels titled *Doubt is Their Product: How Industry's Assault on Science Threatens Your Health*. Doubt—sustaining a fog of non-knowledge around their products or production and disposal practices—is a prominent theme in many of these writings, like Naomi Oreskes and Erik Conway's 2010 *Merchants of Doubt: How a Handful of Scientists Obscured the Truth about Issues from Tobacco to Global Warming* and Barbara Freese's 2020 *Industrial-Strength Denial: Eight Stories of Corporations Defending the Indefensible, from the Slave Trade to Climate Change*. In 2013 Philip Mirowski turned the agnotological lens on the finance industry in his treatise on the 2008 global economic crisis, *Never Let a Serious Crisis Go to Waste*.

---

[6] Proctor, "Agnotology," 1–2.
[7] Proctor, "Agnotology," 3.
[8] Proctor, "Agnotology," 3.

Agnomancy:
How to Make and Keep People Ignorant

The growing study of agnotology helps us to identify the many types of ignorance, the sites of ignorance production, and the parties guilty of promoting ignorance. Ignorance—again, not-knowing, making knowledge unavailable or the processing and application of knowledge difficult—is a desirable attainment for those who are trying to get away with something, who are breaking the law, cheating us, endangering us, exploiting us, polluting our environment, selling us a shoddy product, or otherwise putting us individually and collectively in jeopardy. Wherever the stakes involve power and wealth, there are likely to be purveyors of ignorance. Therefore we find them in business and industry, in government, and in religion.

The field of agnotology has matured considerably, but one element of research on ignorance-making is still lacking. That is the specific practices and tactics that agents of ignorance, masters of not-knowing, put to work to prevent us from having the knowledge we need or from being able to use knowledge effectively in self-defense. An appropriate name for this box of tricks is *agnomancy* (*a-* + *gnosis* + *manteia*, not-knowing-divination/conjuring/magic), sharing a root with necromancy (black magic or death magic), geomancy (earth magic), and scapulimancy (divination by means of the scapula or shoulder blade, which was burned and inspected for cracks). Just as in these other mantic traditions, agnomancy consists of techniques and skills to "conjure up" an effect, in this case, ignorance and opacity of knowledge. For clarity, the difference between agnomancy and agnotology is analogical to the difference between crime and criminology: just as criminology studies crime while crime refers to the actual practices of law-breaking, agnotology studies ignorance while agnomancy refers to the actual practices of knowledge-breaking.

Essentially, agnomancy covers any number of strategies for erecting obstacles between knowledge and the potential knower, whom the agnomancer prefers to keep in the dark. There are many ways to interfere with the availability of information. The most basic and brute-force method is sheer lying, either lying about having information (i.e., denial) or disseminating lies as information. Just short of lying, or a clever indirect way of lying, is what has been dubbed "plausible deniability," which includes practices to deliberately and conveniently make oneself ignorant. If you didn't know, how can you be held responsible? Linsey McGoey's long-term observation of pharmaceutical companies discovered that one means that they adopt to shield themselves from liability is a form of "strategic ignorance" that can include not doing adequate testing of drugs in the first place or not reporting all the findings of their drug tests, even internally to the company; they also might not test for side-effects, for all major drug interactions, or for the efficacy on different populations of future users. Then, if a negative effect surfaces after approval of the medicine, they have an "ignorance alibi," which McGoey defines as "any mechanism that obscures one's involvement in causing harm to others, furnishing plausible deniability and making unawareness seem innocent rather than calculated."[9]

Governments also rely on this ploy. Agencies created and empowered to safeguard citizens, like the Environmental Protection Agency or the National Center for Health Statistics, may be defunded, understaffed, or headed by hostile or incompetent administrators such that they cannot even begin to collect the information they require, thus making them impotent to respond to environmental or health crises. Other institutions like the Census Bureau or the Bureau of Justice Statistics can be and have been hobbled by restrictions on their ability to collect data, let alone to share that data; at other times, as during the coronavirus pandemic, an administration may cut a relevant agency like the Centers for Disease Control out of the information loop, instead channeling data (such as it is) to another agency, in this instance the Department of Health and Human Services, headed by a pliant appointee of the president. In the 1980s Ronald Reagan went so far as to invent the ironically-named Office of Information and Regulatory Affairs precisely to impede the collection of information and thereby any regulatory action.

Another battery of schemes, to which we have become far too accustomed, undermines the sources of knowledge. A primary tactic is discrediting the source of any information that contradicts the claims or threatens the interests of the agnomancers; chief among these sources are scientists, journalists, and academic researchers. These knowledge-professionals may be accused of bias (usually of "liberal bias") or of pursuing their own power and interest. It is true that scientists and scholars tend to be disproportionately "liberal": a 2009 study by the Pew Research Center found that more than half of scientists labeled themselves as liberal and only nine percent as conservative,[10] and scholars in fields such as sociology, anthropology, history, and psychology are consistently accused of sharing a "liberal agenda"—which means that they are critical thinkers who question the contentions of vested interests. Lately, industries and

---

[9] McGoey, *The Unknowers*, 56.
[10] Pew Research Center, "Section 4: Scientists, Politics and Religion."

politicians have gone on the offensive against the quality, trustworthiness, or very truthfulness of information that they do not want the public to know, rebuking it as "fake news." In the worst cases, knowledge-experts may be publicly slandered or intimidated by withdrawal of their funding, loss of jobs, arrest, or even death threats (as when Oklahoma Republican Party chairman and candidate for Congress, John Bennett, recently called for the arrest, trial, and execution by firing squad of Anthony Fauci for the capital crime of, what?, advising Americans to wear masks and get vaccinated[11]).

On a minimally more sensible note, agnomancers may impugn information sources for their past mistakes: if scientists, for instance, were wrong in the past, how can we trust them now? Writing in *Scientific American* in June 2021, Naomi Oreskes (co-author of the aforementioned *Merchants of Doubt*) mentions a study indicating that sixty percent of respondents condemned scientists for being wrong most or all of the time about the coronavirus,[12] and the same holds for subjects from climate change to drug safety or the perils of eating eggs. Those opposed to the opinions of experts also accuse these experts of reaching no consensus (e.g. scientists disagree about climate change, etc.). One of the most nefarious sleights is to circulate "research" conducted by the agnomancers' own hired "experts" to contradict and counteract unwanted information about a product or policy. Tobacco companies pioneered this stratagem decades ago, pumping disinformation into public discourse long before the era of "alternative facts," paying "scientists" (some of whom were reputable men of science but on the corporate payroll) to preach that cigarette smoking was not harmful or at the extreme positively healthy. David Michaels captured this cynical tactic in the title of his book *Doubt is Their Product*, in which he reported that tobacco executives sought deliberately to mislead and confuse smokers: the public, they understood, "is in no position to distinguish good science from bad. Create doubt, uncertainty, and confusion. Throw mud at the [real] research under the assumption that some of it is bound to stick. And buy time, lots of time, in the bargain."[13]

Smithson too emphasized uncertainty as a significant category and force of ignorance, which prevents people from settling on a conclusion or taking action and which, as the tobacco interests well recognized, permits the agnomancers to indulge their bad behavior in the interim. Uncertainty

---

[11] Gore, "Oklahoma GOP Congressional Candidate John Bennett Calls for Execution of Dr. Anthony Fauci."

[12] Oreskes, "The Reason Some Republicans Mistrust Science."

[13] Michaels, *Doubt is Their Product*, 9.

and doubt have a paralyzing effect, which is the desired effect. Add to that cognitive burden the trick of "false equivalence," insisting for example that educators "teach the controversy" or provide "equal time" to positions that are not controversial or equal, from evolution-versus-creationism to Holocaust-reality-versus-Holocaust-denial. Merely injecting into the conversation that there may be a controversy or that the scientifically or historically worthless claim has legitimacy clouds the issue and encourages individuals to invest mental energy in false and ridiculous statements. And many agnomancers know that humans (mal)function with a number of built-in cognitive biases, including the confirmation bias (listeners tend to pay more attention to propositions that they already believe and to data that support their pre-existing opinions) and the exposure effect or illusory truth effect (the more often people hear a statement, the more likely they are to accept it as true).

Other psychological and social tendencies can be weaponized against a potential knower. Two of the most potent are fear and identity. It is well documented that strong emotions like fear, along with anger, influence and hinder critical thinking. Fear and anger induce people to draw and defend sharp boundaries, to become defensive in thought and action, and to be averse to risk; anger particularly makes populations hostile to certain messages and their messengers (again, scientists, journalists, and academics or "liberals" and outgroups such as other races, classes, or ethnicities). Substantial research demonstrates that fear inspires in-group solidarity, obedience to authority, and resistance to change or "support for the 'way things are,'" which is what agnomancers count on.[14] This is one primary reason why manipulators resort to screaming and hyperbolic language, including wild conspiracy theories that cannot be disproven—which is what gives those theories their coveted durability.

Meanwhile, practitioners of agnomancy may intuitively or explicitly comprehend that people do not think and act alone but as members of groups and that groups have their own maintenance and defense mechanisms. Any group—a race, a class, a party, a religion, or what have you—may engage in "identity-protective cognition" that denies and rejects incoming knowledge that jeopardizes its identity and interests. Cognitive dissonance, the psychological discomfort that results when facts contradict existing beliefs and assumptions and too often leads to rejecting the facts rather than adjusting or forsaking an assumptive world (see Chapter 10), works at the individual and collective level and indeed is probably strengthened by group dynamics (that is, when compatriots join you in preserving your assumptive world against challenging realities). As

---

[14] Napier, Huang, Vonasch, and Bargh, "Superheroes for Change," 188.

individuals and as members of groups, people do not want to feel that they are *wrong* or *bad* and do not want to lose status relative to other individuals and groups, which can prompt them to tune out information that threatens them or even to intensify their certainty in their prior knowledge and their commitment to their group.

Earlier we mentioned lies, which are the ultimate and most brazen form of agnomancy. Straight-up lying deprives audiences of the truth, but it can also backfire if the lies are too blatant to be credible or if the lies are eventually exposed, eroding future confidence in the liar. Unfortunately for society as a whole, political leaders are renowned for their dishonesty, so much so that public trust in American political figures is at a nadir. American citizens realize that they have been repeatedly deceived by presidents, from Lyndon Johnson's prevarication about the "Gulf of Tonkin" incident that escalated involvement in the Vietnam War, to Richard Nixon's many lies about the war and about the crimes that brought down his administration, to Ronald Reagan's mendacity about the Iran-Contra affair, Bill Clinton's untruthfulness about his sexual dalliance, George W. Bush's deceit about Iraq's weapons of mass destruction, and most recently Donald Trump's promiscuous and gleeful mass fabrications (capped by The Big Lie about a stolen election). Of course, politicians do not rely on false statements alone to cloak their plans and behaviors; they can also fall back on "politician-speak," talking without saying anything, answering a different question than the one asked (or not answering questions at all), and uttering meaningless feel-good platitudes.

On the other hand, governments surpass corporations, religions, and every other agnomancer in the extent to which they engage in continual and coordinated campaigns of non-knowledge and disinformation, which have been called oxymoronically *strategic communication*. Security analysts Paul Cornish, Julian Lindley-French, and Claire Yorke defined strategic communication as a "systematic series of sustained and coherent activities, conducted across strategic, operational, and tactical levels, that enables understanding of target audiences and identifies effective conduits to promote and sustain particular types of behavior."[15] Toward this end, the U.S. defense apparatus conducts what it calls *information operations*, that is, "the integrated employment, during military operations, of information-related capabilities in concert with other lines of operation to influence, disrupt, corrupt, or usurp the decision making of adversaries and potential adversaries while protecting our own."[16] While most common and useful

---

[15] Cornish, Lindley-French, and Yorke, "Strategic Communications," 3–4.

[16] Theohary, "Defense Primer: Information Operations," 1.

during times of war—and ideally against some other (enemy) population—these tactics are entirely amenable in peacetime and against one's own population. Not surprisingly, as we have seen with a vengeance since the outbreak of its war on Ukraine, Russia is a master of disinformation, which it dubs *reflexive control*, a program to analyze the thinking and decision-making processes of the enemy and use that knowledge against them—tricks like "camouflage (at all levels), disinformation, encouragement, blackmail by force, and the compromising of various officials and officers" in order "to influence his combat plans, his view of situation, and how he fights."[17] The world has witnessed how Vladimir Putin's regime unleashes information-control forces on the Russian people, including euphemisms like "special military operation" and the concomitant criminalization not only of criticizing the invasion or war but of using words like "invasion" and "war," as well as news blackouts and intimidation of journalists with threats of arrest or bodily harm, while also whipping up public fervor with appeals to Russian nationalism and lost greatness, fears of Western belligerence, and crazy incendiary talk of Ukrainian Nazis.

Agnomancy in Religion:
On Believing False Things
and Not Knowing True Ones

Despite the strides in agnotology, little if any of the research has focused on religion, though Proctor directly referred to several "interesting surrogates and overlaps" for ignorance including "secrecy, stupidity, apathy, censorship, disinformation, *faith*, and forgetfulness."[18] There are various explanations for this neglect, none of them good. Commentators may be attending to corporate- and government-derived ignorance to the exclusion of the religion-derived sort. Or perhaps they are protective of religion and do not want to accuse it of ignorance-mongering. Maybe they do not even perceive the agnomancy in religion, or maybe they are cautious not to upset their pious readers. The most depressing possibility is that they really do not think that religion participates in ignorance-conjuring.

But we know that no human endeavor is exempt from ignorance and ignorance-mongering; wherever there are human beings, there will be practices of not-knowing. In fact, some of the bitterest critics of religion denounce it as all lies and falsehoods, leaving nothing of religion *except*

---

[17] Thomas, "Russia's Reflexive Control Theory and the Military," 241–42.
[18] Proctor, "Agnotology," 2 (emphasis added).

agnomancy (and some, like Dawkins, decry religious instruction—by definition the inculcation of non-knowledge to the detriment of knowledge—as child abuse). Be that as it may, it is facile to write off religion as pure ignorance. Instead, our mission is to isolate the agnomancy practices in religion and, as far as possible, uproot them.

Ignorance shows up in many facets of religion, as least as plentifully as and more insidiously than in business and government. Some religions talk openly of ignorance as a problem—or *as a feature*—of religion. Christianity, for example, grapples valiantly with the problem of non-knowledge of its god. To put it gently, Yahweh/Jehovah "works in mysterious ways," another way of saying that we do not understand and cannot predict his/her/its actions (or, less charitably, that he/she/it does not work at all). In a previous chapter, we discussed apophatic theology, a response to the inability to know or express anything concrete about this god in ordinary language. (See Chapter 4) Many professional theologians retreat to the position that we can only say what their god *is not* (not mortal, not material, not finite, etc.) without really explaining what these negations might mean; others simply throw up their hands and concede that our words about this god are metaphorical at best, allegorical or poetic at worst (usually not taking the final leap of conceding that the words are false and nonsensical).

Some deep religious thinkers have absorbed the unknowability of the Christian god and accepted it as a quality of divinity, sometimes labeled *divine hiddenness*. There are traces of the doctrine in scripture itself: Isaiah 45:15 notes or complains, "Truly, thou art a God that hidest thyself, O God of Israel," while Job (13:24) queries his tormenter-god, "Wherefore hidest thou thy face, and holdest me for thine enemy?" Psalms sings, "Why standest thou afar off, O Lord? Why hidest thou thyself in times of trouble?" (10:1) and "How long, Lord? Wilt thou hide thyself for ever? Shall thy wrath burn like fire?" (89:46), among many others. Deuteronomy 31:17–18 has Yahweh himself say to Moses,

> Then my anger shall be kindled against them in that day, and I will forsake them, and I will hide my face from them.
> And I will surely hide my face in that day for all the evils which they shall have wrought, in that they are turned unto other gods.

One solution to the vexing silence or passivity of the deity is given in these verses: he is so mad at and disappointed with his chosen people that he will not show himself.

Christianity is hardly the only religion that struggles with the hiddenness of its god or other supernatural beings (in fact, the quotes above are drawn from the Hebrew/Jewish scriptures). Monotheisms confront this situation as a particularly common and devastating issue, since any single tri-omni god should *be able to* and *want to* exercise his/her/its benevolent power for the good of believers but all too regularly does not. The Islamic philosopher-mystic Ibn 'Arabi (1165–1240 CE) pondered this mystery too, arguing for a two-fold nature of divine hiddenness. On one side, Allah's essence or being is inherently beyond our knowledge, based on his infinite difference from us; for the philosopher and according to Islamic tradition, the being/essence of deity is "the Hidden Treasure": "beyond being known, it is the most hidden secret (*aktam al-sirr*). As the absolutely absent being (*al-ghayb al-ghuyub*), no one can know God in Himself but Himself. No one can perceive the divine essence but God Himself."[19] On the other side, Allah can reveal himself to humans and does so in small doses and indirectly, as through the Qur'an and in his creation of the universe. But there too, in his creations and manifestations, including his creation of humanity, Allah hides himself yet again:

> God becomes hidden by His manifestation. Although the universe and all creatures are signs of God, in as much as they manifest God's attributes they veil God because they show themselves rather than God. God has manifested to be known, but His manifestation is the veil of His face and hides Him.[20]

Therefore, even though the Supreme Being manifests or displays himself, he hides in plain sight behind the veil of the universe, which provides us with no more knowledge than we had before. In other religions, the problem emerges in other forms: ancestors are inscrutable and unpredictable, animistic spirits are capricious, and supernatural forces like mana and chi do not always yield the results we expect, *ad infinitum*.

Hiddenness may be a trait of god(s) and other spiritual beings, or merely one of their nasty and peevish habits, but it can also be viewed as a scathing refutation of him/her/it/them. After all, what kind of loving parent would hide from a child, even if that child were naughty? In a steady stream of publications since 1993, J. L. Schellenberg has pressed exactly this argument, initially postulating that the very existence of humans who are capable of believing in a god—and more, of relating personally to such

---

[19] Azadegan, "Ibn 'Arabi on the Problem of Divine Hiddenness," 51.
[20] Azadegan, "Ibn 'Arabi on the Problem of Divine Hiddenness," 51.

a being—but who do not (that is, atheists) is reason to conclude that there is no such thing as a god, since a perfectly good deity would want to be believed in and related to. His later work developed the notion of "nonresistant nonbelief" (i.e., a person is not *trying to disbelieve or is not determined to disbelieve*) as sufficient reason to be skeptical about the reality of any god(s).[21] Whether on his premises or some other, a hidden and unresponsive god, like an apophatic god, a powerless god, or a dead god, is not much better than no god at all.

Ignorance or not-knowing appears in a different light in Eastern religions. The Sanskrit term *avidyā* (*a- + vid*, to know/see, thus not-knowing, not-perceiving, not-understanding) denotes ignorance in Hindu and Buddhist (Pali, *avijjā*) traditions, but according to Alex Wayman, the word has religion-specific connotations. He preferred to translate it as "unwisdom," stressing that it is not a vacant state, a mere lack of knowledge, but the opposite of knowledge, an illusion, and misunderstanding of the nature of reality. The *Bhagavat-purana* scriptures, for instance, named five varieties of *ajñana-vrtti* (non-knowledge)—darkness, delusion, great delusion, obscuration, and blind obscuration.[22] *Avidya* can also be considered one of the "veils" or "layers" (*kleshas*) that interfere with true knowledge and pure consciousness, along with *asmita* (the illusion of "I-ness" or the self), *raga* (attraction or desire), *dvesha* (aversion or disliking), and *abhinivesha* (fear). At the broadest level, *avidya* entails four kinds of error or illusion—mistaking the temporary for the eternal, the impure for the pure, the misery-making for the happiness-making, and ultimately the non-self for the self.[23]

For Buddhism, the religion/philosophy of enlightenment and the dispelling of delusion (*moha*), *avijja* is equivalent to being asleep, blinded, or in darkness, the state prior to becoming enlightened and thereby free. Interpreting the Theravada *Abhidharma* or *Abhidamma* texts, Bhikkhu Bodhi taught that ignorance or *avijja* "is non-knowledge of eight things: the Four Noble Truths [the foundation of Buddhist thought], the pre-natal past, the post-mortem future, the past and the future together, and dependent arising" or the Buddhist doctrine that each moment, including each moment of the self, is a fleeting product of the past moments.[24] Asvaghosa, in the *Buddhacarita*, expanded on the five Hindu varieties of

---

[21] See e.g., Schellenberg, *Divine Hiddenness and Human Reason*; Schellenberg, *The Hiddenness Argument: Philosophy's New Challenge to Belief in God*.

[22] Wayman, "The Meaning of Unwisdom (Avidya)," 21.

[23] Tripurashakti.com, "Avidya in Yoga Meditation."

[24] Bodhi, *A Comprehensive Manual of Abhidhamma*, 295.

unwisdom listed above, relating them, respectively, to "torpor, birth and death, passion, fury, and weariness."[25]

A different angle on religion and ignorance is the lack of knowledge among devotees of their own religions. It has been consistently remarked that Americans, despite being a highly religious people, are dismally uninformed about religion, measured by their inability to answer basic questions about the Bible, Christian history, religion in public life, and other world religions. A Pew Research Center study in 2010 calculated that Christians on average could answer only 15.7 out of thirty-two questions correctly, and merely forty-five percent could answer seventeen or more questions. Ironically—or not—atheists and agnostics knew more about religion than their pious peers, giving on average 20.9 correct answers and eighty-two percent answering seventeen or more questions right.[26] This goes to show that the more you know about religion, the less you believe.[27] Many Christians are untroubled by ignorance of their own religion (and often proud when it comes to other religions), because they treat their faith as a personal relationship with their god and his son, not a matter of book learning. On the other hand, they would be deeply troubled if they knew that some academic theologians despaired of the concept of a personal god.

Finally, paradoxically at least at first or from the Abrahamic faiths' perspective, religion can generate not more certainty and security but more uncertainty and insecurity. Obviously, only people who believe in witches, like the African Azande, can fear witches, and the Azande saw witchcraft behind virtually every misfortune. Nils Bubandt describes something similar among the Buli of Indonesia, who inhabit a world "where cannibal witches are undeniably real and yet too ephemeral and contradictory to be an object of belief."[28] A Buli witch (*gua*) is an extremely mysterious and ambiguous creature; accordingly, locals suffer not only witchcraft but the "inescapable yet undecidable possibility of witchcraft"—that is, whether it is real, who is a witch, and more

---

[25] Wayman, "The Meaning of Unwisdom (Avidya)," 21.

[26] Pew Research Center, "Who Knows What About Religion."

[27] A meta-analysis of sixty-three previous studies found "a significant negative association between intelligence and religiosity," which the authors reckoned could be attributed to the tendency of intelligent people to be nonconformists, or to their analytic thought style which resists religion, or to intelligence providing all the functions and satisfactions that religious folks get from religion; see Zuckerman, Silberman, and Hall, "The Relation Between Intelligence and Religiosity: A Meta-Analysis and Some Proposed Explanations."

[28] Bubandt, *The Empty Seashell*, 236.

disturbingly whether oneself is a witch.[29] Bubandt concludes that witchcraft, rather than a solution to a problem (the problem of evil or adversity), is another question or puzzle. And because a witch loses a certain amount of his or her consciousness, it is always possible that you yourself are a witch without knowing it, making witchcraft ever-present yet elusive and unknowable.

This complication does not only apply to malign spiritual forces. Around the world, people are often skeptical and doubtful about religious specialists like priests and shamans. Hindus may accuse or scoff at the Brahmin priests for their lack of training and ritual knowledge or for their greed (seeking to profit off of other people's hardship); Muslims too are not above disputing the competence and sincerity of their religious leaders. In other locations, like Mongolia where life has become more difficult, not less, after the fall of communism and the arrival of capitalism, groups like the Buryat are dismayed that while they expected "that shamanism would solve the uncertainties brought about by the market economy, it has created additional spiritual uncertainties."[30] Buryats whose standard of living has declined under market conditions often visit shamans to learn what is wrong and how to alleviate it, but at the same time, they confess their lack of knowledge about shamanism and their lack of confidence in shamans, which leads ironically not to fewer shamanic sessions but more. If one shaman fails to relieve them, or simply fails to impress them, they may consult another and then another. They may test the shaman to determine if he or she is trustworthy and powerful. And at worst, they may suspect that it is a shaman who is afflicting them in the first place, perhaps to create a demand for the very shaman's curing services.

Religion and ignorance have a complex and diverse relationship. But it is time now to turn to the techniques of agnomancy that are rife among religions. Let us begin with the ways in which knowledge is withheld from members, which starts with *secrecy*. Secrecy is more rampant in religion than in business or government, precisely because religious knowledge is typically perceived as especially potent. One of the founding fathers of sociology, Émile Durkheim, made secrecy, or at least unapproachability, the core of his theory of religion in the concept of "the sacred." He defined religion in terms of the sacred, as a set of beliefs and practices "relative to sacred things, that is to say, things set aside and forbidden."[31] Since sacred things—objects, places, persons, and information—are so important and so powerful, the hands and eyes of

---

[29] Bubandt, *The Empty Seashell*, 2.
[30] Buyandelgeriyn, "Dealing with Uncertainty," 127.
[31] Durkheim, *The Elementary Forms of Religious Life*, 62.

ordinary people can only pollute them, profane them, or minimally misuse them. For example, the innermost room of the ancient Hebrew temple was "the Holy of Holies," where the Ark of the Covenant and Yahweh himself were present and only the high priest could enter. Likewise, the Sherpa temple investigated by Robert Paul contained a chapel on the top floor which was open only to celibate monks, since it housed Srungma, a pre-Buddhist god who demanded absolute purity of those who attended him.[32]

One specific form of religious secrecy is *taboo*. Taboo, from the Polynesian word *tapu*, is a restriction or rule of avoidance; it can concern anything from the places you cannot go, to the food you cannot eat, to the knowledge you cannot know. Violating taboos can bring down profound spiritual consequences, from bad luck and sickness to death, and religions strenuously enforce taboos—except when they do not. (See Chapter 6) In a word, taboos circumscribe dangers and separate different kinds of people, for instance, men and women, or priests and laity, or initiated and uninitiated. Economists Chaim Fershtman, Uri Gneezy, and Moshe Hoffman called a taboo "an 'unthinkable' action" in two senses of the phrase: first, most people who observe taboos would never think to breach them, and second, merely thinking of breaching the taboo can elicit a punishment.[33] We could and should add one more sense, namely that anything so cordoned off by religious prohibitions cannot be fully known or thought about.

A common variable of taboo or secrecy in general is gender, that is, there are objects that can be handled, sites that can be visited, and information that can be known by one gender but not the other. Probably most frequently, it is male knowledge that is jealously guarded against women, sometimes on pain of death. Among peoples as remote from each other as the Mundurucú of Amazonia and the Sambia of Papua New Guinea, men sequestered sacred objects (particularly flutes) in the men's ritual house, where they performed their ceremonies far from the prying eyes (if not ears) of their wives. Women did not know, or were not supposed to know, what happened in the men's sacred space. In Australian Aboriginal societies like the Warlpiri where I did fieldwork, religious knowledge is highly sex-segregated. The myths, songs, dances, and rituals that men know and perform (at least the most important and sacred parts of that canon) are carefully hidden from women. Only fairly recently, through the work of Diane Bell and other female ethnographers, did we

---

[32] Paul, "The Sherpa Temple as a Model of the Psyche."
[33] Fershtman, Gneezy, and Hoffman, "Taboos and Identity," 139.

learn that women too possess sex-specific religious knowledge that is believed to be essential for the perpetuation of society and the world.[34]

Religious knowledge is also commonly withheld from members of certain segments of society, particularly the young and uninitiated. Men's knowledge may be available only to *adult and fully initiated men,* who must undergo difficult and painful ordeals to earn access to it. Often a key part of initiation rituals is the revelation of previously concealed knowledge, such as the names of supernatural beings or stories and songs, as well as the making and meaning of sacred symbols. Higher and deeper degrees of knowledge may be attained throughout the lifetime, with knowledge intensely stratified by age and the amount of effort exerted to learn and master it. The gnostic tradition in early Christianity tended to hold that special knowledge or wisdom (*gnosis*) of a mystical or esoteric sort was available exclusively to followers of their sect or community who enjoyed unique privilege; they, therefore, awarded themselves with honorific titles like "the elect," "the enlightened ones," "the immovable race," and "the perfect."[35] Because their teachings were often heretical, and because the reigning church could not allow anyone to claim preferential access to Christian knowledge, such gnostic groups had to be wiped out (see below).

To explore one last dimension of related non-knowledge, in some societies like Australian Aboriginal cultures, some religious knowledge was (and is) not so much secret or taboo as it is *distributed.* By this, we mean that individuals or kin groups had the right to know, to hear, and to perform certain knowledge but not others. For example, men born in particular locations, and thus believed to incarnate the local spirits of those places, "owned" the songs, stories, dances, and symbols associated with those spots. Non-owners could not sing the songs, tell the stories, perform the dances, or paint the designs of those sacred places without the permission of the "owners." Consequently, it was impossible in theory and in practice for any one individual, no matter how old or experienced, to "know" everything about the religion.

Since knowledge is usually expressed in words, one common feature of religion is an *arcane ritual language* spoken by a few specialists or adepts. In Christianity, Latin was the formal liturgical language for centuries, understood by priests and scholars but not the general public; when Catholic rituals like mass were performed in Latin, the parishioners were typically not expected to comprehend what was said. In many Asian settings, the ancient Pali language is the ritual tongue of Buddhism.

---

[34] See for example Bell, *Daughters of the Dreaming.*
[35] Scholer, "In the Know."

Stanley Tambiah documented several decades ago how Thai Buddhist monks chanted to a lay audience, chants that "are meant to be heard but paradoxically they are not understood by the majority of the congregation (nor by some of the monks themselves)" since the monks simply learned to repeat the phrases but not to grasp their meaning. Tambiah classified this situation as "the virtue of listening without understanding," since the villagers were "emphatic that through listening to the chants the congregation gains merit, blessings, and protection"; what they do not gain is *knowledge*.[36] Lars Højer observed a similar process in Mongolia, where a Buddhist lama might craft charms containing verses in the foreign Tibetan script. The written mantra "consists of incomprehensible syllables, which the lama knows by heart but which he cannot and certainly should not translate, because their power derives from their mystical form as words without lexical meaning."[37] Indeed, the authority of these writings—like a Latin mass or a Pali chant—*resides precisely in their incomprehensibility and thus their secrecy in plain sight*. It is the unknown that is most efficacious.

Religious restrictions on speech and literature can take much more muscular forms, including strict *censorship*. Censorship generally designates limitations on what people can read, see, or say on the grounds of either "decency" or "truth" and is by no means unique to religions. Yet, especially in religions with official canons and scriptures and institutional hierarchies and authority structures, any spoken or written information or performance that does not comply with standard usage (and thus contribute to the power of religious authorities) is likely to be *anathema*—a term, significantly, that originated as a ban or injunction declared by religious leadership, often together with ejection from the religious community. Paul in Galatians 1:8–9 ordered, "If anyone proclaims to you a gospel contrary to what you received, let that one be accursed!" and the Council of Elvira (circa 305–306 CE) adopted anathema as a sanctioned church practice.

The most notorious case of religious censorship is of course Catholic book-banning through the *Index Librorum Prohibitorum* or List of Prohibited Books. Christianity had long employed force to compel orthodoxy before the sixteenth century (see below), but the heat of the Protestant Reformation dramatically increased the pressure. Religious and political authorities in the Netherlands, Venice, and France in the early and middle 1500s barred various writings, controlled printers, and sometimes executed writers for their opinions; the Edict of Châteaubriant (1551)

---

[36] Tambiah, *Buddhism and the Spirit Cults in North-East Thailand*, 195.
[37] Højer, "Absent Powers: Magic and Loss in Post-Socialist Mongolia," 581.

allowed censors to inspect all books imported into France. The Catholic Church itself got in the business of forbidding books in 1571 with the founding of the Sacred Congregation of the Index, charged to investigate and "correct" writings that deviated from Roman custom. In 1559 Pope Paul IV issued the Pauline Index, a precursor to the *Index Librorum Prohibitorum*, which named over five hundred authors for exclusion. Among the targets were religious and scientific texts, as well as new and deviant prayers. According to Giorgio Caravale, a decree on litanies (prayers, chants, or recitations used during church services) was issued by Pope Clement VIII in September 1601:

> Faced with the uncontrolled proliferation of new prayers, often containing "inept, dangerous and erroneous" statements, the decree prohibited all litanies that were not contained in breviaries, missals, Roman pontificals and rituals that had already been approved by Rome. Anyone who dared *publish* new prayers or recite them *publicly* would incur the penalties established by the bishop and the inquisitor.[38]

Diverse censorship practices persisted over the centuries, from the *Index Expurgatorius* (a list of books to be revised or corrected) to the Index Leonianus of 1897 to the final version of the banned list in 1948 which contained four thousand entries. The formal prohibition of books by Catholicism ended only in 1966, although the Church's Congregation for the Doctrine of the Faith insisted that the moral intention of the ban remained valid.

As already noted, a particularly urgent matter was the *censorship, suppression, and persecution of heresy*. From the first centuries of Christianity, teachings and practices considered heretical and unorthodox encountered fierce resistance from church defenders. Heterodox opinions were judged as a mortal danger to the church and to individual souls, as such "false knowledge" or "alternative religious facts" could condemn a person, a group, or the entire human race. Proponents of aberrant beliefs and their writings subject to suppression and persecution included the Gnostics, Marcion and his followers, the Montanists, the Adoptionists, and the Docetists. Non-conforming sects continued to sprout, like the Cathars, the Arnoldists, the Waldensians, and the Lollards, who were answered with inquisitions and crusades. The epic struggle between Catholicism and Lutheranism had world-historical implications, if only because Lutherans survived the purge.

---

[38] Caravale, "Private and Public Devotion in Late Renaissance Italy," 397.

When a religion confronts not only a deviant sect or denomination but an entirely different religion, the destruction of the latter religion's knowledge is often singularly passionate. The Hebrew scriptures chronicle military campaigns against neighboring religions and their false idols, lest they infect the true beliefs and rituals of Yahweh's people. Muslims attacked pre-Islamic beliefs like Zoroastrianism as well as polytheistic religions like Hinduism; memories of the Taliban in Afghanistan blasting the Buddhist statues at Bamiyan in 2001, part of a plan to erase the rival faith from local history, are still fresh. And Christians too worked to expunge pagan belief and knowledge, first from the Roman Empire, then from the rest of Europe, and eventually from territories conquered and colonized by Europeans. Much of the knowledge of indigenous religions was lost through the destruction of books (such as the codices of the Mayans and Aztecs), the obliteration of sacred objects and sites, and the death of knowledgeable elders and religious specialists (shamans, diviners, priests, etc.).

The previous topics share a theme: guardians of "religious truth" want the faithful ignorant of religious knowledge *other than their own* or of knowledge *of any kind that would undermine their own*. Censorship and banned/burned texts (and bookmakers) and persecution of dissenters are all methods straight out of the agnomancy playbook, but it is preferable to pre-empt discordant and rebellious knowledge before it can start, ideally by *discouraging questioning and critical thought* altogether. The Old Testament cautions that "increasing knowledge results in increasing pain" (Ecclesiastes 1:18), while the New Testament belittles knowledge: "For the wisdom of this world is foolishness in God's sight" (1 Corinthians 3:19). Early Christian thinkers sustained the attack on curiosity and reason. Tertullian taught that after Jesus showed us the light, "we have no desire to believe anything else; for we begin by believing that there is nothing else which we have to believe."[39] His blunt advice was this: "It is better for you to remain ignorant for fear that you come to know what you should not know. For you do know what you should know."[40] Augustine (*Confessions*, Chapter XXXV, 54) agreed that the "temptation of curiosity" was a snare for disciples:

For besides that concupiscence of the flesh which lieth in the gratification of all senses and pleasures, wherein its slaves who "are far from Thee perish," there pertaineth to the soul, through the same senses of the body, a certain vain and curious longing, cloaked under

---

[39] Quoted in Miller, *Classical Statements on Faith and Reason*, 5.
[40] Quoted in Miller, *Classical Statements on Faith and Reason*, 9–10.

the name of knowledge and learning....This longing ... originates in an appetite for knowledge....

Martin Luther too recognized reason as "God's worst enemy"—"the devil's bride" which "faith must trample under foot": "There is," he opined, "on earth among all dangers no more dangerous thing than a richly endowed and adroit reason," which "must be deluded, blinded, and destroyed."[41] Christianity's track record illustrates a clear opposition to frightening inquiry, from Galileo's study of the planets to Darwin's theory of evolution.

One contemporary fruit of the resistance against the expansion of empirical knowledge is *science denial* among many Christians and other religionists. This antagonism toward knowledge applies both to natural investigation and philosophical/textual analysis and critique. The former speaks for itself: at least portions of Christianity, Islam, and other religions reject evolutionary theory and Big Bang cosmology as well as areas of study that do not directly impinge on theistic dogma such as climate change science and sex/gender research. They also often object to critical historical analysis of their religious literature and mythology, which tends to reveal multiple authorships, redactions and additions, exclusion of competing versions, and errors of transcription (not to mention of fact). For example, most Christians are unaware of the rival ("apocryphal") gospels and "lost Christianities" that were excised from the official scriptures,[42] and Muslims do not want to hear how the Qur'an was assembled over decades, while divergent editions were destroyed. Such knowledge would tend to shake the faith of the pious, which cannot be permitted.

Ultimately the most effective way to build barriers around knowledge is to build barriers—social or physical—around the knowledge community. Appropriately then, many religions, and not only "cults," institute *isolation* of the true believers from the evils of the outside world. Fundamentalist Christian congregations are especially prone to shielding their members from profane knowledge, even of the mundane kind such as movies and music. Members may be instructed to avoid and distrust non-members. Sociologist Nancy Ammerman described one such Midwestern congregation that cordoned itself from wider American culture and sought to be independent in all of its practical, spiritual, and epistemic needs; she stressed that when they and similar faith groups cannot dominate mainstream institutions and knowledge, "they have

---

[41] Quoted in Kaufmann, *The Faith of a Heretic*, 75.
[42] See Ehrman, *Lost Christianities*.

responded by withdrawing to establish their own alternative institutions" and secure their own alternative knowledge.[43] More radical sects and religions, like the Fundamentalist Mormons or the comparatively harmless Amish, may go so far as to erect separatist communities where they can practice their faith and preserve their knowledge without compromising the surrounding society.

A religious group does not have to insulate itself totally from the profane world to lose touch with the knowledge that circulates beyond its borders. A religion that sits confidently at the center of its society often fails to see the privilege that it enjoys and that it denies to religious minorities. Linda Markowitz and Laurel Puchner, a sociologist and an educational leadership expert, respectively, interviewed teachers and administrators in American elementary schools and discovered that the educators mostly dwelt blissfully in "Christian ignorance—a structural ignorance rooted in normative cognitive schemas that creates and maintains Christian privilege."[44] Some of these professionals could literally not see "the ways their schools were organized around Christian norms, and/or, did not see a problem with Christian celebrations in their schools."[45] Christianity, in the form of religion-specific calendars, holidays, songs, symbols, and other behaviors, was normalized and naturalized for them, so much that it was essentially invisible, despite the fact that they knew full well (1) that there were non-Christian students in their classes and (2) that church/state separation demanded religious neutrality in public institutions like schools. Markowitz and Puchner identified four "cognitive frames" that propagated the ignorance of privilege—the frame of denial (e.g. denying that the school contained Christian practices at all or that those practices were "religious"), the frame of equality (e.g. that acknowledging other religions and holidays— usually at Christmas time!—nullified any Christian privilege), the frame of no responsibility (e.g. that parents or other non-professionals have the duty to teach their children about other religions and/or that the educators are only doing what the parents want them to do), and the frame of "no harm, no foul" (e.g. that non-Christians are not disadvantaged by inhabiting a Christian-centric world). I wonder if the teachers, students, and parents would sing the same tune in an Islam- or Hindu-centric society—or if and when some non-Christian religion becomes the majority in their school district.

---

[43] Ammerman, *Bible Believers: Fundamentalists in the Modern World*, 211.

[44] Markowitz and Puchner, "Structural Ignorance of Christian Privilege," 877.

[45] Markowitz and Puchner, "Structural Ignorance of Christian Privilege," 883.

Conclusion:
What You Don't Know Can Hurt You
(and Everyone Else)

Despite this impressive yet depressing and probably incomplete catalogue of agnomancy techniques in religion and beyond, ignorance is not all bad. It is ignorance, and the cognizance of what we do not know, that drives science; conversely, it is arrogant satisfaction with one's current knowledge (or what passes for knowledge) that forecloses further probing of the unknown, as endorsed by Tertullian and his ilk. Then there are the pleasures of not knowing, which allow for surprise, such as not knowing the sex of your future child or the plans for your birthday party. Too much knowledge can ruin the fun and breed complacency.

However, when ignorance is bad, it can be very, very bad. Robert Graef, the author of *Ignorance: Everything You Need to Know About Not-Knowing*, alerts us that ignorance is "costly, dangerous, and undemocratic."[46] Of these three, the third is the most zealously sought by agnomancers.

Ignorance is costly and dangerous because it hinders our ability to make good decisions; effective and economical decision-making requires accurate and sometimes unpleasant or inconvenient knowledge. This applies to issues from personal health (ignoring symptoms or preferring not to know about a medical condition will not make the condition go away and will eventually make it worse) to practical social and natural problems (ignorance or dismissal of the causes and impacts of poverty or racism, on the one hand, or of global warming, on the other, precludes any solutions). Making choices and developing policy in a setting of ignorance is an almost guaranteed path to failure, if not to increasingly undesirable unintended consequences. Indeed, back in 1936 sociologist Robert Merton pinpointed ignorance as one of the reasons for unanticipated consequences—ignorance of the facts of the matter together with ignorance of the deleterious possible outcomes of our actions (such as, for instance, how dams will harm water flow and aquatic species)—along with error (which is not only not-knowing but "knowing" false things), and the "imperious immediacy of interest" or short-term and selfish thinking.[47] We might add other factors of unavoidable ignorance such as uncertainty, risk, and the unpredictability of the future.

Ignorance, or rather agnomancy, is *undemocratic* precisely because it is the maneuver of an individual, party, or other interest group

---

[46] Graef, "Commentary: Ignorance is Costly, Dangerous, and Undemocratic."
[47] Merton, "The Unanticipated Consequences," 898–902.

to have its way (sell its product, dump its waste, pass its law, evade its responsibility, advance its power, promote its beliefs, and so on) by misdirecting the majority or the entire society. It is the malicious misuse of knowledge for partisan advantage, a type of information warfare. If the facts and truth were on their side, they would not have to resort to manipulation through lies, secrets, censorship, obfuscation, gaslighting, and often, as Harry Frankfurt colorfully emphasized, unadulterated bullshit, which differs from lying because the perpetrator does not know or care what is true.[48] This is why agnomancy is a favorite, even essential, tactic of demagogues, populists, and authoritarians, for whom the truth is poisonous.

Many observers have commented that we have long since entered the era of "post-truth"; the Oxford Dictionary, which defines post-truth as "relating to or denoting circumstances in which objective facts are less influential in shaping public opinion than appeals to emotion and personal belief,"[49] named it the word of the year in 2016. Robert Keane, a political scientist and prolific author on modern democracy, shows us how post-truth "is not simply the opposite of truth" but rather the culmination of all of the agnomancy strategies discussed in this chapter, "a combination of different elements in ways that defy expectations and confuse its recipients."[50] He calls it "a species of pugnacious politics dressed in a coat of many colors, as a bricolage of lies, bullshit, buffoonery, and silence ... designed to bewitch and beguile" which is entertaining but also very unhealthy. "In the hands of the powerful, or those bent on climbing the ladders of power over others" he posits, "the post-truth phenomenon functions as a weapon of political manipulation"—and disturbingly, more "truth" or yet another fact is not an antidote.

We who would argue with religion understand this all too well. (It is interesting and worrisome that prominent analyses of post-truth, like that by Lee McIntyre, almost entirely avoid the subject of religion.[51]) We know that giving the facts to theists—of science, of comparative religion, of the weakness of their own arguments, etc.—does not automatically, or often, weaken their confidence in their beliefs. This is because, as we unpacked in another chapter, "belief" is more than propositional fact-claims but also *confidence* and *commitment*, and facts do not instantaneously displace those last two. (See Chapter 2) Rather, like ignorance antibodies,

---

[48] Frankfurt, *On Bullshit*.
[49] Oxford Languages, "Word of the Year 2016."
[50] Keane, "Post-truth Politics and Why the Antidote Isn't Simply 'Fact-Checking' and Truth."
[51] McIntyre, *Post-Truth*.

confidence in and commitment to a "truth" fight off infections of new and menacing knowledge.

This raises the last major point to make. As we noted, agnotologists stress that ignorance is not a void but frequently a construction. More than that, it is not a void because *the space that would be occupied by knowledge is typically not "empty" but is occupied by other "knowledge" which is strictly not knowledge because it is wrong*. In religion but equally in other areas of human life and thought, this space is filled, following the Oxford definition of post-truth, with emotion and personal belief (in the propositional and confidence/commitment senses of the term) but also with shared collective or institutional belief *because most personal beliefs originate from collective or institutional sources*. That is, individuals do not invent Christian dogma; they are indoctrinated with it, usually at great cost and energy.

The significance of this realization is that *if people do not know something, they often or typically "know" something else*, which renders them relatively resistant to novel information which would disconfirm their pre-existing knowledge/belief. This prior "knowledge" inclines listeners to ignore, dilute, reject, and disbelieve the incoming information—all the more so as they are not lone thinkers and knowers/believers but members of epistemic communities (like a religion) in which each individual's ignorance is supported by all of the other individuals and by the leadership and institutional structure. The group and its structure are almost impervious to counter-information (that is, true knowledge) and have impressive self-repairing abilities. Among these abilities is the prior decision *about what sources to trust for knowledge and true information*. If a religion (or a political party or class, race, etc.) has already decided that one source (say, the Bible, Fox News, or some other) is reliable and that other sources (scientists, journalists, the mainstream media, liberals, elites, secularists, and such) are not, then the individual and the group are well inoculated against challenges to their common "knowledge."

In the end, ignorance is no void and is more than a product or construction. It is a habit that is routinely exploited by powerful interests but also eagerly defended by those who cling to their non-knowledge. To paraphrase Isaac Newton, bodies at ignorance tend to remain at ignorance and exert considerable effort to do so. And we would do well to remember that religion (but not only religion) is not just a set of fact-claims but is a worldview, a reality to its adherents, and taking it from them exposes them, at least temporarily, to the traumatic loss of their assumptive world. (See Chapter 6)

8

The Poverty of Philosophy of Religion, or Freeing Philosophy From Faith

In 1984, Alvin Plantinga published a letter of encouragement and a call to arms for Christian philosophers—not for philosophers *of* Christianity or philosophers *who study* Christianity but philosophers *who are dedicated to* Christianity. In that essay, he bemoaned the fact that until recently "mainline establishment philosophy in the English-speaking world was deeply non-Christian," not necessarily anti-Christian or atheistic but insufficiently interested in and committed to the religion.[1] Happily, he sensed that Christianity was "on the move," and he incited his pious peers to act with "Christian courage, or boldness" to "display more faith, more trust in the Lord; we must put on the whole armor of God."[2]

Plantinga saw two main objections against not only doing philosophy in a non-Christian (read, secular or rational) milieu but in a non-Christian/secular/rational way. The first was that Christian philosophy had its own questions to answer and problems to solve, "its own concerns, its own topics for investigation, its own agenda and its own research program."[3] Christian philosophers simply were not or should not be interested in the things that other philosophers were, including, as we will explore later in this chapter, the dreaded matter of verification or trying to prove that their god exists or the exhausted (but unresolved) problem of evil, which many thinkers of both the Christian and non-Christian persuasion today still regard as the main "defeater" (to use a Plantingian term) of monotheism. No, those questions were boring and irrelevant to Christian philosophers, or worse they played into the hands of non- and anti-Christians, who kept faithful philosophers distracted with the burden of proving what they assumed to be true. Thus, the second Plantingian objection was that Christian philosophers did not have to argue *for* or *to* theism since they by definition and devotion argued *from* theism. That is to say,

---

[1] Plantinga, "Advice to Christian Philosophers," 253.
[2] Plantinga, "Advice to Christian Philosophers," 254.
[3] Plantinga, "Advice to Christian Philosophers," 255.

The Christian philosopher quite properly *starts from* the existence of God, and presupposes it in philosophical work, whether or not he can show it to be probable or plausible with respect to premises accepted by all philosophers....

Taking it for granted, for example, that there is such a person as God and that we are indeed within our epistemic rights (are in that sense justified) in believing that there is, the Christian epistemologist might ask what it is that confers justification here: by virtue of what is the theist justified?[4]

Rather than accepting any obligation to prove the claims of Christian faith, he declared that a Christian philosopher "has a perfect right to the ... prephilosophical assumptions he brings to philosophic work"—work which should not, by the way, advance the academy or the pursuit of knowledge but should "serve the Christian community."[5]

Before we turn to the project of demonstrating how very wrong he was (and remains to this day), let us demonstrate how very unnecessary he was. By the time he composed his tutelary epistle, the Society of Christian Philosophers had already been founded, based on a suggestion from fellow faith-philosopher William Alston in 1978. Plantinga was an early member of that group, which announces on its website (tinyurl.com/3v9b5k4a) its mission "to promote fellowship between Christian philosophers and to provide occasions for intellectual interchange among Christian philosophers on issues that arise from their joint commitment"—to Christianity, that is. Generously, it opens its arms to "anyone who considers himself or herself both a philosopher and a Christian," regardless of which particular branch of Christianity they dangle from. Of course, Christian philosophers are welcome to their professional club, as long as they accept that it is no different from and no better than any other interest group, from a Society of Islamic Philosophers (although, curiously, the pro-religion Templeton Foundation seeks to establish an American Society of Islamic Philosophers and Theologians; see tinyurl.com/323ehw73) or Society of Indian Philosophy and Religion (tinyurl.com/4xyh7af7) to a Society of Mathematics Philosophy or a Society of Baseball Philosophy. I am sure they do not.

So Christian philosophers were not, even in Plantinga's time, some marginalized cowering minority. The other contemporary hero of Christian philosophy of religion, Richard Swinburne, roughly a decade after Plantinga's homily, defined the field of philosophy of religion as "an

---

[4] Plantinga, "Advice to Christian Philosophers," 260–61.
[5] Plantinga, "Advice to Christian Philosophers," 255–56.

examination of the meaning *and justification* of religious claims," specifically claims of the sort "more typical of Western religions— Christianity, Judaism, Islam," as if philosophers should be in the business of proving their prior religious beliefs instead of questioning and critiquing all religious (and other) beliefs, including their own.[6] Indeed, *the entire history of Western philosophy through the 1600s (as well as most of Islamic philosophy) is nothing but theistic religion.*

This was certainly not how philosophy was born or what its greatest protagonists intended. Original Greek philosophy was distinctly naturalistic, with thinkers speculating about the nature of reality independent of religious and mythical concepts. Socrates extended philosophical inquiry into social topics, pressing anyone who would listen to inspect and critique their alleged knowledge of matters like justice and goodness—and being accused and condemned of impiety and corruption for his efforts. There were recognizable religious threads in the seminal writings of Plato and Aristotle, but defending religion was far from their primary objectives. All of this changed with the arrival of Christianity: although its champions in the Greco-Roman world absorbed much of the content and style of ancient philosophy, there was an undeniable animosity to secular and rationalist philosophizing (much more virulent than Plantinga's). The most famous case is Tertullian, whom we met in a previous chapter. He asked what Jerusalem has to do with Athens, a metaphor for the chasm between "the Church" and "the Academy" (specifically, Plato's school named the Academy) or between credulous religiosity and questioning philosophy. Accordingly, once Christianity was fully ensconced in the seat of power at Rome, Plato's Academy, which had operated for almost a millennium, was summarily shuttered (by the emperor Justinian around 529 CE). James Hannam, author of *God's Philosophers*, quotes from Justinian's edict, which rooted out philosophers, along with Jews and pagans, for their "ill effect" on society and concluded that

> they should have no influence nor enjoy any dignity, nor, acting as teachers of any subjects, should they drag the minds of the simple to their errors and, in this way, turn the more ignorant among them against the pure and true orthodox faith; so we permit only those who are of the orthodox faith to teach and accept a public stipend.[7]

---

[6] Swinburne, "Religion, Problem of the Philosophy of," 763 (emphasis added).
[7] Hannam, "The Emperor Justinian's Closure of the School of Athens."

So commenced a thousand uninterrupted years during which philosophy essentially *was* theism, specifically Christian theism. After the darkest of the Dark Ages, when little was written or preserved, the reappearance of philosophy was indistinguishable from theology, and most if not all philosophers took a crack at proving that the Christian god, particularly in his incarnation as Jesus, really existed. John Scotus Eriugena (or Johannes Scotus Erigena) in the ninth century and Paschasius Radbertus in the tenth were philosopher-theologians, and Anselm in the eleventh concocted the infamous "ontological argument" for his god, on the premise that his deity was the most perfect being and a perfect being must exist (existence being a perfection). Other medieval theologian-philosophers include Bonaventure, Albertus Magnus, and Thomas Aquinas, all engaged in answering the questions and solving the problems of their own faith. In the 1600s, Baruch Spinoza and René Descartes offered their influential opinions on the nature of their god, equally confident that there was such a thing although differing wildly on what they thought this god-thing was; meanwhile, Gottfried Wilhelm Leibniz, who also contributed to the development of calculus, proposed with apparent seriousness that the Christian god had created the best of all possible worlds (let us hope not!). In the first half of the 1700s, George Berkeley erected the Christian god against the rising tide of empiricism, contending that "to be is to be perceived" but that Jehovah, as the ultimate and universal perceiver, guaranteed both Being and our knowledge of it.

It was only in the seventeenth century that thinkers could conceive a philosophy that did not utterly prostrate itself to Christianity (as in the writings of Thomas Hobbes) and eventually a philosophy that aimed its critical sights at Christianity (as in the writings of David Hume). At the very end of the eighteenth century, Immanuel Kant established that god(s) could not be proven by reason or sensory evidence but counseled people to believe anyhow; although he was still a theist, he built a bridge to the secular philosophy of the future. By the 1800s, the liberation of philosophy from theology was well underway, climaxing in the un-Christian thoughts of Ludwig Feuerbach, Karl Marx, and of course Friedrich Nietzsche.

This lengthy introduction should make it immanently clear that the present chapter will be an indictment of the philosophical subdiscipline called philosophy of religion. As just surveyed, Plantinga's fretting was unfounded then and now, since Western philosophy has been commandeered for Christian purposes for centuries, and philosophy of religion continues to be; the interests, questions, and commitments of philosophy were—and those of philosophy of religion largely remain— the interests, questions, and commitments of Christianity. Philosophy of religion as it currently stands is a travesty and, as we will soon illustrate, an academic embarrassment, and it should either reform itself thoroughly or cease to exist, completing its metamorphosis into (Christian) theology, which is every bit as intellectually barren. I say this not as a detractor of philosophy; I respect and admire philosophy and regard it as closely akin to my own field of anthropology. It is exactly because I respect and admire philosophy that I denounce philosophy of religion as a betrayal of the essence of the philosophical enterprise, which is to increase our wisdom by interrogating our assumptions and dispelling confusion about our concepts, beliefs, and "knowledge." In the spirit of Socrates, we should honor ourselves by admitting and owning our ignorance and unremittingly, even brutally, inspecting what we think we know. Therefore, what Plantinga and his like do, when they grant themselves leave "to start from what we *know as Christians*" with no responsibility whatsoever to "attempt to reason to or justify those beliefs we hold as Christians,"[8] is the polar opposite and the abject abdication of philosophy.

The Faith of Our Philosophers

This is our thesis: philosophy of religion is monopolized by, virtually obsessed with, Christianity. It does not pretend to question, test, doubt, or critically scrutinize (i.e., with the possibility of falsifying and replacing) Christian doctrines but acts in the slavish service of those doctrines. There are of course exceptions, minor ones, including a few nods toward other religions (mostly the "world religions" of Judaism, Islam, Hinduism, and Buddhism) and some professional secularist and atheist philosophers, but they are a diminishingly small proportion of the field. Instead, the weight of philosophy of religion, as philosopher and critic Kevin Schilbrak states in his "manifesto" on religion and philosophy, "defines its task in terms of the rationality of theism and this is the primary focus found in most philosophy of religion journals, textbooks, and courses."[9] Schilbrak goes on to assert that, "If one were to take the essays collected in philosophy of religion textbooks and put a check mark in the corresponding boxes … that represent the different possible topics, almost all of the check marks would be in the box dealing with Christian doctrines."[10] But we do not have to take his word for it; let us examine some major textbooks in the field, which is the first glimpse that philosophy students would get of the

---

[8] Plantinga, "Advice to Christian Philosophers," 265.
[9] Schilbrak, *Philosophy and the Study of Religion: A Manifesto*, 3.
[10] Schilbrak, *Philosophy and the Study of Religion: A Manifesto*, 18.

discipline and is presumably what philosophers of religion want others to know about their vocation.

One of the leading teachers in philosophy of religion was John Hick, whose fourth edition textbook was published in 1990; let's assume that, since he had three prior editions to think about it, what he wrote there he very much intended to write. After a very brief (less than four-page) introduction in which he acknowledges other religions but admits that "the discussion will focus upon the Judaic-Christian concept of God, which lies behind our western Atlantic civilization and still constitutes the main religious option within our culture"[11] (I wonder how students or readers who come from civilizations other than "our" western/Atlantic one feel about that statement), the chapters proceed as follows:

- Chapter 1 The Judaic-Christian Concept of God
- Chapter 2 Arguments for the Existence of God
- Chapter 3 Arguments Against the Existence of God
- Chapter 4 The Problem of Evil
- Chapter 5 Revelation and Faith
- Chapter 6 Evidentialism, Foundationalism, and Rational Belief
- Chapter 7 Problems of Religious Language
- Chapter 8 The Problem of Verification
- Chapter 9 The Conflicting Truth Claims of Different Religions [at least he concedes that there *are* different religions]
- Chapter 10 Human Destiny: Immortality and Resurrection
- and, with charity to our eastern/non-Atlantic friends, or one religion from across the sea anyhow, Chapter 11 Human Destiny: Karma and Reincarnation.

This topic list is a mockery of what philosophy of religion can and should be, but perhaps it is the exception. Maybe Hick is an outlier, or maybe the field has matured and rectified its professional/pious myopia. So, let's consider a textbook from the venerable Oxford University Press by Brian Davies, another fourth edition released in 2021. The table of contents reads:

1. Whose God? Which Tradition?; 2. Philosophy and Religious Belief; 3. Cosmological Arguments; 4. Design Arguments; 5. Ontological Arguments; 6. Experience and God; 7. Talking about God; 8. Divine

---

[11] Hick, *Philosophy of Religion*, 3–4.

Simplicity; 9. Omnipotence and Omniscience; 10. Miracles; 11. God and Evil; 12. Morality and Religion; 13. Life after Death.[12]

Linda Zagzebski's 2007 introductory text gives us:

1. The Philosophical Approach to Religion; 2. The Classical Arguments for the Existence of God; 3. Pragmatic and Fideist Approaches to Religious Belief; 4. Who or What is God?; 5. Fate, Freedom, and Foreknowledge; 6. Religion and Morality; 7. The Problem of Evil; 8. Death and the Afterlife; 9. The Problem of Religious Diversity [again, at least we hear that there *is* religious diversity]; and 10. Faith, Reason, and the Ethics of Belief.[13]

Michael Murray and Michael Rea's introduction, published by Cambridge University Press, contains three parts (The Nature of God, The Rationality of Religious Belief, and Science, Morality, and Immortality) of three chapters each:

1. Attributes of God: Independence, Goodness, and Power; 2. Attributes of God: Eternity, Knowledge, and Providence; 3. God Triune and Incarnate; 4. Faith and Rationality; 5. Theistic Arguments; 6. Anti-Theistic Arguments; 7. Religion and Science; 8. Religion, Morality, and Politics; 9. Mind, Body, and Immortality.

Edward Wierenga's 2016 offering features:

1. Introduction to the Philosophy of Religion; 2. The Cosmological Argument for God's Existence; 3. The Ontological Argument; 4. The Argument from Design; 5. The Problem of Evil; 6. Omnipotence; 7. Omniscience, Foreknowledge, and Free Will; 8. Divine Freedom and Moral Perfection; 9. Miracles; 10. The Evidentialist Objection: Clifford and James; 11. The Evidentialist Objection and Foundationalism.[14]

Really, that is an entire semester's subject-matter? To bring this sorry state of affairs to a close, Keith Yandell's "contemporary introduction" covered roughly the same ground with one curious addition: he also allowed chapters on "nonmonotheistic" religions, of which he could name

---

[12] Davies, *An Introduction to the Philosophy of Religion.*
[13] Zagzebski, *The Philosophy of Religion: An Historical Introduction.*
[14] Wierenga, *The Philosophy of Religion.*

precisely three—Advaita Vedanta (a form of Hinduism), Jainism, and Buddhism.[15]

Please, you may interject, textbooks portray only the most simplistic version of a field; surely higher-level and professional books do a better and more balanced job of representing the discipline. Ponder, then, the selected readings collected by Oxford University Press, filled with dozens of excerpts organized into fourteen sections and a few token non-Christian pieces:

> Part 1: The Nature of Religion [four essays, one on Buddhism]; 2: Religious Experience; 3: Faith and Reason; 4: Arguments about God's Existence; 5: Knowing God without Arguments; 6: The Divine Attributes [eight essays, one from Maimonides and one from the Upanishads]; 7: Divine Action; 8: The Problem of Evil [eight essays, one on Islam]; 9. Atheism and Nonreligious Approaches to Religion; 10: Miracles; 11: Life After Death [six excerpts, one from Buddhism and one from Hinduism); 12: Religion and Science; 13: Religious Diversity [four essays, with one by Dalai Lama); 14: Religion and Morality.

Oxford's handbook on the subject rehearses the same old territory with just twenty more theoretically-oriented essays by prominent figures, on:

> 1. Divine Power, Goodness, and Knowledge; 2. Divine Sovereignty and Aseity; 3. Nontheists Conceptions of the Divine; 4. The Ontological Argument; 5. Cosmological and Design Arguments; 6. Mysticism and Religious Experience; 7. Pascal's Wager and James's Will to Believe; 8. The Problem of Evil; 9. Religious Language; 10. Religious Epistemology; 11. God, Science, and Naturalism; 12. Miracles; 13. Faith and Revelation; 14. Morality and Religion; 15. Death and the Afterlife; 16. Religious Diversity: Familiar Problems, Novel Opportunities; 17. Analytic Philosophy of Religion; 18. Wittgensteinianism: Logic, Reality, and God; 19. Continental Philosophy of Religion; and 20. Feminism and Analytic Philosophy of Religion.[16]

Michael Peterson and Raymond VanArragon's "contemporary debates" volume was a Plantingian dream since all the debates are Christian. It began with three sections of essays fending off "Attacks on Religious

[15] Yandell, *Philosophy of Religion: A Contemporary Introduction.*
[16] Wainwright, *The Oxford Handbook of Philosophy of Religion.*

Belief" before getting on with its work of presenting "Arguments for Religious Belief" and "Issues Within Religion" (which comprise the one true religion, God's government of the world, God's response to prayer, eternal damnation, and divine-command morality, before ending with whether a Christian can be a mind-body dualist).[17] To their credit, Charles Taliaferro, Paul Draper, and Philip Quinn bequeathed eighty pages to Hinduism, Buddhism, Islam, Judaism, and even Chinese and African religions in their companion to philosophy of religion, before returning to the real business of Christianity for almost seven hundred pages.

We could give further examples, but is there any need? It seems more than obvious that, as Schilbrak put it, "a more fitting name for the bulk of what one finds in philosophy of religion textbooks, courses, and journals would be 'philosophical theology' or 'philosophy of theism'"[18]— or to be less kind, Christian exegesis (explanation and interpretation of scripture) and apologetics (unabashed defense of dogma). This is wholly unacceptable as "philosophy" and indeed a bit unsavory, teaching future philosophers of religion not to think critically but to think Christianly. The more urgent question is, What makes philosophers of religion think and write this way? Paul Draper and Ryan Nichols performed an almost forensic analysis of their colleagues and diagnosed a bad case of religious bias in the department. To be specific, the "four symptoms of poor health" in philosophy of religion included the complaints that "it is too partisan, too polemical, too narrow in its focus, and too often evaluated using criteria that are theological or religious instead of philosophical."[19] These symptoms manifest as combativeness against other philosophers who do not bow to their religious "truths," naïve equation of "religion" with theism or more narrowly their favorite brand of Christian theism, and "extraordinary lack of interest in the full range of plausible positions," which is a diplomatic way of saying indifference toward if not ignorance of religions other than their own.[20]

But again we ask, why? If we suspect that the religiosity of these scholars is interfering with their reasoning, then a survey of the beliefs and attitudes of philosophers tends to support this suspicion. More than three thousand philosophers in all specialties responded to the survey on a variety of topics, and of those academics, at all career levels from undergraduate students to professors, approximately two-thirds (66.2 percent) accepted or leaned toward atheism, while a mere 18.6 percent

---

[17] Peterson and VanArragon, *Contemporary Debates in Philosophy of Religion*.
[18] Schilbrak, *Philosophy and the Study of Religion: A Manifesto*, 14.
[19] Draper and Nichols, "Diagnosing Bias in Philosophy of Religion," 421.
[20] Draper and Nichols, "Diagnosing Bias in Philosophy of Religion," 422.

accepted or leaned toward theism (and the remaining 15.2 percent identified as "other," whatever that means); among those at the pinnacle of the field (faculty or PhDs), the percentage of atheists was still higher (69.7 percent). When the sample was narrowed to philosophers specializing in science, the proportion of atheists was higher again (74.2 percent) and highest (79.5 percent) for philosophers of cognitive science, who know how flawed our human cognitive processes are. Astoundingly, philosophers of religion were completely out of step with their colleagues: a full 68.4 percent accepted or leaned toward theism, with less than one-fifth (18.6 percent) avowing atheism. They were also far more inclined to hold related positions like moral realism (74 percent) and the non-physicalism of mind (60.5 percent).[21] Naturally, these religious philosophers also diverge from scientists, the plurality of whom (41 percent) in a different survey dismissed beliefs in a god or higher/universal spirit/power while only 33 percent believed in a god; the largest percentages of atheists worked in the fields of physics and astronomy (46 percent) and geosciences (47 percent).[22]

These numbers expose the prior commitment to religion that Plantinga alluded to. Philosophers of religion approach the topic of religion from a religious perspective—or Draper and Nichols' religious bias—much more so than philosophers with other training and interests. They are thus much more inclined to bring their religious penchants to their research and to shelter those preferences from the corrosive effects of philosophical analysis and criticism—in a word, to ensure that they end up, after their studies, where they began, which is fully faithful.

It is for this reason that I am far from the first commentator to disparage philosophers of religion for the slanted, inappropriate, and often low-quality work that they do. In fact, many of the objections have come from peers in the discipline. We already mentioned Schilbrak's evaluation of philosophy of religion as "philosophical theology" or what I would call theistic philosophy or just plain Christian philosophy (not even philosophy of Christianity, which would or could still be philosophical if it was truly a philosophy study *of* Christianity, rather than philosophy subservient to Christianity). In a series of books and essays, he has recommended a thorough reform of the field. Nick Trakakis appeared to go further, heralding the very end of philosophy of religion, but on closer inspection, he advocated only the end of philosophy of religion "as it is usually practiced in the analytic tradition," a philosophical style characterized by

---

[21] See https://tinyurl.com/yc5jshre for an interactive page of survey results.
[22] Pew Research Center, "Scientists and Belief."

a pesky "attachment to scientific norms of rationality and truth."[23] Heaven forbid that philosophy of religion should apply norms of rationality and truth! Rejecting the whole problem of theodicy (that is, of dealing with suffering in an omnibenevolent god's world) which he bizarrely insisted fails "to take suffering seriously," he endorsed a rival philosophical school (the "Continental" tradition) and eschewed "the sophisticated technical discourse of scientific-minded philosophers" in favor of some sort of mystical experience of a god "who is intimate, intense and immanent."[24] After griping about the bureaucracy of the university and those scholars who only do philosophy for a living instead of as a way of life, he asked, "Indeed, why are *philosophy departments* required anyway?"[25] Well, that's one thing we can agree on.

For an actual critique of philosophy of religion as an enterprise, we must look to J. L. Schellenberg, Paul Draper, and Timothy Knepper. In a book published a decade ago, Knepper imagined not the *end* of the subfield but the *ends* of it, that is, what it should be or be for. The book directly confronted Trakakis and took him to task for his "misdiagnosis of the maladies of contemporary philosophy of religion," arguing persuasively that both the analytic and continental (uncapitalized) schools suffer from the same inadequacies, in that they tend

> (1) to neglect the historical religions of the world, (2) to reduce diversity among the inquiring community, (3) to read the historical religions without critical hermeneutical depth, (4) to fail to engage in formal cross-cultural comparison, and (5) to explain and evaluate their objects of inquiry too narrowly.[26]

He further upbraided Trakakis for his "apparent confusion of scholarly inquiry with spiritual formation,"[27] a charge of which most philosophy of religion stands guilty.

Knepper's recommendations for correcting philosophy of religion should be obvious, but we will return to them in the final section of the chapter. For now, in a new paper Draper and Schellenberg compile a roster of eight grievances against the discipline, indicating that religious philosophers have not heeded any of the previous warnings. (Schellenberg, it will be recalled, is also renowned for his pro-atheist work

---

[23] Trakakis, *The End of Philosophy of Religion*, 1–2.

[24] Trakakis, *The End of Philosophy of Religion*, 115–16.

[25] Trakakis, *The End of Philosophy of Religion*, 122 (emphasis in the original).

[26] Knepper, *The Ends of Philosophy of Religion: Terminus and Telos*, xii.

[27] Knepper, *The Ends of Philosophy of Religion*, 6.

on the problem of "divine hiddenness," discussed in Chapter 7.) The failings that they highlight include:

1. Tribalism, specifically the influence exerted on them by their religious memberships
2. Familiarism, the consequence of their religious affiliations that they are only concerned with topics that are germane to those affiliations
3. Partitionism, the tendency to separate Christianity from other religions or religious subjects for special attention (on the assumption that it *is* special in some way or at least to them)
4. Recentism, the shallow historical perspective that focuses exclusively on contemporary issues as defined by contemporary religion (which again means Christian theism, as opposed to all the earlier forms of religion)
5. Inattention to foundational issues, ignoring more basic questions about the definition and nature of religion as such or their own fundamental concepts
6. Ignorance about religion, the scathing indictment that philosophers of religion really do not know much about religion— certainly not other religious traditions besides Christianity and, incredibly, not even Christianity itself
7. Too few non-Christian philosophers of religion, and
8. Too few other philosophers who see or appreciate the relevance of their work for religion, such as philosophers of science, art, ethics, or epistemology.[28]

Interestingly, observers have detected something rotten in other academic approaches to religion besides philosophy of religion. Ironically in the same year (1984) that Plantinga issued his marching orders to Christian philosophers, Donald Weibe published a denunciation of the field of religious studies, arguing, contrary to Plantinga but more truthfully, that the academic study of religion has always struggled with a "hidden (although invariably unconscious) theological agenda."[29] Scholars in the nineteenth century, during the birth of academic religious studies, battled valiantly against theological (read, Christian) influences and assumptions, not necessarily because those influences and assumptions were false but because they were invasive: one could not (and cannot), for instance, make sense of Hinduism or Buddhism or African, Chinese, or indigenous

---

[28] Draper and Schellenberg, "The Why and the How."
[29] Weibe, "The Failure of Nerve in the Academic Study of Religion," 402.

religions via Christian terms and concepts. The scholar of religion, thus, was required "to eliminate her/his religious commitments from her/his studies"[30]—not to stop believing but to suspend or, as philosophers say, *bracket* those beliefs from the subjects under analysis. In short, "the explicit agenda adopted by the 'founders' of religious studies as an academic (university) concern committed the enterprise to an objective, detached, scientific understanding of religion wholly uninfected by any sentiment of religiosity,"[31] a commitment that pertains as much today as in those days, a commitment that Trakakis renounced as too analytical, rational, and scientific, and a commitment that Plantinga overtly repudiated as unfaithful to the beliefs of philosophical Christians. Weibe attributed the creeping of religion back into the academy (in both religious studies and philosophy) to a "failure of nerve" among academics, but I would suggest instead that (1) many never intended to relinquish their religious pledges in the first place and (2) they exhibit tremendous nerve in their tenacious religiosity in the face of professional criticism and abundant disconfirming evidence and argument.[32]

Philosophers of Religion
Say the Darndest Things

We might hope that textbooks and readers are not indicative of what philosophers of religion do and say on a daily basis, or that cooler heads in the discipline did not heed Plantinga's call for a bold Christian philosophy. To assess what we might categorize, following Thomas Kuhn's account of scientific theories, as "normal philosophy of religion," we can peruse the journals on the subject, where scholars publish their latest thinking for each other on matters of current interest. There is a large number of philosophy of religion journals, such as the *European Journal of Philosophy of Religion, International Journal for Philosophy of Religion, Bijdragen—International Journal in Philosophy and Theology*, emanating from the Jesuit tradition and exploring "the interaction between philosophy and theology (faith and reason)" (https://tinyurl.com/bddkza3z—equating philosophy with faith and theology with reason?), *Religious Studies: An International Journal for the Philosophy of Religion*, and *Sophia: International Journal of*

---

[30] Weibe, "The Failure of Nerve in the Academic Study of Religion," 406.

[31] Weibe, "The Failure of Nerve in the Academic Study of Religion," 422.

[32] Weibe's influence continued to be felt at least as recently as 2012 when a volume edited by Arnal, Braun, and McCutcheon titled *Failure and Nerve in the Academic Study of Religion* was published.

Philosophy and Traditions, not to mention *Journal of Indian Philosophy and Religion*. We might expect more objectivity and nonpartisanship from these titles than from others with names like *American Catholic Philosophical Quarterly*, *Philosophia Christi*, or *Faith and Philosophy* (the last the mouthpiece for the aforementioned Society of Christian Philosophers), which wear their bona fides on their sleeves and their mastheads. However, as we will see, Christian concepts, Christian terms, and Plantingian/Christian questions and problems predominate in all of them.

This section features a survey and summary of representative papers in such journals. What it will portray is a project that is so divorced from the ideals of philosophy—or of scholarship and rational discourse in general—as to be strange, often offensive, frequently ridiculous, and ultimately embarrassing to the academy and to philosophers who esteem the true love of wisdom. Instead, we get a tragic waste of paper and ink, as well as academic salaries.

Let us start with the low-hanging fruit of *Faith and Philosophy*, which shamelessly appoints itself as a vehicle that "serves the Christian community by articulating Christian faith in a manner that withstands rigorous examination and by exploring the implications of that faith for all aspects of human life" (tinyurl.com/424rrj2p). Comprising mercifully few articles per issue, a recent issue (volume 38, number 2, 2021) brings us these essays: "Leibniz on Divine Love" (Lucy Sheaf), "God's Impossible Options" (Kenneth Pearce), "Christianity and the Life Story" (Brian Scott Ballard), "Evaluating a New Logical Argument from Evil" (Bruce Langtry), and "Thomistic Faith Naturalized? The Epistemic Significance of Aquinas's Appeal to Doxastic Instinct" (Mark Boespflug). To show that this is no fluke, regard the essay titles in the previous issue (volume 38, number 1, 2021): "On Responsibility and Original Sin: A Molinist Suggestion" (Mark B. Anderson), "Could God Love Cruelty? A Partial Defense of Unrestricted Theological Voluntarism" (Laura Frances Callahan)—which argues that this god has unlimited freedom to will whatever he/she /it wants as long as we "accept some logical constraints on the ways God could have willed morality to be,"[33] so he/she/it *doesn't* have unlimited freedom?—"Heavenly Freedom and Two Models of Character Perfection" (Robert J. Hartman), "Worship and the Problem of Divine Achievement" (John Pittard), "Banez's Big Problem: The Ground of Freedom" (James Dominic Rooney), and "On St. Isaac the Syrian's Argument Against Divine Retribution" (Jordan Wessling). The line-up continues like that.

---

[33] Callahan, "Could God Love Cruelty?" 43.

We might forgive *Faith and Philosophy* (or ignore it, along with *American Catholic Philosophical Quarterly*, et al.) for at least being frank about its religious prejudices. But look then at a more mainstream and neutral publication like the *European Journal of Philosophy of Religion*. It did have the guts to feature a special section on "The Future of Philosophy of Religion" in a recent issue (volume 14, number 1, 2022) including Draper and Schellenberg's merciless critique discussed above, along with the provocative essay "Queer Advice to Christian Philosophers," in which Blake Hereth demands that "Christian philosophers must mitigate their criticisms of queers and queerness" and even more that they "as a group have a responsibility to communities their group has oppressed to prioritize the interests of the oppressed."[34] I'm sure they will get right on it. Anyhow, unchastened, the rest of the issue resumes business as usual, with "A Faith for the Future: Why Non-doxastic Traditional Religion is the Preferable Form of Evolutionary Religion" (Carl-Johan Palmqvist), "An Epistemic Defeater for Islamic Belief? A Reply to Baldwin and McNabb" (Jamie Benjamin Turner)— which sounds like it might be defending Islam but actually insists that Plantingian thinking (discussed in more detail below) applies to that religion as well—"Divine Simplicity: The Aspectival Account" (Joshua Reginald Sijuwade), "Belief, Resistance, and Grace: Stump on Divine Hiddenness" (Katherine E. Sweet), "Liberal Naturalism without Reenchantment" (Thomas Spiegel), "Methodological Naturalism and Scientific Success: Lessons from the Realism Debate" (Yunus Adi Prasetya), and "From a Necessary Being to a Perfect Being: A Reply to Byerly" (Tina Anderson). At least the *International Journal for Philosophy of Religion* has the decency to print no more than three or four articles per issue, such as these in volume 91, number 2, 2022: "Evil and Maximal Greatness" (Kai Michael Büttner), "Unamuno and the Makropulos Debate" (Alberto Oya), and "Christian Physicalism and the Biblical Argument for Dualism" (Ralph Stefan Weir). Let us congratulate *Sophia* for more adventurous publishing, including its special issue (volume 60, number 3, 2021) on "Living without God: A Multicultural Spectrum of Atheism" with offerings by Oppy and Le Poidevin among others, along with a later issue on religion and language welcoming a "polyphony of faiths" including Hinduism, Islam, and feminist theology.

But we have been skimming the surface of philosophy of religion literature. If we inspect more closely, the situation is sadder. Much of what philosophers of religion write in their essays is sheer nonsense, glossolalia that could only mean something to another theist. For instance, in a 2015

---

[34] Hereth, "Queer Advice to Christian Philosophers," 49.

article from the *International Journal for Philosophy of Religion* Mats Wahlberg describes two so-called "evolutionary theodicies" cooked up by philosophers to reconcile evolutionary processes like competition, predation, death, and extinction with a sovereign and loving god, which both stipulate that the brutal processes of evolution are the "only way" a god could make creatures like us (thank goodness Wahlberg concludes that these theodicies fail).[35] Others persist in rehashing old discredited "proofs" for the existence of their god, like Hugh Hunter's watered-down version of George Berkeley's eighteenth-century argument which, Hunter decides, implies not "that an infinite and perfect God exists, but rather the much weaker thesis that a very powerful God exists and that this God's agency is pervasive in nature" ("very powerful" and "pervasive" is a major demotion of the formerly tri-omni deity).[36] Brayton Polka gives it to us straight: "I undertake to show that the God of the Bible is the subject of modern philosophy, i.e., that philosophy is biblical and that the Bible is philosophical."[37]

Since their god and their scriptures are also the fountain of their philosophy, there are many theistic questions to address. Graham Renz ponders "what, deep down, ontologically, God's power is," specifying that Renz is interested in "the God of classical theism [who is] simple, atemporally eternal, immutable, impassible, infinite" (and that should confer a lot of power!).[38] But if Jehovah/god is too powerful, that poses problems for theists too, so Kenneth Pearce posits that, whereas his god could create or "actualize" any kind of world, and the actual existence of this world must be a choice of the god by some Christian accounts, then the hurdle for those accounts (especially Anselm's "perfect being" god) is that "choosing this world" with all its cruelty and suffering "is inconsistent with the character that would be possessed by a maximally great being."[39] In other words, this god seems to have chosen an option that should be impossible for him/her/it to choose. On a happier note, A. G. Holdier contends that, because the creator so loves his creatures and demands that his creatures love each other, therefore heaven must be "a harmoniously structured society where humans are the functional leaders of a multifaceted, interspecies citizenry."[40] The key concept here is "service," thus just as humans are obligated to care for nonhuman beings in this life

---

[35] Wahlberg, "Was Evolution the Only Possible Way?"
[36] Hunter, "George Berkeley's Proof for the Existence of God," 183.
[37] Polka, "Modern Philosophy, the Subject, and the God of the Bible," 563.
[38] Renz, "What is God's Power?" 3.
[39] Pearce, "God's Impossible Options," 198.
[40] Holdier, "Is Heaven a Zoopolis?" 475.

(and good job so far, humans!), they are obligated to care for those beings in the afterlife (although what needs a dog-angel or cat-spirit might have are unstated).

These studies raise the more fundamental and fascinating question of divine thought: what does this god think and want? Jan Levin Propach wonders why his god thinks what he thinks (presuming of course that we have any idea whatsoever what this god is thinking), dredging up once again old theories, this time Leibniz's notion of divine ideas.[41] And if this god has thoughts, does he/she/it have a mind, and if so does he/she/it have a brain or some other thinking part? That would complicate Joshua Sujiwade's assertion of the Doctrine of Divine Simplicity, that is, that his god does not contain "parts," which Sujiwade clarifies by explaining that God is "a module trope with qualitatively differing, yet numerically identical, aspects.... God *is* a property and the qualities of God, construed as aspects, are indeed identical as well."[42] Now we know.

One problem that vexes Christians and other theists is whether and why one should "believe in god(s)" in the first place, that is, think/believe/conclude that such a thing exists. (This whole problem will be solved, or waved away, by Plantinga below). Fortunately, there are many answers and essays to the rescue. Felipe Miguel asks us to accept the obviously spurious argument from authority that there have been many "exceptional theistic philosophers" throughout history and that "agreement with such philosophers does provide evidence in favor of theism."[43] Of course, philosophers and theologians (or theologians posing as philosophers) have devised many proofs of god(s) over the eons, most of which are still floating in the philosophical atmosphere today. However, one distinct way to put an end to the debate is to make belief involuntary and compulsory. Following Swinburne's verdict that "faith" (understood as commitment, the decision to trust and obey his god) is optional, a human and personal decision (but one that you will be punished for deciding wrongly), but that "belief" is involuntary and beyond our control, Robert Hartman pronounced not only that we are compelled to believe (by what? the facts? the scriptures? the church?) but that we *ought* to have faith and that it is logical if not necessary that a person who is "epistemically unable to exercise faith" (i.e., does not see sufficient evidence to believe and make the choice of faith, I suppose) still can be held "objectively blameworthy for failing to do so."[44] Likewise, Matthew Chrisman insisted that a "can"

---

[41] Propach, "Why God Thinks What He is Thinking?"
[42] Sujiwade, "Divine Simplicity: The Aspectual Account," 176.
[43] Miguel, "The Epistemic Significance of Agreement," 451.
[44] Hartman, "Involuntary Belief and the Command to Have Faith," 191.

implies an "ought" as well as an "ought to do" and an "ought to be" (so, we *can* believe/have faith, therefore we *ought* to believe/have faith and *ought to be* a believing/faithful Christian theist). Not to leave it to free will, Chrisman added that your epistemic community (presumably your church) should try to disabuse you of doxastic attitudes (philosophy-speak for "beliefs") you should not have, by "counter-evidence, counter-arguments, and, at the extreme, institutional care"—which is the breathtaking license *for believers to send non-believers to mental institutions.*[45] On the other hand, Lara Buchak girds the faithful philosophers to overlook any counter-evidence against their beliefs, assuring them that faith means "committing to a risky act before examining further evidence" and holding fast to that commitment without seeking or considering any further evidence.[46] It is hard to imagine a less intellectual or rational position than hers.

Understandably, there is a special place in philosophy-of-religion hell for the non-believer. Travis Dumsday assigns (most) atheists a "duty to pray," invoking the specious and manipulative example of a drowning child: "You see the drowning child, whom you cannot possibly get to in time to save. You grant that there may be a God who might answer your prayers. The chance, you think, is slim, but real. Are you obligated to say the prayer?"[47] Ergo, since there *might be* a supreme being who could save the child (but apparently *will not* intervene until we either bring the situation to his/her/its attention or beg for the favor), we are morally obligated to make the petition. "Might these arguments actually serve to motivate atheists and agnostics to develop a habit of prayer? I'd like to think so."[48] There is so much here that it is truly pathetic. Few atheists or agnostics would be moved by this feeble plea since we do *not* accept that there "might be" a supreme being. Second, suddenly we are talking about a "habit" of prayer rather than an emergency appeal. And the idea that this weak "argument" would sway any critical thinker is laughable.

T. J. Mawson, however, seemingly with a straight face argued that atheists who are not absolutely certain that there is no such thing as god(s) should not only pray but more specifically "are under a *prima facie* epistemic obligation to pray to God that He stop them being atheists."[49] Anticipating the objection of which god exactly we should pray to, Mawson was satisfied to "sidestep" the problem by suggesting that

---

[45] Chrisman, "Ought to Believe," 369.
[46] Buchak, "Faith and Steadfastness in the Fact of Counter-Evidence," 113.
[47] Dumsday, Travis. "Why (Most) Atheists Have a Duty to Pray," 60.
[48] Dumsday, Travis. "Why (Most) Atheists Have a Duty to Pray," 70.
[49] Mawson, "Praying to Stop Being an Atheist," 173.

in praying "Is there anyone there? God, if you're there, please speak to me," with the intention it be heard by any God there might be, one's prayer will be heard by that God whether Judaism, Christianity, Islam, theistic versions of Eastern religions, or some other theistic or polytheistic hypothesis is in fact true.[50]

The fallacies here are almost too many to handle. First, all of the world's gods have personal names and do not usually respond to "God," any more than you or I would respond to "human." Second, presumably it does not matter to Mawson *which* god responds, although I am sure that from his seat at St. Peter's College of Oxford University, the ideal (and expected) responder is Jehovah. What would he do if Odin or Zeus answered? Third of course, there are many putative supernatural beings across the world's religions, as we learned in previous chapters, so why not pray (or communicate in their preferred medium, including blood sacrifice) with them? Finally, can we move on if and when no god responds? Oddly, Mawson granted that "a theist who finds himself or herself receiving no apparent reply to his or her prayers over an extended period ... [would] be led to lower the probability that God exists."[51] Why then are there still any theists, given the undeniable hiddenness, silence, and moral indifference of god(s)?

And when this god does not manifest in reaction to the entreaties of either atheists or theists? Dumsday came to the aid of a negligent (read, absent) god with a couple of papers published six years apart—his 2010 "Divine Hiddenness, Free-Will, and the Victims of Wrongdoing" and his 2016 "Divine Hiddenness and the One Sheep." The solution is divine hiddenness, a factor or theology we discussed in Chapter 7. To cite his earlier essay, he insisted, not entirely originally, that

God may remain temporarily "hidden" to some people not merely in order to allow their free moral choice, but because His proper allowance of such choice has led to a great deal of suffering on the part of the victims of wicked choices. If His existence were constantly obvious to those victims, even in the midst of their victimization, many of them would be led to an attitude of enmity, even hatred, toward God.[52]

---

[50] Mawson, "Praying to Stop Being an Atheist," 181.
[51] Mawson, "Praying to Stop Being an Atheist," 184.
[52] Dumsday, "Divine Hiddenness, Free-Will, and the Victims of Wrongdoing," 423.

See, it is better for us if this god *does not* answer our prayer or otherwise intrude, because revealing himself could hurt us and our victims (including, I suppose, the drowning child?). In the second essay he elucidates that "forcing his reality" by god on vulnerable humans "unwillingly might result in significant spiritual/moral harm, inhibiting their ability to develop a positive relationship with God," giving us a god who is oh so very "concerned about the welfare of the resistant," a.k.a. the atheists and nonbelievers.[53] This amiable god would never condemn resisters to hell or anything.

Finally, G. R. McLean and his god were angrier at the anti-theist than the atheist. (See Chapter 5) Having read Thomas Nagel's comments about his distaste for the Christian god (but seemingly nothing else on the subject), McLean ruled that the preference for such a god not to exist, "though partly explicable, is morally unjustifiable, for clearly recognizable reasons. Regardless, then, of further concerns about the doxastic influence of this attitude, we ought to be ashamed of our antipathy to God, which reflects badly upon us."[54] To hammer the nail of judgment all the way in, McLean swore that it is better to have a god who might eventually conquer injustice in the picture than not, and that to prefer such a god not to exist is to prefer injustice to go unconquered, so therefore "the anti-God desire … reveals a moral perversion in our make-up."[55]

Having plodded through this morass of ludicrousness and extreme partisanship, we might have spared ourselves time and irritation if we had simply quoted Paul Moser, a proponent of "Christ-shaped philosophy." He wrote, in a paper delivered to the Evangelical Philosophical Society that aspired to unite spirit and wisdom:

> Christian philosophy is a distinctive kind of philosophy owing to the special role it assigns to God in Christ. Much of philosophy focuses on concepts, possibilities, necessities, propositions, and arguments. This may be helpful as far as it goes, but it omits what is the distinctive focus of Christian philosophy: the redemptive power of God in Christ, available in human experience. Such power, of course, is not mere talk or theory. Even Christian philosophers tend to shy away from the role of divine power in their efforts toward Christian philosophy. The power in question goes beyond philosophical wisdom to the causally powerful Spirit of God, who intervenes with divine corrective reciprocity. It yields a distinctive religious epistemology and a special

---

[53] Dumsday, "Divine Hiddenness and the One Sheep," 69.
[54] McLean, "Antipathy to God," 13.
[55] McLean, "Antipathy to God," 22.

role for Christian spirituality in Christian philosophy. It acknowledges a goal of union with God in Christ that shapes how Christian philosophy is to be done, and the result should reorient such philosophy in various ways. No longer can Christian philosophers do philosophy without being, themselves, under corrective and redemptive inquiry by God in Christ.[56]

That says it all.

In retrospect, one wonders if some or all of these compositions are intended in earnest or whether, just maybe, they are intellectual exercises, not literal reflections of the opinions of the authors. If the latter, these writings are still out there for the impressionable to read, and they consumed the time and resources of their authors and the institutions that financed and published them. Granted, academic journal articles are often abstruse, but surely academic journals, many published by reputable academic presses, have a professional if not a moral duty to expect and impose some standards of intellectual quality and honesty and not to promote unadulterated obscurantist babble.

Philosophers of Religion with Nothing to Prove: "Reformed Epistemology"

One of the traditions, if not the defining tradition, of philosophy is a stringent level of argumentation and evidence, designed to sweep away weak and unsubstantiated opinions which are based on nothing more than feeling, tradition, or authority. At the same time, one of the intrinsic, if not defining, qualities of belief and faith is steadfastness in the absence of evidence and argument or indeed in the face of disconfirming evidence and logic (see above, for example, Lara Buchak's firmness against counter-evidence—or Tertullian's or Justinian's negation of philosophy or anything other than "the pure and true orthodox faith"). Such hostility to the ordinary practices of the academy (or, in ancient Rome, the Academy) indicates an awareness that facts and logic simply do not support your position.

Some philosophers, theists, and theistic philosophers have tried against hope to derive ever-better arguments for their god(s); we see this exertion in contemporary philosophy of religion. The most stubborn insist that facts and logic *do* support their beliefs, while a few brave ones surrender and accept that there is no justification for theistic (or other religious) beliefs and renounce theism. However, a disturbingly popular

---

[56] Moser, "Christ-Shaped Philosophy: Wisdom and Spirit United," 1.

approach at present is to simply deny that the god-believer has any evidential responsibility at all. For the proponents of this charmed (non)principle, the theist does not have to *prove* anything but can *presume* that his or her beliefs are self-evident and self-justifying.

It is our friend Plantinga who has done more than anyone to advance this perspective: if epistemology (the study of knowledge) is not on your side, then invent your own epistemology, a pious epistemology, a "reformed" epistemology—one (de)formed to accomplish what you are predetermined to accomplish. This is the project on which Plantinga has been working for decades, and here is how it works in a nutshell: rather than accepting the burden to produce knowledge that affirms your religious beliefs, *declare that your religious beliefs are knowledge*. Most bluntly articulated in his 2000 book *Warranted Christian Belief*, Plantinga posited that the claim that the Christian god exists, if not true, is at least warranted because the details of that belief are "properly basic." In short, his re/deformed epistemology was characterized as "starting from an assumption of the truth of Christian belief and from that standpoint investigating its epistemology, asking whether and how such belief has warrant."[57]

Never mind that this line of thought is totally backward: philosophy, or any rational thinking, does not start with an assumption of truth and then try to discover or create the knowledge to serve it but starts with the search for knowledge and, ideally, arrives at the truth, jettisoning falsehoods along the way. The key here, as alluded to, is Plantinga's notion of "properly basic." Or we might better say, sixteenth-century Protestant theologian John Calvin's notion, since Plantinga lifted the idea from the Calvinist tradition (which also has affinities with the Cartesian tradition that the Christian god exists, securely proven by the *cogito ergo sum*, that is, the facts that I exist, that I think, and that I can be confident that a god is not an evil deceiver who only lets me think I exist—a deliciously circular path of reasoning). In this worldview, religious belief does not require evidence because *it is evidence*. The god of Christianity is as self-evident, as "basic," as any sensory perception, any sight, sound, or smell. Sensory perceptions, Plantinga maintained, do not depend on proofs, theories, or inferences: I *know* there is a book in front of me because I can *see* that there is a book in front of me. There is nothing "before" such a perception, nothing that must be justified.

It would take too long to establish here that Plantinga's "theory" of perception—what philosophers call phenomenology—is incredibly primitive and naïve; more alert thinkers like Edmund Husserl and Maurice

---

[57] Plantinga, *Warranted Christian Belief*, xiii–xiv.

Merleau-Ponty demonstrated before Plantinga came along that perception is *not* entirely pre-theoretical, primitive (in the sense of simple and original, not constructed out of anything), and "basic" knowledge. Both Husserl and Merleau-Ponty investigated how humans reach out to the bare facts of the world with *intentionality*, imposing concepts and assumptions on experience and constructing knowledge through this interweaving of concepts and perceptions (Kant said essentially the same thing more than two centuries ago). So Plantinga's Christian epistemology fails right out of the gate.

But "reformed epistemology" makes a much greater and more dubious claim. His basic Christian belief-knowledge is warranted by far more than its basicness. It is warranted by a faculty that his god instilled in humans, namely a *sensus divinitatis* or sense of the divine (a notion borrowed straight from Calvin). In a whiplash-inducing act of circular reasoning, Plantinga asked us to accept that his god, who does not need to be proven, implanted humans with this *sensus divinitatis* which would generate reliable belief-knowledge about him. So, the only warrant that is required is the "proper function" of the human mind, which naturally and inevitably "sees" the god who put the god-sensing organ in place. In Plantinga's words, "a belief has warrant just if it is produced by cognitive processes or faculties that are functioning, in a cognitive environment that is propitious for that exercise of cognitive power, according to a design plan that is successfully aimed at the production of true belief."[58]

The fact that Christians find this argument impressive and convincing should make us despair, because it is so blatantly and fatally flawed. To begin, how do we know when a belief is produced by this or that cognitive process or faculty (a *sensus divinitatis* or any other)? How do we know when such a process/faculty is functioning properly; does it make a rattle when it is out of tune? (And if our defective cognitive faculties lead us to reject the basic evidence for divinity, should we be institutionalized like Chrisman advised?) What is this propitious cognitive environment—other than a Christian-soaked culture where children are taught from the youngest age that certain religious doctrines are true and then scared with threats of hell to internalize them? In a differently-propitious environment, would their properly-functioning faculty produce belief-knowledge of Allah, Zeus, nature spirits, fairies, or leprechauns? And is it not marvelously self-legitimizing to attribute our belief-knowledge to a plan and device that is aimed at the production of that very belief-knowledge?

---

[58] Plantinga, *Warranted Christian Belief*, xi.

We wish that Plantinga was a lone fringe voice in his field, but he is not. William Alston, who hatched the idea of the Society of Christian Philosophers, framed his version of fact-free Christian epistemology in terms of "experience," equating religious experience with any other sensory experience. In a chapter in a 1983 volume conveniently co-edited by Plantinga (with Nicholas Wolterstorff), and his own 1991 book on "perceiving God"—and please note the shift between those first two writings from religious experience/belief to *Christian* experience/belief[59]—Alston made the backward proposal that "leading the Christian life provides some ground for Christian belief," since practicing Christians, or individuals engaged in CP (his "technical" abbreviation for Christian practice)

> sometimes feel the presence of God; we get glimpses, at least, of God's will for us; we feel the Holy Spirit at work in our lives, guiding us, strengthening us, enabling us to love other people in a new way; we hear God speaking to us in the Bible, in preaching, or in the words and actions of our fellow Christians.[60]

CP, he demanded, is no different from "perceptual practice" or PP, ordinary sensory experiences of feeling, hearing, seeing, and such. No one expects proofs or justifications for those non-religious perceptions, he sulked, so it is unfair, a "double standard," to request proofs or justifications for perceptions of his god or what he called "M-beliefs" for divine manifestations that humans can sense (with or without a *sensus divintatis*, I suppose).

Like Plantinga's version, Alston's cranky case for Christian perceptual practice is really too silly for a response. First, a belief is not a practice—*or maybe it is*. Insofar as Christians "practice" experiencing Yahweh/Jehovah, we might reflect on how people come to achieve the perception of certain experiences *as* religious/divine experiences. Anthropologist Tanya Luhrmann has studied this very phenomenon: in her *When God Talks Back*, she described and analyzed how evangelical Christians *learn to interpret* various sensations *as* experiences of deity, which she referred to as "cultural kindling."[61] Such empirical research along with theoretical work like Husserl's and Merleau-Ponty's mentioned above strongly suggest that perception is *not* primitive or basic and

---

[59] Alston, "Religious Experience and Religious Belief"; Alston, "Christian Experience and Christian Belief"; Alston, *Perceiving God*.

[60] Alston, "Christian Experience and Christian Belief," 103.

[61] Luhrmann, *When God Talks Back*.

particularly that people do not perceive or experience god(s) but instead have perceptions or experiences that they *are taught to understand as religious/supernatural/spiritual experiences*. In other words, such experiences and any resultant "knowledge" or "belief" are at least two steps and maybe three from "properly basic" perception. And the proof of this assertion is that people who practice different religions, and thus acquire different perceptual-interpretive habits, tend to perceive or sense the god(s) and spirits they are culturally trained (or kindled) to perceive or sense.

Not all modern philosophers of religion are quite as obtuse (David Kyle Johnson recently pushed back and declared that religious experience *cannot* justify religious belief[62]), although Plantinga's and Alston's ideas are frighteningly well received in philosophy of religion departments. Richard Swinburne at least acknowledged the burden of proof to validate theism, but he was not above taking a shortcut to his favorite destination, which he called the "principle of credulity," the assertion/assumption

> that (in the absence of special considerations) if it seems … to a subject that *x* [in this case, the Christian god] is present (and has some characteristic), then probably *x* is present (and has that characteristic); what one seems to perceive is probably so…. How things seem to be (in contingent respects), that is how we seem to perceive them, experience them, or remember them are good grounds for a belief about how things are or were.[63]

This is hardly an improvement. He summarized his own hubris when he stated, "Things are probably so as they seem to be" when it comes to Christians' preconceived faith—so who needs proof?[64]

One of the most devastating retorts of the whole business of Christian epistemology, properly basic belief, and *sensus divinitatis* is that any religion could and, given the inclination, would make the same argument. Why not a Hindu *sensus divinitatis* implanted by Brahma, or a Muslim *sensus divinitatis* screwed in by Allah, or a Buddhist one, or an ancient Egyptian, Greek, Norse, one *ad infinitum*? This speaks to the perennial problem of religious diversity—that many different religions, religious believers, and religious perceptions/experiences populate our world. Alston and allied Christian philosophers wave away the threat, contending either that Christianity has some special status among

---

[62] Johnson, "Why Religious Experience Cannot Justify Religious Belief."
[63] Swinburne, *The Existence of God*, 295–96.
[64] Swinburne, *Epistemic Justification*, 142.

religions—that it has truth conditions the others do not meet, truth conditions felicitously chosen by Christians—or that other religions mean nothing to a Christian. Alston literally and incomprehensibly assured that, in the presence of divergent religions and with no sure way to sort the true from the false, the believer is justified to cling to her own (an alternative that I bet early Christians did not honor for Roman pagans and that I know they did not honor for colonized indigenous peoples). He concluded, "Incompatible propositions can each be justified for different people if what they have to go on is suitably different"—if, I guess, they occupy different Plantingian "cognitive environments"—which leaves us no standard or method for selecting between religions *and no basis for preferring Christianity other than prior acquaintance with and acquisition of Christianity*. This is a phenomenally weak endorsement of what was alleged to be a self-evident truth.

Conclusion:
The Future of Philosophy of Religion?

Given everything we now know about philosophy of religion as an academic discipline, what should we, or what should *they*, do about it? John Loftus, a most "unapologetic" critic of the field, insists that it must end "because there is no truth to religion."[65] He does grant it a reprieve, though, allowing that philosophers of religion do not have to stop doing it altogether but that it should not be a "separate subdiscipline" in the secular university and that "it should be taught correctly, if it's to be done at all ... treating all faith-based claims equally and privileging none."[66] My position is that philosophers are not obligated to terminate the study of religion and that religion's truth-status is not germane to the question. Religion is a legitimate topic of philosophical inquiry, as are other subjects like art, language, mathematics, law, science, and many more. However, as Loftus demands, it must be done properly, in accordance with the norms and standards of philosophy.

Numerous philosophers have proposed their own remedies for the ailing field. In his 2014 manifesto on the future of the subdiscipline, Schilbrak states:

In one sentence, what I am recommending is this: philosophy of religion ought to evolve from its primary present focus on the rationality of traditional theism to become a fully global form of

---

[65] Loftus, *Unapologetic: Why Philosophy of Religion Must End*, 13.
[66] Loftus, *Unapologetic*, 112–13.

critical reflection on religions in all their variety and dimensions, in conversation with other branches of philosophy and other disciplines in the academic study of religion.[67]

Draper and Schellenberg have more specific advice for the "renewal" of the field, with seven action items:

- Eliminating the religious test for membership in the Society of Christian Philosophers (although philosophers of religion are not compelled to join this organization and ideally it would not exist at all)
- Committing to "balanced inquiry," including examining and even defending positions that the authors themselves do not personally hold
- More clearly distinguishing the aims of philosophy from those of religion
- Encouraging more interaction with philosophers of religion and scholars in the department of religious studies (which, if Weibe is correct, struggles under its own religious commitments)
- Reflecting on the fundamental topics of the subdiscipline such as the definition of religion (which is currently taken entirely for granted), the place of religion in society, and whether there is a core or essence of religious concepts and propositions
- Paying attention to the "deep history of religion" and not merely one or a few recent and familiar religions
- Broadening the education of philosophers of religion[68]

Finally, Knepper's tonic for the field is a five-course therapy, starting with (1) more diversity in its subject matter, that is, more religions besides Christianity, (2) preservation of the philosophical stance of ideological criticism and correction, (3) "thick description" of religions or nuanced and empirically-based reckonings with how people actually practice and use religion (more below), (4) a comparative perspective, which would naturally flow from the first and third courses, and (5) evaluation of various religious claims and concepts, with the caveat that "evaluation requires antecedent description and comparison."[69]

---

[67] Schilbrak, *Philosophy and the Study of Religion*, xi.
[68] Draper and Schellenberg, "The Why and the How."
[69] Knepper, *The Ends of Philosophy of Religion*, 19.

In light of these comprehensive and consistent programs, what is my prescription for philosophy of religion? To emulate Schilbrak, in one sentence it would be: *philosophy of religion should be the polar opposite of what Plantinga advised and what the field has (d)evolved into*. It should not shirk the traditional and essential norms and standards of philosophy in order "to serve the Christian community"; philosophy of religion should not "serve" Christianity or any religion but should serve philosophy and the advancement of knowledge in general. The most elementary norm or standard of all philosophy is *questioning*, not asking questions posed by the dogmas and revered texts of religion or any other subject (science, art, law, etc.) but questions *about* those dogmas and texts, questions that *have the potential to destabilize and disprove received dogmas and texts.* Philosophy should expose assumptions and taken-for-granted "knowledge," which Socrates demonstrated over two millennia ago are often not as known as we think. If there is not a chance that the work of philosophy will erode the ground under a set of assumptions and beliefs, it is not philosophy at all.

It goes without saying that the foremost thing philosophers of religion need to do is to include more kinds of religion in their research, not just Christianity and not just (mono)theism. To do otherwise would be like attempting a philosophy of language by studying only English or at best European languages. This modification alone will dramatically and beneficially reshape the subdiscipline: Christianity will no longer be its sole interest, and being forced to grapple with foreign religious thought-systems will compel scholars to consider other religious terminology and concepts as well as practices and institutions, which will automatically reflect critically on Christian terms, concepts, practices, etc. The effect, and the goal, should be, to use the words of Dipesh Chakrabarty,[70] "provincializing" Christianity—not ignoring that one religion but decentering it as the focus of virtually all current attention.

Once this provincialization and decentering is done, or while it is underway, other shifts will occur. The most sanguine will be an alteration in the questions that philosophy of religion poses. Instead of contemplating how to prove—or how and why *not* to prove—that Christian beliefs are true, the field will formulate such problems as, What are the different kinds of religions? What, if anything. do they have in common, that is, is there an essence or core of religions? What are the unique lexicon and metaphysics of any particular religion? (For instance, one cannot do a philosophy of Hinduism or Buddhism, let alone of Aztec or Australian

---

[70] Chakrabarty, *Provincializing Europe.*

Aboriginal, religion with a Christian vocabulary.[71]) How is religion lived and practiced by members, such as in myth-telling, ritual, and everyday life? (This is similar to questions raised by philosophers of science in regard to how science is actually practiced by laboratory researchers, in contrast to the ideals of science.) Ultimately, why does such a thing as religion exist in the first place—or more fundamentally, *is there such a thing as religion,* or can and should we subsume it under some other sociocultural category or categories and/or explain it in terms of some other psycho-cultural properties?

In order to fulfill this mission, philosophy of religion should and must recruit auxiliary disciplines, first and foremost the cognitive science of religion which is already working on many of these same problems. The major accomplishment of the cognitive science of religion—a joint effort of psychologists, biologists, sociologists, anthropologists, and others—is the realization that religion, as anthropologist Scott Atran phrased it, emerges from "the very same cognitive and affective structures as nonreligious beliefs and practices" and that these mental and emotional characteristics have an evolutionary origin.[72] There are also several parallel subdisciplines in other fields that philosophy of religion should closely observe, such as psychology of religion, sociology of religion, and anthropology of religion. Philosophers of religion could learn two valuable lessons from these colleagues. First, psychologists, sociologists, and anthropologists have produced robust statistical, theoretical, and ethnographic knowledge about religions. Anthropology in particular depends on the very "thick description" that Knepper recommended to his peers (the term was popularized by Clifford Geertz, although he credits it to philosopher Gilbert Ryle[73]), gained from up-close and prolonged contact with a group or society via the method of participant-observation or living with and living like the people they study. (Some religious studies scholars have adopted the method.) I have always considered anthropology to be a kind of "field philosophy" in which fieldworkers discover and describe the conceptual worlds of others by dwelling in those worlds with them. Anthropologists especially could fill the data gaps in philosophy of religion, since we tend to concentrate on non-Western and non-Christian peoples—crucially important as, according to Schilbrak,

---

[71] See for instance historian and philosopher James Maffie's study of Aztec philosophy, *Aztec Philosophy: Understanding a World in Motion*, which illustrates how fascinating another culture's metaphysical thinking can be and how profitable for us it is to acquaint ourselves with it.

[72] Atran, *In Gods We Trust: The Evolutionary Landscape of Religion*, ix.

[73] See Chapter 1 of Geertz's classic book, *The Interpretation of Cultures*.

few or no philosophers of religion specialize in African, Native American, or Aboriginal Australian belief systems. Second, psychological and social approaches to religion by and large do their work with a neutral (and occasionally even a skeptical) attitude toward religion, proving that significant insights can be gained on the subject without—and maybe *only* without—imposing personal piety.

One last area in which philosophers of religion need to educate themselves, ironically, is theology. Although philosophy of religion behaves like, and often sees itself as, an adjunct to theology, it is surprisingly and blithely ignorant of the developments in cutting-edge theology (including developments that were cutting-edge in the 1960s), which shed a harsh light on it. For decades Christian theologians have been generating strange new conceptions of their god—as impersonal, as weak and powerless, even as dead (see Chapter 4)—but philosophers of religion still seem to operate with the old-fashioned and popular god, one who is a person who hears prayers and actively participates in human affairs. Philosophy of religion would be noticeably different if distilled through the acid of contemporary theology.

Finally, I submit that, if philosophers of religion are intent on serving their faith, that this renewed, reformed, and improved approach would serve religion, in the same sense that philosophy properly done serves science, art, language, and its other topics—by helping scholars and researchers in those fields think better about their concepts and practices. Philosophy of science, for instance, does not exist to comfort scientists that they are doing everything right, nor to undermine their work. Rather, its contribution is to assist (maybe force) scientists to recognize the assumptions that they bring to their research and writing and to be more self-reflexive and self-critical. Offered in a constructive spirit, such philosophical inquiry improves science (or art or ethics or law, etc.), and it would improve religion too—which might in the end mean freeing people from it.

9

Freeing Atheism from Atheism: Godlessness beyond Christian Theism

At the end of the second chapter, we cited Onfray's plea for an "atheistic atheism," a curious—and on the face of it, paradoxical or nonsensical—idea. Isn't all atheism atheistic? But his point was to advocate for something other than what he rightly brands "Christian atheism," the kind of atheism with which we are most familiar, the kind of atheism that we tend to think *is* atheism, the kind of atheism that is nothing more than "negation of God" and therefore remains in thrall to the Christian god, the kind of atheism that endlessly goes around and around about the existence of Jehovah, the veracity of the Bible, and all of the other claims that are specific to one theism.

The one thing we can say with certainty is that the conventional form of atheism is hardly free of god(s); quite the opposite, it is obsessed with if not traumatized by god(s). It is one of the three possible variations of atheism that we discussed previously, the "argumentative" or "debate" variation that finds itself constantly in combat with god(s). The point of this chapter is to reveal that there are actually many more varieties of atheism than the three already suggested. This perspective takes seriously but transcends Diller's bare-bones notion of "local atheism," which she and most scholars still envision as arguing with and "disproving" the particular local god(s). Indeed, we have insisted, and others like David Newheiser insist, that there is more to atheism than "not believing," just as there is more to theism or religion in general than "believing," if by that we mean (as people usually do) accepting a proposition as true or "making a cognitive commitment." Newheiser, in his introduction to *The Varieties of Atheism*, reminds us that atheism, like theism or any other cultural system, also "incorporates ethical disciplines, cultural practices, and affective states,[1] which are probably more essential than, and certainly more interesting than, fruitless quarrels about the existence of god(s).

---

[1] Newheiser, "Introduction: The Genealogy of Atheism," 2.

In this chapter, we will look at three major non-Western religions or cultures, namely, Islam, India, and Japan to unpack how they have conceived and continue to conceive nonbelief, irreligion, and atheism. This project also practices the advice that we gave to philosophy of religion in the last chapter, to get out of the Christian box and learn about traditions outside of the one to which they are personally attached. What we find is that, just as there are many ways to do theism, many local theisms (not all of which, as we have established, privilege "belief" as the central factor), there are also many local atheisms (not all of which regard "nonbelief" or propositional dispute about god[s] as their defining feature).

No Submission:
Nonbelief and Atheism in Islam

Here is a riddle: what do Pat Robertson, Glenn Beck, and "New Atheists" like Richard Dawkins and Sam Harris have in common? The answer is an uninformed and virtually hysterical loathing for Islam. I know that is not a funny punchline, but then there is nothing funny—and almost nothing knowledgeable—about the rhetoric that right-wing provocateurs and some of our most admired atheist spokesmen share. We expect no better from the likes of Robertson and Beck (and Jerry Falwell and the rest of that crew). Robertson has said that "these people"—the followers of the Muslim faith—"are crazed fanatics, and I want to say it now: I believe it's motivated by demonic power. It is satanic, and it's time we recognize what we're dealing with," cautioning Americans that "the goal of Islam, ladies and gentlemen, whether you like it or not, is world domination."[2] He further backed up his claim by exposing several "lies" about Islam, for instance, that it is a religion of peace, that jihad is a peaceful struggle, and that Islam is not much different from Christianity or Judaism.[3]

Depressingly, comments by Harris and Dawkins are often indistinguishable from those by conservative Christians, down to the archaic misspelling of Qur'an as Koran. For instance, the middle section of Harris's lauded *The End of Faith* is an ordinary diatribe against Islam, in which he declares war on "the vision of life that is prescribed to all Muslims in the Koran" while explicitly and conveniently ignoring the historical, economic, and political "roots of Muslim violence" in "the Israeli occupation of the West Bank and Gaza," "the collusion of Western powers with corrupt dictatorships," and "the endemic poverty" of the Arab

---

[2] Associated Press, "Pat Robertson Calls Radical Muslims 'Satanic.'"

[3] Beck, *It Is About Islam.*

world.[4] Later in his blog (tinyurl.com/4xrmswbw), he purported to expose "the reality of Islam," which is "all fringe and no center," "a civilization with an arrested history" populated by "utterly deranged" religious tribalists. Dawkins, for his part, has made repeated statements landing him in hot water, such as tweeting (never a good way for intelligent people to communicate complex ideas) that "Christianity was the world's most evil religion. Now massively overtaken by Islam," telling an audience at a 2017 science festival that not all religions are equally bad because Islam is clearly the worst, and tweeting again in 2018 that the Muslim call to prayer offends him in a way that Christian church bells do not, since the utterance *Allahu Akhbar* (God is great) is "aggressive-sounding," literally "the last thing you hear before the suicide bomb goes off."[5]

One point on which Robertson, Beck, Dawkins, Harris, and a disappointing number of scholar-experts on Islam agree is that Islam is incapable of moderation, let alone secularization. Islam—which apparently has a mind of its own and compels believers to act in certain ways—is incorrigibly irrational, atavistic, and immune to modernization, liberalization, and most assuredly atheization, they insist. They are wrong and woefully uninformed.

To be sure, nonbelievers and atheists are not common in Muslim-majority societies (neither are they in many Christian-majority societies), and it is not easy to be a nonbeliever or atheist in such places. But that does not mean nonbelievers do not exist; Westerners' ignorance of critiques of religion and avowals of non-religion in Islamic contexts is partly due to most of that activity being conducted in languages that Westerners cannot understand, but it is also largely due to our more-than-slightly willful blindness to anything other than the worst and most extreme in the religion. Consequently, Moroccan journalist Ahmed Benchemsi upbraided Westerners and Christians for their "inability to even conceive of an Arab atheist."[6]

Instead of a culture of religious inertia, Khaled Diab of the Cairo Institute for Human Rights Studies recently asserted that the Islamic world is experiencing a "tsunami of atheism," sufficient to panic and mobilize religious conservatives and political regimes.[7] Precisely how prevalent nonbelief is among (former) Muslims is a topic of some controversy. Naturally, religious authorities would like us to think that it is diminishingly rare: one often-mentioned survey by the overtly-biased Dar

---

[4] Harris, *The End of Faith: Religion, Terror, and the Future of Reason*, 109.
[5] Osborne, "Richard Dawkins Accused of Islamophobia.'"
[6] Benchemsi, "Invisible Atheists: The Spread of Disbelief in the Arab World."
[7] Diab, "Views: Arab Atheists," 18.

Al-Ifta in Egypt found only 2,293 atheists in the whole of the Middle East and North Africa, including just 34 in Libya. More realistically, KazKaz and Bosch estimate that atheists comprise two percent of the Middle East population, which would total two million nonbelievers, not counting India, Central Asia, and Indonesia with their much greater populations.[8] The World Values Survey reported that the level of nonreligiosity (which is not synonymous with atheism) was much higher—7.5 percent in Egypt, seventeen percent in Turkey, fifteen percent in Indonesia, and sixteen percent in the Shi'ite hotbed of Iran.[9] Likewise, Arab Barometer announced in 2019 that thirteen percent of respondents identified as "not religious," the label even more common among those under age thirty (eighteen percent).

At the level of particular countries, the results are also noteworthy. Arab Barometer claimed that Tunisia, usually considered the most secular of Arab states, hosted the largest proportion of nonreligious, over thirty percent. More than twenty-five percent of Libyans and approximately fifteen percent of Algerians and Lebanese called themselves nonreligious, along with around ten percent of Egyptians and Sudanese. Yemen was the sole case where religiosity increased between 2013 and 2019. Meanwhile, a 2012 WIN/Gallup International poll declared nonreligion alive and well in the heartland of Islam, Saudi Arabia, where nineteen percent identified as nonreligious and a full five percent as atheist. Diab quoted one interviewee as saying, "We non-believers have meetings and groups in a lot of Saudi cities. If you go into them, then you will be shocked by the numbers and elements of society represented."[10] To mention the Islamic republic of Iran again, The Group for Analyzing and Measuring Attitudes in Iran (GAMAAN) informs us that over twenty-two percent of Iranians confess their religious affiliation as "none," with another 5.8 percent agnostics and 8.8 percent atheists. Equally remarkably, more than two-thirds want to separate religion and state, over half oppose religious education in schools, and almost three-quarters disapprove of compulsory veiling of women.[11] And there is good reason to assume that these numbers are underestimated, because of the considerable pressure not to publicly promote one's lack of religion. As Benchemsi explains:

Considering the extent to which the Arab social and political environment impedes the expression of non-belief, the numbers of

---

[8] KazKaz and Bosch, "Media Speech on Atheism," 33.
[9] Schielke, "The Islamic World," 647.
[10] Diab, "Views," 18.
[11] Maleki and Tamimi Arab, "Iranians' Attitudes Toward Religion," 1–4.

doubters and atheists would likely be significantly higher if people felt freer to speak their minds. In January, Egyptian atheist activist Ahmed Harqan told Ahram Online, "If the state preserved and protected the rights of minorities, the numbers of those who reveal they're atheists would increase tenfold."[12]

More to the point of our discussion in this book, the enumeration of atheists and nonbelievers in Muslim settings is complicated by differences in how people in that culture think and talk about non-religion—or about religion for that matter. The problem begins, fortuitously, with the very concept of belief. The venerable scholar of religion, Wilfred Cantwell Smith, postulated that Muslims do not "believe" Islam the way that Christians "believe" Christianity. Indeed, he held that "the Qur'an has no word for 'belief' in the modern sense."[13] The Arabic word *iman* which is often translated as faith, Smith maintained, does not suggest affirming a proposition but rather performing an action. Hence, a Muslim is not someone who "believes" in Allah or the Qur'an but someone who *submits to* the god's and the scripture's authority (both Islam and Muslim derive from the Arabic root *s-l-m* that connotes "peace" and "submission," or here the peace that comes from submission).

Because followers do not "believe" in Allah or the Qur'an, Smith reasoned that Muhammad could not imagine that a person would "not believe." Nonbelief in this (the standard Western) sense is simply unintelligible. Muhammad and later representatives of the religion presume that everyone *knows* that a god exists; knowledge of this god is written on their hearts. One might, for different illegitimate reasons, refuse to submit to the god's rightful authority, which we understand better if we grasp the notion of "religion" in the Muslim view. The Arabic word *din* or *deen*, translated into English as "religion," is related to other terms like *dana* and *dain*, which refer to debt and the obligations related to debt and credit, respectively. (Significantly, the English word "creed" has the same etymological relationship to "credit," as we already acknowledged, which is why even in English, belief in a creed is more than cognitive acceptance of a proposition.) Thus, from the Islamic perspective, *din* is less a truth-claim that you believe than a duty you honor, a debt that you pay. Not accepting and performing your obligations is less disbelief than ingratitude and betrayal.

Through this prism, it is understandable that "nonbelief," "irreligion," and other Western/Christian concepts do not quite fit. For

---

[12] Benchemsi, "Invisible Atheists."
[13] Smith, *Faith and Belief,* 34.

instance, the Arabic term that is typically rendered as unbelief or infidelity is *kufr*, which really means something like "one who spurns," that is, one who stubbornly, selfishly, or ignorantly abdicates their responsibilities to Allāh and his prophets. (One who rejects/spurns religion is a *kafir*.) Almost equally bad is the person who equates the true god with some false idol; hence, Islam condemns idolatry or polytheism as *shirk*, which means "association" (of something ungodly with god) or false equivalence between Allāh and anything else.

Given the moral load of Islam as submission to Allāh's generous but absolute authority, in which infidelity (like infidelity to one's spouse) is not disputing a proposition but dishonoring a commitment, it is easy to see that turning one's back on religion is not so much disputing a fact as rebelling against a creditor. So, the Arabic word that has come to stand for "atheism" is *ilhād* (a [male] atheist is a *mulhid*), which carries the normative implication of "deviation" or "rebellion." In short, "*ilhād* means to be inclined to something negative or blasphemy, to deviate from something good, or to tend to something negative or blasphemy."[14] Note, significantly, that no word or root for god, like *theo-*, appears in the term; instead, a *mulhid* is literally a deviant or traitor, which no one particularly wants to be. Similarly, what English/Christian discourse calls apostasy (leaving religion) equates to *riddah* or *irtidād*, from the root *radd*, to retreat, withdraw, or fall back (as in Christian "backsliding").

Lately, Arabic speakers have invented new terms for secular and irreligious ideas and positions, which are not (any more than in English) entirely interchangeable with atheism. Lacking an indigenous word for "secular" (some insisting that Islam has always been secular in the sense of participating in the material world), *'ilmaniyah* (from the word *'ilm*, knowledge) or *'alamaniyah* (from *'alam*, world) convey roughly the same meaning, the latter closer to the English "worldly." For those who have shed religion, one popular current word is "no religion" (*la din*); the phrase La Deeni (one who has no religion) has been adopted as the name for organizations and websites, since it ideally and rather neutrally "unites many who do not believe in any religion, for example, the atheist, the agnostic, and the deist, who believes that there is a first cause for this universe without believing in any religion, in addition to other categories."[15] For those who prefer their own moniker, an assortment of terms is available, such as *la-adrī* for "agnostic" (literally "I don't know"), *rubūbī* for "deist," and *la-ikritātī* for "indifferent." Obviously, the problem for researchers appears when one or another of these categories is the

---

[14] Fuad et al., "Causes of the New Atheism," 347.
[15] Nader, "Nonreligious Arabs Protest Online To Declare #WeAreHere."

language of a specific survey or study: individuals may accept the label *la dini* but reject the label *mulhid*, for instance.

In this confusing jumble of terminology, and in light of the scandalous if not criminal quality of non-religion in the Islamic context—where the price for desertion from the faith can range from disapproval by family to loss of friends and of jobs to prison or execution—it is little wonder that nonbelievers generally keep a low profile. If and when they speak and act on their nonbelief, they tend to do so anonymously or at least pseudonymously (i.e., under a false name). Predictably, as in the United States and elsewhere, the internet and social media are congenial sites for nonreligious activity, of which there is plenty. One commonly mentioned production is the YouTube channel Black Ducks (a metaphor for misfits like "black sheep" in English) run by atheist Ismail Mohamed. There are programs for all tastes and preferences, from Adam Elmarsi's *rubūbī* (deist) show to the *la adri* (agnostic) figure Kosay Betar (or Qusayy Bitar), the teacherly Hamed.TV of Hamed Abdel-Samad, and the frankly atheistic and satirical show of Sherif Gaber, who performs satirical skits mocking different sorts of believers.[16] Many observers have commented on the use of comedy and ridicule to dethrone religion, including also the Moroccan online project Free Arabs, which features videos like "The Horrific Four" portraying four characters such as a faithless imam and a gay Arab, or "*Al Bernameg*," a Moroccan version of "The Daily Show."

For those seeking more participation, there are myriad Facebook and other groups, among them Atheists in Morocco, MALI (*Mouvement Alternatif pour les Libertés Individuelles* or Alternative Movement for Individual Liberties), the Arab Irreligious Network, the Arab Atheist Forum, the Arab Atheists Network (www.il7ad.org), Ladeeni Online (ladeenion2.blogspot.com), Arab Atheists Magazine with links to multiple videos (arabatheistbroadcasting.com/aamagazine), Arab Atheist blogspot (arabatheist1.blogspot.com), and the Algerian Atheist Twitter site (thealgerianathe). For the truly brave, some opportunities exist to appear on television and radio talk shows, where they are typically interviewed by hostile hosts and pious guests who revile them as immoral, threaten them, and sometimes throw things at them.

Informatively, also, one thing that former Muslims do not tend to do is offer "deconversion" stories, which is a favorite pastime of Western atheists. It is necessary to comprehend that, like "belief," "conversion" is a foreign concept to Islam: individuals do not "convert" to Islam like they do to Christianity. Rather, as we explained, everyone is theoretically born a Muslim; the only question is whether they will honor their (super)natural

---

[16] Elsässer, "Arab Non-believers and Freethinkers on YouTube."

obligations. So, when Vliek interviewed ex-Muslims in Europe, she discovered an absence of deconversion testimonies; as one woman stated, "I never talk about it, it's like eating bread every day, it is just a way of life."[17] In these and similar remarks, it became clear that Muslim nonbelievers did not perceive their situation as a "rupture" or qualitative break from their former status as believers—"rupture" or "break" once more reflecting a Christian way of thinking about one's religious identity (epitomized by Paul's epiphany on the road to Damascus). Another interviewee added, "The question is, why would you say it out loud. Why does it have to be such an extroverted thing?"—especially when the only effect of the declaration is to upset and offend family, friends, and officials.[18]

What, then, motivates Muslims to renounce their religion? Khalil and Bilici pinpointed two main classes of motivations for *riddah* (apostasy)—intellectual/ideological objections and social/experiential ones.[19] The first encompass the kinds of arguments that inspire Western atheists, although naturally with a Muslim inflection. That is, understandably, Muslims do not argue about the Bible or about Jesus; those are Christian problems, the kind that philosophers of religion—and too many Western atheists—spin their wheels over. For Muslims, the problems are Islam-specific, in particular the status of the Qur'an and of its chief prophet, Muhammad. As Malik phrased it, those who dispute Islam often attack the alleged "miraculousness" of the Qur'an—its divine inspiration and perfection—stressing for example its obscurities, its contradictions, and the questionable history of its compilation.[20] (Recall how Salman Rushdie got in trouble for suggesting that mistakes and falsehoods were introduced during the writing of the Qur'an.) Others aim their critiques at Muhammad, denouncing him as a fraud or madman or impugning the historicity of his deeds and sayings.

When people eventually disavow religion for intellectual or ideological reasons, this often if not ordinarily follows a period of intense religious questioning. During this period, believers are usually not attempting to find reasons not to believe but, quite to contrary, are seeking "to deepen [their belief] and to understand religion better."[21] In the process, they discover things in their scriptures or dogmas that confuse or disturb them; religious authorities either cannot or will not answer their

---

[17] Vliek, "'Speaking Out Would Be a Step Just Not Believing,'" 16
[18] Vliek, "'Speaking Out Would Be a Step Just Not Believing,'" 14.
[19] Khalil and Bilici, "Conversion Out of Islam," 118.
[20] Malik, *Atheism and Islam: A Contemporary Discourse*, 36.
[21] Diab, "Views," 17.

questions, often castigating them for asking in the first place. Finally, after some time they turn their backs on religious claims.

However—and this is critically important—more important to most ex-Muslims than falsification of religious doctrine (that is, refuting "beliefs") are the social and experiential concerns. Among these Khalil and Bilici counted the treatment of women in the religion, the clash between religious (shari'a) law and human rights, the strict but unnecessary rules of Islam, and the damnation of all non-Muslims, even "good" ones. Augmenting and amplifying these objections are the violence and intolerance in Islam, the conduct of Islamic extremists and terrorists, and the injustice of many Muslim regimes. Indeed, speaking to the Assembly of Muslim Jurists of America, Zarabozo opined that the single greatest reason why people give up on the religion is *dhulm* "or the wrong that is committed by Muslim individuals, groups and governments as well as religious violence and radicalism."[22] Much of this critique is facilitated by other social forces, such as access to the internet and social media (as already noted), Western education (especially for women), urbanization, modern employment, and the opportunity to live apart from parents in independent apartments, where individuals can meet and date new people—even non-Muslim people. Some sources mention the influence of Western atheism, including the New Atheists, but this influence should not be overstated; in each country and language, a local set of scholars and popular figures inspires peers to question received truths and self-appointed authorities, along the lines and in the terms that make local sense.

Finally, in total refutation of conservative bigots and New Atheists alike, there are entire Muslim societies that simply do not take religion very seriously. Two worth mentioning are the Basseri and the Kyrgyz. The Basseri, a pastoral people in southwest Iran, are nominally Muslim, Fredrick Barth described them as self-consciously "lax" in their religion and "indifferent to metaphysical problems," with little interest in prayer or ritual.[23] In the Central Asian country of Kyrgyzstan, Maria Louw found a distinctly "ironic" attitude toward Islam. Many citizens "display a profound discomfort with 'religion' and with people who have begun to embrace, and publicly display, a 'religious' identity."[24] Frankly, people were a bit ashamed of their religiosity, taking an ironic stance on their own beliefs and behaviors; that is, they would "play with the categories that have been used to describe their ways of being Muslims and with which

---

[22] Zarabozo, "The Rise of New Atheism and its Relationship to Islam," 13–14.
[23] Barth, *Nomads of South Persia*.
[24] Louw, "Being Muslim the Ironic Way," 151.

they circumscribe practices during 'religious' rituals," sometimes laughing that "real" Muslims would doubt their religious identity and sincerity.[25]

No Superstition, No Inequality:
Nonbelief and Atheism in India

When Americans and other Westerners think about India (which is not very often), atheism and non-religion are not the first thing that comes to mind. India, like much of "the East," is imagined as a mysterious exotic land of overwhelming spirituality, ritual excess, and gods galore. On the surface, the numbers seem to support this view: according to one 2022 survey, a mere two percent of Indians describe themselves as non-religious or atheistic (which would still amount to at least twenty-eight million people), that small demographic roughly evenly split between the two categories.[26] But this captures only part of the picture and is, like the Islam case, skewed by the way the question is asked and by the disparity between Western and Indian terms and concepts.

The "atheistic" roots of Indian thought are ancient and deep; any religion or philosophy as old, diverse, and sophisticated as that of India is bound to have multiple, contradictory forms. As Bhattacharya recently wrote, "India indeed is the home to diverse religions, not all of which are theistic."[27] Two South Asian traditions that originally made no reference to god(s) are Buddhism and Jainism. Buddhism, which in its initial incarnation was more of a psychological philosophy than a religion, had no place for god(s) of the conventional kind, since it posited nothing that lasted for more than an instant, let alone for eternity. The doctrine of *anicca* or impermanence teaches that all things are fleeting and temporary, including the self (*anatta*, no self). "Things" that appear to endure are simply sequences or composites of sense experience, each "a succession of discrete, momentary (*ksanika/khanika*) events that pass out of existence as soon as they have originated. As one event is exhausted, it conditions a new event of its kind that proceeds immediately afterwards."[28] The only "reality" is the instantaneously arising and fading perceptions or mental states out of which the mind builds "things." This theory leads inexorably to the doctrine of *sunyata*, emptiness, that there is no essence behind the "things" we experience and also no causal order linking those "things."

---

[25] Louw, "Being Muslim the Ironic Way," 156.
[26] Buchholz, "How Do You Feel About Religion?"
[27] Bhattacharya, "India: 1500 BC to AD 1200," 118.
[28] Ronkin, *Early Buddhist*, 59.

Nothing could be more remote from Christian theology and metaphysics, with their eternal unchanging god and substance. To be sure, some later schools of Buddhism re-admitted gods but at the expense of a certain incoherence of thought.

Jainism, born around the same time as Buddhism, launched from the same point as Buddhism, evaluating life as suffering, in this case emanating from the fundamental entanglement of matter (*ajiva*) and soul (*jiva*). The ideal state would be to rid the soul of all material corruption (which is one reason why Jains observe such strict dietary rules, preferably avoiding not only meat but plants that are still alive). According to Vallely, it is this desperate human condition that invalidates any conception of an active, personal god. "'Why would a God create such a world as this?', Jains ask," answering themselves that there is no creator god; "To accept theism—in whatever expression—would be to accept the cosmos as purposefully, meaningfully created. For Jains, such an idea is untenable, if not sinister, given that unrelenting anguish is part and parcel of the cosmos itself."[29] Yet, Vallely contended that Jain atheism is a "god-saturated atheism," in which their "god" (*deva, devata,* or *bhagwan*) pervades reality—as one of the myriad spiritual beings or "god-species" (*devagati*), as the soul or *jiva*, and as a general term of honor for all "worship-worthy beings."

But we do not have to look outside Hinduism proper for examples of skeptical, atheistic, or materialistic philosophies. The Vedas and the *Upanishads* themselves sometimes express doubt and uncertainty about religious questions, as in hymn 10.129.6 7 of the *Rig Veda*, which ponders "after all, who knows, and who can say, whence it all came, and how creation happened?" Schools of thought like Sāmkhya and Cārvāka carried this line of thought further. Like good skeptics, followers of Cārvāka rejected both "testimony" as a source of knowledge and the existence of unperceivable entities like god(s) or spirits. Only that which can be observed can be known; thus, claims about putative souls and gods should not be believed. As for the Sāmkhya school, it insists that there is no compelling argument in favor of god(s):

There is no proof whatever in the case of God. The inference of God as a creator of the universe is not possible, because Prakṛti, the primordial energy, is the creator of the universe. The Veda is also not a proof of the existence of God as it has no bearing upon its own import but points to the injunctions for meditation, etc.[30]

---

[29] Vallely, "Jainism," 354.
[30] Bhattacharya, "India," 134.

But let us return to the present day. The modern state of India is of course a product of Western (British) colonialism, which introduced many new ideas, including Christianity and liberal freethought. Influenced by Western ideas, not the least Marxism, Bhagat Singh testified "Why I am an Atheist" in a 1931 essay. Insisting that humanity invented the god-concept, he urged that "Society must fight against this belief in God as it fought against idol worship and other narrow conceptions of religion. In this way man will try to stand on his feet."[31] This attitude embraces many of the themes of contemporary irreligion in India. When independence was won in 1947, the country was established as a *secular* state but not an *atheist* one, and neither of these terms means for India exactly what it means for the West.

Political scientist Rajeev Bhargava maintained that Indian secularism was neither simply Western secularism transplanted to the Indian subcontinent nor traditional *sarva dharma sambhava* (literally, "all truths/ways (*dharma*) are equal or harmonious") updated for the modern world but, rather, something "distinctive" that "uniquely combines an active hostility to some aspects of religion with an equally active respect for its other dimensions."[32] The key problem then, as now, was religious diversity (recall that Muslims split from colonial India to form their own state of Pakistan, originally east [today's Bangladesh] and west [today's Pakistan]). Accordingly, India's constitutional secularism is oriented less toward disestablishment of religion (that is, American-style separation of church and state)—and certainly not toward disputing the existence of god(s)—and more toward peaceful co-existence between potentially fractious faith communities; economist Aanchal Anand suggested that "inclusivism" might be a more suitable term than "secularism."[33]

A moderate sort of "live-and-let-live" policy does not equate, though, to absolute neutrality or a hands-off approach to religion. The Indian state, legal scholar Deepa Das Acevedo opined, very much intervenes in religious matters, ironically perhaps more so in regard to Hinduism. The state exerts "control of Hindu religious institutions," and this governmental "regulation of religious institutions goes well beyond the establishment of tax exemptions or annual support and the work of ensuring that institutions do not violate core constitutional principles."[34] Not only, for instance, does the state of Kerala administer public temples through regional boards which must approve all actions of the temples, but

---

[31] Singh, "Why I am an Atheist," 15.
[32] Bhargava, *The Promise of India's Secular Democracy*, 69.
[33] Anand, "The Curious Case of Indian Secularism."
[34] Acevedo, "Secularism in the Indian Context," 149.

courts often settle legal cases by reading and interpreting sacred scriptures like the Vedas and the *Bhagavad Gita*. This strange interventionist secularism has ironically driven some Hindu nationalists to demand "true" secularism on the basis that under the current "pseudo-secularism" scheme, "institutions and practices are subject to a far higher level of state control than those of minority religions."[35]

Finally, of course, there are bona fide irreligious or atheistic individuals and organizations in India. As always, we must be cautious about language: one common contemporary word for "atheist" in Hindi is *nastik*, the negation of *astik* or specifically someone who accepts or believes the authority of the Vedic literature; traditionally, *nastik* therefore meant someone who questions or rejects scriptural authority, which might or might not include theistic disbelief and certainly did not imply utter rejection of religion. Buddhism and Jainism, as well as Cārvāka, are often classified as *nastik* traditions. Among the local heroes of non-religion, in addition to Singh mentioned above, are E. V. Ramaswamy, Goparaju Ramachandra Rao, and B. R. Ambedkar. Ramaswamy (d. 1973), known popularly as Periyar, abandoned his life as a holy man to criticize religious belief but equally if not more so "the caste based discrimination within Hinduism," since caste is as much a religious concept as god(s) are. Renny Thomas tells us that anti-god(s) thinking was integral to anti-inequality (of caste and gender) thinking: "Periyar used atheism and rationalism to talk about local issues, rather than talking about universal metaphysical questions of the existence and non-existence of God."[36] The same applies to Ambedkar (d. 1956), for whom "eradication of caste inequality in India would be possible only with the eradication of the Hindu religion, which sanctions the caste based inequalities."[37] Rao, better known as Gora, was the grandest of them all, founder of the Atheist Center in 1940, publisher of the atheist weekly journal *Sangham*, and organizer of the First World Atheist Conference; as with the others, atheism for Gora was one tool in an arsenal "to spread equality in a caste-ridden society like India."[38]

It is clear that irreligion and atheism in the Indian context mean more than disproving the existence of god(s) (as it often does in Christian and Muslim contexts—and recall that there are many Indian Muslims too). This point is underscored by ethnographic descriptions of atheist institutions like *Andhashraddha Nirmoolan Samiti* (ANiS or Organization for the Eradication of Superstition) in Maharashtra, which is quite different

---

[35] Acevedo, "Secularism in the Indian Context," 144.
[36] Thomas, "Atheism in India: Twentieth Century and Beyond," 837.
[37] Thomas, "Atheism in India," 838.
[38] Thomas, "Atheism in India," 838.

from similar groups in the Christian West. Specifically, the Indian atheist movement "is based on the explicit intent to challenge belief in magical powers of irrational efficacy, as well as the influence of charismatic gurus, so as to tackle the harm and injustices the rationalists see as resulting from such belief"; put another way, Indian atheists want "to show their fellow Indians a way out of their enchanted world toward a rational, this-worldly way of life."[39] But this characteristically Indian atheist organization does more than argue about god(s); it is active in the realm of promoting environmental consciousness and ecological awareness; it collaborates with socio-psychological rehabilitation centers for former criminals, promotes sex education, health education, birth control, and family planning, and supports other areas of social work. Finally, the institution also launched what it calls "comprehensive rural development programs." The gulf between Indian and Western atheism was most glaring at an international conference with the theme "Atheism and Social Progress," where the papers presented by Western atheists "hardly address[ed] the conference topic" and instead droned on about the non-existence of god(s).[40]

As emphasized already, Indian atheism has two targets beyond the "belief" in god(s). The first is obviously social inequality and the influence of the Brahman caste. The other is superstition in general, often specifically in the form of alleged miracles performed by *babas* or "god men" (and sometimes god women). Hence, Binder describes another tactic employed by anti-religion activists in South India, known as Miracle Exposure Programs. Taking their critiques on the road to villages and schools, the nonbelievers demonstrate how alleged miracles are performed, debunking them as tricks and illusions (something like the Amazing James Randi in America). By exposing the fakery, the atheists show their audiences that religion and miracle-workers are unreal and that such unreality "is socially harmful and morally reprehensible because it is strategically produced and maintained by so-called *babas* who rely on secrecy and deceit to exploit people's gullibility for their own selfish gain."[41]

One final observation will illustrate just how far apart are Western and Indian attitudes toward god(s) and godlessness. It is well known that Western scientists (with some conspicuous exceptions) tend to be distinctly atheistic. Some Indian scientists too are unabashed and unapologetic atheists and materialists, but others allow the two thought

---

[39] Quack, *Disenchanting India*, 3
[40] Quack, "Organised Atheism in India: An Overview," 78.
[41] Binder, "Magic is Science," 285.

systems to co-exist. One biologist claimed to have no interest in god(s) although disavowed the title of atheist and admitted to having "a God's area at home like every household has."[42] Others, even if they did own their atheism or agnosticism, felt that they could simultaneously "lead a life based on their religious or cultural ethos":

> They participated in various religious festivals and celebrations and perceived it as cultural. The usage "cultural" in the Indian context is never independent of its religious and caste affiliations. Thus, even though they called themselves atheists, the Hindu scientists, for instance, did not find much contradiction in following the lifestyles or their rules of religion. This meant that they practiced vegetarianism, wore the sacred thread (in the case of Brahmins), admired classical songs in praise of Hindu gods and goddesses, and participated in traditional life cycle and seasonal rituals.[43]

Meanwhile, many of those who did identify as atheists or materialists did so not out of any loyalty to Western atheism (let alone New Atheism) but consistently with ancient Sāmkhya or Cārvāka philosophies. One such individual, a space scientist, said it thus:

> I don't practice any rituals associated with religion. I stopped wearing the sacred thread long ago. I do not call myself an atheist. My view of God is very similar to that of Indian school of Samkhya. I do not consider myself as an atheist. I certainly consider myself as a non-theist. Samkhya was known as Nireeshwara Samkhya; it is not "atheist" as such, but it is non-theist. It doesn't say there is no God. It says "it is not necessary to know God."[44]

The upshot here, regardless of the specifics, is first, for many Indian nonbelievers the primary objective is "not to solve the metaphysical question of whether God exists or not…. They were more concerned about the local issues such as caste based discrimination, and various superstitious beliefs and practices, that affected the everyday lives of people." Second and more generally, atheism means different things in different places and times; Western/Christian atheism is not the universal or only expression of atheism but is one provincial version, and "We need

---

[42] Thomas, "Atheism in India," 841.

[43] Thomas, "Atheism and Unbelief among Indian Scientists: Towards an Anthropology of Atheism(s)," 59.

[44] Thomas, "Atheism in India," 842.

to seriously acknowledge this provinciality when studying atheism and the ways in which it is used, welcomed, and rejected in different locations."[45]

No Religion, Lots of Religion:
Nonreligion and Atheism in Japan

This warning applies equally well to Japan, which by the measure of avowal of non-religiosity stands at the opposite pole from India. Conventional wisdom tells that the vast majority (between seventy and eighty-plus percent) of contemporary Japanese regard themselves as non-religious, with a whopping thirty to forty percent identifying as atheists. That could be a cause for celebration in the Western atheist community. Before we get too excited, a 2015 study by Japan's Agency for Cultural Affairs reported that 89 million people followed Shinto, almost 89 million followed Buddhism, and nearly eleven million belonged to Christianity or other religions—adding up to nearly 189 million or more than the total population of the country.[46] Further, the islands are home to thousands of temples and shrines (some relics or tourist destinations, many active) and sacred sites like Mount Fuji, and Ian Reader commented that people there assert "that they are not religious, even whilst performing acts of an overtly religious nature, such as praying at a shrine or walking a pilgrimage."[47]

If the cases of Islam and India give us pause, Japan should stop us in our tracks. Yet we know where the problem lies: in "the unwarranted ethnocentric assumption that religion everywhere must resemble the features of the Abrahamic faiths that are predominant in Western societies"[48]—and the associated unwarranted ethnocentric assumption that irreligion and atheism everywhere must resemble Western/Christian theistic atheism. Starting as always with the local vernacular, the Japanese word ordinarily translated as religion, shūkyō (a compound of shū, sect and kyō, teaching) was introduced in the 1850s after contact with the West; there was no native word that was completely equivalent to religion, and shūkyō does not quite do the job either, as no religion in the West—certainly not Christianity—regards itself as merely the teaching of one sect. The borrowed term embedded itself in the language two or three decades later, during the Meiji reform era. This was a period of modernization and nation-building and therefore of defining what was and what was not truly Japanese. Shintō ("way of the gods") was formalized

---

[45] Thomas, "Atheism in India," 847.
[46] Aiyar, "The Most Religious Atheist Country in the World."
[47] Reader, *Religion in Contemporary Japan*, 1.
[48] Kavanagh and Jong, "Is Japan Religious?" 1.

(some say invented) by the government and promoted as "Japanese culture" (*bunka*) in contrast to "religion" (*shūkyō*), which at best implied organized religion or creed and at worst foreign belief, superstition, and fanaticism. Among these foreign belief systems were Buddhism and Christianity, which might qualify as "religion" in the sectarian sense, while traditional (or invented traditional) Japanese belief was simply culture. In a word, during the late-nineteenth and early-twentieth centuries, Shintō and its concomitant veneration of the emperor as the descendant of divinity "were not religion but a moral pillar of the Japanese 'national body' (*kokutai*)."[49] But Japanese hostility toward "religion" goes back much further: partly because of the growing power of Buddhism in medieval Japan, the imperial court imposed strict rules on monks and monasteries, and early in the Tokugawa shogunate (1603–1867) all Buddhist temples were commanded to affiliate with a recognized sect, and all individuals were required to register with or belong to a temple, contributing financially to and receiving their funeral from their official temple. At the same moment, Christian missionaries were expelled from the country and Christianity banned. (This is a classic case of preferring your own local god[s] or other beings over alien ones; see Chapter 5.)

Before catching up to the present day, a word about god(s) in Japan is in order. The Japanese term that is ordinarily translated as "god" is *kami*, but, as with many such concepts across the world's religions, Inoue Nobutaka, writing for the Institute for Japanese Culture and Classics at Kokugakuin University, affirms that "the word *kami* and the English word *god* are quite different concepts."[50] First, there are many of them, not one. Furthermore, *kami* are not creator-beings; while the understanding of the entities has naturally evolved over time, partly from the influence of foreign religions like Buddhism and Christianity, they were and basically still are closer to nature spirits:

> Celestial bodies, for example, the sun, the moon, and the stars, were often worshiped as the kami itself. Natural phenomena such as thunder or wind were mostly considered as the workings of kami. Seas, rivers, lakes, mountains, forests, and stones were sometimes considered as places where kami stayed and at other times as the kami itself. Many animals, especially snakes, crocodile, deer, wolves, bears, monkeys, foxes, and crows, were also worshiped as kami or as beings in which kami were manifest.

---

[49] Watanabe, *Becoming One*, 64.
[50] Nobutaka, "Perspectives toward Understanding the Concept of Kami."

In many ways they are quite human-like, sometimes even dwelling in shrines (*jinja*). When such a being/spirit was enshrined, it could be "divided" or "multiplied" by the process of *bunrei*, such that it could be distributed to another shrine. An eighteenth-century writer instructed that the term could refer broadly to any being that was thought to have extraordinary power or goodness and was "awesome and worthy of reverence." And as always, when the modernizing Meiji regime arose in the late 1800s, it reformed the *kami* and *jinja* system, giving citizens new guidance "on the relationships between *kami* and the state and *kami* and the social order."

This brings us to the modern period, including the Constitution of 1889 which promised freedom of religion, or more accurately freedom of religious belief (*shinkyō no jiyū*), both *shinkyō* (belief-teaching) and *shūkyō* bearing the connotation of subversive or false knowledge or education.[51] The gap between culture and religion was widened by the creation in 1900 of two agencies, the Shrine Bureau and the Religions Bureau, the former administering Shintō and the latter overseeing Buddhism and Christianity which were disparaged as not part of authentic Japanese culture.

Secularization (*sezokuka*) of Japanese society was accelerated under the American occupation after World War II. The Constitution imposed by the Americans guaranteed freedom of religion and separation of religion and state, Article 20 confirming, "No religious organization shall receive any privileges from the State nor exercise any political authority. No person shall be compelled to take part in any religious acts, celebration, rite or practice. The State and its organs shall refrain from religious education or any other religious activity." Courts were also instrumental in Japanese secularization, the Supreme Court ruling in 1977 that a particular Shintō ritual was "a secular activity." The concept of *shūkyō* also continued to develop. Expanding beyond the three "foreign" or unofficial religions, it grew to encompass the explosion of new religious movements in the country after the freeing of religion, as well as what had formerly been categorized as pseudo-religions and "evil cults." For that very reason, *shūkyō* retained and retains associations with extreme, bizarre, and even dangerous religious movements like Aum Shinrikyo, responsible for poison gas attacks on Japanese subways in 1995. Yuki Shiose also judged that the local aversion to "religion" results from the pre-war experience of state-enforced Shintō and the connection of religion and political indoctrination: for Japanese people today, the "choice of non-declaration of religiosity could be understood as an astute if non-deliberate

---

[51] Horii, *The Category of "Religion" in Contemporary Japan*, 58.

move of citizens wary of the meddling of Big Brother (state intervention)."[52] Concomitantly, there has been an absolute decline in formalized "religious" behavior like attendance at Buddhist temples, much of it driven not by changes in devotion but in demographics, as the population gets older and more urban, leaving many temples with shrinking congregations.

Finally, then, Kavanagh and Jong tested the purported irreligion of Japanese people, posing the question in varying ways. When asked if they were "religious," a remarkably low ten percent said yes, while more than half (fifty-five percent) identified as non-religious, and almost a quarter (twenty-two percent) as atheist. However, when offered a list of religions to identify with, thirty-four percent chose Buddhism, five percent Shintō, three percent Christian, and slightly less than half (forty-five percent) none. And although the majority affiliated with a religion, they were not particularly active in religious behavior—for instance, forty-six percent rarely or never attended temples or shrines, and the same number rarely or never prayed, while most (seventy-one percent) attended at most one religious festival in a year.[53]

The Moral World(s) of Atheism

"Thus in India we have people asserting a Hindu identity while not worshipping; in Japan we have people worshipping while denying any religious identity."[54] We could make similar presentations on other non-Western societies, like Turkey, which was founded after World War I on the principle of *laiklik* or secularism, more antagonistic toward religion than most secular countries but less so on the premise that religion is false than that it is not modern. (Turkey, like India, has lately drifted in a more religious-nationalist direction.) We could even discuss Western states like France, with its doctrine of *laïcité* (related to the word "laity" and the source of Turkey's term) which is both anti-clerical (i.e., opposed to the power of priests and clergy) and concerned about the divisive effect of religious identities and public displays of religiosity. Indeed, the 2013 *Charter of Secularism at School* not only prohibits "all proselytizing" but also bans "wearing signs by which students ostentatiously demonstrate a religious membership" (which has led to the targeting of the Islamic *hijab* more than the Christian cross).

---

[52] Shiose, "Japanese Paradox: Secular State, Religious Society," 325.
[53] Kavanagh and Jong, "Is Japan Religious?"
[54] Gellner, "Studying Secularism, Practising Secularism," 339.

The examples we have discussed at length, and others that we could discuss, teach us two key lessons. The first is that atheism, nonbelief, irreligion, and so forth (which are most definitely not synonymous) are highly diverse across cultures and religious/philosophical traditions. Focusing on atheism, it is more proper to speak of *atheisms*, of many local formations of godlessness ranging from the very lack of any such concept as "god(s)"—which is more common in cultures and even in religions than most people realize—to the adamant denial that there is any such thing as god(s), with many positions in between. This means, we cannot repeat or emphasize enough, that familiar Western/Christian argumentative atheism is only one variation on godlessness and far from the only, universal, or—Zeus help us!—"correct" kind of godlessness. Western/Christian atheism, which remains, in Onfray's viewpoint, a disappointingly theistic atheism, is also a distinctly local atheism, one appropriate to situations where a monotheistic god is the dominant idea but not applicable to every religion. If we are to be fully informed and completely consistent atheists—experts of godlessness in all its manifestations—then we must become global atheists in the sense of understanding and accounting for the wide world of atheisms.

The second lesson will come as little surprise to many atheists but as a great surprise, even a challenge or contradiction, to opponents of atheism like Mr. Haught from Chapter 1. The message is, contrary to everything that not only Christians but Muslims and many other believers hold dear and would love to convince others, that atheists are not only often if normally quite moral but that *atheism in many of its instantiations is a fundamentally moral position*. We saw this in the cases of anti-theism (Chapter 5) and misotheism (Chapter 4), where the objection to god(s) specifically and religion generally is not always, and seldom only, logical or propositional but is often profoundly moral. Recall that Schweizer in his book on misotheism (hating or disapproving god[s]) insisted on "the essential decency" of god-haters who are "motivated by admirable humanistic impulses"[55]—which is a fancy way of saying "morality." It is precisely the moral failings of the god(s) and their anointed representatives here on earth that atheists around the world tend to indict. What kind of sane and decent person could endorse the position of Russian Orthodox Father Rodin, who declares, "If we don't win, we'll burn it all down.... [W]e're ready to martyr ourselves and the whole world.... There's no need for a world like that"?[56]

---

[55] Schweizer, *Hating God: The Untold Story of Misotheism*, 23.
[56] Mian, "Behind the New Iron Curtain," 32.

We witnessed this clearly in the discussion of nonbelief in Islam, which evidenced that social and moral qualms surpass intellectual ones in the minds of many apostates. We hear this again and again in the testimony of former Muslims, from prominent ones like Ayaan Hirsi Ali to less famous ones like Amir Ahmad Nasr. In his deconversion autobiography, Nasr laments falling out of love with Islam once he grasped the depth of the "fervor and bloodlust" in his religion, sickened by "the filthy liars who are blinded by their dogmatism and...the polarizing divisiveness," by "their pretentious claims to respect other people of different faith," and more than anything by their theft of his freedom. He reached the stage where he shouted, "Against them, again and again, I pledged myself, 'No submission! *Never*."[57] Another ex-Muslim, Harris Sultan, summed it up as well as it can be said: "I am not anti-religion; I am anti-misogyny, anti-slavery, anti-sexism, antiviolence, anti-ignorance, anti-child abuse, anti-oppression, and anti-war. Religion is anti-me."[58] In other words, if this is what religion has to offer, out it goes, along with whatever god(s) inhabit it.

Conditions are the same yet different in Hinduism. There are subtle arguments against god(s) or against the ancient scriptures that speak of god(s). But at least as influential for critics of the religion are the social injustices that it sanctions, especially caste inequalities. In this instance, religious dogma and social inequity are inseparably enmeshed, and a Hindu who would reject caste hierarchy must, in their eyes, reject the religion that causes and perpetuates that discrimination. Other considerations include the incompetence or greed of priests (here, Brahmans) and the superstitions upon which self-described god men play to fleece their credulous flocks. This does not mean, even for some persons of science, chucking the entire edifice of god(s), beliefs, and rituals, but for many if not most it means freeing oneself—and others—from the baleful influence of non-reason. As for many ex-Muslims, ex-Hindus seek social and mental liberation.

All around the world, we find practical and moral skepticism about religion more often than logical or intellectual rejection of the "truths" of religion. Two brief examples illustrate the point. Iban or Dayak (Kalimantan, Indonesia) religion featured ancestor spirits and shamanism rather than god(s), but some Iban people confessed that "the shaman's performance may involve deceit" such as sleight-of-hand, and rival shamans accused each other of trickery and fraud.[59] Moreover, skepticism

---

[57] Nasr, *My Isl@m*, 197.
[58] Sultan, *The Curse of God: Why I Left Islam*, 11.
[59] Wadley, Pashia, and Palmer, "Religious Scepticism," 44.

toward shamans was socially motivated: people might accept or rationalize deceit as intended to fool the spirits when they wanted to support a particular shaman, "yet they may use a seemingly insignificant flaw in an otherwise excellent performance to reject another shaman." A similar problem appeared in Nepal, where some people disparaged or laughed at their *dhamis* (shamans). Denunciation of shamans usually occurred in two circumstances: some doubters displayed their "modern consciousness" by consigning shamanism to backward culture and *andhabiswas* (blind belief), while others eventually gave up on shamans because supposed shamanic cures yielded no results. Insofar as Nepali villagers continued believing in shamans, they transformed themselves "into 'modern believers,' people who believe in shamans skeptically."[60]

Even on the credulous continent of Africa, largely the same dynamic pertains. Most sources suggest that as few as three percent of Sub-Saharan Africans identify as non-religious or at least religiously unaffiliated, only slightly higher than in India, although the numbers may be notably higher in South Africa (fifteen percent) and Mozambique (upwards of eighteen percent).[61] Yet nonreligious and atheistic organizations exist, like the Atheists in Kenya Society, which makes the moral announcement on its internet homepage, "You can be good without God" (atheistsinkenya.org). More generally, African nonbelievers tend not only to dismiss god(s) but to distrust and look askance at religious authorities and political leaders and institutions alike, condemning them for a panoply of moral failings such as "overemphasis on prosperity teachings, religion's overinvolvement in political affairs, disapproval of fundamentalist trends, or recurring moral scandals by religious leaders who 'preach water and drink wine.'"[62]

Leo Igwe, one of the most outspoken proponents of nonbelief in Africa and founder of the African Humanist Alliance, reminded us that pre-colonial Africans often exhibited the same skepticism and humor toward religion as just noted in Indonesia and Nepal, among other places. Africans traditionally, he claimed, "make fun or jokes about the gods; sometimes what may seem a religious performance is in reality a religious ridicule of the deities. In fact, some performances such as oracle consultation and divination, the choice of a new king, or the cause of death or disease in a community that are considered acts of God are human acts disguised as God's."[63] In short, Africans fell anywhere on the piety

---

[60] Pigg, "The Credible and the Credulous," 191.
[61] Omer, "The Condition of Nonbelievers in Africa," 2.
[62] Gez, Beider, and Dickow, "African and Not Religious," 62.
[63] Igwe, "Southern Africa," 971.

spectrum from firm belief to doubt, "religious disinterestedness, indifference, and rejection of deities or their earthly mouthpieces."[64]

One of the remarkable indigenous African philosophies was and is Ubuntu, which Igwe characterized as "an ethnophilosophical outlook with atheistic proclivities." It might go too far to judge it as atheistic or godless, but as a kind of native humanism it has that potential. Ubuntu, he explained,

> is based on the notion that persons are made by other persons, interpersonal relations, and understanding; relationships with divinities do not define a person's humanity. Put simply, within the framework of Ubuntu, human development and fulfilment of potential does not require divine fiat or enablement; human beings are gods to other humans.[65]

In some interpretations and practices, of course, the ancestor spirits and even such putative gods as are available to various tribes and peoples can be part of these relationships (and some researchers have suggested that "ancestor worship" is less a religious idea than the simple extension of the respect due to elders to the eldest of the elders, namely, the dead). But even then, what we see is an essential *social* quality of religion, stressing not beliefs and propositions but relationships and social obligations (which, again, is roughly how Muslims conceive of Islam and, frankly, how many Christians conceive of Christianity—not as a "religion" or dogma but as a personal relationship with Jesus).

At any rate, it is not a stretch to see how Ubuntu and similar philosophies could become secular and atheistic or develop an affinity with secularism and atheism:

> Ubuntu is fundamentally unconcerned with the divine as a central and pivotal preoccupation. Even though Ubuntu is not expressly atheistic, this cultural philosophy has the community, the group, or communal existence at the center of its perception and orientation.... The isiXosa expression "*Umntu ngumtu ngabantu*" roughly translates as "a person is a person through others." Ubuntu embodies a humanistic philosophy that emphasizes human sharing and caring.... Thus, reverence and worship of deities are not necessary conditions for human happiness and existential fulfilment.[66]

---

[64] Igwe, "Southern Africa," 973.
[65] Igwe, "Southern Africa," 974.
[66] Igwe, "Southern Africa," 974.

And in fact some observers insist that Ubuntu and similar ideas have taken just such a turn. Kolsen reckons that Nelson Mandela was an adherent of "Ubuntu atheism,"[67] and so-called Zambian humanism, promoted by the first president of independent Zambia, rests on implicit criticism of religion and the gods: "It encapsulates a combination of socialist ideas and African values such as loyalty to family and community. Predicated on the centrality of people, not deities, Zambian humanism is based on principles such as 'the dignity of man,' 'hard work and self reliance,' 'equal opportunities for all,' and 'non exploitation of man by man.'"[68] These are fine values that have no need of god(s) to invent or authorize them.

Therefore, as Igwe wrote elsewhere, "The wind of atheist emancipation is blowing across Africa."[69] And, as the present chapter has shown, this wind is blowing around the world, linked to currents in faraway places but swirling with material from each local context. Consequently, there is not one atheism but many, some primarily intellectual or logical, some social or moral, and some (if not most) a mixture of the two. I have argued in the past, and continue to maintain, that moral objections are not disproofs of god(s): arguing that a god or religion is bad (or, as in some latter-day theologies, weak or impotent; see Chapter 4) does not establish that a god doesn't exist. It is entirely possible that, if some god did exist, it would be capricious, uncaring, or downright malevolent, as are many of the gods and other entities we encountered in other chapters. However, a bad god, bad religion, or bad followers of said god and religion are sufficient reason to put that god and his/her/its/their religion and followers behind us.

More importantly, perhaps, is the discovery—or reaffirmation— that morality and goodness do not flow from nor depend on god(s) and religion. The very possibility of critiquing god(s) and religion on moral grounds entails that there are moral standards independent of *and higher than* religious/divine ones, by which god(s) and religion can and routinely do fail. Most importantly of all, everything that we have explored in this chapter, and in this book, cries out that nonbelief, skepticism, and atheism are *more*—more than intellectual positions and argumentative practices and more than Western/Christian theistic atheism. In all of their multifarious forms, they are lived and embodied sensibilities, distinct and noble ways of being in the world that represent and necessitate a "trust in the capacity of human moral judgment."[70] Furthermore and finally, non-

---

[67] Kolsen, "Mandela's 'Ubuntu Atheism' and Why It Matters."
[68] Igwe, "Southern Africa," 977.
[69] Igwe, "Atheism in Zambia."
[70] Schielke, "Being a Nonbeliever in a Time of Islamic Revival," 311.

religion offers its own set of moral principles and values, greater and more universal than any religion's obsession with sexuality or alcohol or facial hair. Those values include respect for the individual, denunciation of prejudice and violence, the rights to privacy and the pursuit of truth wherever it takes us, and above all else—because it depends on and enables all of these—freedom.

10

Winning Hearts and Minds:
Atheism's Change of Attitude

Some years ago, a student at a local college approached me to interview an atheist for a school class project. I gladly complied. Apparently, the assignment was for a social work course, to interview someone the student might work with someday who is very much unlike her. That's what I gathered (and feared) when she arrived in a Christian t-shirt and began quizzing me on what it is like to be an atheist. I thought I was being my usual affable self, but her Christian privilege showed when she attested that she literally did not see Christianity in the public square, such as Christmas decorations. Flabbergasted, I could hardly avoid pointing out to her some of the ways that her religion occupied and commandeered society, painfully obvious to a non-adherent such as myself, as well as some other mistakes in her thinking. I walked away feeling pretty good about the encounter. When she shared with me the paper she wrote about the meeting, I discovered that I had confirmed her worst fears about atheists—that we are argumentative, critical, and just not very nice. I was embarrassed that I made such a bad impression for atheists and so utterly misrepresented myself and my kind. (Or had I represented myself perfectly accurately? Or was she bound to find fault in me, in us, no matter what I said and did?)

My meeting with this individual was neither a debate nor an occasion for either of us to try to convert the other, nor did I approach it as such. Nevertheless, according to the wise *Handbook of Persuasion Skills*, "The goal of all communication is to persuade the audience."[1] Or, as marketing and leadership experts Kevin Hogan and James Speakman put it more bluntly and enthusiastically, "Life IS persuasion!"[2] In retrospect, I could have done a better job of resisting my inclination to argue and identify her errors. That was not persuasive. What I did instead was reinforce what she already thought of atheists and atheism; I

---

[1] Center for Good Governance, *Handbook on Persuasion Skills*, 7.
[2] Hogan and Speakman, *Covert Persuasion*, xii.

influenced her all right, but in exactly the opposite way that I would have hoped.

Many if not all of us self-conscious and public atheists like to argue. As discussed in Chapter 2, in a theism-saturated society atheism is bound to take an argumentative or defensive posture; unlike the "natural" or default atheism of people who have never heard the god-concept, we must be not only *without* god(s) but *against* god(s). Further, we pride ourselves on our rationality; although there are various sufficient reasons to reject god(s), we insist that facts and logic have led us to the inevitable and correct godless conclusion. And we want to spread that conclusion and the knowledge on which is based, which is entirely within our right. Words like "gospel" and "evangelize" have been usurped and colonized by religionists, but originally they meant nothing more than good news (Old English *gōd spel*, Greek *eu angelion*, "good message/story/news") and, while they may now be irretrievably corrupted by religious usage, the idea of good news and sharing good news is in no way solely religious.

So, atheists have good news and want to disseminate (Latin *dissemen*, literally "abroad/cast-seed") it to others. The practical question is how best to accomplish that task. We generally feel that we can "deconvert" others if we can muster the most facts and craft the finest arguments, essentially treating the problem like a debate or a jury trial. I, myself, have likened the clash of theism and atheism to a jury trial, and I stand by the comparison—in a good and bad way. The challenge of the trial lawyer is to present the best evidence and build the most compelling case, and the defense lawyer (the one who is taking the "negative" position, that the charge is false) has, in our system of justice, *no burden of proof; if the prosecution cannot prove its case, the charge should be assumed false*. However—and this is a huge however—no experienced lawyer pins the outcome of the trial on the evidence and arguments alone. She knows that the humans on the jury are not exclusively or even especially rational and that all sorts of other social and emotional considerations can sway their opinions. Indeed, battering and badgering them with facts can bore the jury or turn them against the lawyer, the client, and the truth.

What I am saying here is that, if our goal is to change people from god(s)-believers to god(s)-nonbelievers (and it is), then simply flinging more facts and sharper—or louder, more aggressive, and at worst more condescending—arguments at our interlocutors is not the most effective way to do so. What I am *not* saying is that we should never argue or debate with a theist again; I personally rather despair of the practice, since arguing and debating seldom change minds for two primary reasons. First, people enjoy hearing their side presented publicly, and Hogan and Speakman warned that once an idea or belief is communicated in speech or writing "it will be maintained, even in the face of overwhelming evidence to the contrary."[3] Merely saying it or hearing it becomes a commitment to it and strengthens that commitment. Second, too few people who attend (or participate in) arguments and debates know when an argument or debate has been won, that is, what the standards of arguing/debating and of reason are. Consequently, both sides usually walk away confident that they prevailed.

So, while I think it is mostly unsuccessful and often counterproductive, those who relish the business of arguing and debating, in person and during call-in internet programs, and who are good at it are welcome to it. Theists surely have not retired from arguing their case, even dreaming up new apologetics for their discredited beliefs; rather, they often salivate at the chance to engage us in debate, for the reasons just described. And I am not insisting that arguing and debating never work; they can, whether in the short run or the long run. But Dale Carnegie, the famed specialist in influence, declared almost a century ago, "Nine times out of ten, an argument ends with each of the contestants [and don't forget their audiences too] more firmly convinced than ever that he is absolutely right." He continued:

> You can't win an argument. You can't because if you lose it, you lose it; and if you win it, you lose it. Why? Well, suppose you triumph over the other man and shoot his argument full of holes and prove that he is *non compos mentis*. Then what? You will feel fine. But what about him? You have made him feel inferior. You have hurt his pride. He will resent your triumph.[4]

And a ten percent success rate is a low return on investment.

This last chapter assembles some of the findings from researchers and disciplines in the area of influence and persuasion, chief among them psychologists, educators, marketers, and leadership trainers. It is the closest thing to "advice" that appears in this book. The first section will summarize our knowledge of what does not work in efforts to change minds and why. The second section will turn to helpful insights into fruitful influence and persuasion. One very useful reorientation will be to shift the discourse from the baggage-loaded term "belief" to the more neutral psychological term "attitude" and thus from disabusing people of

---

[3] Hogan and Speakman, *Covert Persuasion*, 6.
[4] Carnegie, *How to Win Friends and Influence People*, 110–11.

(false) belief to *attitude change*. The conclusion will bring the entire volume full circle by reminding us why theists are motivated to exaggerate the difficulty of being an atheist and to perpetuate the (melo)drama of atheism.

Some readers, I expect, will object to some of the lessons conveyed herein. The recommendations and tactics may sound too much like manipulation, like sales, or perhaps like religion. The third objection is misplaced; religions certainly profit from a variety of influence techniques, many of which are not available to us (from heavenly rewards and hellish punishments to early childhood indoctrination), but that is no reason to reject them out of hand. Recall how Alain de Botton among others counseled atheists on "importing certain of [religionists'] ideas and practices into the secular realm" (see Chapter 2); he and they overlooked persuasion methods. And just because something is done by religion does not make it a "religious thing to do." The objection that influence/persuasion is like sales is also moot. I am no salesman and find sales a bit unsavory, but we *are* selling something of a sort or, if you will, asking people to "consume" or accept a "product"—god(s)less reality— and the same methods that sell one good can sell another. Besides, we are promoting a product that we genuinely endorse; we do not personally profit from the "sale"; and we demand no money in exchange (instead, we will probably save the theist money, time, frustration, and heartache). Finally, "manipulation" is an unnecessarily harsh word. Hogan and Speakman, champions of "covert persuasion," still advocate ethical use of their skills. But in the end, influence or persuasion *is* a skill, or skill set, one that an influencer or persuader should master. It is only reasonable that, in pursuit of winning hearts and minds to atheism, we should avail ourselves of the best knowledge about how to effect attitude change, whatever its source, and we are reasonable people.

Man Does Not Live by Facts Alone, or Why Facts Don't Change Minds

One of my favorite cautionary tales is Kurt Wise, PhD, a Harvard-educated geologist *and devout Christian* who studied under the illustrious Stephen Jay Gould (although apparently not very hard). Gradually he found himself being seduced by religion until he faced the dilemma that either scripture was right and evolution was wrong or evolution was right and scripture was wrong, in which case he would have to "toss out the Bible" (a classic example of cognitive dissonance, which we will explore below). Once convinced that Christianity was the answer, he became a creationist—and a young-earth creationist to boot—despite his professional-level knowledge of geology. So armed with belief, he announced that "if all the evidence in the universe turned against creationism, I would be the first to admit it, but I would still be a creationist because that is what the Word of God seems to indicate."[5] In other words, he could know (and does know) the facts, and accept that they contradict his beliefs, and yet hold obstinately to his beliefs. And he is just one of fifty scientists in John Ashton's volume who "choose to believe in creation" in full view (and disregard) of the facts.

It has been said many times and bears saying again, that facts do not automatically change minds—including minds that have been trained to respect and seek facts. This goes against everything that atheists cherish; we are sure that if theists could simply hear the evidence, and take the evidence seriously, they would relinquish their theistic ways. It is not true—and our refusal to adjust to that truth is as stubborn as Wise's refusal to discard his theism.

Few people understand the difficulty of getting others to listen to, process, and use new information better than educators, whose job description is change-through-knowledge, which is as good as any definition of learning. Education experts Clark Chinn and William Brewer carefully surveyed the terrain of students confronting new information that falsified (or should have falsified) the students' pre-existing "knowledge" or belief, or what the authors called "anomalous data." Ideally, students exposed to anomalous data would recognize the flaw in their old thinking and abandon it in favor of new and improved thinking; that is certainly what atheists want to happen when we show anomalous anti-god(s) data to theists. Chinn and Brewer found to their dismay that learners "typically resist giving up their preinstructional beliefs. Instead of abandoning or modifying their preinstructional beliefs in the face of new, conflicting data and ideas, students often staunchly maintain the old ideas and reject or distort the new ideas."[6]

In total, the authors documented seven varying responses to information that challenged prior beliefs, only one of which involved significantly changing those beliefs. First, people may just ignore the incoming information: "When an individual ignores data, he or she does not even bother to explain it away. Theory A [the old belief] remains intact and totally unscathed."[7] Second, they may reject the information, which requires a little more cognitive energy than merely ignoring: "The

---

[5] Ashton, *In Six Days: Why 50 Scientists Choose to Believe in Creation*, 355.
[6] Chinn and Brewer, "The Role of Anomalous Data," 1–2.
[7] Chinn and Brewer, "The Role of Anomalous Data," 4.

difference is that in ignoring data, the individual does not even attempt to explain the data away; in rejection, the individual can articulate an explanation for why the data should be rejected."[8] Unfortunately, this explanation almost always uses the terms of the pre-existing belief, so the contradictory data can ironically fortify that belief, since the belief "handled" the data. The most common way to reject data, they said, is to attack it, arguing "that there was a fundamental methodological error in the way the data were obtained" or "that the data were merely due to random variation" or that the data are "fraudulent"[9]—a trick we should recognize from agnomancy. (See Chapter 7)

A third strategy to avoid the uncomfortable consequences of new information is to exclude the information, normally by labeling it as "outside the domain" of the question at hand or as irrelevant to the belief. One way to achieve this effect is compartmentalization, in which the learner hears the data—and may even learn it and accept it—but files it mentally far away from the precious preinstructional belief. "When anomalous data are excluded from the domain of a theory, they obviously do not lead to any theory change."[10] Fourth, the learner can simply delay dealing with the new information, "holding anomalous data in abeyance." In this event, there may be some acknowledgement that the data have consequences for pre-existing beliefs, but learners postpone contemplating those consequences, often on the premise that their beliefs can meet the challenge and will meet it at some indefinite future date. It is just a matter of time, they may insist, until their belief can integrate or overcome the contradiction, which also serves to reinforce the initial belief. The fifth approach is reinterpretation, where the learner

> accepts the data as something that should be explained by his or her theory. In the case of reinterpretation, supporters of theory A [the old position] and theory B [the new position] can agree at some level about the data, but at a theoretical level; they assign different meanings to the data—meanings that align with and even support the theories/beliefs they already hold.[11]

The authors introduced some of their own research to demonstrate this effect: "After reading about some anomalous data that were designed to be clearly inconsistent with the meteor impact theory of mass extinctions,

---

[8] Chinn and Brewer, "The Role of Anomalous Data," 6.
[9] Chinn and Brewer, "The Role of Anomalous Data," 6.
[10] Chinn and Brewer, "The Role of Anomalous Data," 7.
[11] Chinn and Brewer, "The Role of Anomalous Data," 9.

one student who supported the meteor impact theory wrote, 'This further proves the meteor impact theory,' and he actually increased his rating of how strongly he believed the theory."[12] A sixth outcome allows the pre-existing belief to survive by making peripheral changes to it but leaving its essence intact. Finally, it sometimes does transpire that students shed their previous theory/belief and adopt a new one. Such acceptance means "change in one or more of the theorist's core beliefs. In this form of response to contradictory information, the individual accepts the new data and explains it by changing the core beliefs of theory A or by accepting an alternate theory."[13]

This disheartening summary is not news to anyone who has tried to teach (especially controversial subjects from science to history), argue with theists, or otherwise struggle to convince people to change their thinking and their behavior on any number of topics. But that still leaves the question: *why* are people so impervious to belief/thought/attitude change? The first thing to understand, as aggravating and disappointing as it is, is that humans are not particularly rational beings. Atheists like to think that we are, and that everyone else is too, but the evidence does not support that conclusion.

The "rational individual" approach is typical of classical economics, which depicts each person, or at least each well-informed person, as a maximizer. That is, given knowledge of the choices and of the costs and benefits of the choices, the rational individual will reliably choose the option that maximizes her interests (e.g. saves the most money, promises the best return, takes the least effort, etc.). Unfortunately, this mythical rational individual flies in the face of actual observed behavior. This is why scholars like Dan Ariely have opened a field called "behavioral economics," also known as judgment and decision-making studies, which does not assume or prescribe what people *should* do but investigates what they do in real life. In a series of insightful and amusing books, essays, and videos, Ariely declares that humans are not only fairly irrational but that we are *predictably irrational*—that our irrationality follows the same pattern, again and again."[14]

One reason—or one battery of diverse reasons—why we are so predictably irrational is that we suffer from a great number of cognitive biases. Cognitive biases

---

[12] Chinn and Brewer, "The Role of Anomalous Data," 10.
[13] Chinn and Brewer, "The Role of Anomalous Data," 12.
[14] Ariely, *Predictably Irrational*, xx.

are systematic cognitive dispositions or inclinations in human thinking and reasoning that often do not comply with the tenets of logic, probability reasoning, and plausibility. These intuitive and subconscious tendencies are at the basis of human judgment, decision making, and the resulting behavior.[15]

And because biased thought-processes deviate from logic, probability, and plausibility, the thoughts and actions they produce are equally systematically faulty.

In a ground-breaking 1974 paper, Amos Tversky and Daniel Kahneman pioneered the concepts of mental heuristics and cognitive biases. In general, a heuristic is a method or shortcut for solving problems and making judgments, allowing the individual to reach conclusions more quickly and easily, without all that pesky and time-consuming thinking. Tversky and Kahneman specified three common heuristics—representativeness (a kind of generalization or presumption that one object, fact, or event is typical of all others, which they said facilitates the "illusion of validity"), availability (using only the most familiar or frequent information to make a judgment), and anchoring (sometimes also called framing or priming, allowing a pre-existing or previous thought or experience to guide your thinking). The rub, of course, is that trusting these heuristics, especially in circumstances of limited information and the attendant uncertainty, while convenient, can also "lead to systematic and predictable errors," which they called cognitive biases.[16]

There are far too many documented cognitive biases (some lists go to twenty-five or more) to examine here, and I have reviewed them elsewhere.[17] Two such biases do bear mentioning, though. The first is the *fluency* bias, which states that information that is easier to process tends to play a bigger role in our thought processes. Information can be fluent for various reasons. It may be familiar, something that we have heard a hundred times before, something that is embedded in our daily experiences. It may be short and catchy; although the research is divided on the subject, in many instances terse information, expressed in a few words or even a single word, sticks in our minds more reliably than long and complex presentations and arguments. Information flows through our brains better if it is multisensory (visual, auditory, tactile, etc.) and if it is narrative (a story) rather than a dry catalogue of facts. It also helps (or

---

[15] Korteling and Toet, "Cognitive Biases," 610.

[16] Tversky and Kahneman, "Judgment under Uncertainty," 1131.

[17] Eller, "A Mind is a Terrible Thing: How Evolved Cognitive Biases Lead to Religion (and Other Mental Errors)."

hurts, depending on the case) if the information delivers an emotional punch; fear and anger particularly ratchet up the cogency of data.

The second bias, which is often related to the first, is *confirmation bias* or selective attention to and preference for things we already think are true—and things we want to be true. Harvard neuroscientist Iqra Noor identifies three ways that the confirmation bias operates: it can prejudice our search for facts (only looking for data that aid our prior beliefs and commitments), our interpretation of facts (bending or distorting data, sometimes so far as to allegedly prove what they actually disprove), and our memory of facts (conveniently forgetting data that threaten our beliefs or commitments). Interestingly, Noor designates "religious faith" among the catalysts for processing experience with bias.[18] Together, these two major defects in our thinking go a long way toward explaining Chinn and Brewer's six alternatives to accepting the consequences of anomalous data.

One well-studied mechanism that drives much rejection of new, anomalous, and upsetting information or experience is *cognitive dissonance*. It is not inconsequential that social psychologist Leon Festinger coined the term for his study of a new mid-twentieth-century religious movement and its failed doomsday prophecy. Members of the movement eagerly awaited the arrival of extraterrestrials and the end of the world, which obviously did not occur. Level-headed people would have accepted the falsity of their beliefs and moved on; instead, some (but by no means all) members became *more* ardent in their "faith" and intensified their recruitment efforts. On the surface, this makes no sense, but Festinger accounted for it in terms of the psychological discomfort of holding two opposing thoughts—that the prophecy must be true but that the evidence proved it wrong. When two such conflicting realities inhabit one mind, "there will arise pressure to reduce or eliminate the dissonance" (literally bad-sound). Naturally (and rationally), the troubling mismatch of faith and fact "would be largely eliminated if they discarded the belief that had been disconfirmed, ceased the behavior which had been initiated in preparation for the fulfillment of the prediction, and returned to a more usual existence."[19] This is not what happened.

Alternatively, the dissonance would be reduced or eliminated if the members of a movement effectively blind themselves to the fact that the prediction has not been fulfilled. But most people, including members of such movements, are in touch with reality and cannot

---

[18] Noor, "Confirmation Bias."

[19] Festinger, Riecken, and Schacter, *When Prophecy Fails*, 27.

simply blot out of their cognition such an unequivocal and undeniable fact. They can try to ignore it, however, and they usually do try.[20]

Third—and frustratingly commonly, as in this case—"believers may try to find reasonable explanations and very often they find ingenious ones."[21] Another debunked prophetic movement, the Millerites, did just that after their "great disappointment" in 1844 when Jesus did not return to end the world. Some tenacious devotees reinterpreted their prediction so that they could claim *that they had been right* and that "the world as they knew it" had ended, the door to heaven slammed shut, denying the chance of salvation to anyone other than the movement members; others reasoned that they had merely misunderstood their own prophecy and that not the earth but heaven had been cleansed on the appointed day, and out of this contingent the Seventh-day Adventist church was born. Finally, Festinger also attributed the renewed proselytizing of this refuted cult to an impetus toward truth in numbers: "If more and more people can be persuaded that the system of belief is correct, then clearly it must, after all, be correct."[22]

All of these creative and depressing ways in which people can bat away inconvenient truths are enabled and exacerbated by a phenomenon famously credited to Justin Kruger and David Dunning and hence often dubbed the *Dunning-Kruger effect*. At its most basic, an alarming number of people are blind to the flaws in their own thinking, precisely because their thinking is too flawed to see them; worse, these same people assume that they are thinking well. As the authors phrased it, "People tend to hold overly favorable views of their abilities in many social and intellectual domains.... Not only do these people reach erroneous conclusions and make unfortunate choices, but their incompetence robs them of the metacognitive ability to realize it."[23] They lack thinking skills, including the skill to properly judge their own thinking. They are, as Kruger and Dunning memorably put it, *unskilled and unaware that they are unskilled*.

But that is still not the whole story. Two other problems to beware of are *motivated reasoning* and *ego defense*. In a chapter from Proctor and Schiebinger's volume on agnotology, Charles Mills straddled these two forces as what he called "motivated irrationality" regarding white privilege.[24] Ziva Kunda nailed down motivated reasoning in a 1990 psychology article, positing two strikingly divergent purposes for seeking

[20] Festinger, Riecken, and Schacter, *When Prophecy Fails*, 27.
[21] Festinger, Riecken, and Schacter, *When Prophecy Fails*, 28.
[22] Festinger, Riecken, and Schacter, *When Prophecy Fails*, 28.
[23] Kruger and Dunning, "Unskilled and Unaware of It," 1121.
[24] Mills, "White Ignorance."

and processing information: one, the one that we rationalists value, "is to arrive at an accurate conclusion, whatever it may be," while the other "is to arrive at a particular, directional conclusion."[25] She explained that "people motivated to arrive at a particular conclusion attempt to be rational and to construct a justification of their desired conclusion that would persuade a dispassionate observer,"[26] but given recent experience, this might be too charitable a statement. We have witnessed individuals engage in all manner of agnomancy, up to and including bold-faced lying and bullshit, to preserve their pet beliefs and values and to persuade others to partake in them. (See Chapter 7) It is naïve of us to insist that all audiences are driven by the desire to get the facts right; the ugly truth is that many of us humans (and probably all of us sometimes) "reason to prepare for action, and so reasoning is motivated by the goals people are trying to achieve":

> The crucial point is that the process of gathering and processing information can systematically depart from accepted rational standards because one goal—desire to persuade, agreement with a peer group, self-image, self-preservation—can commandeer attention and guide reasoning at the expense of accuracy.[27]

Observing their reasoning (or unreasoning) process, it is often all too easy to discern what their aims and interests are.

Some interests advanced by motivated reasoning are practical and venal, namely, to make money, to gain and hold power, and to get away with misbehaviors and crimes. However, there are other sorts of interests that can be equally stimulating. These motivations constitute another angle on the process of cognitive dissonance. In Festinger's analysis, cognitive dissonance meant the strain between two different facts or truths (e.g. 1. we prophesied the end of the world and 2. the world did not end). However, the dissonance and strain can also be, and may more frequently be, *between facts and identity*. At the most primitive level, the mismatch may be between the facts and the individual's sense of self, for instance of being a good, moral, sensible person; given the choice between defending the self and accepting the truth, the self usually wins.[28] But it is not only

---

[25] Kunda, "The Case for Motivated Reasoning," 480.

[26] Kunda, "The Case for Motivated Reasoning," 482.

[27] Epley and Gilovich, "The Mechanics of Motivated Reasoning," 14–15.

[28] In one of his many quotable aphorisms, Nietzsche mused, "Memory says, 'I did that.' Pride replies, 'I could not have done that.' Eventually, memory yields." Elsewhere (*The Gay Science*, #132), he also confessed, "What is now decisive against Christianity is our taste, no longer our reason." He may be right about that.

our individual ego that is at stake in many of these information encounters; it is also our attachments, our group, our professional, national, racial, political, ideological, and of course religious identities. Accordingly, scholars of persuasion and influence "consistently find evidence for hyper skepticism toward scientific evidence among ideologues, no matter the domain or context,"[29] the effect more pronounced the further from reality one's ideologies have strayed.

In such circumstances, anomalous data potentially undermine not only trivial bits of purported "knowledge" but deeply-felt dimensions of the hearer's personhood. Dan Kahan et al. referred to the response to this peril as "identity-protective cognition," which is especially intensely stirred "to deflect threats to identities they hold, and roles they occupy."[30] There are several crucial implications of this new emphasis on identity-motivated cognition. The first is that thinking is *deeply social*. That is, humans are not intrepid isolated thinkers as often portrayed in philosophy; they get many if not most of their ideas, beliefs, and values (including the value of freedom; see Introduction) from other people, exercise their cognition in groups and in terms of belonging, and absorb, interpret, and/or resist information consistently with those identities. Second and therefore, cognition is not only motivated but *reparative*. By this we mean that people are motivated, somewhat along the line of cognitive dissonance, to repair damage to their identities and their commitments before they repair damage to knowledge and truth. To say it another way, humans are often willing to sacrifice knowledge rather than sacrifice identity—and to sacrifice knowledge at the altar of identity. Facts are not then, as we would like to believe, neutral entities for everyone to know and accept. Facts tend to be perceived as *for* or *against* one group or another, so when facts jeopardize "the beliefs common to members of salient 'in-groups,'" members of those groups "resist revision of those beliefs in the face of contrary factual information, particularly when that information originates from 'out-group sources'."[31]

Third, the social and reparative qualities of thought are reminders that the people who are targeted by facts, arguments, and debates are not empty vessels waiting for our superior knowledge to pour in. They are already filled with "knowledge" (albeit false knowledge), beliefs, values, trusts, commitments, and identities, these various elements arranged in networks that render them coherent and resistant to change. Accordingly, a change of mind in response to new facts, even compelling and

---

[29] Kraft, Lodge, and Taber, "Why People 'Don't Trust the Evidence,'" 121.
[30] Kahan et al., "Culture and Identity-Protective Cognition," 467.
[31] Kahan et al., "Culture and Identity-Protective Cognition," 469–70.

indisputable facts, is not simply the addition of one fact to a blank mind or the replacement of one (false) fact by another (true) one in a pliant mind but the alteration of the integrated structure of that mind. To say it another way, one bit of new knowledge can (and often should) have a cascade effect on multiple ideas, beliefs, values, trusts, commitments, and identities, inducing possibly widespread changes in thought and behavior. In short, hearkening back to our discussion of religious trauma, new knowledge—particularly if it is very important and very different from what audiences already hold true and dear—is not just something new to know but an assault on the hearers' "assumptive worlds" and likely to be repulsed as such. (See Chapter 6)

And if repulsion of dangerous knowledge were the foulest outcome, it would be bad enough. However, repeated studies demonstrate that the result is often "a 'back-fire effect' in which corrections actually *increase* misperceptions among the group in question."[32] Brendan Nyhan and Jason Reifler, for instance, mentioned several studies in which people who were provided with evidence that unsettled their belief "perversely became *more* confident in their beliefs" and even developed "opinions that are more extreme than they otherwise would have had."[33] Hogan and Speakman summarize one such study, in which subjects were first tested to determine their attitude toward capital punishment as a deterrent to crime. Next, half of each group (those who believed the death penalty did deter crime and those who did not) was shown information that murder rates were reduced by capital punishment, while half was given information that murder rates were unaffected by such penalties. In the end, attitudes were changed alright, just "not in the direction of the evidence they were presented, but the opposite. Those who were shown that capital punishment didn't deter murder believed more strongly that it did if they had believed that in the first place."[34]

Hogan and Speakman went on to advise against frontal attacks on a person's pre-existing knowledge and belief:

> *Never tell your target person he is wrong....* When you think about it, how would you feel if someone told you that you were wrong? You would probably get defensive and try to show or prove that you were in fact right. You would end up clinging more tightly to that position.[35]

---

[32] Nyhan and Reifler, "When Corrections Fail," 303.
[33] Nyhan and Reifler, "When Corrections Fail," 306, 308.
[34] Hogan and Speakman, *Covert Persuasion*, 20.
[35] Hogan and Speakman, *Covert Persuasion*, 8.

And most of the examples of knowledge/belief persistence and backlash involve issues relatively tangential to the audience's core ideas and values, like whether firefighters are risk-takers, whether Iraq possessed weapons of mass destruction, or whether global warming is real. We can only presume that if the issue were really at the heart of the audience's concerns and "truths" the resistance would be greater and the backlash stronger. In the case of the theist's assumptive world, they cannot let god(s) go without losing their sense of reality (as unreal as it is). Moreover, they may and often do walk away from the confrontation more firmly convinced of and committed to their beliefs, because they think that those beliefs withstood the test of the atheist, because even if they did not win the debate they survived an encounter with an antichrist, or because, as in the case of my meeting with the student, every negative thing they imagined about an atheist was confirmed.

I've Got a New Attitude:
Atheism and Attitude Change

So now we have some notion of what does not work and why when it comes to convincing people that their theistic (or any other) ideas and beliefs are wrong. What *does* work? In approaching this essential question, I take a cue from two writers on opposite ends of the philosophical and historical spectrums. In his *Rhetoric* (rhetoric being the skill or art of persuasion through speech and writing, which is our vocation), Aristotle asserted that persuasion functions in three modes—the personal character of the speaker, the frame of mind that we instill in the audience (including their emotional reactions), and "the proof, or apparent proof, provided by the words of the speech itself." Let us emphatically note that proof is only one, and perhaps the least effective, lever for changing minds.

The other guide through the terrain of persuasion is Dale Carnegie in his popular *How to Win Friends and Influence People*. To summarize his (decidedly less sophisticated) position on influence and persuasion, he stressed:

> You can tell people they are wrong ... [but] do you make them want to agree with you? Never! For you have struck a direct blow at their intelligence, judgment, pride, and self-respect. That will make them want to strike back. But it will never make them want to change their minds. You may then hurl at them all the logic of a Plato or an Immanuel Kant, but you will not alter their opinions, for you have hurt their feelings....

Never begin by announcing "I am going to prove so-and-so to you." That's bad. That's tantamount to saying: "I'm smarter than you are. I'm going to tell you a thing or two and make you change your mind...."

That is a challenge. It arouses opposition and makes the listener want to battle with you before you even start.[36]

Or in five words, "Don't criticize, condemn, or complain."[37]

Let us also agree that our mission is persuasion, which is understood as "the formation or change of attitudes through information processing in response to a message about the attitude object."[38] Consider that we may be implanting (forming) an original attitude or (more likely) modifying or excising a prior one, specifically attitudes about god(s). What do psychologists mean by "attitude," and why is it—as I suggested at the outset of this chapter—potentially a better concept for our purposes than "belief"? In their review of the literature, Gerd Bohner and Nina Dickel define attitude as "an evaluation of an object of thought. Attitude objects comprise anything a person may hold in mind, ranging from the mundane to the abstract, including things, people, groups, and ideas."[39] The *Gale Encyclopedia of Psychology* characterizes an attitude as "a predisposition to respond cognitively, emotionally, or behaviorally to a particular object, person, or situation in a particular way," elaborating its three components:

- Cognitive component, which concerns one's beliefs; the cognitive aspects of attitude are generally measured by surveys, interviews, and other reporting methods
- Affective component, which involves feelings and evaluations; the affective components are more easily assessed by monitoring physiological signs, such as heart rate
- Behavioral component, which consists of ways of acting toward the attitude object; this component may be assessed by direct observation.[40]

---

[36] Carnegie, *How to Win Friends and Influence People*, 116–17.
[37] Carnegie, *How to Win Friends and Influence People*, 16.
[38] Bohner and Dickel, "Attitudes and Attitude Change," 403.
[39] Bohner and Dickel, "Attitudes and Attitude Change," 392.
[40] Longe, *The Gale Encyclopedia of Psychology*, 89.

It is worth stressing also that attitudes are both products and producers of information and experience: facts and other learning situations generate our attitudes, but once they are in place they act as filters or screens for subsequent knowledge and meaning. In this sense, they operate as "schemas" do for Piaget, skills and models that we *apply to* the world once they are *acquired from* the world.

These considerations suggest why "attitude" could be preferable to "belief" in contemplating and conducting change. First, as we have established elsewhere, the concept of "belief" is a very controversial and loaded one. (See Chapter 2). Speaking the language of belief forces atheists to explicate themselves and their position in terms of belief (whether we "do not believe in god[s]" or "disbelieve in god[s]" or "believe that there are no god[s]," etc.). In any arrangement of the words, we are stuck in the theist's web of belief, which is their concept and not ours. Instead, if asked about my *attitude* toward god(s) I can respond that I have no use for him/her/it/them—or more appropriately, the concept of him/her/it/them—that I am profoundly uninterested in him/her/it/them, that I dismiss him/her/it/them, that I ultimately am free of him/her/it/them. Further, whether or not the theist "believes" in god(s) becomes secondary to her attitude toward god(s), which is fearful, loving, worshipful, obedient, confident, committed, faithful, or what have you. This closes the gap between "belief" and "faith" since it necessarily involves more than propositional assent. It reminds us again, as the *Gale Encyclopedia* analysis does, that the factual or propositional component of belief is only one facet of attitude—along with trust and commitment—and maybe not the most vital facet. (See Chapter 2)

If then our business is *attitude change* (and it is), that is, moving people from one attitude (positive, believing, faithful) to another (negative, disbelieving, free) on the topic of god(s), then it is imperative to understand that, according to Bohner and Dickel, there are two parallel mental processes at play. One, to be sure, is rational and logical, which they call *propositional reasoning* "based on syllogistic inferences about propositional information that is relevant for a judgment."[41] This is home ground for most argumentative atheists. However, the second process is not exactly rational (nor is it irrational, more properly considered non-rational, or not subordinated to reason) but rather entails *associative evaluation* which is, prominently, "independent of truth values."[42] Compared to propositions or fact-claims, which are either true or false on their own merit, associations are *implicit* (unspoken, even unconscious),

---

[41] Bohner and Dickel, "Attitudes and Attitude Change," 398.
[42] Bohner and Dickel, "Attitudes and Attitude Change," 398.

emotional or affective (more about what we feel than what we know), and *relational* (reactions to other aspects of a claim or experience than its veracity). As two of the proponents of the "associative-propositional evaluation" (APE) model, Bertram Gawronski and Galen Bodenhausen, expressed it, these distinct processes can be in conflict, such that "the affective gut response is inconsistent with other salient propositions that are considered relevant"; when this happens, cognitive dissonance sets in, which can be resolved "either by rejecting one of the involved propositions … or by searching for an additional proposition that resolves the inconsistency."[43] This probably accounts for the otherwise-inexplicable position of geologist Kurt Wise, whose scientific head conflicts with his theistic heart—where the heart triumphs over the head.

The associative dimension of attitudes and attitude change leads us to consider other features of the attitude-change encounter besides the "truth" of the facts and the power of the argument. Specifically, beyond the "message characteristics," specialists in attitude change alert us to "source characteristics" and "recipient characteristics." We will not say much about the latter at this point, other than that *whose* mind we are trying to change makes a difference, and therefore the same tactics will not work on everyone. Whether the individual is old or young, male or female, highly educated or uneducated, intelligent or dim, motivated or unmotivated, happy or angry, warm or cold—all of these factors impact the effectiveness of our persuasion efforts and the particular strategies and styles we should employ. Two variables to which we should be alert are what have been called the recipient's "need for cognition" (are they inclined toward "the truth" and thus open to attitude change, or are they inclined toward idea- and identity-preservation and thus defended against such change?) and their "self-monitoring tendency." In regard to the former, "People high in need for cognition prefer to think deeply about issues and are likely to be influenced by message arguments, whereas those low in the need for cognition rely on more fleeting aspects of an issue."[44] Regarding the latter, in their almost forty-year-old essay on attitude change, Joel Cooper and Robert Croyle maintained, "Individuals who are high self-monitors tend to be sensitive to, and thus influenced by, situational cues. Low self-monitors, however, tend to rely on their inner states and dispositions when making behavioral decisions."[45] Predictably, high self-monitoring folks will be more susceptible to persuasion than

---

[43] Gawronski and Bodenhausen. "The Associative-Propositional Evaluation Model: Theory, Evidence, and Open Questions," 63.

[44] Cooper, Blackman, and Keller, *The Science of Attitudes*, 106.

[45] Cooper and Croyle, "Attitudes and Attitude Change," 401.

their low-monitoring peers—and the damnable thing is that, short of a personality test before the argument, we usually cannot tell which we are dealing with.

Much more is known, and can be exploited, in the realm of source characteristics (that is, who/what is providing the information). One obvious and desirable trait in a source of information is expertise, which is part of the broader quality of *source credibility*. We are certainly more prone to the influence of people whom we think know what they are talking about. Another part of source credibility, more problematically, is trustworthiness. The problem is that an audience might accept the expertise of a speaker, say a scientist, but question his trustworthiness (maybe, the listener feels, the scientist is biased or power-hungry or a liberal tool, as some felt about Anthony Fauci during the COVID-19 pandemic). An auxiliary problem is that an audience may be highly motivated to dispute the trustworthiness, if not the very expertise, of a speaker if the speaker's message contradicts what they already "know" and believe and are determined to "know" and believe.

However, source credibility is a fraction of what enters into a listener's evaluation of the bearer of news. The audience may be focused on the identity of the speaker—his or her gender, race, age, ideology, party affiliation, and religion among others—especially if the speaker is a member of the audience's out-group in any of these categories. Here, atheists are at an obvious disadvantage, since we are by definition outside the congregation of the devout. And then there are the factors of *source attractiveness*, which include similarity to the audience, gender (in various ways, depending on the subject and situation), the so-called "halo effect" (the assumption or cognitive bias that one positive quality of the source rubs off on other qualities, enhancing the positive evaluation of the source as a whole), and, sad to say, the pleasantness and physical attractiveness of the source (which is another angle on the halo effect: we tend to feel more positively about pleasant and nice-looking people).

With all of this knowledge in hand, we can now receive some specific advice from some of the established experts on influence and persuasion. Among the most renowned is Robert Cialdini, who offered six "weapons of influence":[46]

---

[46] Cialdini, *Influence: The Psychology of Persuasion*.

- *Reciprocity* means the inclination to return a good deed done to us. I remember some years ago at a grocery store, where a church group was handing free bottles of water to customers as they exited the building. The water certainly carried no theistic message or argument, but as a gift, it was intended (1) to leave a favorable impression, (2) to create a sense of obligation ("we did something for you, now you do something for us, like attend our church"), and (3) to advertise their church to those who were unaware of it. All sorts of entities play the reciprocity game, distributing free samples or handing out goodies (like mailing labels and cards from charities) in hopes of creating a positive mood and eliciting a response.

- *Commitment and consistency* amount to the source's reputation for honesty and authenticity, for "walking the walk" or acting in conformity with their stated ideas and values. Further, since the purpose of persuasion is to shift people from one position to another (whether disbelieving in god[s] or buying one brand of car over another), Cialdini recommended deciphering the prior commitments of the audience and then moving them in small steps from where they are now to where you want them to be. Like other specialists in influence, he also noted that getting people to agree or commit to anything, no matter how minor, increased their likelihood of accepting more and larger ideas or commitments thereafter.

- *Social proof* is crowd psychology, the tendency to check ourselves in relation to others. Humans pay attention to what other people are doing or thinking, which can entice them to join the crowd. This is partly due to peer pressure (psychological experiments have reported that people will even alter their perceptions depending on what others say and do) and partly to the appeal of the popular. The fact that other people choose it is often compelling proof that it is worth choosing. Religions thrive on this principle: religions often strive for monopoly and ubiquity in society (I have called this "colonizing culture"), so that everywhere members of society see "proof" that the religion is true, good, and inevitable.

- *Liking* refers to the plain fact that "as a rule, we most prefer to say yes to the requests of someone we know and like."[47] As noted in the previous discussion of source attractiveness, audiences tend to

---

[47] Cialdini, *Influence*, 167.

be swayed by sources who make them feel good—and to be turned off by sources who make them feel bad, dumb, worthless, or otherwise inferior. It is no accident that many religious leaders, such as Joel Olsteen, put on a happy face and extend a warm handshake. They know, instinctively or explicitly, that friendliness is a foot in the door of the potential convert's mind. Key to Cialdini's insight is that when you attempt to persuade someone and change their mind, you are attempting to make them be like you, which they are more inclined to do if they like you. The antithesis of such liking is the cranky, condescending, and scolding arguer.

As is unambiguously communicated in his title, Dale Carnegie considered this perhaps the most fundamental step in persuasion. He had his own six principles for making people like you:

1.   Become genuinely interested in other people
2.   Smile
3.   Remember the person's name
4.   Be a good listener
5.   Talk in terms of the other person's interests, and
6.   Make the other person feel important, and be sincere about it.[48]

Again, you might think you are just arguing a fact and not making friends, but you are—in fact, (1) you are a role model for the new attitude and (2) if the theist becomes an atheist as you hope, she will be a part of your community.

- *Authority* fairly speaks for itself. Unsurprisingly, expertise gives an influencer source credibility. Authority is of course a double-edged sword: people may listen to someone who has knowledge and experience, but they also may not want to be lectured and talked down to. Expertise can turn into pedantry, and too many facts and details can be overwhelming and off-putting. Cialdini counsels to use expertise politely.
- *Scarcity* is the impression that whatever the source is offering is in short supply. If people feel that there is an urgency in decision-making—that there is a limited amount of whatever good is being

---

[48] Carnegie, *How to Win Friends and Influence People*, 62, 70, 79, 88, 93, 105.

proffered or a limited time to accept it—people may be more motivated to jump at it. This tactic is less available to atheists and rationalists, since knowledge is mostly free to everyone and, lacking an imminent apocalypse to frighten them with, there is plenty of time to choose. Religions, on the other hand, can exploit this principle exquisitely, claiming the possession of exclusive esoteric knowledge, the special privilege of a chosen few who will reap the rewards, and the immediacy of Armageddon. No wonder Christianity thrives on constant prophecies of end-times and second-comings.

The eminent psychologist Howard Gardner presented his own plan of seven "levers" for changing minds, all starting with "re-":

1. Reason in the form of "sheer logic, the use of analogies, or the creation of taxonomies"
2. Research or "the collection of relevant data" and statistical tests
3. Resonance or appeals to "the affective component" of the personality as opposed to the purely intellectual appeals of reason and research; an idea or experience resonates for the audience "to the extent that it feels right to an individual, seems to fit the current situation, and convinces the person that further considerations are superfluous"
4. Representational redescriptions (which Gardner deemed the most critical of all the levers) or expressing the idea in multiple different forms and media—arguments and debates possibly, but also stories, visual images, arts, hands-on experience, and cooperative/social projects[49]
5. Resources and rewards, both resources that the influencer can invest in the persuasion effort and rewards that the audience can earn
6. Real-world events, which can impact people's thought processes and induce change
7. Resistances, that is, identifying and removing the obstacles to attitude change.[50]

A classic 1967 study in the field of persuasion, or what the authors Gerald Marwell and David Schmitt called *compliance-gaining behavior*, crafted a more elaborate list of sixteen techniques:

---

[49] Gardner, *Changing Minds*, 140–41.
[50] Gardner, *Changing Minds*, 16–18.

1. Promise (reward for compliance)
2. Threat (punishment for noncompliance)
3. Positive expertise (explaining the benefits of the new attitude)
4. Negative expertise (explaining the costs of not adopting the new attitude)
5. Liking (being friendly and helpful)
6. Pre-giving (reward before compliance)
7. Aversive stimulation (punishment or negative consequences end when the new attitude begins)
8. Debt (equivalent to Cialdini's reciprocity)
9. Moral appeal (you are bad if you do not change)
10. Positive self-feeling (you will like yourself better once you change)
11. Negative self-feeling (you will not like yourself if you refuse to change)
12. Positive altercasting (comparing the audience to other good people who comply)
13. Negative altercasting (comparing the audience to other bad people who do not comply)
14. Altruism (comply for the good of others)
15. Positive esteem (people will like you more if you comply)
16. Negative esteem (people will not like you if you don't comply).[51]

At the upper limit of our attention span, Hogan and Speakman suggested twenty-seven tips and warnings for the would-be persuader—the pithiest being that people do not question things enough, that they don't know how to ask the right questions, that they don't read (bad news for us book writers!), and that their perception is their reality[52]—and a full fifty-five "covert persuasion tactics," complete with a table and worksheet to master them.[53] Chip Heath and Dan Heath mercifully boiled their guidance down to six qualities that they declared would make an idea "stick" in the minds of hearers: keep the idea *simple, unexpected, concrete,* and *credible,* and express it in *narrative (stories)* with *emotion.*[54]

Finally, some researchers on influence and persuasion have put their lessons into practice, like B. J. Fogg and his Stanford Behavior Design Lab (formerly known by the more ominous name, Persuasion Technology Lab). According to its website (behaviordesign.stanford.edu),

---

[51] Marwell and Schmitt, "Dimensions of Compliance-Gaining," 357–58.
[52] Hogan and Speakman, *Covert Persuasion,* 190–201.
[53] Hogan and Speakman, *Covert Persuasion,* 210–214.
[54] Heath and Heath, *Made to Stick: Why Some Ideas Survive and Others Die.*

the initiative "is a new approach to understand human behavior and how to design for behavior change," with "a comprehensive set of models and methods that work together to give you a systematic set of tools for thinking and designing." Linguist and philosopher George Lakoff was celebrated for his instruction to American liberals and progressives, who are noticeably behind their conservative colleagues in the influence game. His work stressed the power of "frames" for thought and action. A frame is a cognitive or conceptual structure within which thought and discourse occur; it is the "box" that people think and talk in.[55] Within that frame, words and actions have meaning, and some frame of thought is always necessary for shared meaning. Even more, the frame is a mighty constraint on what can be talked and thought about.

- Every word comes from some frame. You cannot speak in a generic language, only some particular language—which is *somebody's* particular language (like Christian or theist language).
- Words of a frame evoke that frame. Words, concepts, etc. from one frame or language "bring along" the whole rest of the frame or the worldview that it builds.
- Evoking the frame reinforces the frame. Every time we use the frame or speak the language, it strengthens the frame/language. It becomes more cognitively real and compelling to the participant.
- Contrary to what we might expect, negating a frame does not reduce its force, since negating it is still evoking it (i.e., talking *against* it is still talking *about* it). And since every evocation is reinforcement, then even negation is reinforcement.

This is why mind-controllers, from *1984*'s Big Brother to conservative pollster Frank Luntz to Vladimir Putin, understand the value of dominating the language. Who sets the words sets the frame, and who sets the frame sets the reality.

This is also, in the end, why I caution atheists about debating theists, because when we do, we almost invariably enter into their frame. No wonder that theists love to debate us: they know that they pose the questions ("Does God exist?") and provide the terms ("God," "belief," "sin," "creation," blah blah), so we are still talking about *their god*. The ultimate triumph of Alvin Plantinga is making "Christian philosophers" of us all. (See Chapter 8). What we must do, at the grandest level of strategy, is seize the questions back from the theists, provide our own terms, create

---

[55] Lakoff, *Don't Think of an Elephant: Know Your Values and Frame the Debate.*

our own language, and invent our own culture. To take one tiny tip from the biblical character Jesus (Luke 23:3), when theists (mostly Christians in our experience) ask if we "believe in God," a wise response would be, "Those are your words, not mine." Throughout this book, I have used phrases like "god(s)" or "he/she/it/them" when referring to a god precisely to turn the tables on theists and make it clear to them that *their* god is not the only one to talk about. There are lots of gods in the world's religions, and lots of beings other than gods; why is it interesting or important to talk about *your* god, let alone any god? I neither "believe" nor "disbelieve" in god(s); I am free of god(s).

Conclusion:
I Wouldn't Want to Be Like You

We have probably all seen the meme of the grumpy atheist goat. Aimed at children, it teaches them that atheists are "bitter," "sad," "crotchety," "poor lost souls" and "grouches" who "lash out at" and "try to trick" youngsters (and presumably adults too). You should not even talk to them; you definitely do not want to be one of them.

This particular image/meme apparently originates from the parody site Objective: Ministries (objectiveministries.org), but it probably represents fairly accurately the impressions of many theists. Indeed "spiritual safety" is a real thing, as in the Mormon "Spiritual Safety Tips for Frequent Travelers" (tinyurl.com/4ya9s822). Be that as it may, we can recognize such tactics now as acts of agnomancy, keeping the flock ignorant of what atheists really say and who they really are. It is also an act of framing, seizing the narrative about what atheists and atheism must necessarily be. It is a very primitive but efficient version of the (melo)drama of atheism explored and rejected in this book. (See Chapter 1)

Demonizing and erecting cognitive and emotional barriers against the other is Persuasion 101, and it is clear now, bringing our book to a close and full circle, that the (melo)drama of atheism is an influence trope, constructed to create and perpetuate distance between theism and its anti-matter opposite, atheism. It must be impossibly difficult to be an atheist, insist theist partisans from John Haught to Jeanine Diller to Norman Geisler and Frank Turek in their irrationally titled *I Don't Have Enough Faith to be an Atheist*. Notwithstanding that we would not tolerate such hateful and stupid insults aimed at any other group (imagine someone insisting that African Americans are grumpy and bitter or publishing a book about the foolishness of Mexicans or gays), there is no argument being advanced in such barbs. They are, as Bohner and Dickel said above, "independent of truth value" but are emotion-laden poisonings and assassinations of a position they desperately want not just to falsify but to destroy. They are also hopelessly trapped inside their own worldview, their own assumptive world, with no mindfulness that another worldview might exist and be happily inhabited.

It is impossibly difficult to be an atheist because of the burden of proof against all the god(s), they declare, as if they care about "all the god(s)." Then they express mock-sympathy that it is impossibly difficult to be an atheist because humans without god(s) must be crushed by existential despair. To those misguided insults, they add two more theist fantasies—that even if atheists were right that there is no such thing as god(s), you wouldn't want to be an atheist because you wouldn't want to be *like* an atheist, and you wouldn't *like* an atheist if you knew one. The disagreeable truth for theists is that atheists are people just like them, dwelling in a strange world full of hostile forces, from viruses and the climate to strangers in angry enemy tribes. Their desire to think the worst of us is the height of motivated cognition—motivated by perhaps the niggling sense that it is *not so hard* to be god(s)less after all and that freedom from god(s) feels pretty good.

Bibliography

Acevedo, Deepa Das. "Secularism in the Indian Context." *Law & Social Inquiry* 38, no. 1 (2011): 138–67.

Adams, Robert Martin. *Nil: Episodes in the Literary Conquest of Void during the Nineteenth Century.* New York: Oxford University Press, 1966.

Afzal, Ahmed. *Lone Star Muslims: Transnational Lives and the South Asian Experience in Texas.* New York and London: New York University Press, 2015.

Aijaz, Imran. "Islamic Conceptions of Divinity." In *The Routledge Handbook of Contemporary Philosophy of Religion*, edited by Graham Oppy, 114–126. London: Routledge, 2015.

Aiken, Charles Francis. "Apologetics." *The Catholic Encyclopedia.* Vol. 1. New York: Robert Appleton Company, 1907. http://tinyurl.com/255esb8b, accessed January 12, 2024.

Aiyar, Pallavi. "The Most Religious Atheist Country in the World: Japan's Confounding Relationship with Religion." http://tinyurl.com/ah55t2dv, accessed December 23, 2023.

Alford, C. Fred. *Rethinking Freedom: Why Freedom Lost Its Meaning and What Can Be Done to Save It.* New York: Palgrave Macmillan, 2005.

All About Philosophy. "Christian Existentialism." https://tinyurl.com/2cuk5v8x , accessed March 27, 2022.

Alston, William R. "Christian Experience and Christian Belief." In *Faith and Rationality: Reason and Belief in God*, edited by Alvin Plantinga and Nicholas Wolterstorff, 103–34. Notre Dame, IN: University of Notre Dame Press, 1983.

Alston, William P. *Perceiving God: The Epistemology of Religious Experience.* Ithaca, NY: Cornell University Press, 1991.

———. "Religious Experience and Religious Belief." *Noûs* 16, no. 1 (1982): 3–12.

Altizer, Thomas J. J. *The Gospel of Christian Atheism.* Philadelphia, PA: Westminster Press, 1966.

Aly, Ramy M. K. *Becoming Arab in London: Performativity and the Undoing of Identity*. London: Pluto Press, 2015.

American Psychological Association. "Trauma." apa.org/topics/trauma, accessed October 21, 2021.

Ammerman, Nancy T. *Bible Believers: Fundamentalists in the Modern World*. New Brunswick, NJ and London: Rutgers University Press, 1987.

Anand, Aanchal. "The Curious Case of Indian Secularism." In *World in Their Hands: Ideas from the Next Generation*, edited by Natalia Bubnova, 149–62. Moscow: Carnegie Moscow Center, 2012.

Angel, H-F. "Credition, the Process of Belief." In *Encyclopedia of Sciences and Religions*, edited by A. Runehov and L. Oviedo, 536–539. Dordrecht, Netherlands: Springer Science + Business Media, 2013.

Angel, H-F, L. Oviedo, R. F. Paloutzian, A. L. C. Runehov, and R. J. Seitz, eds. *Processes of Believing: The Acquisition, Maintenance, and Change in Creditions*. Cham, Switzerland: Springer International Publishing, 2017.

Anker, Elisabeth R. *Orgies of Feeling: Melodrama and the Politics of Freedom*. Durham, NC and London: Duke University Press, 2014.

———. *Ugly Freedoms*. Durham, NC and London: Duke University Press, 2022.

Ariely, Dan. *Predictably Irrational: The Hidden Forces that Shape Our Decisions*. New York: HarperCollins, 2008.

Aristotle. *Metaphysics*. Translated by W. D. Ross. London: Global Grey Books, 2018.

Arnal, William E., Willi Braun, and Russell T. McCutcheon, eds. *Failure and Nerve in the Academic Study of Religion*. Sheffield, UK: Equinox, 2012.

Arterburn, Stephen and Jack Felton. *Toxic Faith: Understanding and Overcoming Religious Addiction*. Nashville, TN: Oliver-Nelson Books., 1991.

Ashton, John F., ed. *In Six Days: Why 50 Scientists Choose to Believe in Creation*. Green Forest, AR: Master Books, 2000.

Asser, Seth and Rita Swan. "Child Fatalities from Religion-Motivated Medical Neglect." *Pediatrics* 101, no. 4 (1998): 625–29.

Associated Press. "Pat Robertson Calls Radical Muslims 'Satanic.'" https://tinyurl.com/fjwr833p , accessed May 17, 2022.

Atran, Scott. *In Gods We Trust: The Evolutionary Landscape of Religion*. Oxford: Oxford University Press, 2002.

Aveling, Francis. "Atheism." *The New Advent Catholic Encyclopedia*, Vol. 2. New York: Robert Appleton Company, 1907. https://tinyurl.com/5buh3843, accessed April 9, 2022.

Azadegan, Ebrahim. "Ibn 'Arabi on the Problem of Divine Hiddenness." *Journal of the Muhyiddin Ibn 'Arabi Society* 53 (2013): 49–67.

Badham, Paul. "What is Theology?" *Theology* 99, no. 788: 101–6.

Baggini, Julian. *Atheism: A Very Short Introduction*. Oxford and New York: Oxford University Press, 2003.

Barth, Fredrik. *Nomads of South Persia: The Basseri Tribe of the Khamseh Confederacy*. Oslo, Norway: Oslo University Press, 1961. Baumrin, Stefan. "Antitheism and Morality." *The Philosophical Forum*. 39, no. 1 (2008): 73–84.

Beck, Glenn. *It Is About Islam: Exposing the Truth about ISIS, Al Qaeda, Iran, and the Caliphate*. New York and London: Threshold Editions, 2015.

Bell, Catherine. *Ritual Perspectives and Dimensions*. New York: Oxford University Press, 1997.

Bell, Diane. *Daughters of the Dreaming*, 2nd ed. Minneapolis, MN: University of Minnesota Press, 1993 [1983].

Benchemsi, Ahmed. "Invisible Atheists: The Spread of Disbelief in the Arab World." *New Republic* (23 April). http://tinyurl.com/23w6yvrc , accessed July 8, 2022

Berkof, Louis. *Systematic Theology: New Combined Edition*. 1938. Reprint, Grand Rapids, MI: William B. Eerdmans Publishing Company, 1996.

Berlin, Isaiah. *Liberty: Incorporating* Four Essays on Liberty, edited by Henry Hardy. Oxford and New York: Oxford University Press, 2002.

Betenson, Toby. "Recasting Anti-Theism." In *Does God Matter? Essays on the Axiological Consequences of Theism*, edited by Klaas J. Kraay, 164–177. New York: Routledge, 2017.

Bhargava, Rajeev. *The Promise of India's Secular Democracy*. New Delhi: Oxford University Press, 2010.

Bhattacharya, Ramkrishna. "India: 1500 BC to AD 1200." In *The Cambridge History of Atheism*, vol. 1 and 2, edited by Stephen Bullivant and Michael Ruse, 118–138. Cambridge and New York: Cambridge University Press, 2021.

Biale, David. *Not in the Heavens: The Tradition of Jewish Secular Thought*. Princeton, NJ and Oxford: Princeton University Press, 2011.

Bidney, David. "The Varieties of Human Freedom." In *The Concept of Freedom in Anthropology*, edited by David Bidney, 11–34. The Hague: Mouton, 1963.

Biernacki, Loriliai. "Introduction: Panentheism Outside the Box." In *Panentheism across the World's Traditions*. edited by Loriliai Biernacki and Philip Clayton, 1–17. Oxford and New York: Oxford University Press, 2014.

Binder, Stefan. "Magic is Science: Atheist Conjuring and the Exposure of Superstition in South India." *HAU: Journal of Ethnographic Theory* 9, no. 2 (2019): 284–298.

Bird-David, Nurit. "'Animism' Revisited: Personhood, Environment, and Relational Epistemology." *Current Anthropology* 40, supplement (1999): S67–S91.

Bodhi, Bhikkhu. *A Comprehensive Manual of Abhidhamma*. Onalaska, WA: Pariyatti Publishing, 2003.

Boddy, Janice. "The Work of Zâr: Women and Spirit Possession in Northern Sudan." In *The Problem of Ritual Efficacy*, edited by William S. Sax, Johannes Quack, and Jan Weinhold, 113–30. Oxford and New York: Oxford University Press, 2010.

Bohner, Gerd and Nina Dickel. "Attitudes and Attitude Change." *Annual Review of Psychology* 62 (2011): 391–417.

Booth, Leo. *When God Becomes a Drug: Breaking the Chains of Religious Addiction and Abuse*. Los Angeles, CA: J. P. Tarcher, 1992.

Bottoms, Bette L., Phillip R. Shaver, and Gail S. Goodman. "An Analysis of Ritualistic and Religion-Related Child Abuse Allegations." *Law and Human Behavior* 20, no. 1 (1996): 1–34.

Bowen, John R. *Can Islam be French? Pluralism and Pragmatism in a Secularist State*. Princeton, NJ: Princeton University Press, 2010.

Boyce, James P. "Abstract of Systematic Theology." Philadelphia, PA: American Baptist Publication Society, 1887. https://tinyurl.com/ypdctfuh , accessed March 16, 2022.

Brown, Wendy. *States of Injury: Power and Freedom in Late Modernity*. Princeton, NJ: Princeton University Press, 1995.

Bruce, Steve. *God is Dead: Secularization in the West*. Malden, MA and Oxford: Blackwell, 2002.

Bubandt, Nils. *The Empty Seashell: Witchcraft and Doubt on an Indonesian Island*. Ithaca, NY and London: Cornell University Press, 2014.

Buchak, Lara. "Faith and Steadfastness in the Face of Counter-Evidence." *International Journal for Philosophy of Religion* 81, no.1–2 (2017): 113–133.

Buchholz, Katharina. "How Do You Feel About Religion?" http://tinyurl.com/y79j72zz, accessed December 25, 2023.

Bullivant, Stephen. "Defining 'Atheism." In *The Oxford Handbook of Atheism*, edited by Stephen Bullivant and Michael Ruse, 11–12. Oxford and New York: Oxford University Press, 2013.

Burns, Elizabeth D. "How to Prove the Existence of God: An Argument for Conjoined Panentheism." *International Journal for Philosophy of Religion* 85, no. 1 (2019): 5–21.

Buyandelgeriyn, Manduhai. "Dealing with Uncertainty: Shamans, Marginal Capitalism, and the Remaking of History in Postsocialist Mongolia." *American Ethnologist* 34, no. 1 (2007): 127–47.

Byler, Darren. *Terror Capitalism: Uyghur Dispossession and Masculinity in a Chinese City*. Durham, NC: Duke University Press, 2021.

Callahan, Laura Frances. "Could God Love Cruelty? A Partial Defense of Unrestricted Theological Voluntarism." *Faith and Philosophy* 38, no. 1 (2021): 26–44.

Camus, Albert. *The Myth of Sisyphus*. Translated by Justin O'Brien. Harmondsworth, UK and New York: Penguin Books, 1979 [1942].

———. *Notebooks 1951–1959*. Translated by Ryan Bloom. Chicago, IL: Ivan R. Dee, 2008 [1989].

Caravale, Giorgio. "Private and Public Devotion in Late Renaissance Italy: The Role of Church Censorship." In *Domestic Devotions in Early Modern Italy*, edited by Maya Corry, Marco Faini, and Alessia Meneghin, 389–407. Leiden, Netherlands: Brill, 2019.

Carnegie, Dale. *How to Win Friends and Influence People*. New York: Simon & Schuster, 1981 [1936].

Casanova, José. *Public Religions in the Modern World*. Chicago, IL: The Chicago University Press, 1994.

———. "Secularization Revisited: A Reply to Talal Asad." In *Powers of the Secular Modern: Talal Asad and His Interlocutors*, edited by David Scott and Charles Hirschkind, 12–30. Stanford, CA: Stanford University Press, 2006.

Cassaniti, Julia. *Living Buddhism: Mind, Self, and Emotion in a Thai Community*. Ithaca, NY and London: Cornell University Press, 2015.

Center for Good Governance. *Handbook on Persuasion Skills.* https://tinyurl.com/3jbvmaka.pdf, accessed May 26, 2022.

Chabot, Alexis. "Cruel Atheism." *Sartre Studies International* 22, no. 1 (2016): 58–68.

Chakrabarty, Dipesh. *Provincializing Europe: Postcolonial Thought and Historical Difference.* Princeton, NJ: Princeton University Press, 2000. Chalfant, Eric. "A Greimas Rectangle for a New New Atheism." *Culture and Religion* 19, no. 3 (2018): 317–328.

Chinn, Clark A. and William F. Brewer. "The Role of Anomalous Data in Knowledge Acquisition: A Theoretical Framework and Implications for Science Instruction." *Review of Educational Research* 63, no. 1 (1993): 1–49.

Chrisman, Matthew. "Ought to Believe." *The Journal of Philosophy* 105, no. 7 (2008): 346–370.

Cialdini, Robert B. *Influence: The Psychology of Persuasion*, revised edition. New York: Harper Business, 2006 [1984].

Cliteur, Paul. "The Definition of Atheism." *Journal of Religion and Society* 11, (2009): 1–23.

———. *The Secular Outlook: In Defense of Moral and Political Secularism.* Malden, MA and Oxford: Wiley-Blackwell, 2010.

Comte-Sponville, André. *The Little Book of Atheist Spirituality.* Translated by Nancy Huston. London: Bantam Press, 2008 [2006].

Conifer, Steven J. "Theological Noncognitivism Examined." https://tinyurl.com/49cjpape , accessed March 13, 2022.

Conrad, Nickolas G. "An Argument for Unbelief: A Discussion about Terminology." *Secularism and Nonreligion* 7, no. 11 (2018): 1–8.

Cooper, Joel, Shane Blackman, and Kyle Keller. *The Science of Attitudes.* New York and London: Routledge, 2016.

Cooper, Joel and Robert T. Croyle. "Attitudes and Attitude Change." *Annual Review of Psychology* 35, (1984): 395–426.

Cornish, Paul, Julian Lindley-French, and Claire Yorke. "Strategic Communications and National Strategy." London: The Royal Institute of International Affairs, 2011.

Craig, William Lane. *Reasonable Faith: Christian Faith and Apologetics*, 3rd ed. Wheaton, IL: Crossway Books 2008 [1984].

Cunningham, David Michael with Taylor Ellwood and Amanda R. Wagener. *Creating Magickal Entities: A Complete Guide to Entity Creation.* Perrysburg, OH: Egregore Publishing, 2003.

Cyril. *The Catechetical Lectures of S. Cyril, Archbishop of Jerusalem*, volume II. Translated by Members of the English Church. Oxford: John Henry Parker, 1838.

Davies, Brian. *An Introduction to the Philosophy of Religion*, 4th ed. Oxford and New York: Oxford University Press, 2021.

Dawkins, Richard. *The God Delusion*. London: Bantam Press, 2006.

de Botton, Alain. *Religion for Atheists: A Non-Believer's Guide to the Uses of Religion*. New York: Pantheon Books, 2012.

De Jong, Joop T. and Ria Reis. "Kiyang-yang, a West-African Postwar Idiom of Distress." *Culture, Medicine, and Psychiatry* 34, no. 2 (2010): 301–321.

Deeb, Lara and Mona Harb. *Leisurely Islam: Negotiating Geography and Morality in Shi'ite South Beirut*. Princeton, NJ: Princeton University Press, 2013.

DeLancey, Craig. "Camus's Atheism and the Virtues of Inconsistency." https://tinyurl.com/wn8bzxvp , accessed March 1, 2022.

Dennett, Daniel. *Freedom Evolves*. New York and London: Viking, 2003.

Dentan, Robert Knox. *Overwhelming Terror: Love, Fear, Peace, and Violence among Semai of Malaysia*. Lanham, MD: Rowman & Littlefield, 2008.

Diab, Khaled. "Views: Arab Atheists and their Quest for Acceptance amid Religious Intolerance." *Rowaq Arabi* 25, no. 2 (2020): 1524.

Diller, Jeanine. "Global and Local Atheisms." *International Journal for Philosophy of Religion* 79, no. 1 (2016): 7–18.

Dixon, J. M. "A Survey of COVID-19 Deaths among American Clergy." *Socio-Historical Examination of Religion and Ministry* 3, no.2 (2021): 238–51.

Donato, Clorinda and Robert M. Maniquis, eds. *The Encyclopédie and the Age of Revolution*. Los Angeles, CA: University of California and Los Angeles Library, 1992.

Draper, Paul and Ryan Nichols. "Diagnosing Bias in Philosophy of Religion." *The Monist* 96, no. 3 (2013): 420–46.

Draper, Paul and John L. Schellenberg. "The Why and the How of Renewal in Philosophy of Religion." *European Journal for Philosophy of Religion* 14, no. 1 (2022): 1–20.

Dudley, Will. *Hegel, Nietzsche, and Philosophy: Thinking Freedom*. Cambridge: Cambridge University Press, 2002.

Dumsday, Travis. "Divine Hiddenness, Free-Will, and the Victims of Wrongdoing." *Faith and Philosophy* 27, no. 4 (2010): 423–38.

————. "Divine Hiddenness and the One Sheep." *International Journal for Philosophy of Religion* 79, no. 1 (2016): 69–86.

————. "Why (Most) Atheists Have a Duty to Pray." *Sophia* 51, no. 1 (2012): 59–70.

Durkheim, Émile. *The Elementary Forms of Religious Life*. New York: The Free Press, 1965 [1912].

Ehrman, Bart D. *Lost Christianities: The Battles for Scripture and the Faiths We Never Knew*. Oxford and New York: Oxford University Press, 2003.

Eliade, Mircea. *Myth and Reality*. Translated by Willard R. Trask. Prospect Heights, IL: Waveland Press, 1998 [1963].

Eller, David. *Atheism Advanced: Further Thoughts of a Freethinker*. Cranford, NJ: American Atheist Press, 2007.

————. "The End of Harris." *American Atheist* 48, no. 7 (2010): 32–33.

————. "A Mind is a Terrible Thing: How Evolved Cognitive Biases Lead to Religion (and Other Mental Errors)." In *Christianity is the Light of Science: Critically Examining the World's Largest Religion*, edited by John Loftus, 47–68. Amherst, NY: Prometheus Books, 2016.

————. *Natural Atheism*. Cranford, NJ: American Atheists Press, 2004.

Eller, Jack David. "Atheism is Global Atheism." *Socio-Historical Examination of Religion and Ministry* 2, no.2 (2020): 66–86.

————. *Cruel Creeds, Virtuous Violence: Religious Violence Across Culture and History*. Amherst, NY: Prometheus Books, 2010.

Elsässer, Sebastian. "Arab Non-believers and Freethinkers on YouTube: Re-Negotiating Intellectual and Social Boundaries." *Religions* 12, no. 2 (2021): 1–18.

Encyclopedia Britannica. "History of Encyclopedias." https://tinyurl.com/2p9bbx4t, accessed March 18, 2022.

Enroth, Ronald. *Recovering from Churches that Abuse*. Grand Rapids, MI: Zondervan Publishing House, 1994.

Epley, Nicholas and Thomas Gilovich. "The Mechanics of Motivated Reasoning." *The Journal of Economic Perspectives* 30, no. 3 (2016): 133–140.

Ferrándiz, Francisco. "Open Veins: Spirits of Violence and Grief in Venezuela." *Ethnography* 10, no. 1 (2009): 39–61.

Ferrier, James F. *Institutes of Metaphysics: The Theory of Knowing and Being*. Edinburgh and London: William Blackwood and Sons, 1854.

Ferschtman, Chaim, Uri Gneezy, and Moshe Hoffman. "Taboos and Identity: Considering the Unthinkable." *American Economic Journal: Microeconomics* 3, no.2 (2011): 139–164.

Feser, Edward. "Adventures in the Old Atheism, Part I: Nietzsche." https://tinyurl.com/yhdw8a88, accessed March 22, 2022.

———. "Adventures in the Old Atheism, Part IV: Marx." https://tinyurl.com/mpk3wr3z , accessed March 26, 2022.

Festinger, Leon, Henry W. Riecken, and Stanley Schacter. *When Prophecy Fails*. Minneapolis, MN: University of Minnesota Press, 1956.

Fish, Stanley. *The First: How to Think about Hate Speech, Campus Speech, Religious Speech, Fake News, Post-Truth, and Donald Trump*. New York: One Signal Publishers, 2019.

Flint, Robert. *Anti-Theistic Theories: Being the Baird Lecture for 1877*, 5th ed. London: William Blackwood and Sons, 1894.

Flueckiger, Joyce Burkhalter. *When the World Becomes Female: Guises of a South Indian Goddess*. Bloomington and Indianapolis, IN: Indiana University Press, 2013.

Franke, William. *On What Cannot Be Said: Apophatic Discourses in Philosophy, Religion, Literature, and the Arts*, volume 1. Notre Dame, IN: University of Notre Dame Press, 2007.

Frankfurt, Harry G. *On Bullshit*. Princeton, NJ and Oxford: Princeton University Press, 2005.

Freud, Sigmund. "Analysis Terminable and Interminable." *International Journal of Psycho-Analysis* 18: (1937): 373–405.

Fromm, Erich. *Escape from Freedom*. New York: Avon Books 1969 [1941].

Fuad, Mohamad Razif Mohamad, Mohd Fauzi Hamat, Mohd Khairul Naim Che Nordin, and Mohammad Abdelhamid Salem Qatawneh. "Readings on the Definition and Arguments Towards Atheism." *Afkār* 24, no. 1 (2022): 343-80.

Gardner, Howard. *Changing Minds: The Art and Science of Changing Our Own and Other People's Minds*. Boston, MA: Harvard Business School Press, 2006.

Gawronski, Bertram and Galen V. Bodenhausen. "The Associative-Propositional Evaluation Model: Theory, Evidence, and Open Questions." In *Advances in Experimental Social Psychology*, volume 44, edited by James M. Olson and Mark P. Zanna, 59–127. San Diego, CA: Academic Press, 2011.

Geertz, Clifford. *The Interpretation of Cultures*. New York: Basic Books, 1973.

Geisler, Norman L. and Frank Turek. *I Don't Have Enough Faith to be an Atheist*. Wheaton, IL: Crossway Books, 2004.

Gellner, David N. "Studying Secularism, Practising Secularism. Anthropological Imperatives." *Social Anthropology* 9, no. 3 (2001): 337–40

Gez, Yonatan N., Nadia Beider, and Helga Dickow. "African and Not Religious: The State of Research on Sub-Saharan Religious Nones and New Scholarly Horizons." *Africa Spectrum* 57, no. 1 (2022): 50–71.

Girard, René. *Violence and the Sacred*. Translated by Patrick Gregory. Baltimore, MD: The Johns Hopkins University Press, 1977.

Girardet, Raoul. *Mythes et Mythologies Politiques*. Paris: Éditions de Seuil, 1986.

Global Center for Religious Research. "Religious Trauma Research." www.gcrr.org/religioustrauma, accessed October 21, 2021.

Gore, Hogan. "Oklahoma GOP Congressional Candidate John Bennett Calls for Execution of Dr. Anthony Fauci." https://tinyurl.com/ayxjexy5, accessed May 4, 2022.

Gotinga, J. C. "Pastor Claiming to Be 'Son of God' Charged with Sex Trafficking." https://tinyurl.com/6v9ctt4a , accessed April 24, 2022.

Graeber, David and David Wengrow. *The Dawn of Everything: A New History of Humanity*. New York: Farrar, Straus, and Giroux, 2021.

Graef, Robert. "Commentary: Ignorance is Costly, Dangerous and Undemocratic." https://tinyurl.com/3b2xrh5d, accessed May 8, 2022.

Hamilton, Clive. *The Freedom Paradox: Towards a Post-Secular Ethics*. Crows Nest, NSW, Australia: Allen & Unwin, 2008.

Hannam, James. "The Emperor Justinian's Closure of the School of Athens." https://tinyurl.com/tdr5njcd, accessed May 11, 2022.

Harbour, Daniel. *An Intelligent Person's Guide to Atheism*. London: Duckworth, 2001.

Harris, Sam. *The End of Faith: Religion, Terror, and the Future of Reason*. New York: W. W. Norton, 2005.

Hartman, Robert J. "Involuntary Belief and the Command to Have Faith." *International Journal for Philosophy of Religion* 69, no. 3 (2011): 181–192.

Harvey, Gill. "The Power and Control Dynamics of Growing Up in an Abrahamic Faith Environment." *Socio-Historical Examination of Religion and Ministry* 3, no. 2 (2021): 279–94.

Haught, John F. *God and the New Atheism: A Critical Response to Dawkins, Harris, and Hitchens*. Louisville, KY: Westminster John Knox Press, 2008.

Heath, Chip and Dan Heath. *Made to Stick: Why Some Ideas Survive and Others Die*. New York: Random House, 2009.

Hefner, Philip. *The Human Factor: Evolution, Culture, and Religion*. Minneapolis, MN: Fortress Press, 1993.

Hereth, Blake. "Queer Advice to Christian Philosophers." *European Journal of Philosophy of Religion* 14, no. 1 (2022): 49–75.

Hick, John H. *Philosophy of Religion*, 4th ed. Englewood Cliffs, NJ: Prentice-Hall, 1990.

Hodge, Charles. *Systematic Theology*, volume 1. Reprint, Bellingham, WA: Lexham Press, 1997 [1872].

Hogan, Kevin and James Speakman. *Covert Persuasion: Psychological Tactics and Tricks to Win the Game*. Hoboken, NJ: John Wiley & Sons, 2006.

Højer, Lars. "Absent Powers: Magic and Loss in Post-Socialist Mongolia." *The Journal of the Royal Anthropological Institute* 15, no. 3 (2009): 575–91.

Holdier, A. G. "Is Heaven a Zoopolis?" *Faith and Philosophy* 37, no. 4 (2020): 475–499.

Holyoake, George Jacob. *The Principles of Secularism*. London: Austin, 1871.

Horii, Mitsutoshi. *The Category of "Religion" in Contemporary Japan: Shūkyō and Temple Buddhism*. Cham, Switzerland: Palgrave Macmillan, 2018.

Human Rights Campaign, "The Lies and Dangers of Efforts to Change Sexual Orientation or Gender Identity." https://tinyurl.com/cnntbcs7, accessed April 24, 2022.

Humphrey, Caroline. "Alternative Freedoms." *Proceedings of the American Philosophical Society* 151, no. 1 (2007): 1–10.

Hunter, Hugh. "George Berkeley's Proof for the Existence of God." *International Journal for Philosophy of Religion* 78, no. 2 (2015): 183–93.

Huxley, Thomas. "Agnosticism." *Collected Essays: Volume V Scientific and Christian Tradition*. New York: D. Appleton and Company, 1902.

Igwe, Leo. "Atheism in Zambia--Skeptical, Rational Thought in a Very Superstitious Country." http://tinyurl.com/mr26rcys, accessed December 23, 2023.

———. "Southern Africa." In *The Cambridge History of Atheism*, vol. 1 and 2, edited by Stephen Bullivant and Michael Ruse, 971–81. Cambridge and New York: Cambridge University Press, 2021.

Indick, William. *The Digital God: How Technology Will Reshape Spirituality*. Jefferson, NC: McFarland and Company, 2015.

Infantino, Lorenzo. *Ignorance and Liberty*. London and New York: Routledge, 2003.

Janoff-Bulman, Ronnie. *Shattered Assumptions: Towards a New Psychology of Trauma*. New York: The Free Press, 1992.

Johnson, David and Jeff VanVonderen. *The Subtle Power of Spiritual Abuse*. Minneapolis, MN: Bethany House, 1991.

Johnson, David Kyle. "Why Religious Experience Cannot Justify Religious Belief." *Socio-Historical Examination of Religion and Ministry* 2, no. 2 (2020): 26–46.

Johnson, Paul. *The Quest for God: A Personal Pilgrimage*. London: Weidenfeld and Nicolson, 1996.

Kahan, Dan M., Donald Braman, John Gastil, Paul Slovic, and C. K. Mertz. "Culture and Identity-Protective Cognition: Explaining the White-Male Effect in Risk Perception." *Journal of Empirical Legal Studies* 4, no. 3 (2007): 465–505.

Kahane, Guy. 2011. "Should We Want God to Exist?" *Philosophical and Phenomenological Research* 82, no. 3 (2011): 674–96.

Kaufmann, Walter. *The Faith of a Heretic*. Garden City, NY: Doubleday & Company, 1961.

———. *The Portable Nietzsche*. Harmondsworth, UK and New York: Penguin, 1977.

Kavanagh, Christopher M. and Jonathan Jong. "Is Japan Religious?" *Journal for the Study of Religion, Nature and Culture* 14, no. 1 (2020): 152–80.

KazKaz, Lana and Miriam Diez Bosch. "Media Speech on Atheism: A Case Study in Arabic Channels' Talk Shows." *International Journal of Social Sciences: Current and Future Research Trends* 12, no. 1 (2021): 32–44.

Keane, John. "Post-truth Politics and Why the Antidote isn't Simply 'Fact-Checking' and Truth." https://tinyurl.com/22ny4hh3, accessed December 12, 2021.

Kearney, Richard. *Anatheism: Returning to God After God*. New York: Columbia University Press, 2010.

Kelley, S. J. "Ritualistic Abuse of Children: Dynamic Impact." *Cultic Studies Journal* 5, no.2 (1988): 228–236.

Kelsey, David H. 2020. *Human Anguish and God's Power*. Cambridge and New York: Cambridge University Press.

Khalil, Mohammad Hassan and Mucahit Bilici. "Conversion Out of Islam: A Study of Conversion Narratives of Former Muslims." *The Muslim World* 97, no. 1 (2007): 111–24.

Kierkegaard, Søren. *The Sickness Unto Death*. Translated by H. V. Hong and E. H. Hong. Princeton, NJ: Princeton University Press, 1980 [1849].

Klein, Patricia, Evelyn Bence, Jane Campbell, Laura Pearson, and David Wimbish, *Growing Up Born Again: A Whimsical Look at the Blessings and Tribulations of Growing Up Born Again*. Old Tappan, NJ: Fleming H. Revell Company, 1987.

Knepper, Timothy David. *The Ends of Philosophy of Religion: Terminus and Telos*. New York: Palgrave Macmillan, 2013.

Kolsen, Mark. "Mandela's 'Ubuntu Atheism' and Why It Matters." http://tinyurl.com/mh2vu7wy, accessed December 26, 2023.

Korteling, J. E. (Hans) and Alexander Toet. "Cognitive Biases." In *Encyclopedia of Behavioral Neuroscience*, 2nd ed, edited by Sergio Della Salla, 610–619. Amsterdam: Elsevier Science, 2022.

Kraay, Klaas J. and Chris Dragos. "On Preferring God's Non-Existence." *Canadian Journal of Philosophy* 43, no. 2 (2013): 157–78.

Kraft, Patrick W., Milton Lodge, and Charles S. Taber. "Why People 'Don't Trust the Evidence': Motivated Reasoning and Scientific Beliefs." *Annals of the American Academy of Political and Social Science* 658 (2015): 121–33.

Kruger, Justin and David Dunning. "Unskilled and Unaware of It: How Difficulties in Recognizing One's Own Incompetence Lead Inflated Self-Assessments." *Journal of Personality and Social Psychology* 77, no. 6 (1999): 1121–34.

Kunda, Ziva. "The Case for Motivated Reasoning." *Psychological Bulletin* 108, no. 3 (1990): 480–98.

Kurtz, Paul. *The New Skepticism: Inquiry and Reliable Knowledge*. Buffalo, NY: Prometheus Books, 1992.

Lakoff, George. *Don't Think of an Elephant: Know Your Values and Frame the Debate—The Essential Guide for Progressives*. White River Junction VT: Chelsea Green Publishing Company, 2004.

Lao Tzu. *Tao Te Ching*. Translated by J. H. McDonald. https://tinyurl.com/mwv58aeb , accessed April 28, 2022.

Le Poidevin, Robin. *Agnosticism: A Very Short Introduction*. Oxford and New York: Oxford University Press, 2010.

———. *Arguing for Atheism: An Introduction to the Philosophy of Religion*. London and New York: Routledge, 1996.

Lévi-Strauss, Claude. *Structural Anthropology*. Translated by Claire Jacobson and Brook Grundfest Scheepf. New York: Basic Books, 1963.

Levinas, Emmanuel. *Totality and Infinity: An Essay on Exteriority*. Translated by Alphonso Lingis. Pittsburgh, PA: Duquesne University Press, 1969.

Levine, Michael. "Pantheism." *Stanford Encyclopedia of Philosophy*. https://tinyurl.com/3ymwekm5, accessed April 26, 2022.

Levy, Robert I., Jeannette Marie Mageo, and Alan Howard. "Gods, Spirits, and History: A Theoretical Perspective." In *Spirits in Culture, History, and Mind*, edited by Jeannette Marie Mageo and Alan Howard, 11–27. New York and London: Routledge, 1996.

Lino e Silva, Moises and Huon Wardle. "Testing Freedom: Ontological Considerations." *Etnofoor* 29, no. 1 (2017): 11–27.

Lion's Roar Staff. "What Are the Four Negations?" https://tinyurl.com/2zcsd63c , accessed April 28, 2022.

Loftus, John W. *Unapologetic: Why Philosophy of Religion Must End*. Durham, NC: Pitchstone Publishing, 2016.

Longe, Jacqueline L., ed. *The Gale Encyclopedia of Psychology*, 3rd ed. Farmington, MI: Gale, 2016.

Longkumer, Arkotong. "The Power of Persuasion: Hindutva, Christianity, and the Discourse of Religion and Culture in Northeast India." *Religion* 47, no. 2 (2016): 203–27.

Louw, Maria. "Being Muslim the Ironic Way: Secularism, Religion, and Irony in Post-Soviet Kyrgyzstan." In *Varieties of Secularism in Asia: Anthropological Explorations of Religion, Politics, and the Spiritual*, edited by Nils Bubandt and Martijn van Beek, 143–61. London and New York: Routledge, 2012.

Luhrmann, Tanya M. *When God Talks Back: Understanding the American Evangelical Relationship with God*. New York: Alfred A. Knopf, 2012.

Maffie, James. *Aztec Philosophy: Understanding a World in Motion*. Boulder: University Press of Colorado, 2014.

Maleki, Ammar and Pooyan Tamimi Arab. "Iranians' Attitudes Toward Religion: A 2020 Survey." Netherlands: GAMAAN, 2020.

Malik, Shoaib Ahmed. *Atheism and Islam: A Contemporary Discourse*. Abu Dhabi: Kalam Research & Media, 2018.

———. "Defining Atheism and the Burden of Proof." *Philosophy* 93, no. 2 (2018): 279–301.

Malinowski, Bronislaw. *Magic, Science, and Religion and Other Essays.* Garden City NY: Doubleday Anchor Books, 1948.

Markowitz, Linda and Laurel Puchner. "Structural Ignorance of Christian Privilege." *International Journal of Qualitative Studies in Education* 31, no.10 (2018): 877–94.

Martin, Michael. *Atheism: A Philosophical Justification.* Philadelphia, PA: Temple University Press, 1990.

Marwell, Gerald and David R. Schmitt. "Dimensions of Compliance-Gaining Behavior: An Empirical Analysis." *Sociometry* 30, no. 4 (1967): 350–64.

Mawson, T. J. "Praying to Stop Being an Atheist." *International Journal for Philosophy of Religion* 67, no, 3 (2010): 173–86.

McCarthy, Vincent A. *The Phenomenology of Moods in Kierkegaard.* Boston, MA: Martinus Nijhoff, 1978.

McIntyre, Lee. *Post-Truth.* Cambridge, MA and London: MIT Press, 2018.

McGoey, Linsey. *The Unknowers: How Strategic Ignorance Rules the World.* London: Zed Books, 2019.

McGrath, Alister E. *The Twilight of Atheism: The Rise and Fall of Disbelief In the Modern World.* New York: Doubleday, 2004.

McLean, G. R. "Antipathy to God." *Sophia* 54, no. 1 (2015): 13–24.

Medieval Sourcebook. "Twelfth Ecumenical Council: Lateran IV 1215." https://tinyurl.com/429r4suv , accessed April 28, 2022.

Merton, Robert K. "The Unanticipated Consequences of Purposive Social Action." *American Sociological Review* 1, no. 6 (1936): 894–904.

Mian, Marzio. "Behind the New Iron Curtain: Caviar, Counterculture, and the Cult of Stalin Reborn," translated by Elettra Pauletto. *Harper's* (January 2024): 22–32.

Michaels, David. *Doubt is Their Product: How Industry's Assault on Science Threatens Your Health.* New York: Oxford University Press, 2008.

Miguel, Felipe. "The Epistemic Significance of Agreement with Exceptional Theistic Philosophers." *Faith and Philosophy* 37, no. 4 (2020): 451–74.

Milem, Bruce. "Defining Atheism, Theism, and God." *International Journal for Philosophy of Religion* 85, no. 3 (2019): 335–46.

Mill, John Stuart. *On Liberty.* Kitchener, Ontario: Batoche Books, 2001 [1859].

Miller, Ed L., ed. *Classical Statements on Faith and Reason*. New York: Random House, 1970.

Mills, Charles W. "White Ignorance." In *Agnotology: The Making & Unmaking of Ignorance*, edited by Robert N. Proctor and Londa Schiebinger, 230–249. Stanford, CA: Stanford University Press, 2008.

Moreno, Father Antonio. "Demons According to St. Teresa and St; John of the Cross." https://tinyurl.com/mwf3vnvz , accessed April 1, 2022.

Moser, Paul K. "Christ-Shaped Philosophy: Wisdom and Spirit United." Paper presented to the Evangelical Philosophical Society, August 5, 2012. https://tinyurl.com/4ndbde6f , accessed November 20, 2012.

Murray, Michael J. and Michael C. Rea. *An Introduction to the Philosophy of Religion*. Cambridge and New York: Cambridge University Press, 2008.

Nader, Mina. "Nonreligious Arabs Protest Online To Declare #WeAreHere." http://tinyurl.com/25ssb2uz, accessed July 7, 2022.

Nagel, Thomas. *The Last Word*. Oxford: Oxford University Press, 1997.

Napier, Jaime L., Julie Huang, Andrew J. Vonasch, and John A. Bargh. "Superheroes for Change: Physical Safety Promotes Socially (but not Economically) Progressive Attitudes among Conservatives." *European Journal of Social Psychology* 48, no. 2 (2018): 187–95.

Nasr, Amir Ahmad. *My Isl@m: How Fundamentalism Stole My Mind—and Doubt Freed My Soul*. New York: St. Martin's Press, 2013.

National Institute of General Medical Sciences. "Physical Trauma." https://tinyurl.com/4pt3nm3n , accessed October 21, 2021.

Nelson, Maggie. *On Freedom: Four Songs of Care and Constraint*. Minneapolis, MN: Graywolf Press, 2021.

New, Christopher. "Antitheism: A Reflection." *Ratio (New Series)* 6, no. 1 (1993): 36–43.

New World Encyclopedia. "Freedom." https://tinyurl.com/378mvy5e, accessed June 4, 2022.

Newheiser, David. "Introduction: The Genealogy of Atheism." In *The Varieties of Atheism: Connecting Religion and Its Critics*, edited by David Newheiser, 1–18. Chicago, IL and London: The University of Chicago Press, 2022.

Newman, Saul. *Political Theology: A Critical Introduction*. Cambridge: Polity Press, 2019.

Nhat Hanh, Thich. "The Heart Sutra: The Fullness of Emptiness." https://tinyurl.com/yftwfa4w , accessed April 2, 2022.

Niebuhr, H. Richard. *Faith on Earth: An Inquiry into the Structure of Human Faith*, edited by Richard R. Niebuhr. New Haven, CT and London: Yale University Press, 1989.

Nietzsche, Friedrich. *The Gay Science*. Edited by Walter Kaufmann. New York: Vintage, 1974 [1882].

———. *The Will to Power*, Books 1 and 2. Translated by Anthony M. Ludovici. Edinburgh and London: T. N. Foulis, 1914.

Nikkel, David H. *Panentheism in Hartshorne and Tillich: A Creative Synthesis*. New York: Peter Lang, 1995.

Nobutaka, Inoue. "Perspectives toward Understanding the Concept of Kami." http://tinyurl.com/yuhue2bs, accessed December 25, 2023.

Noor, Iqra. "Confirmation Bias." https://tinyurl.com/273y37fy, accessed May 28, 2022.

Novšak, Rachel, Tina Rahne Mandelj, and Barbara Simonič. "Therapeutic Implications of Religious-Related Emotional Abuse." *Journal of Aggression, Maltreatment, & Trauma* 21, no. 1 (2012): 31–44.

Nyhan, Brendan and Jason Reifler. "When Corrections Fail: The Persistence of Political Misperceptions." *Political Behavior* 32, no. 2 (2010): 303–30.

Oakley, Lisa and Kathryn Kinmond. *Breaking the Silence on Spiritual Abuse*. London and New York: Palgrave Macmillan, 2013.

Omer, Mohy. 2021. "The Condition of Nonbelievers in Africa." Washington, DC: United States Commission on International Religious Freedom.

Onfray, Michel. *In Defense of Atheism: The Case Against Christianity, Judaism, and Islam*, translated by Jeremy Leggatt. Toronto: Viking Canada, 2007 [2005].

Online Etymology Dictionary. "Belief." https://tinyurl.com/2ek2f3zn, accessed March 6, 2022.

Oppy, Graham. *Atheism: The Basics*. London and New York: Routledge, 2019.

Oreskes, Naomi. "The Reason Some Republicans Mistrust Science: Their Leaders Tell Them To." https://tinyurl.com/y8h6tjh9, accessed May 4, 2022.

Osborne, Samuel. "Richard Dawkins Accused of Islamophobia after Comparing 'Lovely Church Bells' to 'Aggressive-sounding Allahu Akhbar.'" https://tinyurl.com/yc22wtsr, accessed May 17, 2022.

Overing, Joanne. "Images of Cannibalism, Death, and Domination in a 'Non-Violent' Society." In *The Anthropology of Violence*, edited by David Riches, 86–102. Oxford: Basil Blackwell, 1986.

Oxford Languages. "Word of the Year 2016." https://tinyurl.com/2p98nuw5, accessed May 8, 2022.

Parkes, C. M. "Bereavement as a Psychosocial Transition: Process of Adaptation to Change." *Journal of Social Issues* 44, no. 3 (1988): 53–65.

Pasquale, Teresa B. *Sacred Wounds: A Path to Healing from Spiritual Trauma*. St. Louis, MO: Chalice Press, 2015.

Paul, Gregory S. "Cross-National Correlations of Quantifiable Societal Health with Popular Religiosity and Secularism in the Prosperous Democracies." *Journal of Religion & Society* 7 (2005): 1–17.

Paul, Robert A. "The Sherpa Temple as a Model of the Psyche." *American Ethnologist* 3, no. 1 (1976): 131–46.

Pearce, Kenneth L. "God's Impossible Options." *Faith and Philosophy* 38, no. 2 (2021): 185–204.

Peterson, Michael, William Hasker, Bruce Reichenbach, and David Basinger, eds. *Philosophy of Religion: Selected Readings*, 5th ed. Oxford and New York: Oxford University Press, 2014.

Peterson, Michael L. and Raymond J. VanArragon, ed. *Contemporary Debates in Philosophy of Religion*. Malden, MA and Oxford: Blackwell, 2004.

Pew Research Center. "Scientists and Belief." https://tinyurl.com/56vs7a5j, accessed May 12, 2022.

———. "Section 4: Scientists, Politics and Religion." https://tinyurl.com/5n796v47 , accessed May 4, 2022.

———. "Who Knows What About Religion." https://tinyurl.com/bde7wvxj , accessed May 6, 2022.

Pigg, Stacy Leigh. "The Credible and the Credulous: The Question of 'Villagers' Beliefs' in Nepal." *Cultural Anthropology* 11, no. 2 (1996): 160–201.

Plantinga, Alvin. "Advice to Christian Philosophers." *Faith and Philosophy* 1, no. 3 (1984): 253–71.

———. *God and Other Minds: A Study of the Rational Justification of Belief in God*. Ithaca, NY: Cornell University Press, 1967.

————. *Warranted Christian Belief.* New York: Oxford University Press, 2000.

Pohle, Joseph. "Theology." In *The Catholic Encyclopedia: An International Work of Reference on the Constitution, Doctrine, Discipline, and History of the Catholic Church*, volume 14, edited by Charles G. Herbermann, 580–97. New York: The Encyclopedia Press, Inc., 1913.

Polka, Brayton. "Modern Philosophy, the Subject, and the God of the Bible." *Sophia* 54, no. 4 (2015): 563–76.

Pouillon, Jean. "Remarks on the Verb 'To Believe.'" in *Between Belief and Transgression: Structuralist Essays in Religion, History, and Myth*, edited by Michael Izard and Pierre Smith, 1–8. Chicago, IL: The University of Chicago Press, 1982.

Proctor, Robert N. "Agnotology: A Missing Term to Describe the Cultural Production of Ignorance (and Its Study)." In *Agnotology: The Making & Unmaking of Ignorance*, edited by Robert N. Proctor and Londa Schiebinger, 1–33. Stanford, CA: Stanford University Press, 2008.

Propach, Jan Levin. "Why God Thinks What He is Thinking? An Argument against Samuel Newlands' Brute–Fact–Theory of Divine Ideas in Leibniz's Metaphysics." *European Journal for Philosophy of Religion* 13, no. 3 (2021). DOI: https://doi.org/10.24204/ejpr.2021.3301.

Quack, Johannes. *Disenchanting India: Organized Rationalism and Criticism of Religion in India.* Oxford and New York: Oxford University Press, 2012.

————. "Organised Atheism in India: An Overview." *Journal of Contemporary Religion* 27, no. 1 (2012): 67–85.

Reader, Ian. *Religion in Contemporary Japan.* Honolulu, HI: University of Hawai'i Press, 1991.

Reilly, Thomas F. "The Sexual Abuse of Children in the Roman Catholic Archdiocese of Boston." https://tinyurl.com/4d9mhpby, accessed December 15, 2003.

Renz, Graham. "What is God's Power?" *European Journal of Philosophy of Religion* 13, no. 3 (2021). https://doi.org/10.24204/ejpr.2021.3295.

Ronkin, Noa. *Early Buddhist Metaphysics: The Making of a Philosophical Tradition.* Abingdon, UK: RoutledgeCurzon, 2005.

Rosen, Christine. "The Foolishness of 'Ugly Freedoms.'" https://tinyurl.com/4knwjn8j, accessed June 2, 2022.

Rissler, James. "Open Theism." Internet Encyclopedia of Philosophy. https://www.iep.utm.edu/o-theism, accessed April 27, 2022.

Ruel, Malcolm. *Belief, Ritual, and the Securing of Life: Reflexive Essays on a Bantu Religion*. Leiden: E. J. Brill, 1997.

Ryan, Alan. "Freedom." *Philosophy* 40, no. 152 (1965): 93–112.

Salamon, Janusz. "Atheism and Agatheism in the Global Ethical Discourse: Reply to Millican and Thornhill-Miller." *European Journal for Philosophy of Religion* 7, no. 4 (2015): 197–245.

Sartre, Jean-Paul. *The Words*. Translated by Bernard Frechtman. New York: George Braziller, 1964.

Sax, William S. 2010. "Ritual and the Problem of Efficacy." In *The Problem of Ritual Efficacy*, edited by William S. Sax, Johannes Quack, and Jan Weinhold, 3–16. Oxford and New York: Oxford University Press, 2010.

Schellenberg, J. L. *Divine Hiddenness and Human Reason*. Ithaca, NY: Cornell University Press, 1993.

———. *The Hiddenness Argument: Philosophy's New Challenge to Belief in God*. New York: Oxford University Press, 2015.

Schielke, Samuli. "Being a Nonbeliever in a Time of Islamic Revival: Trajectories of Doubt and Certainty in Contemporary Egypt." *International Journal of Middle East Studies* 44, no. 2 (2012): 301–20.

———. "The Islamic World." In *The Oxford Handbook of Atheism*, edited by Stephen Bullivant and Michael Ruse, 638–50. Oxford: Oxford University Press, 2013.

Schilbrak, Kevin. *Philosophy and the Study of Religions: A Manifesto*. Malden, MA and Oxford: Wiley Blackwell, 2014.

———. "What *Isn't* Religion?" *The Journal of Religion* 93, no. 3 (2013): 291–318.

Scholer, David M. "In the Know." https://tinyurl.com/3jtjr75b, accessed May 6, 2022.

Schmitt, Carl. *Political Theology: Four Chapters on the Concept of Sovereignty*. Translated by George Schwab. Chicago, IL: The University of Chicago Press, 2005 [1934].

Schweizer, Bernard. *Hating God: The Untold Story of Misotheism*. Oxford and New York: Oxford University Press, 2011.

Sevinç. Kenan, Thomas J. Coleman III and Ralph W. Hood Jr. "Non-Belief: An Islamic Perspective." *Secularism & Nonreligion* 7, no. 5 (2018): 1–12.

Shiose, Yuki. "Japanese Paradox: Secular State, Religious Society." *Social Compass* 47, no. 3 (2000): 317–28.

Shnirelman, Victor A. "Hyperborea: The Arctic Myth of Contemporary Russian Radical Nationalists." *Journal of Ethnology and Folkloristics* 8, no. 2 (2014): 121–38.

Shook, John R. "Atheology." In *Religion: Beyond Religion*, edited by Phil Zuckerman, 263–79. Farmington Hills, MI: Macmillan Reference, 2016.

———. *Systematic Atheology: Atheism's Reasoning with Theology*. New York and London, 2018.

Singh, Bharat. "Why I am an Atheist." http://tinyurl.com/4d5maruk, accessed December 25, 2023.

Sissons, Jeffrey. *The Polynesian Iconoclasm: Religious Revolution and the Seasonality of Power*. New York and Oxford: Berghahn Books, 2014.

Skorupski, John. *Symbol and Theory: A Philosophical Study of Theories of Religion in Social Anthropology*. Cambridge: Cambridge University Press, 1976.

Slade, Darren M. "Failed to Death: Misotheism and Childhood Torture." In *God and Horrendous Suffering*, edited by John W. Loftus, 118–66. Denver, CO: GCRR Press, 2021. https://doi.org/10.33929/GCRRPress.2021.05.

Slade, Darren M., Adrianna Smell, Elizabeth Wilson, and Rebekah Drumsta. "Percentage of U.S. Adults Suffering From Religious Trauma: A Sociological Study." *Socio-Historical Examination of Religion and Ministry* 5, no. 1 (2023): 1–28. https://doi.org/10.33929/sherm.2023.vol5.no1.01.

Sloat, Donald. *The Dangers of Growing Up in a Christian Home*. New York: Thomas Nelson, 1986.

Smith, George H. *Atheism: The Case Against God*. Amherst, NY: Prometheus Books, 1989.

Smith, Michelle and Lawrence Pazder. *Michelle Remembers: The True Story of a Year-Long Contest Between Innocence and Evil*. Scarsborough, Ontario: Nelson/Canada, 1980.

Smith, Wilfred Cantwell. *Faith and Belief*. Princeton, NJ: Princeton University Press, 1979.

Smithson, Michael. *Ignorance and Uncertainty: Emerging Paradigms*. New York: Springer-Verlag, 1989.

Stack, Carol. *All Our Kin: Strategies for Survival in a Black Community*. New York: Harper & Row, 1974.

Stark, Rodney. *One True God: Historical Consequences of Monotheism*. Princeton, NJ: Princeton University Press, 2001.

Steffen, Lloyd. *The Demonic Turns: The Power of Religion to Inspire or Restrain Violence*. Cleveland, OH: The Pilgrim Press, 2001.

Stein, Gordon, ed. *The Encyclopedia of Unbelief*. Buffalo, NY: Prometheus Books, 1985.

Steinhart, Eric. "On the Number of Gods." *International Journal for Philosophy of Religion* 72, no. 2 (2012): 75–83.

Stenger, Victor J. *God: The Failed Hypothesis—How Science Shows that God Does Not Exist*. Amherst, NY: Prometheus Books, 2007.

Stroebel, Lee. *The Case for Christ: A Journalist's Personal Investigation of the Evidence for Jesus*. Grand Rapids, MI: Zondervan, 1998.

Sujiwade, Joshua R. "Divine Simplicity: The Aspectual Account." *European Journal for Philosophy of Religion* 12, no. 3 (2021): 143–79.

Sultan, Harris. *The Curse of God: Why I Left Islam*. Bloomington, IN: Xlibris, 2018.

Swan, Rita. "Faith-Based Medical Neglect: For Providers and Policymakers." *Journal of Child & Adolescent Trauma* 13, no. 3 (2020): 343–53.

Swinburne, Richard. *The Coherence of Theism*. Oxford: Clarendon Press, 1977.

———. *Epistemic Justification*. New York: Oxford University Press, 1999.

———. *The Existence of God*, 2nd ed. New York: Oxford University Press, 2004 [1979].

———. "Religion, Problems of the Philosophy of." In *The Oxford Companion to Philosophy*, edited by Ted Honderich, 763–66. Oxford: Oxford University Press, 1995.

Taliaferro, Charles, Paul Draper, and Philip L. Quinn, eds. *A Companion to Philosophy of Religion*, 2nd ed. Malden, MA and Oxford: Wiley-Blackwell, 2010.

Tambiah, Stanley. *Buddhism and the Spirit Cults in North-East Thailand*. London: Cambridge University Press, 1970.

Tamimi, Azzam. "The Origins of Arab Secularism." In *Islam and Secularism in the Middle East*, edited by Azzam Tamimi and John L. Esposito, 13–28. Washington Square, NY: New York University Press, 2000.

Theohary, Catherine A. "Defense Primer: Information Operations." Washington, DC: Congressional Research Service, 2018.

Thomas, Renny. "Atheism in India: Twentieth Century and Beyond." In *The Cambridge History of Atheism*, vol. 1 and 2, edited by Stephen Bullivant and Michael Ruse, 831–49. Cambridge and New York: Cambridge University Press, 2021.

———. "Atheism and Unbelief among Indian Scientists: Towards an Anthropology of Atheism(s)." *Society and Culture in South Asia* 31, no. 1 (2017): 45–67.

Thomas, Timothy. "Russia's Reflexive Control Theory and the Military." *Journal of Slavic Military Studies* 17, no. 2 (2004): 237–56.

Thompson, Mark. "Luther's Raging Torment." https://tinyurl.com/y33em2cm, accessed April 1, 2022.

Tillich, Paul. *The Courage to Be*. New Haven, CT and London: Yale University Press, 1952.

Tooley, Michael. "Axiology: Theism Versus Widely Accepted Monotheisms." In *Does God Matter? Essays on the Axiological Consequences of Theism*, edited by Klaas J. Kraay, 46–69. New York: Routledge, 2017.

Torres, Phil. "Godless Grifters: How the New Atheists Merged with the Far Right." https://tinyurl.com/564j8wma, accessed June 6, 2021.

Trakakis, Nick. *The End of Philosophy of Religion*. London and New York: Continuum, 2008.

Tripurashakti.com. "Avidya in Yoga Meditation." http://tinyurl.com/462rrex7, accessed May 6, 2022.

Turner, Tamara Dee. "Music and Trance as Methods for Engaging with Suffering." *Ethos* 48, no. 1 (2020): 74–92.

Turner, Victor. *The Ritual Process: Structure and Anti-Structure*. Chicago, IL: Aldine Publishing, 1969.

Tversky, Amos and Daniel Kahneman. "Judgment under Uncertainty: Heuristics and Biases." *Science* 185, no. 4157 (1974): 1124–31.

Vahanian, Gabriel. *The Death of God: The Culture of Our Post-Christian Era*. New York: George Braziller, 1957.

Vallely, Anne. "Jainism." In *The Oxford Handbook of Atheism*, edited by Stephen Bullivant and Michael Ruse, 351–66. Oxford: Oxford University Press, 2013.

Vliek, Maria. "'Speaking Out Would Be a Step Beyond Just Not Believing'—On the Performativity of Testimony When Moving Out of Islam." *Religions* 10, no. 10 (2007): 1–19.

Wadley, Reed L., Angela Pashia, and Craig T. Palmer. "Religious Scepticism and Its Social Context: An Analysis of Iban Shamanism." *Anthropological Forum* 16, no. 1 (2006): 41–54.

Wahlberg, Mats. "Was Evolution the Only Possible Way for God to Make Autonomous Creatures? Examination of an Argument in Evolutionary Theodicy." *International Journal for Philosophy of Religion* 77, no. 1 (2015): 37–51.

Wainwright, William J., ed. *The Oxford Handbook of Philosophy of Religion*. New York: Oxford and New York: Oxford University Press, 2005.

Wallace, Anthony F. C. *Religion: An Anthropological View*. New York: Random House, 1966.

Walters, Kerry. *Atheism: A Guide for the Perplexed*. New York and London: Continuum, 2010.

Watanabe, Chika. *Becoming One: Religion, Development, and Environmentalism in a Japanese NGO in Myanmar*. Honolulu, HI: University of Hawai'i Press, 2019.

Wayman, Alex. "The Meaning of Unwisdom (Avidya)." *Philosophy East and West* 7, no. 1/2 (1957), 21–25.

Weibe, Donald. "The Failure of Nerve in the Academic Study of Religion." *Studies in Religion* 13, no. 4 (1984): 401–22.

Wesley, John. "Sermon 95: On the Education of Children." https://tinyurl.com/2p8nu5wa, accessed July 16, 2008.

Wheelwright, Philip, editor. *The Presocratics*. New York: The Odyssey Press, 1966.

Wielenburg, Erik J. "The Absurdity of Life in a Christian Universe as a Reason to Prefer that God Not Exist." In *Does God Matter? Essays on the Axiological Consequences of Theism*, edited by Klaas J. Kraay, 147–63. New York: Routledge, 2017.

Wierenga, Edward R. *The Philosophy of Religion*. Malden, MA and Oxford: Wiley Blackwell, 2016.

Wiesel, Elie. *The Trial of God: (as it was Held on February 25, 1649, in Shamgorod)*. New York: Random House, 1979.

Wilde, Oscar. *De Profundis*. https://tinyurl.com/42vsj3ez, accessed June 30, 2022.

Winell, Marlene. "It's Not Just Personal: The Collective Trauma of Religion." *Essays in the Philosophy of Humanism* 29 (2021): 1–8.

———. *Leaving the Fold: A Guide for Former Fundamentalists and Others Leaving their Religion*. Berkeley, CA: Apocryphile Press, 2007 [1993].

———. "Religious Trauma Syndrome." journeyfree.org/rts, accessed October 21, 2021.

Wolf, Susan. *Freedom within Reason*. Oxford and New York: Oxford University Press, 1990.

Yandell, Keith E. *Philosophy of Religion: A Contemporary Introduction*. London and New York: Routledge, 1999.

Zagzebski, Linda Trinkaus. *Philosophy of Religion: An Historical Introduction*. Oxford: Blackwell, 2007.

Zarabozo, Jamaal. "The Rise of New Atheism and its Relationship to Islam." Houston, TX: 17th Annual Imams' Conference of The Assembly of Muslim Jurists of America, 2021. http://tinyurl.com/3akdjp2y, accessed November 11, 2023.

Zdybicka, Zofia J. "Atheism in *The Universal Encyclopedia of Philosophy*." *Studia Gilsoniana* 7, no, 4 (2018): 709–57.

Zuckerman, Miron, Jordan Silberman, and Judith A. Hall. "The Relation Between Intelligence and Religiosity: A Meta-Analysis and Some Proposed Explanations." *Personality and Social Psychology Review* 17, no. 4 (2013): 325–54.

Zuckerman, Phil. *Society without God: What the Least Religious Nations Can Tell Us About Contentment*. New York and London: New York University Press, 2008.

Index

E

F

G

G

H

T

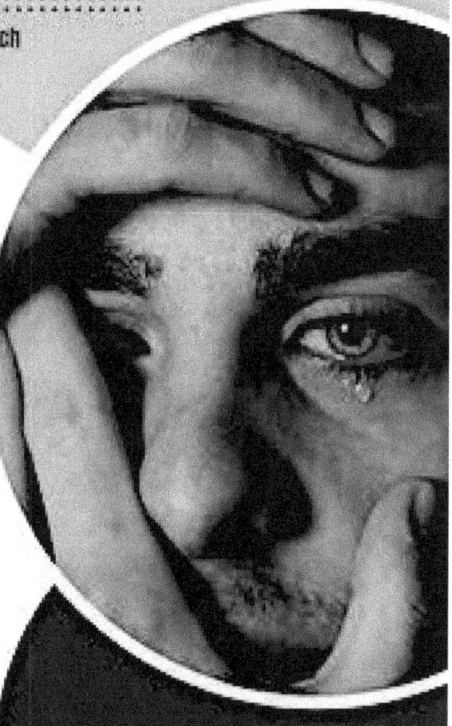

www.ingramcontent.com/pod-product-compliance
Lightning Source LLC
Chambersburg PA
CBHW070904120626

46546CB00001B/135